Contemporary Gender Issues

Contemporary Gender Issues

Identity, Status and Empowerment

Edited by

Gurpreet Bal

RAWAT PUBLICATIONS

Jaipur • New Delhi • Bangalore • Guwahati • Kolkata

ISBN 978-81-316-0762-6

Published by
Prem Rawat for **Rawat Publications**
Satyam Apts, Sector 3, Jawahar Nagar, Jaipur 302 004 (India)
Phone: 0141 265 1748 / 7006 Fax: 0141 265 1748
E-mail: info@rawatbooks.com
Website: www.rawatbooks.com

New Delhi Office
4858/24, Ansari Road, Daryaganj, New Delhi 110 002
Phone: 011 2326 3290

Also at *Bangalore, Guwahati* and *Kolkata*

Typeset by Rawat Computers, Jaipur

Printed at Nice Printing Press, New Delhi

To my Loving Mother
Diljeet Kaur

Contents

Contributors

Anuradha Ghandy, MSS Institute of Social Work, Bajaj Nagar, Nagpur.

Bindu Duggal, Centre for Research in Rural and Industrial Development (CRRID), Chandigarh.

Chetna Gala, Kasegaon, Sangli, Maharashtra.

E.N. Ashok Kumar, School of Social Sciences, The Swami Ramanand Teerth Marathwada University, Nanded, Maharashtra.

Gail Omvedt, renowned social scientist and social activist based in Kasegaon, Sangli, Maharashtra.

Geetha Thachil, MSS Institute of Social Work, Bajaj Nagar, Nagpur.

Jayshree Soni, Centre for Social Studies, Veer Narmad South Gujarat University, Surat.

J.P. Singh, Professor at the Postgraduate Department of Sociology, Patna University, Patna.

Kalpana Shah, formerly Professor, Department of Rural Studies, South Gujarat University, Surat.

Neerja Ahlawat, Associate Professor, Department of Sociology, MD University, Rohtak.

Nishi Batra, former student of Department of Sociology, Haryana Agriculture University, Hisar.

Pushpinder Walia, Principal, DAV College, Firozepur.

Raj Mohini Sethi, formerly Professor, Department of Sociology, Panjab University, Chandigarh.

Raj Singh, formerly Professor, Department of Sociology, Haryana Agriculture University, Hisar.

S. Gohilavani, Reader, Department of Women's Studies, Alagappa University, Karaikudi.

Suguna Pathy, formerly Professor, Department of Sociology, South Gujarat University, Surat.

Sumita Bakshi, Assistant Professor in Public Administration, DAV College, Sector-10, Chandigarh.

Swinder Singh, Associate Professor, Public Administration, DCS, Panjab University, Chandigarh.

Tanvir Likhari, Associate Professor, Jawaharlal Nehru Architecture and Fine Arts University, Hyderabad.

Vibhuti Patel, Professor, Department of Economics, Mumbai University, Mumbai.

Preface

Examining identity and status of women in modern India brings forth two significant points. First, throughout the history of Indian civilisation women of great courage, grit and sensibilities whose agency gave a new mould to the society of that time could be found. In present times, the proportion of such women has increased manifold who through their education, work, hard work, commitment and courage have contributed significantly in the making of modern India. Second, still in twenty-first century we tend to find gender discrimination, differentiation and segregation, and dowry deaths and rapes. However, in contemporary India it would be wrong to make a conclusive comment that women in general occupy low status. Women's position varies in terms of caste, class, religion, region, education and occupation. It is in India only that men in Meghalaya are organising and struggling to eliminate inequalities to have equal status to women. However, it may be argued that in modern society, there are certain issues of universal concern such as equality, justice and rights, which need to be addressed. It is important to have gender parity and equity for the development of any country. The central concern of this volume is to focus on the diversity of India and differences among women in the context of identity, status and empowerment.

The Department of Sociology, Guru Nanak Dev University, Amritsar would be completing its 40 years of teaching and research with commitment and dedication in 2016. To commemorate the occasion, the faculty took a unanimous decision to celebrate its contribution to girl students, researchers and society at large. Besides teaching and research, the department has been continuously publishing its own journal *Guru Nanak Journal of Sociology* since 1980. As a part of the celebrations, the department under the steward leadership of Professor Paramjit Singh Judge decided to publish series of theme books. The present book is one in the series. The articles selected to be included in the volume were originally published in *Guru Nanak Journal of Sociology*. I am grateful to the worthy Vice Chancellor, Professor A.S. Brar, G.N.D. University, Amritsar, for his constant encouragement and help.

I take this opportunity to thank Professor Paramjit Singh Judge for his invaluable suggestions and comments on the compilation of the volume. Without his constant reminders, pressure and cooperation, this volume would not have been completed within time frame. I would also like to extend my gratitude to my family, Paramjit and Neil. Their love, care and concern has gone deep into my understanding of gender. With heavy heart I would like to dedicate my work to my mother who is not there to read this volume but who braved through nurturing three daughters in a patriarchal environment.

I am also grateful to all the contributors and Rawat Publishers for making the publication easy.

Gurpreet Bal

Introduction

Gender Issues and Concerns

Studies on gender issues in India do not have a long history. Gender, as subject of concern, has been realised as recent as in late 1980s. There has been no evidence of 'gender perspective' in the usual academic curriculum in academic institutions and was not even a subject of teaching in the universities. However, in the early 1970s the Research Centre for Women Studies was started in SNDT Women's University, Mumbai, it was largely emerged out of the women's movements and their struggle for gender equality. The prevalent gender bias in academia blocked the attempts at looking into social issues from gender perspective. As a matter of fact, the leadership to organise women to study women issues in India comes mainly from the western part of the country. Thus, the women issues could not get equal attention in different parts of India and hence the sensitivities of the people towards women concerns and problems have also remained blurred. Consequently, we find that the western and southern states have shown more progressive parameters of gender equality as compared to northern states. The present volume aims to bring together studies conducted in different regions of India, providing a comprehensive understanding of women's existence and negotiations in everyday contested life. It also endeavours at exploring woman's agency on the way to her empowerment.

Why do we need to study gender? There are glaringly sharp gender gaps found in terms of education, employment, health and in decision-making bodies of our society. The feminisation of poverty, feminisation of migration and more negative effects of globalisation on women speak of their vulnerability. Domestic work lies heavily on women's shoulders, and still media is representing gender stereotypes.

There are gender discrepancies, gender segregation and gender discrimination in almost all walks of life. With this broader overview, the present introductory chapter focuses on understanding myriad issues confronting women and their identity in India and the concerns and challenges they tend to face. The discussion is placed into two parts. The first part tries to unfold the issue of women's identity. The basic question raised is: do women constitute a homogeneous category? If not, how can we understand women's issues and problems in Indian context? The part two of the chapter brings forth major challenges women of India tend to face in the twenty-first century. An overall view of the challenges is presented and an attempt has been made to bring out a perspective to analyse the issues comprehensively.

I

Woman's Identity

Before we delve into the gender issues, it is significant to make the position clear that male and female might have equal opportunity to be born (even that is questionable), but opportunities available to women and men are drastically different in our society. Besides the differences between men and women, the enquiry is also whether women constitute a homogeneous category. The debate has been going on whether all women are equal. I may begin by stating that all women are not equal; they tend to differ in terms of available opportunities and the exercise of choices. There are divisions among women themselves as there are differences between men and women. Women differ on the basis of caste, religion, class, race and ethnicity. Women as a group form a heterogeneous category, but at the same time there are many commonalities that bind them together. Differences tend to wither away when we identify the nature and extent of patriarchy operating in the society and hence, by and large, common everyday experiences of women. The problems and issues women are facing are the same for all in the private as well as in public spaces. Even if we review the history of feminism, there is a variety of feminisms. Each of it suffers from its limitations of experiences. But these were largely the experiences of white, middle-class women in Europe and North America who were speaking for all women and, as Freedman (2002) writes, ignoring the experiences of women in Third World and the ways their lives have been affected by colonialism, capitalism and racism; and in the case of India casteism. Black feminists are critical of white women's conscious neglect of their oppression by white men. It is improbable to describe a universal and homogeneous oppression of women. Woman from a low caste and class is likely to experience the brutality of oppression more than a woman of high caste or class is likely to have. It is not their oppression as women alone but their socially underprivileged position in the society, which turns their oppression multidimensional.

Many feminists have argued that family is one of the major structures of patriarchal society and thus a prime site of women's oppression. For underprivileged women, however, the family may act as a site of strength against the caste and ethnic oppression. The Beijing UN Conference (1995) marked the shift towards intersectionality of identities such as gender, religion, caste, race and nationality. The term 'intersectionality' was introduced by Crenshaw (1991) in 1989. Crenshaw defined the concept of intersectionality to denote various ways race and gender interact to shape multiple dimensions of African–American women's employment. The term was later adopted by the UN Commission on Human Rights in 2002 in the resolution on the human rights of women. The concept of intersectionality refers to aspects of identity and how they interact and affect equality. In India, Rege (2004) started investigating caste, class, ethnicity and gender as being interlinked. Intersectional approach does not just add up disadvantage, but looks at how the disadvantages intersect and affect each other in different contexts and at different times. Discrimination occurs when one identity intersects with another identity. It helps us understand and examine how inequalities multiply for Dalit and tribal women in India. Intersectionality recognises the diversity of women. Thus, the patriarchal structures, placement in social hierarchy, women's identity and experiences are seen as mutually constituting and shaping each other.

The Gender Issue

From 1970s onwards, the term 'gender' has become common whenever we need to focus on women issue. For centuries, the biological differences have been the basis of justification of creating different social roles for men and women. Women's capacities of childbirth, breast feeding and less physical strength were seen as determining their social role in the house. Biological differences also made them unfit to participate in the public sphere. Women are judged to be less reasonable than men, more ruled by emotions, thus incapable of political decision-making. The scientist Robert Wright in his best seller *Moral Animal – Why We Are, The Way We Are: The New Science of Evolutionary Psychology* (1994) writes that feminists have managed to procure legislation against sexual harassment and affirmative action for women, but they will never share power with men because they lack men's genes for competitiveness and risk taking behaviour. This led to a distinction between physiological sex and social gender. This distinction can also be expressed by the terms female and feminine, female being the biological category to which women belong and feminine behaviour and roles being the social constructions based on the biological category. Thus, many feminists have argued that whereas biological sex is a naturally occurring difference, all the roles, relations and forms of behaviour associated with being a woman have been created historically by different societies. Until the beginning of twentieth century both boys and girls would wear white dresses in the West and later on till 1950s boys wore pink and girls wore blue, but after 1950s it was reversed. Blue colour was identified with masculinity and pink with femininity. In the United States till 1960s, only fashionable shoes, high heels and pointed toes were available for women. Similarly, in India till the MNCs entered, comfortable, short heel, broad toes shoes were not available. All women have to wear was a particular type of shoes. Being in the process of becoming is constantly under social construction. French feminist, Simon de Beauvoir (1972) writes, 'One is not born, but rather becomes, a woman. Women's inferior position is not a natural or biological fact but one that is created by society. One may be born as a female of the human race but it is civilisation which creates woman, which defines what is feminine and prescribes how women should and do behave. And this construction of women meant her continued oppression. The social roles and modes of behaviour that civilization has assigned to women have kept them in an inferior position to that of men' (Freedman, 2002: 14). Similarly, Oakley (1972: 16) argues that:

> Sex is a word that refers to the biological differences between male and female – the invisible difference in genitalia, the related difference in procreative function. Gender, however, is a matter of culture – it refers to the social classification into masculine and feminine. Sex is natural thus, largely unchanging and fixed, but gender is constructed socially, thus always has a scope for change.

However, the issue is who does participate in the construction process? The Radical feminists' answer is that it is a result of patriarchy. Patriarchy is a system of power and control that expresses itself through patrilineality and patrilocality. But Steinem (Shukla, 2014) argues that patriarchy is just 5 per cent of human history and it arrived between 500 and 5000 years back. In India, matrilineal cultures existed from Kerala to Himalayas before colonialism and Christianity arrived. Though patriarchy has caused much damage to the natural balance, yet we may say that the construction of gender is the result of centuries of experiences, practices, codes of conduct and modes of behaviour. Gender to evolve as a term and a concept has undergone a process. Every culture has constructed its gender categories by keeping sex at the foundation.[1] The purpose is to differentiate the males from females and it is important to differentiate in order to treat them differently. Men have power, physical as well as social, to create discourses on the way gendering is to be done through various social processes: socialisation, social institutions and social interaction (cf., Reskin and Padavic, 1994). Freedman (2002) argues that it is sex, gender and power that actually intersect to perpetuate the differentiation and inequalities.

Thus, the concept of gender seems to have opened up new avenues of thought and analysis for women studies and feminists. The concept of gender allowed room for an idea of hierarchy and power relations, which meant that the division could be considered from another angle. Here the discrimination and inequalities women face can be examined in relation to men. In that sense gender analysis provides more comprehensive understanding. However, women studies centres prefer to use the word 'women studies' because in their view gender subsumes the power equations. But as Oakley (1972) puts that gender is a term that has been used by academic feminists to bring respectability to their work. More often, gender is seen as something that is relevant only to women, because gender was so readily accepted by feminists to explain women's subordinate position in the society, so it is mainly perceived as a term that applies to women only and the social construction of femininity. At least in India masculinity has not been a subject of rigorous analysis as well as its construction under gender studies. However, the principle of becoming is also true for men: one is not born masculine, but has to become a man. A boy has to appear legal rational and has to hide his tears otherwise the stereotypes would embarrass him.

To place the gender in contemporary Indian context, we need to have a cursory look into the position of women historically. Did they occupy the same low position or over the years their position has changed? If it has improved, what are the new challenges the women in modern India face? The evidence on human civilisation clearly reveals a continuous history of civilisation for the last 3,000 years. All through these years, there is hardly any evidence of equal status for women. The structure of the societies has always been such where men's actions and ideas dominated. Most of the societies of the world had a system of authority and control over women not only at the level of practice, but also as an ideology.

Gender in History

The genealogy of status of women depicts that how over the centuries the woman has been constructed by the powerful. The excavations of

Indus civilisation depict the presence of fertility goddesses. Woman was presented as an ideal of beauty and movements. During the Vedic period though many historians have hinted at fairly satisfactory status of women, yet we find mixed response towards the status of women in Vedic religious practices. But here we need to be clear that respect for women and status of women are two different things. There was respect for women, but is important to remember that to perform religious duties wife was important but not essential. The myth prevalent with regard to Lord Brahma (Pushkar Temple near Ajmer in Rajasthan) narrates that Devi Savitri was easily replaced by another woman to perform *Yagya* point towards her dispensability. The status is to be understood in terms of discrimination and inequalities prevalent in any society. Thus, during this period, as Dharamshastras depict, women were allowed to participate in religious practices. Gradually, brahmanical patriarchy (Ramusack and Sievers, 1999) started Vedic ritual along gender lines; many restrictions were imposed on women and the right to read Holy Scriptures was denied to women. During the Maurian period, Arthshastra became virtually a practical guide for dealing with women and laws of Manu outlining the child marriage, no widow remarriage, no property right and treating husband as god clearly show the lower position of women. Discourses were created of her role as devout wife and caring mother. Women have always been contained within the bonds of marriage. Thus, the Indian history of gender clearly depicts that women were always kept under the control of men; they themselves never had any existence. The history alongside also has constructed ideal women in terms of role relationships, such as Draupadi, Shakuntala, Sita and Sati Savitri. They are depicted as ideal role models. They were independent, strong willed yet devoted ideal wives.

Maria Mies (1980) analyses the reasons for their segregation from men and hence constituting the two worlds apart. She brings out three main reasons for it.

1. The lower position of women may be traced back to the time when men started accumulation process and to have bigger share they began fighting. In other words, as and when this competition resulted into conflicts and wars in human society, the women's status started deteriorating, as they were withdrawn from public sphere and confined to the four walls of the house. It was due to biological reasons as well as to take care of the children and the elderly in the house. Consequently, a number of practices such as child marriage, Sati system and widowhood were glorified.
2. Her detachment from property, by not having the right to own the property.

3. The prevalent patriarchy in the society humbled her and reduced her to a segregated self.

Further impositions were added during medieval period, when the veil/purdah system created physical exclusion of women. The spaces were gendered. Again contrarily, we have illustrations of Razia Sultana, Rani Laxmi Bai and Mira Bai who rejected the system and fought for their rights.

The British attempted to improve the position of women but they could also not go out of the Indian social context, besides enacting some legal provisions under the Hindu Marriage Act, Widow Remarriage Act, Abolition of Sati and focusing on education of women. The contribution of religious leaders, social reformists, nationalist leaders remain significant to improve the status of women. As a matter of fact, we may emphasise that whatever the status of women have achieved in contemporary times, they never had that at any point of time in history. Over the time the status of women in Indian society has improved due to multiple factors. The United Nations International Conference on Population and Development Beyond, 2014, reports that the status of women has improved worldwide, as more number of women has access to education, work and political participation.

Cultural Context of Gender

Gender is presented as an emblem of family, community and society. Thus, it must be constructed and represented according to the needs, wishes and values of its people. Societies have been undergoing the process of constructing the gender in different spaces. The fabric of Indian society remains patriarchal. The patriarchal values dominate both in public and in private forms (Walby, 1990). The social rules are so constructed that women are denied from participating in a number of activities and from many fundamental rights. Subtle expressions of patriarchy through various symbols, rituals, practices, folk songs, dances and even abuses, directly or indirectly give the message of inferiority and subordination of women. Ritual practices such as fasting, *karva chauth* and *Navratras* reinforce her role as an obedient, pious daughter and devout wife. Ironically, woman has been performing various rituals for the good health of the husband and welfare of the family. No record is found in the history of civilisation showing men's rituals for having good wife and her long life (Desai and Thakkar, 2001).

Ironically, construction of gender takes place to represent a religion and a community identity. In first Punjabi novel, *Sundari*, published in 1898 Bhai Vir Singh, the great Punjabi novelist and poet, in order to construct Sikh community and Sikh religion has used gender. Sundari a beautiful, strong, determined, courageous and benevolent woman presents an image of a Sikh woman (Bal, 2006). Women are regarded as the underbelly of religious community. In the face of the threat to the community, she is first to face the attack and thus she has to be protected, curtailed and also glorified. However, the writings of first Punjabi woman poet of nineteenth century – Peero (Bal, 2003) claim that woman is universal. She does not have any religion. She argues that religious constructions are also of and for men. Women do not fall along religious categories, yet societies construct religious communities on the basis of gender. It is only the men who have put her into religious boundaries. Rejecting Islam, Hinduism and Sikhism, Peero transcends all the religious boundaries. In her view, being a woman is her identity, and all other imposed identities are irrelevant in the context of gender. In the time of crisis and upheavals in the community, the weaker is likely to suffer the most. For instance, during the Indo-Pak partition, Punjab was partitioned and the Punjabi women were the worst sufferers during the time which lead to reinforcement of gendered spaces. The Hindu women happily married to Muslim men were forced to leave their marital families and sent back to their country. Giving women to other religious, caste or ethnic group means the reduction in the community membership. To protect the honour of the community, all such restrictions are imposed both culturally and brutally, whereas taking or bringing girl within the community from outside has different implications. It is an addition to the community and the linage would be patrilineal where woman's identity would be submerged with the identity of the man.

II

Prevalent Issues and Concerns

In order to examine the issues involved in gender in our society, this part of the chapter is divided into two sections. In the first section, a brief review of the issues raised and resolved through movements and struggles in the western world in the recent past would be discussed. In the second section, a few issues of serious nature which Indian women have been encountering would be examined by taking illustrations from the real-life situations.

Feminists' Issues

How did women in different societies encounter inequalities and some women of substance took the lead to sort out the issues with state or, in other words, with masculinity? The process of struggle and movements is called *feminism* or the *feminist development of thought*. History of feminist thought is diverse and multifaceted grouping of ideas. The thought on feminism has mainly come out of the actions of the women activists. It is necessary to be clear that there is no single feminism. What are the common features of all feminisms? All feminisms concern themselves with women's low position in society and with discrimination encountered by women because of their sex. All feminists call for changes in the social, economic, political or cultural order to reduce and eventually overcome this discrimination against women. They all deal with women issues, but the issues are diverse (Freedman, 2002).

The term 'feminism' is relatively a recent one. It was first used in 1871 in a French medical text to describe termination in development of the sexual organs and characteristics of male patients who were suffering from feminisation of their bodies. In 1840s, women's rights groups started emerging in the United States and in Britain and France women's suffrage movements emerged. We can trace the development of women's rights movements from the mid-nineteenth century. The word feminism emerged much after the women started questioning their low social position. Even many of the rights groups in late-1960s and 1970s did not want to call themselves as feminist. What it suggests is that one does not have to be a feminist to support women's rights to equal treatment and that not all supporters of women's demands are feminists. To address women issues throughout the history of world, a number of feminist movements at different moments of history have emerged as a series of waves. Thus, first wave of feminism is used to refer to late nineteenth and early twentieth centuries feminist movements that were concerned with gaining equal rights for women, particularly the right of suffrage. Woolf argues that women needed financial independence, others pressed for domestic parity with men. The second wave of feminism refers to the resurgence of feminist activity in the late 1960s and 1970s, when protest centred around women's inequality, but this time not only in terms of women's lack of equal political rights but also in the areas of family, sexuality and work. It does not mean that in between these two phases there was no activity (c.f. Humm, 1992).

Popularly feminism is divided into three groups – Liberal feminism, Marxist or Socialist feminism and Radical feminism. Liberal feminists include all those who campaign for equal rights for women within the framework of liberal state, arguing that the theoretical basis on which this state is built is sound but the rights and privileges it confers must be extended to women to give them equal citizenship with men. Marxist and socialist feminists link gender inequality and women's oppression to the capitalist system of production and the division of labour consistent with the system, whereas radical feminists such as Millett (1970) see men's domination of women as the result of system of patriarchy. She argues in *Sexual Politics* that ideological indoctrination and economic inequality is the cause of women's oppression. More recent issues have also been added, such as psychoanalytical feminism, postmodern or poststructuralist feminism, black feminism, queer feminism and ecofeminism, which are referred as the third wave of feminism. They argue that all women are not the same. The issues and problems tend to vary due to differences among women themselves. Though all these feminist perspectives have focused on some specific issue but the basic idea of these feminists is that human subjects are socially constructed through sociocultural discourses and exercise of power and thereby the meanings are plural, multiple and open to revision.

Jayawardana (1986) argues that feminism was not a western creation but has endogenous roots in the Third World. It has a long history of its own. In nineteenth century India, there were movements in favour of women's emancipation, and there were debates on women's rights in China as well. Women in developing countries were already debating their social position and mobilising to bring change. Women in India have been politically engaged with problems of sati system, child marriage, property rights, dowry-related harassment and forced the colonial rulers to pass legislations against the anti-women practices in the nineteenth century. Thus, Indian women activists have also made cliché in feminist genealogy. They took up the issues of sexual harassment, rape, poverty, alcoholism, health and even ecology.

Vandana Shiva has argued that ecology is a specific feminist issue and has developed what can be christened as ecofeminism. The basic argument is that the oppression of the nature has a linkage with the oppression of women. Ecofeminism began in the 1970s and the term first appeared in 1974. It was the year when in Chipko Movement women tried to save thousands of square kilometres of sensitive watershed by hugging the trees when woodcutters tried to cut the trees. Ecofeminists argue that before the western colonialism and development of science and technology the women and the indigenous people had close and harmonious relationship with nature. But in the development process women's relationship to communal land use and land rights has been transformed. When technology entered the agriculture, women were the first to be displaced. Women were growing vegetables and some fruits enough for family's subsistence. That economy and wisdom is no more relevant. Overuse of land, pesticides, hybrid seeds and technology all have destroyed the ecology, which poses serious health risks. Mies and Shiva (1993) suggest that the only way to come out of the ecological crises is to revert to women's earlier relationship to the environment and to promote return to nature. If the ecosystem and biodiversity are to be conserved, it is vital to start listening to women and taking their knowledge seriously. Foucault (1980) says knowledge is power and power is knowledge. It is equally important to know which knowledge is powerful. It is in the form of discourse created by the men that her knowledge is not socially valued. Her location in the gendered space is restricted to an access to socially relevant knowledge (Das Gupta, 1994). To conclude, we may say that the feminist struggle has been continuously going on and shall go on till women's issues and concerns get resolved and consequently women get equality in the society.

Fundamental Parameters of Gender Inequality in India

Further discussion identifies some of the issues and challenges which Indian women encounter in everyday life experiences irrespective of internal differences among them.

Sex-based Inequalities

India has a population of 1.21 billion people consisting of 623.7 million males and 586.5 million females according to 2011 census. The sex composition reveals that males outnumber females in lower age group that is less than 25 years of age and females outnumber males in older age groups. As the age increases from 60 years onwards, the proportion of females starts increasing in the total population and proportion of males starts declining. Though apparently it appears good but the trend indicates survival of widows, decaying health and increasing dependency on children. In any society, the sex ratio is a sensitive index of the status of women. Sex ratio stands for proportion of females per 1,000 males in any society. The data on Indian society starting from 1901 to 1961 show that sex ratio has been constantly and continuously declining. The rate of decline got faster from 1971 onwards when the ratio of females dropped to 930 in 1971, 934 in 1981 and 927 in 1991. Twenty-first century has started showing a little sign of improvement when the ratio of females to males increased to 933 in 2001 and 946 in 2011. Kerala has the most favourable sex ratio where ratio of females outnumbers males. In between 1980 and 2010, nearly 4.5 million girls went missing in India. Punjab is a prosperous state but provides no better treatment to its girls. Punjab shows the most disturbing trend in this case where the sex ratio is 893 for 1,000 males as per 2011 census. The child sex ratio (0–6 years) at present is 846 females per 1,000 males. These trends show the sociocultural bias of Indian people towards the females. Some scholars blame the value system, whereas others explain the phenomenon in terms of highly unfavourable practices such as dowry system, expensive marriages and violence against women.

Female Infanticide and Foeticide

The reproduction has always remained a complex and contested issue. The meanings have undergone a change and new meanings were generated to maintain the patriarchy. The function of reproduction is controlled by men, which has lead to alienation of woman's body. Women have reproductive capacity but this is channelised through social structure, the way it is constructed, largely by men. Motherhood is a pleasure for women but is controlled by social practices. Female infanticide was commonly practiced in the nineteenth and early twentieth centuries among the upper classes, irrespective of the religion. Studies (Malhotra, 2002; Oberoi, 1994; Singh, 1981) have revealed that it was practiced among certain communities, viz., the Khatri, Bedi, Sodhi, Brahmin, Jats and Muslims in Punjab. No community member raised any question but the British rulers passed a law with regard to Bedi community that if a girl child dies, then there would be investigation into the circumstances of her death. Technology is further controlling the reproduction. In a way, technology has liberated the woman from the drudgery of repeated childbirths, but the same technology is also taking away the right of the women to reproduce. The feminists are also of view that the new scientific advances and technologies are an attempt to maintain and reinforce men's control over women's reproductive capabilities. The new reproductive technologies are also accused of posing risks to women's health by increasing social pressure on infertile women to have children, and also to select the sex of the child. The reproductive capability of women is no more a natural process, but it is being intervened strongly by the patriarchal values to reproduce under all conditions and at the same time also fulfilling the needs of the patriarchal structural requirements. The mindset of the women is not only prepared to just reproduce but also to produce the male child. Supposedly a simple species function of reproduction imbibes a complex social value system in which woman's biological activity is transformed into her being the object of patriarchal discourse. Women are forced to go for repeated foeticides so that they could perpetuate the family lineage. Thus, the foeticide needs to be understood from social structural point of view. Worldwide there is daughter deficit and son surplus, but in India it has touched dangerous proportions. The world sex ratio has come down to 100 women for 101.3 men due to different forms of femicide. More number of women has been killed in the last 50 years (Shukla, 2014). Studies have shown the wealthiest and most educated are the major conspirators.

The politics of the country also promotes the control over the family size. Thus, the women have a double burden of not only producing limited number of children but also taking the role to determine the sex of the child. A son must be produced. The status and her respect in the family and in the kinship network depend on the number of sons born to her (Arora, 2009).

Education

The access to education is one's fundamental right. The efforts of Indian Government through various initiatives and development programmes are aimed at bringing equality and welfare of women. Education provides knowledge and knowledge is a source of development. Though education as a strategy has remained effective, yet still only 65.46 per cent women as per 2011 census are literate in India while the proportion for men is 82.5. A clear cut disparity is observable. In spite of equal right to education why after 67 years of independence of the country do the girls tend to suffer on accounts of education? The answer to the question is not just lack of facilities, but it is more entangled in our belief pattern and sociocultural practices. Chanana (2000, 2001) has explained the phenomenon in terms of protection of female sexuality prevalent in our texts and ideology. The particular concern seems to be still prevailing strongly when we analyse the data on education. As per 2011 census, the primary school completion rate for boys is 95 and 94 for the girls and secondary school enrolment percentage for girls is 56 and for boys is 64. As the girl grows in age, her access to education is accordingly withdrawn. Up to primary school, both boys and girls have almost equal chance to get education, but when a girl reaches puberty, she is put under restrictions. The construction of gender starts at a very young age. Data reveal that illiterate women have high fertility rate and also high infant mortality rate. As educational level increases, fertility rate declines and also the death rate drops.

Knowing the benefits of women's education for the person and society, the social reformers and nationalist leaders worked for the education of women. Many taboos, beliefs and practices such as purdah system were challenged. By the early 1920s, the education of women had become a public issue and the slogan had become 'educating a girl means educating a family'. In Punjab, Arya Samaj, Ahmadiyya movement and Singh Sabha made a point to reform the condition of women and, thus, propagated the education of women. As Chanana (2001) points out that the concern for daughters' sexuality and virginity made parents reluctant to send them to schools or send them unescorted. Thus, an arrangement commonly known as 'Zenana system' of schooling was introduced where she was going through self-learning at home, teacher coming to home, going to school in a covered palanquin, or escorted by domestic maids. Western-educated men's preference for educated wife encouraged families to educate their daughters to have good grooms. Also initially, education of women was emphasised so that they could be able to read the holy books. Once the parents got ready to impart education to girls, the other big question was to which school? Could they send girls to co-educational schools to be taught by male teachers? Girls started going to all girls' schools and colleges. For her, spaces started getting gendered. On top of that another problem was what subjects they should be taught. They took up gendered specific courses. They were introduced to feminine subjects as it was understood that girls in any case would not be working. Girls would become homemakers, thus they should be given training which was useful to run the household.

Even in recent times parents tend to send their sons to private schools and girls to government schools, though the girls show more interest in studies and they tend to perform better than the boys do. Girls are outshining the boys at all levels of education in India. They are taking to professional courses with an intention to take up job, but still lot of stereotypes are prevalent. The mindset of the girl is prepared in such a way that her marriage becomes the top most priority for the parents as well as for the daughters. Every year the most bright girl students in our universities have to sacrifice their career for home making. Only a minuscule percentage of girls in India are free from all these handicaps.

Economic Agency of Gender

The economic independence of women is a route to their empowerment. It gives them autonomy, confidence, self-esteem and self-fulfilment besides providing an identity of one's own. Therefore, it is necessary for her to work. Work generates income and is performed at a place and at a time. The meaning of work is dynamic, which changes from time to time. The meaning of work may be understood in terms of values attached to it. For women in Diaspora, the meaning of work is different from the women in a Punjabi village. The same work is valued in Canada but not in India. Thus, the meaning of work is also socially constructed.

Working women tend to work in double shifts – at workplace and at home. Women who are not employed but are working hard from morning till night are not considered workers, because they are not generating any income. In India, majority of women are not regarded as workers but still they are working. Lot of discussion has been carried out on the issue. For instance, if someone else's services are hired to do the same tasks, she would be paid. That means draining out the family resources. This unpaid labour is seen by many feminists as the product of patriarchy and capitalist system of production, which give men power over women through sexual division of labour. It is also argued that if women take more number of roles, the accumulation of roles gives her more power; no doubt it also adds to her stress and strains. Presently 25.6 per cent of women are employed as per the census of 2011, out of which a large majority of women are engaged in the informal sector where they are not protected by any law. Only 7.5 per cent women are in the organised sector where they experience both the equality of wages and conditions of work with men.

Globalisation has done some good to women in the sense that now more job avenues are available which women have also grabbed. Most of these jobs are available in the service sector. Therefore, more and more women are engaged in providing various services. Most of these jobs are of low status but carry fairly good working conditions. On the one hand, it is seen as a positive development, but, on the other hand, we find that the paid employment of women has increased her burden; it has resulted in a double day's work of paid employment outside the home and unpaid housework in it.

The labour market is also not based on principle of equality. There is gender segregation. Some of the jobs are typified for men, while others for women. All those jobs, where women exceed men, carry low prestige and they are paid less than the men. For the workers in the categories of semi-skilled and unskilled, the deputy commissioner of a district fixes the wages and surprisingly the rates vary for men and women. For instance, the women construction workers actually work much harder than the men. They carry the container full of material on their heads and walk on the scaffold, while men are mainly engaged in the mixing of the material on the ground itself. Though the Equal Remuneration Act 1976 is in place, but women are paid less than the men because here the nature of their work nominally differs. Why do the women on the average earn less than the men? The answer may be sought from Walby's (1990) argument when she distinguishes the public form of patriarchy from the private.

In the public sphere also principle of patriarchy operates. Here it is collective appropriation of women's labour power. In the public form of patriarchy, the strategy is segregationist and subordinating in which both employer and state are involved. A study (Soman, 2009) conducted on IT professional women in India revealed that both husband and wife are equally educated, same professional competence, earning same amount, but the family responsibilities fall only on women. Women themselves regard that the care of children and elderly is the sole responsibility of the women. Even the boss understands her leave to perform such tasks from work is genuine and colleagues also do not criticise the attitude of women assigning priority to family. Long, late working hours alongside the men also subject them to suspicion on their sexual misconduct. It shows how patriarchy is being reinforced as a social structural phenomenon. In the present times, sexual harassment at the workplace has becomes a matter of concern. This also provides the explanation that women tend to get concentrated in one type of jobs, which further leads to low prestige of certain types of jobs or they are labelled as women's jobs. Women are also likely to leave such jobs that employ more men and take up to traditionally female workplaces. Therefore, some of the jobs get stereotyped as women's jobs and carry low prestige, less wages and bad working conditions.

The best way of employment for women is self-employment. In modern times, we use the term 'entrepreneurship', which means carrying out some business or commercial activity that requires initiative, innovation and managerial skills, besides taking moderate risk. Entrepreneurship basically means doing things a new and different way. Entrepreneurship has been found the most conducive work for women. Many women in the western world, even when they are engaged in the high prestige jobs in the formal sector, tend to face glass ceiling and thus prefer to leave the jobs and becoming entrepreneurs. In the United States and Canada, woman entrepreneurs constituting 30 per cent of the total do not only create jobs for themselves but also create employment at least for minimum five more persons. In India, entrepreneurship among women has been found as the most successful strategy for their empowerment. The Indian Government, since 1980s, has developed various policies and launched programmes for the upliftment of rural and underprivileged women. A large number of women have become entrepreneurs. They have diversified the nature of their business activities to technology-based manufacturing sector. Still a large number of women take to those enterprises that cater to the needs and requirements of women. This also helps them to utilise their traditional skills and knowledge and experience in the commercial endeavours. They have been able to overcome the gender stereotypes. They start their business usually from one or two rooms of the house with little investment and gradually through saving and investment rise to medium or big entrepreneurship. In this way, they are able to play their family roles vis-à-vis the work in more efficient manner, because they are the masters of their time. They may be present in the family to meet the needs of the children. With their earning power and raised confidence, they participate in all major family decisions (Bal, 1997). They are able to negotiate the gendered divisions more effectively. All women do not have technical skill and resources to become entrepreneurs. In case of women, it is functional entrepreneurship, which deals with their traditional knowledge and skills which emerges out of everyday life experiences. Indian fashion, dresses, handicrafts, jewellery designing, embroidery, beauty and health, cooking items, bee keeping, piggery and poultry are some of the activities to which women have ventured in a big way. Entrepreneurship carries prestige and in fact has become a cliché among women in these days. In a nutshell, it may be argued that it is the economic independence that would empower the Indian women. For which we need to change the mindset of women and the best way is through education and training. Political empowerment may create ability of decision-making but the central focus must be shifted on to her gainful employment.

Gender-based Violence

The extreme form of aggression and oppression against women is violence, which may happen within the family and in the community or society. Violence accompanies power. Gender and power intersect. Power is central to any discussion on violence. Violence is a coercive instrument to uphold or enforce cultural code of honour, or in other words disciplining the women. Therefore, any individual or group facing the threat of coercion or being disciplined to act in a manner required from an individual or group is subject to violence (Krishnaraj, 1995). Violence can be visible, invisible or camouflaged. We may classify the range of violence into three: sexual violence, violence for economic gains and violence based on socioreligious sanctions.

Physical or sexual violence is a tool of domination. Feminists have seen sexual violence as a continuum running from sexual harassment through rape to murder. Susan Brownmiller (1975) argues that it is sexual violence, and especially rape and the threat of rape, which gives men control over women. She maintains that all women suffer from this, even if they are not the victims of actual rape, because they are all victims of the threat of rape. It is this fear generated by the threat of rape that keeps women subordinated. Conversely, all men benefit from the fact of rape, even if they are not the perpetrators of rape themselves, because the system of rape keeps all women fearful and subordinated to men. Brownmiller (1975: 324) writes,

> Once we accept the basic truth that rape is not a crime of irrational, impulsive, uncontrollable lust, but is a deliberate, hostile, violent act of degradation and possession on the part of a would be conqueror, designed to intimidate and inspire fear, we must look toward these elements in our culture that promote and propagandize these attitudes, which offer men, and in particular, impressionable, adolescent males, the ideology and psychologic encouragement to commit their act of aggression without awareness, for the most part, that they have committed a punishable crime, let alone a moral wrong. The myth of a heroic rapist that permeates false notions of masculinity, from the successful seducer to the man who takes what he wants when he wants it, is inculcated in young boys from the time they first become aware that being a male means access to certain mysterious rights and privileges, including the right to buy a woman's body. When young men learn that females may be bought for a price, and the acts of sex command set prices, then how should they not only conclude that that which may be bought may also be taken without the civility of a monetary exchange?

It is just not about biology, but about the construction of masculinity in our societies, as evidenced by the folk tales, ballads, songs and films that portray men as strong and dominating. War, as is the case with rape, forms part of the male system of control over women. During the time of war, the rate of rape increases, and this is not just because men have more opportunity in times of war, but because war cultivates male violence and the army glorifies such violence (Freedman, 2002). During the Bangladesh war, women were raped for whom later mass abortions were organised. War cultivates male violence (Enarson and Chakrabarti, 2009). In Indian society, no day passes by without the news of the horrific incidence of rape in some corner of the country. One may ponder over whether men have heightened libido due to better food or exposure to pornography or it is due to the liberation of women. Nothing like that may be the reason. It is reassertion of male supremacy that men find is being questioned by women being empowered economically, politically and socially in the everyday life. Men in communities and families are desperately trying to control and subordinate the women and thus trying to show them that the outer world is hostile to them, thus you need to be controlled.

India is unique in the sense that here violence is committed against women for economic gains. Dowry, which started as a customary practice, has taken such an ugly shape that innocent women are coerced to bring more dowry to fulfil the insatiable desire of the husband and his relatives, failing which they may be burnt alive. In some parts of Rajasthan, still the *Nata Pratha* (establishing a relationship) is prevalent where woman is virtually sold to have *nata* for some time with a man. The case of widows of Vrindavan narrates the story of economic gains, even calling them as *dayans*/witches and hence killing them by throwing stones at them. Trafficking of women narrates another tale of exploitation of women for economic gains.

Violence is committed on women as there are social and religious sanctions to do so. Sati practice (self-immolation) is the most violent of patriarchal practices. In the relatively recent case of Roop Kanwar in Deorala village in 1987, some 40,000 young Rajput boys gathered together to protect the right to commit Sati. Though female infanticide has been found quite prevalent among certain communities, but the use of technology for reproduction has been readily adopted by women whose role expectation is to produce son for the family. The values attached to produce the son to complete family and to escape women's victimisation the sex determination test is socially accepted (Sandhu and Anuradha, 1999). Honour killing is justified by the community and family as love threatens the honour of the family. To overcome the shame, killing becomes necessary to restore and maintain the pride (Judge, 2012). For Bedia community (*India Today,* 2013) of Rajasthan and Madhya Pradesh sex trade is an age-old customary practice with the consent of the community. The young girls tend to forgo marriage as it is exploitative and dominating for the sake of leading independent life which makes them to earn ₹ 1,200–2,000 per day by catering to 6–10 clients. The life and experiences of women symbolise the status, respect and pride of family and community. The sexuality and reproductive rights of women are regulated by customs, traditions and normative order. The concept of the purity of women is being produced and reproduced in the normal social interaction in everyday life. It is in women's social stock of knowledge that purity must be maintained even if one has to sacrifice one's life. Maintaining virginity is more than the human life. There have been attempts by the feminist groups and others to counter the gender violence. As the second wave of feminism gave call for 'personal is political', personal problems can be solved through political means and political actions. Political means are being increasingly used to report the cases, for protesting, and networking. Both the use of media and involvement of community have remained very effective to get the culprits punished. The political intervention, though not satisfactory, has made it possible to take up legal course of action. The Domestic Violence Act, 2005, was later amended in 2012 to include maid servant to protect her from violence. The Dowry Prohibition Act was passed in 1961 and amended in 1986, The Pre-natal

Diagnostic Technique Act, 1994, and Sexual Harassment at the Workplace Act, 2013, to protect the women's rights at the workplace are major interventions of the Indian state. To combat the gender violence, more important is to deconstruct the categories of good and bad women. For example, the women who commit sati are considered pious and devoted wives, whereas others are regarded as bad. There is also a need for deconstructing the notions of honour and shame (Mathur, 2004). The feminist groups demand from the state counselling, rights, the adequate support and care to the victims of violence.

Personal is Political

The basic argument is that the definition of the political must be extended beyond institutions and issues to which it has traditionally been limited to include the family and personal relationships. For a long time women were denied the voting right and still they are underrepresented in formal political institutions and decision-making bodies. The politics has been and continues to be masculine where men tend to dominate. It may be traced to western political thought from Plato and Aristotle to Hobbs, Locke and Rousseau for a natural difference between men and women. 'Men are naturally rational and thus suited to politics and public life. And women are irrational, thus more suited to emotional life of the home'. Such discourses have contributed to the relegation of women to private sphere of life – to the family. Rousseau argues that women made the customs and men made the laws. Thus, women should limit themselves to the domestic government and should not mix themselves in the public space of politics. Criticisms of the private/public divide led the second wave feminists of 1960s and 1970s to declare that 'the personal is political'. Challenging the traditional views on family and personal life as outside the domain of politics they argued that the private sphere was in fact a primary zone of power relations and of gendered inequality. Personal problems and issues like live-in-relationship, dowry, domestic violence, rape, honour killing, bride burning, desertion of wife, sexual harassment at workplace, discrimination and disparities can thus be solved only through political means and political actions. Postcolonial India has witnessed a number of movements where women collectively raised voice against sexual assault, child marriage, bride burning, widow immolation, sexual harassment at work, and other such similar cases. And forced the state to take political decision and pass laws and acts to protect women's human rights.

Governance played an important role in achieving the development objectives through launching of various programmes and policies. Women in India were granted equal right to vote in 1937. Starting from 1952 to the 16th Lok Sabha in 2014, the voting percentage of women has increased from 37 per cent to 65.63 per cent. The gender gap in Lok Sabha elections in 2014 has reduced to 1.46 per cent points against more than 4 per cent points in 2009. Even in some of the states, including Punjab, women voters surpassed men (http://eci.nic.in/eci_main1 2014) Kapoor and Ravi (2014) studied the gender bias in political participation by analysing women voter turnout in Indian democracy from 1962 to 2012 and have discovered a silent revolution in the sense that there is a steady and sharp decline in the gender bias in voting over time and across all states of India. Sex ratio of voters has increased from 715 in 1960s to 883 in 2000s, out of the total 717 million voters, 342 million voters are women, while male turnout has remained unchanged over time. This improvement is not due to top-down policy action, but largely due to voluntary participation of women voters in elections, which is a testimony to the voluntary act of self-empowerment of women. However, their representation in Lok Sabha, increased from 4.4 per cent to 8.8 per cent, shows the existence of patriarchal political culture in Indian democracy. Women are still underrepresented in the parliament and in the government and in other elected decision-making bodies, both local and national. Government (male dominated) takes decisions on women but women are not participating. A number of arguments are given for their nonparticipation, some of which are as follows:

1. Women themselves are responsible for their political isolation.
2. The public space is unfeminine. Politics is unfeminine, criminalisation of politics and political violence restrain women from being active in political space, which is aggressive, hostile, calculating, competitive, rational and pragmatic.
3. Still 35 per cent of women in India are illiterate. In the absence of information and knowledge, how can it be assured that women effectively participate in politics?

Nevertheless, those women who are actively participating in political activities are raising issues from women's perspective. Since 1996, the demand for one-third representation of women in parliament is still pending but what state actually could do is reserved one-third of seats in local governing bodies, that is, in Panchayati Raj Institutions and urban local bodies, with the 73rd and 74th Constitutional Amendments in the Constitution in 1992. This affirmative political action also shifted the focus from welfare development of the women to their empowerment. Now it is her agency which has got prominence. The policy of reservation has certainly brought power within the reach of rural and urban women. For instance, Amritsar, a metropolitan city, has 63 constituencies of municipal corporation out of which 9 are represented by women councillors. Karnataka and

West Bengal have already reserved seats for women and their experience has been positive. These women are shattering the myths of inefficiency and inability historically and traditionally attributed to women. Development is top on their agenda. Inclusion of women in politics speaks of inclusive development of India. Stacey and Price (1981) are of the opinion that if women wish to make changes in the societies they live in, they must seek and achieve power positions. It is essential that women should enter the political arena since the societies are all male dominated and men certainly cannot be relied upon to initiate or carry through the necessary changes. India has been debating legislation on women's equal representation in elected assemblies. Feminists typically use three types of arguments in campaigning for quotas for women's representation or for gender parity. First, equal representation for women is a matter of justice. Second, only women can adequately represent women's interests. The third relates to the supposedly beneficial influence that the presence of women would have on the functioning of political institutions. It is argued that the Gulf War would probably have been avoided or at least much moderated had there been enough women in American parliament at that time. Critic of these arguments also argue that it would be a challenge to party system with more cross party voting and alliances between women of different parties (Freedman, 2002). There is a move from private sphere of homes to public arena but women are still highly underrepresented in positions of power and decision making.

To conclude the discussion, it is significant to mention that some feminists have sought to resolve these dilemmas and challenges in the third wave of feminism, particularly in the postmodernist or poststructuralist theories that provide a set of alternative ways of addressing the problem of difference and of problems related to women's experience and identities. These postmodernist feminists consider not only the differences between men and women, or differences between women themselves, but also differences within and constitutive of the female subject or a difference within woman (Evans, 1995). They are challenging the notion of a fixed definition of femininity. Postmodern feminism assumes that femininity and masculinity have no fixed meanings and they argue for the need to deconstruct the discourses constructed as feminine and masculine. Central to this process of deconstruction is the analysis of the various discourses constructed over the time to define femininity and masculinity. Accepting the differences does not provide any scope for discrimination and inequalities. The families, community and society can have equality among men and women accepting the fact that there are differences. There can always be a free play of opposing forces (Powell, 2000), which would bring sometime the women in the centre taking decisions and other times men may be in the centre, exercising the power in certain spheres.

Most of the democratic countries of the world have adopted the policy of multiculturalism. It provides equal opportunities to the people of diverse nationalities. The differences among the citizens are rather glorified, which adds to the diversity of the nations. They have become inclusive in the policies and practices. Similarly, women, in spite of the differences among themselves and from men, can have access to equal opportunities and can make their own choices accepting the fact that men and women are two different beings.

Freedman (2002) argues that to continue to be powerful political force and a force for change, feminism must assume some kind of collective identity of women, while at the same time acknowledging differences. This common identity can be found in a common cause, namely the struggle against all types of oppression, exploitation and discrimination against women. Although oppression and domination vary with time and from society to society, it is possible to form an alliance against the various oppressions that exist and to overcome differences to reach this goal. It provides all the women an identity, an identity of their own of which they should be proud of. This collective identity would ensure their way to equality.

At the end it is important to give an overview of the book as it has been planned to provide a comprehensive understanding of significant issues that women tend to face in contemporary Indian society. Besides the Introduction, the book is divided into three parts. The first part entitled 'Literature and the Reconstruction of Gender' consists of three chapters, the second part on 'Work, Employment and Entrepreneurship' presents seven chapters covering different regions of India. In the third part, 'Equality, Status and Empowerment', comprising seven chapters, challenges and concerns women in India tend to face in everyday life. Each of the three parts separately provides an introduction to the topic of concern, besides tracing an overall thrust of each chapter included in the part.

Note

1. One of the finest illustrations, I often use to explain gender construction in my class teaching is from Reskin and Padavic (1994). The fabel is that a stranger arrived at a village begging for food, the villagers said they had no food at all, the stranger announced he had a magic stone with which he offered to prepare a 'Stone Soup'. As the stone simmered in a pot of boiling water, the stranger told the onlookers that the soup would be even more delicious if they could find just one onion. Somebody admitted to have one and added to the pot.

The stranger asked that soup would be really superb if one carrot is added. Somebody brought a carrot. The stranger got the villagers to add potatoes, turnip, garlic and even some meat. The stone soup which was served was delicious. So stone is like a biological sex used as foundation around which societies construct gender. The whole construction of gender favours men. In fact, gendering of all activities is done to maintain the male advantage.

References

Arora, B. 2009. *Female Foeticide in Punjab: A Sociological Study*. Amritsar: Guru Nanak Dev University.

Bal, Gurpreet. 1997. 'Women Entrepreneurs: Emerging Trends and Issues', in P.S. Judge and S.K. Sharma (eds), *Dimensions of Social Change* (169–188). Jaipur and New Delhi: Rawat.

——. 2003. 'A 19th Century Woman Poet of Punjab: Peero'. *Indian Journal of Gender Studies*, 10(2): 183–200.

——. 2006. 'Construction of Gender and Religious Identities in the First Punjabi Novel *Sundari*'. *Economic and Political Weekly*, XLI(32): 3528-3534.

Brownmiller, S. 1975. *Against Our Will: Men, Women and Rape*. New York: Simon and Schuster.

Chanana, Karuna. 2000. 'Treading the Hallowed Halls: Women in Higher Education in India'. *Economic and Political Weekly*, XXXV(12): 1012–1022.

——. 2001. 'Hinduism and Female Sexuality: Social Control and Education of Girls in India'. *Sociological Bulletin*, 50(1): 37–63.

Crenshaw, Kimberle. 1991. 'Demarginalizing the Intersection of Race and Sex: A Black Feminist Critique of Antidiscrimination Doctrine', in Katherine Bartlett and Roseanne Kennedy (eds), *Feminist Theory and Antiracist Politics in Feminist Legal Theory: Reading in Law and Gender* (57–80). San Francisco, CA: Westview Press.

Das Gupta, Tania. 1994. 'Political Economy of Gender, Race and Class: Looking at South Asian Immigrant Women in Canada'. *Canadian Ethnic Studies*, XXIV(1): 137–151.

de Beauvoir, Simone. 1972. *The Second Sex*. H.M. Parshlay (ed.). Harmondsworth: Penguin.

Desai, Neera and Thakkar, Usha. 2001. *Women in Indian Society*. New Delhi: National Book Trust.

Enarson, E. and Chakrabarti, P.G. Dhar (eds) 2009. *Women, Gender and Disaster: Global Issues and Initiatives.* New Delhi: Sage.

Evans, J. 1995. *Feminist Theory Today*. London: Sage.

Foucault, Michel. 1980. *Power/Knowledge, Selected Interviews and Other Writings 1972–1977.* Colin Gorden (ed.). Brighton: Harvester.

Freedman, Jane. 2002. *Feminism*. New Delhi: Viva Books.

Humm, Maggie (ed.) 1992. *Modern Feminisms: Political, Literary, Cultural.* New York: Columbia University Press.

Jayawardana, K. (ed.) 1986. *Feminism and Nationalism in Third World*. London: Zed Books.

Judge, Paramjit S. 2012. 'Love as Rebellion and Shame: Honour Killings in the Punjabi Literary Imagination'. *Economic and Political Weekly*, XLVII(44): 44–50.

Kapoor, M. and Ravi, Shamika. 2014. 'Women Voters in Indian Democracy: A Silent Revolution'. *Economic and Political Weekly*, XLIX(12): 63–67.

Krishnaraj, M. (ed.) 1995. *Women and Violence: A Country Report*. Bombay: Research Centre for Women's Studies.

Malhotra, Anshu. 2002. *Gender, Caste, and Religious Identities: Restructuring Class in Colonial Punjab*. New Delhi: Oxford University Press.

Mathur, Kanchan. 2004. *Countering Gender Violence: Initiatives Towards Collective Action in Rajasthan*. New Delhi: Sage.

Mies, Maria and Shiva, V. 1993. *Ecofeminism*. London: Zed Books.

Mies, Maria. 1980. *Housewives Produce for the World Market: The Lace Makers of Narsapur*. Geneva: ILO.

Millett, Kate. 1970. *Sexual Politics*. New York: Doubleday.

Oakley, A. 1972. *Sex, Gender and Society*. London: Temple Smith.

Oberoi, Harjot. 1994. *The Construction of Religious Boundaries: Culture, Identity and Diversity in the Sikh Tradition*. Delhi: Oxford University Press.

Powell, Jim. 2000. *Derrida for Beginners*. Chennai: Orient Longman.

Ramusack, B.N. and Sievers, S. 1999. *Women in Asia: Restoring Women to History*. Bloomington: Indiana University Press.

Rege, Sharmila (ed.) 2004. *Sociology of Gender: The Challenge of Feminist Sociological Thought*. New Delhi: Sage.

Reskin, B. and Padavic, I. 1994. *Women and Men at Work*. Thousand Oaks: Pine Forge Press.

Sandhu, Jasmeet and Anuradha. 1999. 'Use of Technology for Human Reproduction and Construction of Gender: A Case Study in Amritsar City'. *Guru Nanak Journal of Sociology*, 20(½): 99–110.

Shukla, Vandana. 2014. 'Patriarchy is Just Five Per Cent of Human History'. *The Tribune*, Spectrum, February 9: 1.

Singh, Bhagat. 1981. 'Condition of Women in Punjab in the Early 19th Century'. *The Punjab, Past and Present*, XV(II): 353–364.

Soman, Uthara. 2009. 'Patriarchy: Theoretical Postulates and Empirical Findings'. *Sociological Bulletin*, 58(2): 253–272.

Stacey, M. and Price, M. 1981. *Women, Power and Politics*. London: Tavistock.

Walby, S. 1990. *Theorizing Patriarchy*. Oxford: Blackwell.

Wright, Robert. 1994. *Moral Animal: Why We Are, the Way We Are: The New Science of Evolutionary Psychology*. New York: Vintage Books.

Websites

http://eci.nic.in/eci_main1/sveep/*VoterTurnout Highlights Lok Sabha 2014* (accessed on 20 July 2014).

http://indiatoday.intoday.in/story/sex-trade-and-tradition-family-business-be dia-families (accessed on 29 July 2014).

Part One

Literature and the Reconstruction of Gender

In every society, gender, its roles and relations are constructed, and the Indian society is no exception to this general rule. However, as a process the construction of gender occurs within the framework of social traditions, history and cultural practices. Malinowski (1964) argues that every item, cultural practice, beliefs and customs, have some task to perform and have a vital role to play. The functional view of culture propounds a theoretical paradigm that in order to fulfil various levels of needs, institutions and organisations have emerged. Accordingly, a number of customs, beliefs, practices and rituals have been evolved to perform the various functions of institutions effectively. Thus societies, to run efficiently, have constructed a number of cultural items. Analysis of such a cultural heritage becomes essential tool to understand any practice in contemporary times. As a matter of fact, it is difficult to give an explanation of the causal relationship between gender construction and the normative order, but it may be said that both reinforce each other. The culture and value system of any society plays a vital role in the way gender is constructed. The literature is one such expression of our cultural heritage. It is an essential piece of creativity which aims at presenting reality in a fictionalised manner. To the understanding of the complexities of gender construction, the literature is one of the richest sources to empathise with the subjectivities of the characters. It is a written text. The poststructuralists take cultural/linguistically constructed as the nature of reality. Meanings are product of language, signs, symbols and binary oppositions are essential to the operation of language (Downs, 2004).

Derrida (2002) developed a technique of reading what he called deconstruction, which conveys that the meanings of the text are not stable, singular and fixed. The texts can be interpreted in multiple ways by developing subversive ways of reading it. By decentring the text the signifiers and signified tend to change their relationship. In understanding the gender the signifiers need to be interpreted as they tend to convey more than the signified. Foucault (1961) also argues that the phenomena are constructed through language. In *Madness and Civilization*, he argues how madness is socially and linguistically constructed over time and across space. The meaning of an insane person kept on changing from time to time due to changing interconnections of knowledge, power and truth. The French feminists tended to focus their attention on language, analysing the ways in which meanings are produced. The Ecriture feminism meaning 'women's writing' creating woman's image by a woman for women emphasised on removing men's biased approach while writing on women (http:en.wikipedia.org/wiki).

Judge and Bal (2008) argue that the text is not simply a narrative the purpose of which is to entertain, the reader is simultaneously involved in decoding and interpreting it as a social reality. Literature represents the social reality. The reality of everyday life depicts the oppression, dilemmas and ambivalence of roles a woman plays. The writings of women on women have moved from margins to the centre of academic corridors. The folk songs, folk dances, mythology, stories and narratives depict the complexities of gender roles and relationships by constructing symbols, images and models.

Sometimes, the literary source enriches the understanding of the sensitivities, silence and expressions of women in a much more profound manner than does the quantitative information available in the academics. Chakraverty (2012) is of the view that women's texts have occupied a central position in all literary writings representing a high standard of social and literary theories, attempting to examine not only with technique but also with tabooed subject matters in various forms such as fiction, drama, prose and short stories. In the first section of the book an attempt is made to interpret gender issues by taking three chapters based on Indian English novels written by women. Though since time immemorial women have been producing rich oral tradition in the form of folk ballads, folk songs, proverbs and tales, novel can be regarded as the most vital source of social history, for it traces in-depth details of the experiences of the characters. Three novels published in the 1990s trace the varied dimensions of gender throughout the twentieth century. The novels *What the Body Remembers* (1999), *The God of*

Small Things (1997) and *Sangati* (1994) have been interpreted and analysed. The authors, on the basis of narratives, have tried to reconstruct gender in the context of colonialism, patriarchy, social structure, intersectionality, sexuality and body experiences.

The text chosen by Tanvir Likhari for analysis is *What the Body Remembers* by Shauna Singh Baldwin set in colonial pre-partition era. It is Baldwin's first novel published in 1999. It received the 2000 Commonwealth Writer's Prize for Best Book (Canada and Caribbean Region) and has been translated in fourteen languages. The story set in 1937 of a 16-year-old girl got married to an Oxford-educated and already married engineer, Sardarji in his late 40s, for whom it is a second marriage for the want of a son. It deals with the marking of the bodies and minds of women with patriarchal and nationalist ideologies. Baldwin's narrative juxtaposes newlywed Roop with Sardarji's first wife Satya who are circumscribed within the private arena; who strike a subversive note by resorting to incitement as a mode of articulation accessible to them. This chapter attempts to map the 'voice consciousness' and how the identity of women is constructed as they negotiate not only the forces of 'tradition' and 'modernity' but also the dynamics of the private sphere itself. Female identity in India has had to negotiate colonialism, the imaging of a nation as well as 'tradition' and 'modernity'. Multiple patriarchies were also recast during the colonial era and in turn reformulated the sanctified image of the upper caste/class woman. In this entire discourse ostensibly about women, there is a total lack of women's voices and their subjectivity is difficult to construct. Women were left faceless and voiceless. Moreover, women were seen as sites of discourse authenticating communal/religious and cultural identities. Apart from the various ideologies – familial, social, traditional and modern that women carry – there emerges a voice distinct from the many scripts that attempt to construct the identity of woman – a voice provided by the woman novelist. It is here that the task of the postcolonial woman novelist in resurrecting the lost voices of women, in tracing the quiet voice of subversion, in mapping silences and filling the gaps becomes significant. In fact the quiet voice of subversion is accommodated in the realm of tradition itself.

The paradigm of feminist discourse has always offered points and counterpoints for intellectual speculation. With power as the underlying basis of man–woman relationships in the social structures, gender and its defining dialectics becomes an imperative field of study. Pushpinder Walia in her chapter draws upon the wider socio-cultural paradigm and explores the appropriation and stereotyping of male–female roles into the powerful and the powerless, focusing on Arundhati Roy's Booker Prize winner *The*

God of Small Things published in 1997. The story is about the dynamics of a family (probably a biography of Arundhati Roy) in Kerala, a state of India. A major chunk of the novel takes place in 1969 when the twins, the central characters of the novel are just seven years old and moves on up to 1990s. In its reading of the multiple hues and shades, ironies and paradoxes of the woman's condition in the novel, the chapter attempts to answer as well as raise questions on the paradigmatic context of gender and its corollary of power play.

The third chapter in the section traces the voices from margins of Indian feminist discourse. Dalit feminism has been described as a 'discourse of discontent', 'a politics of difference' from mainstream Indian feminism, which has been critiqued for marginalising Dalit women. Dalit feminist discourse not only questions Indian feminism's hegemony in claiming to speak for all women, but also the hegemony of Dalit men to speak on behalf of Dalit women. In such a scenario, Dalit women like Bama themselves taking the pen to articulate and record their experiences of hurt and humiliation subverts centuries old historical neglect (by the elitist nationalist discourse) and a stubborn refusal to be considered as a subject. *Sangati* is a record of their experiences of the joint oppression of caste and gender faced by numerous Dalit women; it is in a sense an autobiography of Bama – an educated, economically independent and living alone has to come to terms with her identity in a caste-ridden hierarchical society. Tanvir Likhari's chapter on Dalit feminism, based on *Sangati*, analyses Dalit women's oppression as a triple jeopardy of oppression by double patriarchies – 'discreet' patriarchy of their own caste and an 'overlapping' patriarchy of the upper caste – as well as poverty. 'Discreet' patriarchy dictates that power rests with men in the community and in the institutions led by them – the caste courts, the Church, the panchayats. The text traces an account of the aggressive exploitation of Dalit women in terms of double day labour, domestic violence, priests in the Church, upper caste landlords and their own ignorance and suggests remedies. Bama locates male violence unleashed by their caste men in their own sense of powerlessness vis-à-vis upper castes. Exploitation, threat of rape by the upper castes is analysed in terms of values of 'overlapping' patriarchy which maintains a strong sense of gendered spaces and sees the habitual visibility of Dalit women which they inhabit as sites of work as a sign of their availability and inscribes them as lustful women whose sexuality cannot be controlled by the Dalit men. Bama foregrounds the 'difference' of Dalit women from privileged upper caste women and also celebrates their 'identity' in their strength, labour and resilience. As a feminist writer Bama protests against all forms of oppression and relying on the strength and resilience of Dalit women, makes an appeal for change and self-empowerment through education and collective action.

References

Chakraverty, Lalima. 2012. *Gender and Culture in the Works of Indian Subcontinent's Select Women Novelists*. New Delhi: Atlantic Publishers.

Derrida, Jacques. 2002. *Of Grammatology*. Trans. G.C. Spivak. Delhi: Motilal Banarsidass Publishers.

Downs, Laura Lee. 2004. *Writing Gender History*. New York: Oxford University Press.

Foucault, Michel. 1961. *Madness and Civilization*. Trans. A. Sheridan. New York: Random House.

Judge, Paramjit and Bal, Gurpreet (eds) 2008. *Reconstructing Identities: Society Through Literature*. Jaipur: Rawat.

Malinowski, Bronislaw 1964. *A Scientific Theory of Culture and Other Essays*. London: Oxford University Press.

Sangari, Kumkum and Vaid, Sudesh 1989. *Recasting Women: Essays in Colonial History*. New Delhi: Kali for Women.

Website

http://en.wikipedia.org/wiki/%c3%criture_f%3%A9minine (accessed on 9 August 2014).

the borders of class/community in a sense of shared shame. Women express solidarity with each other across [illegible] communities, classes [illegible] Roop with her maid, [illegible] and her Muslim friend, [illegible] [illegible] later [illegible] through Roop who moved by the sight of women [illegible] of rags about their breasts drops her own clothes, making a [illegible] to treat women as God made them, as merely [illegible] – [illegible] by religion/community:

> [E]very man, woman and child [illegible] see woman's body without shame. [illegible] that, not from the corners of your eyes [illegible] she wants to scream, *See me, I'm human, though I'm only a woman. See me: I did what women are for. See me not as a vessel, a plaything, a fantasy, a maid servant, an ornament, but as Vahiguru made me.* (emphasis original, [illegible], 1999: 298)

Both Satya and Roop are subjects in [illegible] they [illegible] and alter their modes of subjectivity negotiating [illegible] of their patriarchy. Both the female protagonists [illegible] resistance within the threshold itself, Satya by [illegible] her personal 'rights' and claims and Roop by failing [illegible] patriarchy. Satya who moves from the [illegible] impulse – of Kakeyi and Kali, ultimately [illegible] the Sita model choosing self-immolation like her. Satya [illegible] rather than live without [illegible] having [illegible] Roop. Like Sita she gives him, her husband [illegible] by courting death, by taking the poison [illegible] Mohan's [illegible] articulates her protest silently [illegible] conformity with patriarchal norms [illegible] soul re-enters the world [illegible] changed.

> again I'm born a woman, foolish-girl child who has entered the world with her eyes wide open and [illegible] than before a man ...
>
> [illegible] man's voice comes [illegible] disappointed I'm [illegible]
>
> benefit of words, that men who [illegible] treasure me as I grow to woman – though he call me princess [illegible] the Guru and [illegible]
>
> *I have come so far – I have borne so much [illegible] But [illegible] not yet changed.* (emphasis original, [illegible] 1999: 538)

[illegible] independence, Roop too [illegible] 'sweet-sweet' Sita construct to one who protests silently [illegible]

1

Gender, Tradition and Modernity in Shauna Singh Baldwin's *What the Body Remembers*

Tanvir Likhari

The decade before and after the partition of the country, saw the reconstruction of identities – of both religion and gender. The hitherto blurred, porous religious boundaries were solidified giving rise not only to communalism but also to inscribing the bodies of women with these identities. At the same time colonial and postcolonial period saw the gendered identities negotiating new paradigms of tradition and modernity. This chapter attempts to map the 'voice consciousness' and identity of women as they negotiate not only the forces of 'tradition' and 'modernity' but also the dynamics of the private sphere itself. The focus is on how the identity of women is constructed by cultural processes that are subject to change, and how class plays a formative role. It explores how as Sangari and Vaid point out, 'the consciousness of women exceeds quite often the ideologies which create it or enable it' (1989: 18). The text chosen for analysis is *What the Body Remembers* by Shauna Singh Baldwin. *What the Body Remembers* covers a wide canvas from the colonial pre-partition era to the time immediately following the independence of the country. It deals with marking the bodies and minds of women with patriarchal, nationalist ideologies. Baldwin's narrative is about two Sikh women, Satya and Roop circumscribed inside the private arena, with one conforming to and the other questioning its dictates.

Tradition and modernity are not polarities but complex structures locked into complicated negotiations with each other; both are rooted in a state of flux and constantly enlarge their boundaries. During the colonial period, tradition and modernity were contemporaneously produced and recast by patriarchies to fix the cultural identity of women. In fact, according to Sangari and Vaid, 'Both tradition and modernity have been, in India, carriers of patriarchal ideologies ... . Both tradition and modernity are eminently colonial constructs which need to be dismantled to look at the cultural processes in their actual complexity' (1989: 17). 'Tradition', as C.S. Lakshmi points out in the essay, 'Bodies Called Women', 'is not static, its content keeps changing and it contains within it elements that oppose it. Its boundaries keep getting erased and reformed ... . And attempts are made to write this notion of tradition on the body of the woman, to dictate its movement, needs, attire, aspirations and spheres of existence even while the body is moving along time, space and history' (2953). The attempt to write tradition on the body of the woman is born of a need to perceive women as subjects who authenticate a cultural or a national identity and as guarantors of the purity of this identity.

The colonial discourse attempted to reformulate tradition and identity of women in two oppositional ways – the traditionalists/revivalists who invoked precolonial feudal scripts which foregrounded religion, scripture and tradition, while the reformers resolved the contrary pulls of tradition and modernity. In fact, women were encrypted with 'spiritual essence' – qualities of suffering, strength and endurance. The precolonial feudal script fiercely defended by the revivalists glorified women as carriers of tradition as well as their capacity for suffering at the altar of familial/marital obligations. The reformers too emphasised the 'spiritual qualities' of tradition that needed to be preserved but also insisted on change consistent with what Tejaswini Niranjana (1991) has called 'good modernity'. They attempted to reconcile an emergent bourgeois identity complicit with the consolidation of British colonial rule in India and reformed the identity of women 'for companionate marital relationships and attendant family duties' (Sangari and Vaid, 1989: 14). The inscription of this new Indian identity on the body of woman was codified through the construction of the *bhadramahila* or the gentlewoman. Women internalise the offered models and constitute themselves with varying degrees of conformity. The nationalist paradigm supplied an ideological principle of selection of traditional as well as western/modern values to construct the identity of the new woman. It was not a dismissal of modernity; the attempt was rather to make modernity consistent with the nationalist project. As Partha Chatterjee points out, 'No matter what the changes in the external conditions of life for women, they must not lose their essential spiritual (i.e. feminine) virtues; they must not ... become *essentially* westernised ... there would have to be a marked *difference* in the degree and manner of westernisation of women, as distinct from men, in the modern world of the nation' (emphasis original, 1989: 240–243). The degree of modernisation/westernisation was contingent upon the class to which the woman belonged and the extent to which related patriarchies were willing to stretch the bar of the threshold.

The threshold being the bar that 'multiple patriarchies' (the high-caste Brahmin Hindu, Sikh and Muslim) place upon the women of their class/community measures the degree of tradition and modernity that they must imbibe. Sangari points out that patriarchies are not distinct from or superadded to structures of class caste and nation but are intrinsic to their very formation. Patriarchies are resilient structures as they are embedded in social stratification, religious/cultural practices as well as the contractual and consensual elements in them. These contractual elements which are imposed upon women are open to constant reformulations and change. Gender difference is structured and in turn structures the wide set of social relations. Patriarchies as systems of subordinating women 'function simultaneously through coercion or threat and practice of violence, through making a wide social consensus drawn from and dispersed over many areas of social life and through obtaining in various ways, different degrees of consent from women' (Sangari, 1993: 868). Patriarchies formulate thresholds in congruence with their specific class, caste and community codes and make women conform and consent to the laws of the private sphere through a complex system of reward and punishment. Women's consent to the patriarchal law is neither an essential nor a historically static category but a part of the dynamic process of the reconstitution of patriarchies. According to Sangari, when women conform to or invest in patriarchal values, it need not be construed as consent; since patriarchies are simultaneously located in class structures and particular forms of caste–class inequality. Conversely, patriarchies help in inculcating an acceptance of social inequalities which transcend gender. Although patriarchies are related to class–caste structures of social inequality, they remain distinct and are not collapsible. The relation between classes and patriarchies is complex and variable, and class formulation and social differentiation are themselves uneven and contradictory processes. The problem of evaluating the hegemonic power of patriarchies is 'knotty, entangled with many other questions' (Sangari, 1993: 869).

Patriarchies themselves cannot be seen in isolation as they are entrenched within larger ideologies of class/caste/community tend to fix the identities of their women (1993: 868). Women are seen primarily as subjects who validate cultural identities – Sikh co-wives who are supposed to live 'like sisters' in *What the Body Remembers*. Shauna Singh Baldwin presents two women inside the threshold and explores their identity as it is constructed by various institutionalised discursive practices of family, class and religion/community. Roop in *What the Body Remembers*, growing up as a Sikh in pre-partition times, validates the cultural identity of her own community, distinguishing it not only from the 'Other' Muslim community but also from the earlier Hindu identity of her extended family. Satya too is proud of her lineage of belonging to an old, established Sikh family and not a newly converted one like Roop's.

However, in this entire discourse so ostensibly about women there is a total lack of women's voices and their subjectivity is difficult to construct. In the social realm, female identity is usually lost or rendered invisible within the larger group identities of family, community and nation. Women are left faceless and voiceless. The women also rework and negotiate the paradigms of tradition and modernity that their class/caste/community allow them. But apart from the various ideologies – familial, social, traditional and modern that women carry – there emerges a voice distinct from the many scripts that attempt to construct the identity of woman, a voice provided by the woman novelist. It is here that the task of the postcolonial woman novelist in resurrecting the lost voices of women, in mapping silences and filling the gaps becomes significant. Baldwin foregrounds both tradition and modernity as they are played upon the women in the construction of their identity.

Baldwin presents the 16-year-old Roop whose identity has been constructed and schooled into obedience by the complex dynamics of reward and punishment until she emerges as a *hanji* (meaning 'yes') saying figure approved by upper-class Sikh patriarchy. Married into an upper-class, elite family she pliantly conforms to the 'new' standards of colonial modernity expected of her – as in the *bhadramahila* construct, vacillating between the decorative memsahib and the useful strong woman as she grows older. Her sister Madani too is cast in the useful accomplished model of the *bhadramahila*, but being married into a family of lower status than Roop, Madani does not have to mould herself according to the constructs of modernity. Satya, as the useful accomplished woman rejects the false modernity of her patriarchy but presses for her own rights as a woman. In doing so she breaks out of established scripts and enters the domain of individual or personal rights contrary to 'Indian' cultural values and is rejected by her husband. It is Satya's voice that reverberates in protest through the text. Roop negotiates tradition and modernity as constructs imposed by her patriarchy, but ultimately understands the dynamics of patriarchal oppression behind them and begins to identify with the feminist voice consciousness of the older first wife Satya. The private sphere itself is embroiled in the play of a power politics between the two wives of Sardarji, Satya and Roop. The patriarchal arrangement prevents the co-wives from developing any relationship of solidarity as women and locks them in a politics of intrigue between the powerful and the powerless inside the private sphere. Shauna Singh Baldwin suffuses the text with a preeminently feminist consciousness in the form of one of the protagonists Satya. The author explores how the body of woman becomes 'tabula on which the history of a nation and the mores and rules of patriarchal society are indelibly inscribed' (Malik, 2002: 195).

As Rajeshwari Sunder Rajan points out silence cannot be the perpetual condition of human beings, however oppressed. Women as users of language are excluded from and trapped within a sign system that perpetuates a kind of 'false consciousness'. Yet through the 'interpretive framework' of their experiences within the threshold itself they voice partly subversive modes. The 'private' sphere is a distinct 'political' site for the games of power and contests of will, centring on issues of class, procreativity, household labour and other forms of sexual division of labour that are seldom integrated into the political economy of the public sphere. The text explores the 'rhetoric of incitement' that women resort to in order to play power games in the inner confines/private sphere and takes into account what Kumkum Sangari has called 'socially structured and often sanctioned forms of indirect agency, in their specific articulation of consent and resistance, as significant signs of the ways in which men and women make their history or are inhibited from doing so' (1993: 867).

Satya and Roop, the two wives of Sardarji are seen primarily as bodies; either as bodies that failed to deliver 'what women are for' or as the object of male desire. Although both the female protagonists are relegated inside the private sphere and objectified into bodies as objects, the feminist 'voice consciousness' of Satya emerges as the perspective of the twenty-first century author. Satya breaks out of the discourses of her time and insists on recognition of her identity for who she is and not merely as a body or a womb. Rejecting the subject position of a subservient wife Satya has arrived at a feminist perspective. This perception originates from the conflict and contradiction between dominant institutional definitions of a woman's role primarily as a life-bearer, structures of society of her time, which allow a man to take many wives and the liberal discourse of a free and self determining individual will. As a woman born much ahead of her times 'who comes into this world with her eyes open will never lower them before a man' and despite 'a whole life of worship and expiation is born into the body of woman once again' (Baldwin, 1999: 12). She rebels against the social order; having failed to bear a child till the age of 42 years her husband brings home a young girl, Roop, pinning his hopes on the fecundity of her youthful body.

The identity of the two female protagonists is constructed through various social discourses. They are socialised through authoritative patriarchal ideologies, learn to and give meaning to their experiences and form their identity circumscribed inside the private sphere. Satya is constructed in the Nationalists' mould of the useful/functional woman who is tuned to her husband's/household needs. Although Satya rebels against the law that primarily views her as a body, she consents to the authority which the threshold enforces. As an upper-class, elite woman of her time, she lacks direct access to the public sphere but nevertheless she wields authority as *Bari Sardarni* on lower-class/caste men watching them on the basis of 'corroborative patriarchal ideologies', wording her commands as if they had been mouthed by Sardarji himself (Sangari, 1993: 867). Patriarchal social or cultural contexts give her power over Sardarji's subordinates and she manages his estate in his absence, 'Mukhtiar, manager Abdul Aziz, does my bidding because he respects my judgement, he knows he cannot cheat me, I am too watchful. Not a pai of Sardarji's money is spent on mere ornamentation' (Baldwin, 1999: 19). Satya acquiescences to patriarchal practices which give her power over low-class males as well as over younger women like Sardarji's new wife Roop, something she has been trained in by watching her mother-in-law. Satya's acceptance of the authority conferred upon her need not be constructed as consent to patriarchy; as she rebels against the order that sees her primarily as a body. Moreover patriarchy too is subjected to and simultaneously located in specific modes of production, in class structures and in particular forms of caste–class inequality. Conversely, patriarchies also help in inculcating an acceptance of social inequalities and in making structures of deference which are wider than the relations between men and women. The relation between classes and patriarchies is complex and variable. According to Sangari, conditions which govern women's consent are wider than patriarchies so women's consent may be linked with other social structures in specific historical conjunctures (1993: 869).

But in this scenario of power politics inside the threshold, Satya in spite of hailing from a high-class family 'famous for its bravery' is fast losing control in the private sphere because of her failure to provide an heir for Sardarji's vast wealth and property (Baldwin, 1999: 193). The contractual element of bearing a son, implicit in the institution of marriage, is widely accepted in the cultural context of the society. Satya is slighted even by her maid Mani Mai for her barrenness. As she scolds Sardarji's valet for putting a damaged apricot in the good ones, Mani Mai retorts 'Dehna Singh was only doing what he sees happening in this home. Satya does not let Mani Mai see she had been hurt'. Instead she swallows the overripe fruit willing its seed to 'travel all the way to her womb'. As she chokes over the seed, her maid simply watches as she coughs and chokes exclaiming 'Allah! every woman has her *kismet*' (Baldwin, 1999: 23). Her own sense of guilt comes forth as 'her body betrayed her every moon-month with its bleeding' and she feels, 'what right had she to share his bed and bring nothing from the coupling?' Satya's mother *Bebeji* is an old-timers who has internalised patriarchal ideologies and lives by its mores, 'a woman is merely cracked open for seedling like the earth before the force of the plough. If she is fertile, good for the farmer, if not, bad for her' (Baldwin, 1999: 19, 25). She counsels Satya to go and find a *sant*/'holy man' to sleep with her for the money and get a son referring to the custom of high-caste women frequenting shrines of *faqirs* and ascetics who are known to have the power to give children to childless women.

Sardarji draws upon consensual and contractual elements of the threshold – his sister Toshi and her husband Sardar Kaushal Singh to arrange a second wife for him. According to Sangari:

> Women are subject to determination of patriarchal structures ... not only because they are embedded in social stratification, divisions of labour, other political structures, religious/cultural practices ... but also because of the contractual and consensual element in them, which along with patriarchal systems is open to constant and consistent reformulation. (1993: 868)

Toshi functions in 'active collusion' in structures of patriarchal practices and actively collaborates in finding him a new wife to bear a son. Satya too pretends to look for the perfect bride for Sardarji, one who is conversant with the new *git-mit* talk of the British. But when Roop arrives, Satya is ignored by Toshi and her husband when they come for a visit and no longer ask about her when Sardarji visits their home.

Satya who will not bow to any imposed constructs raves and rants on Sardarji's marriage to the 16-year-old Roop, and taking up the rhetoric of her own rights is seen as a *churail* or the regulatory psychobiography of Kakeyi:

> I want your love, not your duty ... your fidelity, not your generosity. I want, not for you, but *for me, for myself* (Emphasis added). Because though I failed to do what the women are for, I am still here, still

> your wife, still Satya. *And, if he were here now I would say, 'In return let me share as the Guru himself allows me; share your burdens, your obligations, your vulnerability. Let us face them, not you alone, or I alone, but you and I'*. (347, emphasis original)

In the Indian context individuality, particularly a woman's, is seen as a disruptive force which has to bow before decisions of collective authority imposed upon them. As Sangari points out, since women are usually perceived as having duties, any claim to 'rights' unless effectively disguised become a sign of woman's evil nature. 'You have a tongue sharper than Kakeyi. I tell you, I'm so tired of your shouting … . You don't want me because I tell you what you have become. I tell you what I see inside you, that's why you throw me away' (Baldwin, 1999: 26).

Satya, whose name means truth, has not learnt lessons of obedience to men that she was meant to learn from past lives and like the goddess Kali, who steps on her husband has the courage or foolhardiness to tell a man what she really thinks of him, 'Why don't you take a stand, either say you are for independence and join the protesters or say you are a puppet of the British so people can respect you or revile you, but at least know how you feel' (Baldwin, 1999: 222). Taking an ideologically different position from that of her husband who joins the ranks of the Indian elite in the British civil service (the Public Works Department), she not only supports the nationalist fervour of the patriots but also takes her husband to task for not doing so. The figure of Kali represents both beneficent and malevolent aspects of female power, providing a rationale for the control of female sexuality through men and marriage. In her malevolent aspect Kali receives blood sacrifice but is benevolent as Lakshmi when she is under the control of the male god. As Susan Wadley suggests, it is marriage and the dominance of the male that transforms the goddess' dangerous power into benevolence (1988: 24). But even through marriage Satya has not been completely tamed. Although Satya has internalised several ideologies of patriarchal society especially those that confer power and authority on her, she has within her a subversive female rage which is manifested in her refusal to deify her husband. 'She talked to the shadows and cried for herself because she had not wanted all that he wanted, because she would not forget the past lives just because the British say there are none' (Baldwin, 1999: 26).

Satya can no longer call her paternalistic patriarchy to account in recognised forms of surrogate action to intervene on her behalf, and in time her father too loses the power that accrues from his land, when the British formalise land rights to registered deeds. Her brother too wastes himself in drink and opium and is finally murdered by bandits:

> *I am not wife, for my husband has abandoned me. I'm not widow, for he still lives. I'm not mother, for the son he gave me is taken away, I'm not sister, for I have no brother. With no father, I'm but daughter of my Bebeji. And so I am no one .... I have become all I hated in Roop – dependent, grasping, begging for the leftovers of his love.* (emphasis original, Baldwin, 1999: 360)

The identity of Roop, on the contrary, is constructed through dominant institutional sites of patriarchal discourse for women of her class, encased in the private sphere. 'The "private" sphere is a distinct "political" site for the direct and tangential formation of the gendered subject' (Sangari, 1993: 867). The reworked and recast patriarchies in the changing social, political, cultural scenario in pre-independence India not only construct Roop's subjectivity but the shifting identities of community/religion and nation are rewritten on women – dictating their movement, attire and needs. Roop as an eight-year-old child growing up in her village, Pari Darwaza, learns the complex dynamics of culture. In fact, 'Culture' says Rajan, 'viewed as the product of beliefs and conceptual models of society and as the destination where the trajectory of its desires takes shape, ... is the constitutive realm of the subject' (1993: 10). She learns to conform to sex role stereotyping of a 'good-good' *hanji* saying young woman. According to Sangari and Vaid 'women internalise the offered models and constitute themselves with varying degrees of conformity' – the formation of models deferred according to community/religious identities (1989: 14).

Roop has been raised to conform to the Nationalists' model of the *bhadramahila*, who is reasonably educated and cultured to fit into the companionate model for the bourgeois husband. The model of the ideal woman constructed by the Nationalists was the middle path between the Western model of the memsahib 'who was fond of useless luxury and cared little for the well-being of the home' and the lower-class woman who was termed as coarse and vulgar. The education that Roop and her sister Madani receive is meant to inculcate in them 'typically bourgeois virtues – of ordinariness, thrift, cleanliness and a personal sense of responsibility, the practical skills of literacy, accounting and hygiene and the ability to run the household according to the new physical and economic conditions set by the outside world' (Chatterjee, 1989: 247). But within the ideologies which make her sister Madani conform completely, she makes space for independent ambitions – refuses to learn cooking as it is needed only as a substitute for beauty. She determines to marry a rich man practising to say 'How did you do. Delighted to meet you'. Roop does not want to spend her life in the backwaters of a tiny village Pari Darwaza like her mother. 'She'll travel to places the traders speak of – the Mall Road in Muree ... even the capital of all India – Delhi' (Baldwin, 1999: 106, 127). Marrying well is the highest scope of feminine ambition that patriarchy allows Roop. In concession to the 'new zamana' and the new expectations of modernity demanded from women during the colonial period by the changing patriarchies, girls must learn to read and write and be married only at sixteen. In accordance with her ambition of marrying into a high-class family, Roop implores her father to send her to school where she can learn to sit on chairs. So Roop and her sister Madani are sent to Bhai Takht Singh's Sikh Girls' School with chairs for Roop and walls twelve feet high, unlike her brother Jeevan who is sent to the mission school to learn English and prepare for the army even if his father has to take a loan for it.

Roop's mode of subjectivity is constructed by the closed circle of women who have internalised patriarchal ideologies, in the interior of her father's *haveli* – from Revati Bhua, an unmarried sonless woman who lives in the house of Roop's father, Bachan Singh with her 'small tachey case;' her *Nani,* who at her deathbed gifts Bachan Singh with heavy gold *panjebs,* as compensation for having died in a married daughters home; from Gujri the low-class child widow 'who accompanied her mother's pots and pans' as part of her dowry (Baldwin, 1999: 41, 83). The social cultural context of these women teaches her that it is imperative for women to be born with 'good *kismet*', to have dependable men – fathers/husband/brothers to look after them. *Nani* at her deathbed advises the girls to listen and obey their father and brother. 'There should be no difference between one and the other'. Since the girls do not have a mother they are sent to a distant relative, Lajo Bhua, to learn 'the great importance of [their] ... *chunni,* her modesty, the dangers of unknown men and the importance of obedience "for her own good"' (Baldwin, 1999: 82, 95). The girls are taught rule number one, two and three as laws of the threshold:

> Rule number one: you want to make a good marriage; you must be more graceful, more pleasing to your elders. I want to hear only '*achaji, hanji, yes-ji*' from you. Never '*nahinji, no-ji*' ... . Rule number two! Speak softly, always softly! ... Rule number three: Never feel angry, never, never. No matter what happens, at what your husband says, never feel angry". (Baldwin, 1999: 97–98)

Having lost a mother who could have informed her, Roop does not realise that it is more important to *appear* docile and *say yes-ji* all the time, thereby obtaining leverage for maneuver. It is much later that Roop learns the politics of the threshold as well as the 'rhetoric of incitement' which works behind the scenes from her sister-in-law Kusum.

Roop is interpolated, body and mind by the law of the threshold. Roop's independent, free spirit as a child has been effectively curbed and socialised by the authority of what is 'normal/natural' and she is 'raised to bend like saplings with every wind so long as it speaks with a voice of authority' (Baldwin, 1999: 20). She can be slapped, cajoled and rewarded into submission. As Partha Chatterjce points out, 'as with all hegemonic forms of exercise of dominance, this patriarchy combined coercive authority with the subtle force of persuasion' (1989: 248). The energetic eight-year-old who could eat as much as her brother and compete with him at boxing, swimming and punching him hard is slowly socialised to learn demure behaviour. The girl who loves to ride her horse, Nirvair, is later forbidden by her father to do so for the fear 'that there would be no blood on the sheets when she gets married'. 'Roop-bi, you're so *ziddi* that if you're not careful everyone will say: "Let her be alone."' She promises to be more careful, grateful and obedient (Baldwin, 1999: 119).

Baldwin also mentions women who follow the scripts laid down by Gandhi, address protest marches, speak fearlessly to men in the street and inhabit a space created for women in the 'public' world. The nationalist discourse, as in the Gandhian script for women did create a space of mobility for women outside the domestic sphere in the domain of the public – the nation and the freedom struggle signified in the text by the woman addressing the public rally in Lahore. However, this is the space that remains out of bounds for Roop. She watches the woman protester with 'no softness in the planes of her earth brown face' negotiating the public space inhabited by men in white *kurtas* with 'the raw unfinished smell of anger' (Baldwin, 1999: 94). A bonfire is built and the woman marches towards it:

> Roop is afraid for this woman, this determined woman who speaks so loud in the street away from her home, who must be attracted to the flames, like moths to a candle. She waits for the woman to walk into the fire, as Sita did, when Ram tested her in the *Ramayan* … . But the woman does not. Instead she takes off her *chunni* and says that throws it into the fire. (Baldwin, 1999: 94)

However, this new public space is kept strictly out of bounds for Roop by the patriarchy of her class and community. These women are not role models to be followed, as Roop soon learns when on throwing her own *chunni* in the flames she feels the stinging palm of her father across her cheek in a slap twice as humiliating as that of her sister, 'Don't you follow outside men. You don't even know what they were saying! You could have been taken, you could have been raped, anything could have happened!' (Baldwin, 1999. 95). "The repositioning of cultural forms … is implicated in the formation of a predominantly middle-class public sphere – in a desired version of Indian culture and in a desired version of the ideal woman. It is also implicated in a new formation of the home as the insulated private sphere which is free even from temporary challenges to male authority' (Sangari and Vaid, 1989: 12). Roop can neither question the authority of her father, nor her brother, but she marvels at her brother's daring to disagree and argue with her father about political issues. She has been taught the importance of being 'sweet-sweet, good-good' and her heavily lashed brown eyes unlike Satyas grey ones are demurely lowered and innocent. 'A man could tell those eyes anything and they would believe him, a man could kiss those red lips for hours and they would look fuller and more luscious for the brushing.' From Roop's tongue, 'a man will hear no truths he cannot explain away' (Baldwin, 1999: 15, 16). She has learnt 'at last to please Bachan Singh ... covering her head, being silent and obedient'.

In traditional Indian ideology female sexuality was legitimately embodied only in marriage, wifehood, motherhood and domesticity – all forms of control over women's bodies. Baldwin foregrounds the anxiety for purity, chastity of upper-class/caste girls as soon as Roop approaches puberty. The dazzling beauty of Roop traps her as a prized object within the threshold. Bachan Singh's daughters do not have to go to the fields like other girls in the village, 'because they are getting older and who knows what would happen to young girls going alone to the fields with no man to protect them' but use latrine built for his wife because she had to be in *purdah* (Baldwin, 1999: 84). Roop is no longer allowed to cross the threshold of her father's *haveli* 'because of what people will say'. Any weakness or infirmity in a woman's body, an object of barter, is to be concealed at all costs. After the typhoid Roop must conceal her 'bad ear' even from close family for what rich man will marry the girl with one ear? Similarly Roop on discovering that her two-year-old daughter appears cross-eyed at certain angles teaches her to hide her eyes and look away just as she herself had learnt to live with one ear. The rationale behind concealing physical imperfection in her daughter is simple for, 'If there was something wrong with her, there is something wrong with Roop with the body that made her, shaped her' (Baldwin, 1999: 272).

According to Chakravarty, 'the central factor for the subordination of the upper caste woman [is] the need for effective sexual control over such women to maintain not only patriarchal succession ... but also caste purity, the institution the unique to Hindu society' (1993: 579). Although theoretically the Sikhs are forbidden to practise caste/untouchability, the control of the sexuality of women cuts across communities/religions along lines of class. In fact effective sexual control of women assumes proportions of panic among the upper classes. Bachan Singh keeps a strict vigil over the exceptional beauty of his daughter. Roop too internalises the codes of subjectivity expected of her:

> Roop's heart has become a storeroom where Bachan Singh hoards the full measure of her giving. That young heart presses like a coiled steel spring against her breast. Heart that does not venture outside the haveli for fear of Bachan Singh's displeasure, heart afraid to glance at or speak to unrelated men in the village … . Heart that beats hard and fast as a tabla in her chest if her *chunni* falls but once, for a moment, to her shoulders, lest a man be smitten because Roop tempted him.
>
> By now Bachan Singh, Gujri, Revati Bhua and Kusum have done their duty well: Roop has learned shame. (Baldwin, 1999: 128)

Roop's young body becomes an object of barter between her father who is heavily in debt and the wealthy childless landowner Sardarji, 26 years her senior. She fails to realise that she is being married without dowry to replace the infertile emptiness of his first wife, Satya. She is elated with the proposal and sees it as an opportunity to escape 'papaji's policing' and 'endless restrictions' and fulfil her ambitions to have pretty clothes and jewels (Baldwin, 1999: 122). Roop's identity is now fixed into the patriarchal mould not of a mother but as a mere womb. On conception she is carried on Sardarji's arm 'as though he carries hope flowering on his arm' for 'without sons to remind the world of its doer a man's work dies at the same instant as a man's body' (Baldwin, 1999: 168, 162).

Roop is asked to give her firstborn to her 'like-a-sister' who would be 'like-a-mother', another patriarchal construct that foregrounds what Rajan calls the elision between real and imagined women. Her second born, a son, is also handed over to Satya and she realises her 'obligatory altruism', that her mode of existence is reduced to a womb. 'This is a fire test, the kind of test Ram asked Sita to take when he became unsure that Sita was worthy to be his queen … . Roop could fail this test because she isn't good-good sweet-sweet as Sita; she isn't generous enough to let Satya have a child' (Baldwin, 1999: 201). But she cannot afford to fail this test, she could be sent away and 'papaji's *izzat* will be dragged in the mud' and she remains fixed into man-imagined construct of 'Sita in her man-inscribed circle' (Baldwin, 1999: 200, 229). After giving away her children the promised joy of sacrifice does not come. She is reduced to a mask of taut strings. He is the cause and she is the effect. She cannot tell how she who once rode her horse fearlessly came to mean 'mother-ness without child-ness and yes-ness without no-ness, like a word reversing meaning as it passes from mouth-to-mouth' (Baldwin, 1999: 227). She is totally denied an identity of her own and is even deprived of the luxury of being known by her role as a mother. Women, as Malik says, 'are mere objects to facilitate man, to be used and discarded at their convenience; they are objects of barter, means of reproduction and tools or instruments used for torturing one-woman against another' (2002: 197).

Roop has not been schooled in what Sangari calls the 'politics of incitement' and her position is one of resigned acceptance rather than active collusion. According to Sangari, 'incitement exists at the interaction between the "political" and "domestic", between gender relations and power relations, occupies an uneasy boundary between the respective logics of women's consent and resistance re-articulating their relationship in different ways' (1993: 872). Her passive acquiescence is dependent not only upon her absence of choices but related to power equations of material factors and class structures. Roop's father, Dipty Bachan Singh, is no match for Sardarji's traditional as well as modern structures of elitism. '*He maybe Lambardar, he maybe Dipty of all Pari Darwaza, but in the end he is just a poor, ordinary Punjabi village man*' (emphasis original, Baldwin, 1999: 307). Roop as a 'woman who has climbed beyond her father kin' has no power against structures of oppression.

But her brother Jeevan, as an English educated captain in the Her Majesty's Army, has moved up the social scale with 'the war ... helping Indians rise faster in the Army than they ever could in peacetime' (308). So it is Jeevan she calls upon for 'the rhetoric of incitement' – her protector and saviour, for all the golden threads she has woven into *rakhri* for him. 'Incitement ... occupies an uneasy boundary between the respective logics of women's consent and resistance re-articulating their relationship in different ways' (Sangari, 1993: 872). Roop cannot speak for herself like Satya, cannot act independently but she can call upon her paternal patriarchy to intercede on her behalf. Jeevan like a clever negotiator never names Roop's personal interest, but abstractions like family, *izzat*/'honour', religion/community mediates it. For if women cite their own personal stake, then they acquire malignant connotations: they become conniving intriguers and wicked manipulators who lead men astray. 'In naming and not naming resides the distinction between willingness and heroic inciting women ... [A]ny claim to 'rights', unless effectively disguised, becomes a sign of woman's evil nature' (Sangari, 1993: 873). Roop fears that Satya is trying to poison her but as Kusum informs her, 'it is a big thing for you – you think you're so important. For papaji *izzat* is bigger' (Baldwin, 1999: 312). So it is the paradigm of *izzat*/'honour', that is invoked and not Roop herself – neither as subject not as agency. Jeevan subtly exaggerates that Satya was trying to poison not Roop but her son. Satya is cast in the mould of the manipulating woman or Kakeyi who represents 'control over male sexuality ... [thus] putting male honour ... at stake .... by laying him open to social castigation for being unmanly' (Sangari, 1993: 873). Thus Jeevan, Bachan Singh and Sardarji negotiate with the entire village as an audience and seal the fate of two women. It is decided that Satya will live separately and that the children will be handed back to Roop in order to save the honour/*izzat* of the menfolk.

In this entire discourse women become the site on which issues such as men's honour, the children and claims of the community become deciding factors. In times of pre-independence turmoil, it would be useful for Sardarji to have a well disposed young brother-in-law in the Army in uncertain times. Besides Pari Darwaza with the dominant Muslim population has a Sikh *Lambardar/Dipty* and undermining his authority as the leader of the village over a 'mere woman' was something that he was not inclined to do. When Jeevan drops Roop back to Rawalpindi, Sardarji ceremoniously hands her over the keys of the pantry. By setting up a structure of incitement which serves as Roop's mode of redressal and indirect agency she calls patriarchy as a structure of public accountability that could affect Sardarji's social standing.

The colonial elite patriarchies served as a partially modernising force as it recast 'women for companionate marital relationship and attendant familial duties' (Sangari and Vaid, 1989: 19). Chatterjee admits to 'reproach mixed with envy – of the wealth and luxury of the new social elite emerging around institutions of colonial administration and trade' (1989: 240). Roop moulds her identity to the new script that the elite, upper-class Sikh patriarchy casts for her – as a socially presentable, decorated woman who must do her husband proud as she accompanies him to various social gatherings outside the home, to clubs and dinners – structures from which patriarchies of an earlier generation had strictly debarred their women, keeping them in the enclosed confines of the *zenana*. Unlike Satya shared of Sardarji's early years of struggle, Roop conforms to the colonial bourgeois script and becomes the wife for modern times, the one for English dinner parties with Sardarji's 'superiors' and for ornament learning new etiquettes along with the use of knife, fork and serviettes, the insipid taste of white sauce and tolerate the smell of fish. Although the Sikh faith scripturally accorded a higher status to women (though none of its prophets were women), a kind of pan-Indian upper-class affinity kept women in the inner confines of the household. The Sikh identity which interpellates Roop's subjectivity also dictates tradition and religious faith and accordingly Roop can sing *shabads* or the 'holy hymns'. 'Socially approved conduct is not only dictated by gender but also by religious/community patriarchies' (Chatterjee, 1989: 247). Thus after moving up the social scale by marrying into an elite, upper-class family, Roop can glide in chiffon sari – an attire which is seen to be 'shameless' by her Muslim friend Huma, whose body is engulfed in the folds of her burqa. Even here class affiliations dictate the mode of existence of women as in *Sunlight on a Broken Column* where Laila, an upper-class, elite Muslim woman, is not only allowed English education but also some movement outside the *zenana* in the public sphere by her patriarchy. Sardarji who since his return from England has called his people 'Indians/them' having forgotten 'when he knew "them" to be "us"' permits his wife to use cosmetics and beautiful clothes (Baldwin, 1999: 162).

The identities of women are intertwined with religious/community ideologies from beyond the 'private' sphere. Thus Roop learns that 'Guru's words are simple – work hard, share with your neighbour, repeat the name of God. That worship at graves is not for Sikhs that worship before Hindu idols is not for Sikhs' (Baldwin, 1999: 82). Shifting identities during the time of partition not only crystallise into Sikhs, Hindus and Muslims but even full caste Sikhs and the casteless ones. The growing rigidity in religious identities can cause friction between brothers – the older Bachan Singh who is a Sikh convert, now identifies with his adopted community. He orders that the family will no longer walk the border of one faith and another but be proper Sikhs. His younger brother, Shyam Chacha, a staunch Hindu has been attending Arya Samaj Hindu reform meetings and been told that 'Mahatma Gandhi thinks the turban "dirty"'. 'Shyam Chacha now asks Bachan Singh to prove his brotherhood, by folding his hands in the temple' (Baldwin, 1999: 86). The fundamentalist Shuddhi movement of the Arya Samaj results in forcible cutting off the hair of a promising Sikh youth who is the son of a retired military man. As a result he can no longer be recruited in the Sikh regiment. Bachan Singh escorts the boy home walking through the bazaar with his sword unsheathed. Sardarji's friend Rai Alam, an ICS officer begins to observe the Ramzaan again, stops eating meat at Faletti's, a Sikh owned hotel.

As communal/religious identities harden, multiple patriarchies 'brand their women with their identity, inscribed their fear on their bodies, clothe them in burqas, make them badges of their honour and *izzat* and direct passions and revenge of communal frenzy on the bodies of the "other" women' (Baldwin, 1999: 154). Patriarchies doubly reinforced by dominant ideologies of community/religion are inscribed on the bodies of women and ensure that Roop's friend Huma is to be clothed in 'heavy woollen socks peeping out from under the hem of new black burqua' and is no longer sent to play with her; that Revati Bhua will no longer worship her idols, or Roop cut her hair, wear a *bindi* or vermillion in the parting of her hair; that *Nani* will no longer hold a *siapa* – a custom of mourning for her dead daughter. Henceforth there would be no more need for Revati Bhua to perform any purification ceremony with cow's urine or Ganga water in the house.

Women being badges of honour of men/community are pulled out from the 'private' sphere and made soft targets of communal hatred in the 'public' arena of politics and the nation. Sharpening communal identities slowly give way to simmering suspicion and a frenzy of hate and revenge which is played out on the bodies of women during partition. 'Women's bodies were the "site" on which the hyper masculine revenge drama of mutual humiliation was enacted. Their bodies were the tabula on which men imprinted their bestiality' (Malik, 2002: 200). Women are subjected to violence not only by men of the warring communities but also their own men to save 'their' honour. Roop's father, Dipty Bachan Singh fearing that the Muslims will violate the honour of his son Jeevan's wife Kusum, she being young and of childbearing age himself asks her for a sacrifice. 'I told her what Sant Puran Singh said the Sikhs must do, and that I had to do it now. She understood. Always she made no trouble' (Baldwin, 1999: 521). Kusum goes into the interior rooms of Roop's mother, turned her back and took off her *chunni* to bare her neck and Bachan Singh beheads her with a single stroke of the *kirpan*. He could not endure the idea of 'seeds of that foreign religion ... being planted in ... her womb' (520). Kusum's body is desecrated by the Muslims, used as a site to convey a message to her husband and men of her community. Her body is brutally dismembered each limb severed at the joint and the womb ripped out:

> He received the message. Kusum's womb, the same from which his three sons came, had been delivered. Ripped out.
>
> And the message, 'We will stamp your kind, your very species from existence. This is no longer merely about *izzat* or land. This is a war against your quom, for all time. Leave. We take the womb so there can be no Sikhs from it, we take the womb, leave you its shell' (Baldwin, 1999: 511)

The bodies of women thus become the receptacle of their community's history as well as the sign through which 'the violent dialogue between men was conducted' (Das, 1995: 186). At this juncture women – Hindu/Sikh/Muslim bear the shame and hatred of 'other' communities imprinted on their bodies. As they are identified as class and community subjects, at the same time women transcend the barriers of class/community in a sense of shared shame. Women express solidarity with each other across religions, communities, classes or time – Roop with her maid, Jorimon and her Muslim friend, Huma. Baldwin 50 decades later adds her own 'voice consciousness' through Roop who moved by the sight of women pulling the remnants of rags about their breasts drops her own clothes, making a plea to treat women as God made them, as merely human – uninscribed by religion/community:

> ... [E]veryman, woman and child should, just once in this lifetime, see woman's body without shame. See her as no man's possession; *see* her, not from the corners of your eyes! ... she wants to scream, *See me, I'm human, though I'm only a woman. See me; I did what women are for. See me not as a vessel, a plaything, a fantasy, a maid servant, an ornament, but as Vaheguru made me.* (emphasis original, Baldwin, 1999: 498)

Both Satya and Roop are subjects in process as they mould and alter their modes of subjectivity negotiating with the expectations of their patriarchy. Both the female protagonists resort to modes of resistance within the threshold itself, Satya by invoking her personal 'rights' and claims and Roop by falling back upon her paternal patriarchy. Satya who moves from the imagined constructs that men impose – of Kakeyi and Kali, ultimately comes back to the Sita model choosing self-immolation like her. Satya chooses to die for her dignity rather than live without *izzat* having been spurned and cast off for Roop. Like Sita she gives him, her husband, the 'gift' of her absence by courting death, by taking the poison of tuberculosis from her cousin Mumta's lips, her TB afflicted cousin through a European kiss. Satya articulates her protest silently not disturbing Sardarji's honour in conformity with patriarchal norms but protests nonetheless. Satya's soul re-enters the world for a rebirth only to find that things have not changed:

> Again I'm born a woman, foolish-girl child who has entered the world with her eyes wide open and so will never lower them before a man ...
>
> The man's voice comes deep, comes low ... he is disappointed I'm not a boy ... . And I know, because my body remembers without benefit of words, that men who do not welcome girl-babies will not treasure me as I grow to woman – though he call me princess just because the Gurus told him to.
>
> *I have come so far – I have borne so much pain and emptiness! But men have not yet changed.* (emphasis original, Baldwin, 1999: 538)

Post independence, Roop too changes from the 'good-good sweet-sweet' Sita construct to one who protests silently with the 'rhetoric of incitement' as the only mode of articulation available to her. From a decorated memsahib-like construct she takes on the functional role of Satya after her death and deals with partition and the tempestuous times, and supervises refugee relatives in her new residence in Delhi. The subdued and obedient Roop, with Satya's consciousness within her, evolves into a strong woman confronting Muslim sepoys and rescuing her maid, Jorimon, from being raped by them. With a degree of hauteur and wit, she gambles, pretending to be a Muslim and succeeds in fooling the Muslim army, having no one but herself to rely upon, being neither a recipient of male bounty or chivalry. From a merely decorated accompaniment to dinner parties she becomes the strength of her husband as he himself falters and loses hope after partition. Roop comes to understand and feel an affinity with Satya after her demise and absorbs within her body the latter's anger, pride and ambition thus establishing the ultimate solidarity of womanhood.

The identities of women in *What the Body Remembers* are formed through their negotiations within the inscribed paradigms of class/caste/religion/community inside the private sphere. Though these women have internalised to varying degrees the ideologies that construct them yet a 'voice consciousness' emerges to offer what Jacqueline Rose describes as 'the critique of male discourse'. This voice consciousness is distinct from the patriarchal constructs imposed upon them – a voice provided by the woman novelist. As these women live through their oppressions they realise the solidarity of 'the community of the oppressed' – Roop begins to feel Satya's consciousness within her and realises solidarity with her sister-in-law, Kusum, and even her maid, Jorimon; and even take on roles of agency as Roop saves Jorimon. Women 'tell' their narratives with the safety of time behind them. As times change and permit their narratives to be 'told', patriarchies themselves shift the threshold to accommodate change and the still, quiet yet subversive 'voices' of women inside the threshold as they accept as well as contest the constructs placed upon them.

References

Baldwin, Shauna Singh. 1999. *What the Body Remembers*. New Delhi: HarperCollins.

Chakravarty, Uma. 1989. 'Whatever Happened to the Vedic Dasi?', in Kumkum Sangari and Sudesh Vaid (eds), *Recasting Women: Essays in Colonial History*. New Delhi: Kali for Women.

——. 1993. 'Conceptualising Brahmanical Patriarchy in Early India: Gender, Caste, Class and State'. *Economic and Political Weekly*, 27(14): 579–584.

Chatterjee, Partha. 1989. 'The Nationalist Resolution of the Women's Question', in Kumkum Sangari and Sudesh Vaid (eds), *Recasting Women: Essays in Colonial History*. New Delhi: Kali for Women.

Das, Veena. 1995. *Critical Events*. Delhi: Oxford University Press.

Malik, Seema. 2002. 'Body as Object: A Reading of Shauna Singh Baldwin's *What the Body Remembers*', in Rajul Bhargava (ed.), *Indian Writing in English: The Last Decade*. Jaipur and New Delhi: Rawat.

Niranjana, Tejaswini. 1991. 'Cinema, Femininity and the Economy of Consumption'. *Economic and Political Weekly*, 26(43): WS 85–86.

Rajan, Rajeshwari Sundar. 1993. *Real and Imagined Women: Gender, Culture and Postcolonialism*. London and New York: Routledge.

Sangari, Kumkum and Vaid, Sudesh. 1989. 'Introduction', in Kumkum Sangari and Sudesh Vaid (eds), *Recasting Women: Essays in Colonial History*. New Delhi: Kali for Women.

Sangari, Kumkum. 1993. 'Consent, Agency and Rhetoric of Incitement'. *Economic and Political Weekly*, 28(18): 867–882.

Wadley, Susan. 1988. 'Women and the Hindu Tradition', in Rehana Ghadially (ed.), *Women in Indian Society: A Reader*. New Delhi: Sage.

2

Tracing the Contours of Conflict

Gender, Power and Powerlessness in *The God of Small Things*

Pushpinder Walia

The Woman's Question – a raging cry that has echoed through the various stages of history – continues to be an overwhelming concern for the sociocultural-political paradigm even today. The praxis of the dynamics of gender and power is clearly delineated in Arundhati Roy's (1997) *The God of Small Things*, where the preponderance of power appears in the oppression of the feminine gender. The objective of this chapter thus becomes twofold: (a) to analyse and study the entity of gender vis-à-vis the paradigm of power and (b) to bring out the transgression of boundaries set by the culturally defined and socially fixed roles of female stereotypes. The most tragic victim of the system is Ammu, who suffers at the hands of her husband, her family and the Ayemenem social values; her predicament in the patriarchal world where she lives, is central to an understanding of the gender connotations underlying the text. At 27 years of age, divorced, with two children in tow, Ammu is confronted with the fact that she has no 'Locusts Stand I'.[1] Not only Ammu, even Mammachi, Ammu's mother – 'used to' being beaten with a brass vase everyday by her husband, and Baby Kochamma, suffering from a frustrated relationship that yields her nothing except lifelong bitterness and loneliness, represent pathetic victims, who are by-products of an oppressive patriarchal structure. For this reason, even though they tyrannise Ammu, yet one finds that as oppressors, they are no less oppressed themselves.

However, before plunging into a detailed narrative in this context, it becomes imperative to outline and highlight the historical paradigm of feminism as well as its theoretical bases.

Perspectives on Gender and Construction of 'Woman'

Feminism, by bringing forth the perceptive and insightful thinking of intelligent women (as well as men), seeks new definitions of female identity. Avasthi and Srivastava (2001) put it succinctly:

> Feminism is a politics, directed at changing existing power relations between women and men in the society. These power relations structure all areas of life – family, education and welfare, worlds of work and politics, culture and leisure. (Introduction 11)

The major concerns of feminism, as Madsen points out, can be identified as 'the unique experience of women in history; the notion of female consciousness; the definitions of gender that limit and oppress; and the cause of women's liberation from those restrictions' (2000: ix). Tracing the historical contexts of American feminism, Madsen states that it was the hierarchical worldview of the Puritan colonists that determined the position of women in colonial America. 'As men deferred to God and His ministers, so women should defer to men'.[2] The inferiority of women, according to the Puritans, was a mark of Original Sin and so in nineteenth century America, a woman was unable to vote, and after marriage had no control over her property or her children. 'Her status was akin to that of a minor or a slave' (Madsen, 2000: 3). And thus it was that the organised movement for women's rights had its origin in connection with slavery when the *American abolitionist movement split over women's* right to separate.

The first wave of American feminism can be traced in the 1840s, irked by the first Women's Rights Conference, held in Seneca Falls in 1848. Organised by Elizabeth Cady Stanton and others, the tone of the convention had been set by the efforts of Margaret Fuller whose plea for abolition of all intellectual and economic restrictions imposed for reasons of gender in her book *Woman in the Nineteenth Century* (1845) received an overwhelming response. The Seneca Falls Convention marked the beginning of the political struggle for women's rights and led to the formation of National Woman's Suffrage Association founded by Elizabeth Cady Stanton and Susan B. Anthony, and the American Woman's Suffrage Association (established by Lucy Shane); the two organisations merged in 1890 to become the National American Woman's Suffrage Association. However, it wasn't till 1920 that the Suffrage amendment to the constitution was made.

The second wave of American feminism emerged in the early 1960s; it focused upon 'an indictment of male sexism and the domestic oppression of women' (Madsen, 2000: 7). Its major concerns were the raising of women's consciousness of gender oppression as well as raising the personal experience of that oppression as a political issue. Friedan and Millett came to the fore as the most influential thinkers in the early stages of the second wave. Friedan (1976: 68) points out that the core problem for women is 'a problem of identity – a stunting or evasion of growth that is perpetuated by the feminine mystique' and that their 'culture does not permit women to accept or gratify their basic need to grew and fulfill their potentialities as human beings, a need which is not solely defined by their sexual role'. Millett's (1970: 30) research on 'the image of woman' in the patriarchal society, to which all women try to conform, led her to infer that the one stereotype that the mystique always seeks to glamorise is that of 'the happy housewife'.

Similarly, Millett (1970) attributes the cause of women's oppression to patriarchy. According to Millett, power is exerted directly or indirectly, in civil and domestic life, to constrain women. She borrows from social science the important distinction between 'sex' and 'gender' and explains how 'sex' is determined biologically, while 'gender' is a psychological concept which refers to culturally acquired sexual identity. But patriarchy deliberately confuses the biological categories of 'male' and 'female' with those of gender, like masculine and feminine. This acting out of the roles in the unequal relation of domination and subordination is what she calls 'sexual politics'. Later, in the 1970s and 1980s, the use of sexual violence by men as a strategy for sustaining patriarchal control for women rose prominently as a major feminist issue. Brownmiller's (1975) ground-breaking analysis of rape highlights the fact that all women are victimised by rape because the threat of rape is directed towards all women in patriarchal culture and as such, benefits all men in that culture. Steinem (1983) too brings out the commonality of female sexual exploitation.

The rise of the feminist theory in the areas of literary study, sociology, political theory, philosophy and history, thus becomes a notable landmark of the second wave feminism; early feminist theory, that developed from the Women's Liberation and Civil Rights movements, focused upon 'points of continuity between the reading experience and personal experience (including family, society, networks of relationships, power structures, systems of value learned and lived and perpetuated in "private" life)' (Madsen, 2000: 15).

Contemporary American feminism is characterised by diversity, and the whole notion that 'a post-feminist' era has started, when the aims of the women's movement have been realised and further efforts to extend women's rights are not required. Faludi (1991) speaks of the contemporary 'backlash', which is her term for what others have termed 'post-feminism'. Roiphe (1993) compares the feminism experienced by her mother in the early 1960s to her own encounter with feminism as dogma and infers that contemporary feminism is promoting an image of woman as a passive victim of male domination – the very image that early feminists sought to destroy. Another conspicuous strand of contemporary feminism is also found in the feminism of colour, highlighted in Davis (1981), hooks (1984), Allen (1996) and Anzaldua (1990). These feminists of colour point to the emergence of Black Feminism, Chicana/Hispana Feminism, Native Feminism and Asian Feminism as distinct theoretical perspectives upon the oppression of women with reference to the specifics of their racialised sexuality.

French feminism, an integral part of Western feminist theory, made its voice heard in Simone de Beauvoir's *The Second Sex* (1949), which is another canonical text in feminist literary discourse. De Beauvoir posits the fundamental questions of feminist identity when she points out that woman defines herself by saying, 'I am a woman'. She further elaborates how man defines the human, not woman, and she shares only a lopsided relationship with him. Man is the One, she the Other. Later, influential French feminists such as Cixous, Kristeva and Irigaray analyse how 'a specific kind of writing, designated feminine (Ecriture feminine) subverts the linguistic and metaphysical conventions of Western discourse' and the feminine thus becomes 'the symbol' of otherness, alterity, the unconscious, the unspoken, the 'Imaginary' of Lacan's revision of orthodox Freudian thought (Madsen, 2000: 19). French feminism of the 1980s, thus, is grounded in Freudian psychoanalysis, where the 'feminine' is a category of discourse, whose definition is constructed in language, philosophy, psycho-analysis and elsewhere. Hence, subconscious as well as the linguistic determinants of consciousness, are analysed psychoanalytically to discover the reasons for female oppression.

The discussion so far has focused on the overall concerns in Feminist Theory that have emerged, and continue to do so, in the Western tradition; there has been felt a need, however, to articulate the indigenous feminist issues, as distinct from the Western experience. 'Western notion of feminism is the outcome of the crisis precipitating in those societies' and 'in different' cultures, the tasks, powers and privileges and prescriptions are differently distributed between these domains' (Avasthi and Srivastava, 2001: 6). That Western feminist discourse employs certain strategies to codify others as non-Western and themselves as Western is a point that Mohanty (1995) too brings out in his chapter. Rejecting the image of the 'Third World Woman re-presented/produced in the Western discourse,

Mohanty refers to the 'Third World Difference' which characterises the work of Western feminists regarding women in the Third World. This 'Third World Difference', according to Mohanty, projects a picture of homogeneity of the oppression of the Third World Woman – a picture that does not take into count the relationship between 'Woman' as a cultural, ideological composite Other, and 'women' as real, individual subjects in their 'collective histories' (1995: 260). Mohanty argues:

> It is in this process of homogenization and systematization of the oppression of women in the third world that power is exercised in much of recent Western feminist discourse, and this power needs to be defined and named … . (1995: 260)

Hence, there emerges a pattern of power and domination on the part of the Western feminism in the re-presentation of oppression, in a society where the forces as well as the consequences of oppression are in reality quite distinct from their Western counterparts. Mohanty identifies three 'principles' that are used by the Western discourse to homogenise the Third World Women: the assumption of woman as an already constituted group sharing identical interests, the usage of certain methodologies to universalise and validate cross-cultural relevance and the politically loaded models of 'power and struggle' used in the Western methodologies and analytic strategies, where the average Third World Woman is represented as having an 'essentially truncated life based on her gender', being sexually constrained, ignorant, poor, bound by tradition, whereas Western women are (implicitly) represented as educated, modern and in control of their lives (1995: 261). Although women are bound together by the sociological concept of 'sameness' of oppression, yet this kind of homogeneity cannot be mistaken for the historically specific realities of women as separate groups. Western Feminism, as Mohanty (1995: 261) says, focuses not on analysing the specifications that mark particular groups of women in particular contexts as 'powerless' but on locating 'powerless' groups of women to prove that all women are powerless, as a homogenous, universally oppressed gender.

The above discussion highlights the significance of the critique of culture with relation to woman's identity as a social being located in a specific cultural setting with its existing, dominant values and norms. Therefore, Indian Feminism, so to speak, in order to study the feminist issues of its women, cannot look towards the West as a universal referent or norm. The text in women's writing in India becomes a reflection of 'Multiple subjectivities as well as their links with their material and ideological underpinnings' (Thapan, 1997:

11). The texts are inseparable from their historical context of production and reception and eventually lead to a discourse of culture which finally has political connotations. The aesthetic of women's texts 'does not lessen discontinuity, dispossession or marginality, but dramatizes and clarifies it', by delineating 'how did they (women) tread their oblique paths across competing ideological grids, or obdurately hang on to illegitimate pleasures? What forms did their dreams of integrity or selfhood take T' (Tharu and Lalita, 1991: 36). The concept of 'selfhood' and the female protagonist's trials and tribulations in defining it, often in a nonconformist mode with reference to the prevalent patriarchal norms in itself becomes a major concern in locating a text in its specific historicity and culture. As Spivak states, a text does not exist in isolation but has to be read as 'a literary form in its connections to what is being read: history, political economy – the world' (c.f. Tharu and Lalita, 1991: 36).

The framework of emerging Indian nationalist consciousness, thus, becomes a significant historical and cultural paradigm to study women's writing in India during the late nineteenth century and the first half of the twentieth century. Chatterjee (1986: 2) describes the modern – liberal context of freedom struggle in terms of 'certain global standards set by the advanced nations of Western Europe, accompanied by the awareness that those standards have come from an alien culture and that the inherited culture of the nation did not provide the necessary adaptive leverage to enable it to read those standards of progress'. Therefore, Eastern type of nationalism was a response to this deficiency; it was 'an attempt to equip the nation culturally and also to change it, followed by a regeneration of ancestral culture and a deliberate rejection of the alien culture to which the people have been drawn' (Sathe, 2001: 240). The realisation that the West could no longer be the referent for Indian ethos, thus led to the rejection of the former.

This raises another pertinent issue, that of the aggrandisement and foregrounding of ancient Indian cultural lineage, literature and mythology, as an integral part of the national paradigm. Indian national identity highlighted, as Uberoi (1990: 42) says, 'the centrality of the feminine' in its symbolic representation, thereby suggesting that 'the colonial encounter shaped the construction of Indian femininity'. Uberoi refers to 'a common universe of discourse' in which both the colonisers and the colonised participated, with three main characteristics marking this discourse; the 'privileging' of the woman as an object of discourse, convergences of multiplicities to understand femininity and, very importantly, the chalking out of the specific canon of textual and ritual practice that would define authoritatively and authentically, an emerging Indian cultural tradition. As Uberoi (1990) states, the 'recasting' of women posited a set of identities on the one hand and a set of exclusions and negations on the other. The status of women thus became the defining signifier of the nature and condition of Indian society and 'the essence of Indian culture and society was to be located in the past and present and future of Indian women'. Referring to Uma Chakravarty's 'Altekarian paradigm', which consists of the construction of a classical age of Indian civilisation and a narrative of its decline under the twin forces of Brahmanism and Islam, Uberoi foregrounds a basic question: How was the classical canon constituted? Uberoi herself gives the answer when she points out that the cultural tradition identified with the sacred tradition of religion, and as Kapur (1989: 68), an art historian, says, 'The touchstone for nineteenth century Indian renaissance is thus Hindu civilization'.

'Cultural' nationalism thus identified tradition with religion and Hinduism, newly constituted through the identification of significant events and narratives from the massive corpus of Indian myth, history and legend. The 'recasting' of Indian women was henceforth a rescripting of the past through a carefully planned, strategic propagation of feminine ideal types, representing India not only to outsiders but also to itself. There was a 'deification' of women in certain social roles: 'the pure virgin, the loyal and obedient wife, and most importantly of all, the "mother"', all of which have their archetypes in the Hindu pantheon of Goddesses (Uberoi, 1990: 42). Thus, in the definition of the canon, the 'Aryan' element was highlighted, with Ramayana and Mahabharata being the regenerated referents with pan-Indian relevance. Also, certain themes were identified which were consistent with the newly constituted notion of a 'perfect' Hindu woman, such as the self-sacrificing wifely devotion of Sita and the celebration of conjugal love in the legends of Nala and Damayanti, Shakuntala and Dushyanta, etc.

In fact, there is a juxtaposition of the traditional and the modern in the projection of woman's question in the dominant Indian discourse. Indian woman is thought to be 'naturally' and essentially virtuous and in the development of the nationalist paradigm, both India and Indian womanhood are perceived as homogeneous entities. The terms 'nationalism', 'culture' and 'womanhood' share a dynamic, co-relational meaning and all three have been 'recast' with a different set of connotations in a span of the last two centuries. Though the original Latin sense of 'nasci' refers to an ethno-linguistic collectivity, a tribe inhabiting a specific territory, yet it is the political dimension that is now most highlighted in the term 'nationalism' (Chaudhuri,

2001: 83). 'Culture', in the sense of national culture, constitutes a process that is 'both hegemonic and homogenising', 'thereby rendering powerful the language, culture and religion of the dominant section' (Chaudhuri, 2001: 83) and relegating others to the margins, as already noted in the discussion of Uberoi's ideas on the set of excluded identities.

The idea of an ideal national/Indian womanhood, like 'nation' and 'culture' carries with it 'the sense of social transcendence' and women are the essence of Indian culture (Chaudhuri, 2001: 83). The reformer in the colonial India thus had to seek validation of the proposed liberation of women from the sanctified past, which further took two dimensions – the Vedic Ages or Shastric injunctions. A commonly held assumption in the nineteenth century Britain was that woman's position was an excellent indicator of society's advancement (Rowbotham, 1974) and this resulted in a new zest for self-criticism leading to the reinterpretation of traditional institutions and ideas, thereby giving rise to a complex amalgam of fusion of the traditional and modern (Chaudhuri, 2001).

Interestingly, the emergent model of a reformed woman was greatly influenced by the culture of Victorianism, and a parallel of the Indian preoccupation with female chastity and purity in the context of the celebration of a monogamous marriage is to be found in Victorian England which also laid great emphasis on sexual restraint and moral uprightness in women. Thus it was that 'India was part of the modernisation process that conjoined the fates of England and India together, one as the coloniser and the other as the colonised' (Chaudhuri, 2001: 93). The specificity of the Indian middle class in colonial India consisted of the intelligentsia, including the public servants and members of the recognised independent professions and it was this class that was instrumental in the redefinition of tradition and culture. Sathe (2001) deconstructs the image of the *bhadramahila* or 'the respectable middle-class housewife' as a product of urbanisation and modern liberal ideology, on the Brahminical–Victorian lines.

This image finds a parallel in the much critiqued stereotype of the happy housewife in Betty Friedan's *The Feminine Mystique* (1976) and though there is sameness in the enforced perfection of womanhood to which the women were expected to conform, yet the cultural and historic specification cannot be sidelined. In India, the deification of women in the role of the mother was a unique feature of the nationalist paradigm of the first half of the twentieth century. There was 'a symbolic use of the mother ranging from feminist assertion of women's power to be mother of the nation to terrorist invocations of the protective and ravening mother goddess, to the Gandhian lauding of the spirit of endurance and suffering embodied in the mother against the brutality of British power' (Sathe, 2001: 242). Aurobindo's Savitri, projecting the image of the selfless Savitri's purity, her selfless wifely devotion, her powerlessness that contains the power to save Satyavan (in this case not only the nation but the human condition) is a representation of the deification of the mother role in the nationalist psyche. Ironically, though Gandhi did provide the moral legitimacy for women's cause, with the spinning wheel symbolically representing women's participation in the nation's regeneration, yet women's sphere was equally clearly defined by the wheel. Women would participate, yes, but without having to leave their home. The woman thus was not just victimised but rather chose for herself the path of suffering in order to regenerate the world around her (Tharu, 1989).

Along with the glorification of certain stereotypes from the classical canon, there were a parallel set of identities that were ignored or marginalised, namely, other religions and cultural traditions that were not encompassed in Hinduism, lower-caste practices by Brahminical and Kshatriya models, folk genres and aesthetic values that were specifically indigenous in nature (Uberoi, 1990). Therefore, it can be safely said that the nationalist paradigm, at some level, pretended an authenticity that it did not carry in reality and consequently, set a hierarchy of hegemony of a culture, constituted of images and stereotypes that remained silent on the marginalised sections of society.

Before beginning with a 'gendered' reading of the novel, constituted of a detailed textual analysis and interpretation of its discourse of identities, entities and institutions, it becomes imperative to elaborate upon the feminist implications of the difference between gender and sex. As already pointed out in this chapter, it was Millett (1970) who foregrounded the notion of sex as a biological construct and gender as a socially constructed identity. One of the most powerful works to show that anatomy is not destiny and that sex-role stereotypes are merely arbitrary was Mead's research on culture and personality. Her anthropological observations illumined the infinite variety of sexual patterns and the enormous plasticity of human nature, a vision based on the differences of sex and temperament she found in three primitive societies: the Arapesh, where both men and women were 'feminine' and 'maternal' in personality and passively sexual; the Mundugumor, where both husband and wife were violent, aggressive, positively sexed and 'masculine' and the Tchambuli, where woman was the dominant, impersonal managing partner and man the less responsible and emotionally dependent person. Mead suggested that no aspects of behaviour are sex linked. Anatomy is not destiny and women can realise their full capabilities in a society which replaces arbitrary sexual definitions with recognition of genuine individual gifts (c.f. Friedan, 1976). Male images of women, however, only serve to embolden the view that it is better to preserve the sexual biological limitations imposed and established by a culture. That these limitations are different in different cultures is a point that has already been delineated at length and so need not be repeated. Gender can no more be marginalised in the study of human societies than the concept of 'human action' or the concept of 'society'. It would not be possible to pursue any sort of social science without a concept of gender (Moore, 1988).

The most important element in patriarchal male–female relationships or gender relations, so to speak, is power – contained in the male and denied in the female. Gender roles thus expose the patterns of male power and female powerlessness that exist as a social norm in a culture. This 'power' ideology is particularly powerful because through conditioning, women themselves become perpetrators of male values, which ironically serve only to devalue them. And this conditioning takes place through the force of family, the establishment or the academy and the Church, (implying religious sanction to such arbitrary definitions of roles). As such 'gendered' reading of a text draws attention to its signification of familial attitudes, political inequities and the perspective of the Church, that is the religious establishment.

The Text

The God of Small Things, at one level of signification, can be read as a codification of 'Love Laws' and their concomitant patterns of power and powerlessness where gender emerges as a subtext. A cryptic statement, repeated at critical moments in the text, occurs at the end of the first chapter:

> That it really began in the days when the Love Laws were made. The laws that lay down who should be loved, and how. And how much. (33)

Two points are to be noted here: Love Laws are not natural but have been 'made' and made long, long ago, as is suggested by the narrative mode of the sentence. The pervasive irony of the natural, spontaneous impulse of passion being bound by the unnatural constraints of convention is not lost upon the reader. And what do these laws do? Rather, what are they meant to do? They are to define 'who' to love and 'how', that is, they are to appropriate the very essence of love, by depriving it of the right to choose the beloved as well as the manner of the relationship. Therefore, 'Love Laws' become a signifier of conflict, of strife between 'Love' and 'Laws'. In fact, it is interesting to see the interplay between 'love' and 'lovelessness', so to speak. Love that exists outside the boundaries of social sanction is rendered powerless, whereas 'lovelessness', that defines the legitimate relationships approved by societal norms, becomes powerful and dominant. In the same vein, the text exposes the dialectic of 'love' and 'lovelessness' most explicitly in the institution of marriage. In fact, marriage becomes a kind of threshold, and relationships that fall within its bounds, reveal the gender inequity of 'lovelessness' that pervades the lives of the spouses, especially women, trapped in it. It is in this light that the marriages of Reverend Ipe 'Punnyan Kunju'–Aleyooti Ammachi, Pappachi–Mammachi, Baba–Ammu, Chacko–Margaret and even Pillai–Kalyani attain multiple levels of signification. On the other hand, when 'boundaries blur' (1) and love refuses to bind itself within laws, the threshold is crossed, as shown in the relationship of Ammu–Velutha and Esha–Rahel. Marriage, thus, becomes a statement not only of love and lovelessness but, most importantly, of how these two aspects affect the individuals involved, depending on whether they are male or female. Finally, it is always the power quotient that matters and the glorification of 'lovelessness' as opposed to the condemnation of love, speaks volumes about the sociocultural paradigm that defines the 'who' and 'how' of love, as well as the concept of marriage as a cultural signifier of gender relations.

The paradigm of the 'Love Laws' goes back to time immemorial, 'It could be argued that it began long before Christianity arrived in a boat and seeped into Kerala like tea from a tea bag' (33) and therefore, it becomes imperative to examine the institution of marriage and the gender equations within its parameters, as set forth in classical as well as the religious canon of tradition, in Hinduism as well as Christianity. The iniquity of power relations of the sexes is thus the deep-rooted core of patriarchy, 'a cultural (ideological) system that privileges men and all things masculine, and a political system that places power in the hands of men and thus serves male interests at the expense of women' (Madsen, Preface xii). This 'privileging' of men, through social sanction – embodied in culture and tradition – therefore becomes an essential field of study in the text.

The superiority of the male in the institution of marriage is clearly suggested in the oldest generation of the Ipe family, that of Reverend Ipe 'Punnyan Kunju', the Little Blessed One, and his wife Aleyooty Ammachi. The individual portraits of the husband and wife signify the truth of their married life:

> Reverend Ipe smiled his confident – ancestor smile out across the road instead of the river.
>
> Aleyooti Ammachi looked more hesitant. As though she would have liked to turn around but couldn't. Perhaps it wasn't as easy for her to abandon the river. With her eyes she looked in the direction that her husband looked. With her heart she looked away. (30)

The passage speaks volumes about the different meanings that marriage has for the husband and wife: the portraits are a study in contrast. Reverend Ipe's confidence and Ammachi's hesitation, his ready acceptance of the road and her unwillingness to 'abandon' the river (suggesting the heartlessness of her husband who doesn't honour the river with sincerity), thereby implying a conflict of interests where the wife's inclination in disregarded as Ammachi doesn't dare to look at the direction contrary to her husband's though 'with her heart', she may look away. Moreover, Ammachi's heavy, dull gold kunukku earrings become a signifier of the well-meant concern/tyranny of her patriarchal husband: these earrings are apparently 'tokens of the little Blessed One's Goodness', (30) but what have they actually done? They have so 'stretched her earlobes', (30) that they now hang all the way down to her shoulders, yet despite the oppression, her desires don't die, because even through the holes in her ears, one can see the hot river and the surrounding trees.

Punnyan Kunju's 'confident ancestor-smile', at one level of signification, is the confidence of centuries of male dominance and superiority in the institution of marriage. The traditional perspective of Hindu as well as Christian religion and philosophy throw up amazing, 'political' statements on marriage 'Laws'. It becomes pertinent at this point to examine the various models of matrimony in the Hindu/Christian religio-cultural mode. The predominant metaphor presented in *Manusmriti* is that of *Beeja* and *Kshetra*. *Beeja* means seed or semen and '*Kshetra*' means field or land. Man is called a seed that has the power to reproduce its own kind and, in the same context, woman is called a field that acts as a nourishing agent for the growth of a seed. As Meena Kelkar points out, Manu states three possibilities of *Beeja–Kshetra–Nyaya.* While some experts give greater importance to *Beeja*, others to *Kshetra* and still others give equal status to both, Manu clearly favours the view that *Beeja is* superior to *Kshetra* because, in his opinion, normally a seed sown in a defective or infertile field (or a non-field) gets destroyed and therefore, wasted. A field that does not receive seed remains barren and yet, due to the power of good seed, Manu points out that sages who have been praised and worshipped were born even out of animal wombs, that is, even a person born in 'Tiryakyoni' or animal species can also become a 'muni' or sage if it is the offspring of a worthy seed. Therefore, the seed or *Beeja* reigns supreme, whereas the field or *Kshetra is* merely the receiver and in this respect too, it can be substituted *Mahabharata* too gives the view that a human being may be born even without the semen carried or nourished by a woman thereby making redundant the existence of a woman as the carrier of the seed. Dronacharya's birth illustrates this view, strengthening the concept of the overall superiority of the seed having the power to perpetuate itself (Kelkar, 2003).

The implications of the *Beeja–Kshetra–Nyaya* model in the context of gender politics, especially in marriage – which is primarily for the sake of begetting progeny – cannot be overemphasised. Deriving its genesis from agriculture, the model also suggests 'ownership' of a woman. When human beings started cultivating the land, land became for them, a property or a possession. Similarly man, who owned the land, also owned the woman. Just as man sowed the seeds and reaped the harvest, just as he was the owner of the crop, similarly woman was simply like the field and her children belonged to the father. This idea is given a cosmological signification when Krishna, in *Bhagavad Gita*, calls himself the father of the world because he is the giver of the seed (Kelkar, 2003). Therefore, the *Beeja–Kshetra* theory pervades the hierarchical structuring of a patriarchal family wherein man is the head and woman and children are his property. Kelkar gives an example of a (shocking) story in *Mahabharata* where *Yayati*, a king, presents his daughter Madhavi to a hermit Galav who in turn sells her four times to four kings, getting 250 horses from each one of them. The kings, one by one, get sons from Madhavi and then return her to the hermit. The identification of a woman as a possession, a commodity, is complete: she can be exchanged, used and returned (Kelkar, 2003).

No wonder, with such a paradigm, validated by ancient Indian religion and philosophy, gender relations became lopsided by the belief that man is superior and he must rule over woman. Curiously, the Old Testament too asserts the instrumental value of woman and her complete ownership by man. After making Adam, God realised that he needed a helper (Genesis 2: 18) and so God marched all of the animals past Adam (Genesis 2: 19–20) looking for a suitable animal. Finding none suitable, God created Eve out of one of Adam's ribs. Adam later asserted his superiority over Eve by naming her '... She shall be called Woman, because she was taken out of Man'. In ancient times one was believed to have authority over a person or thing by naming it. Adam's role is to be Eve's master. Robinson points out that The King James Version, the New International Version and Revised

Standard Version use the term 'rule' to describe Adam's role vis-à-vis Eve: '... thy (Eve's) desire shall be to thy husband and he shall rule over thee'. The Living Bible uses the term 'master'. The Modern Language Bible uses the word 'dominate'. By implication, all of their descendents would have the same power imbalance between spouses (Robinson 2). In Exodus 20 and 21, a number of verses, describe a woman as the property of her father. After marriage, her ownership is transferred to her husband. Exodus 20: 17 lists the last of the Ten Commandments: 'thou shall not covet thy neighbour's wife, nor his man servant, nor his maid servant, nor his ox, nor his ass, nor anything that is thy neighbour's'. It is important to note that man servant and maid servant were male and female slaves and as such, possessions of their masters. By forbidding man from coveting his neighbour's house, his wife, male or female slaves, animals or anything else owned by the neighbour, the Tenth Commandment clearly regards wife as equivalent to a piece of property. Exodus 21: 2–4, states: 'If thou buy an Hebrew servant, six years he shall serve, and in the seventh he shall go out free for nothing ... . If his master have given him a wife, and she have born him sons or daughters, the wife and her children shall be her master's, and he shall go by himself'. Though the slave owner was permitted to give a woman to his male slaves as a wife, there is no indication that the women were consulted during this type of transaction. As clearly stated, the male slave could leave after serving for six years, but his wife and children would remain slaves of the owner. (In a slight variation, *Beeja–Kshetra* model too suggests a similar right of ownership, on the part of the husband. All children born to a woman, including those fathered by another man, rightfully belong to her husband as he is the one who owns her, just as all the harvested crop belongs to the owner of the land, and not to the labourers or peasants who cultivate it). Exodus 21: 7 states: 'And if a man sells his daughter to be a maid servant, she shall not get out as the men servants do'. A father could sell his daughter as a slave. One conclusion is clear, even though a male slave was automatically given freedom after six years, a female slave remained a slave forever.

No wonder then, with such a mighty tradition of validated and sanctified gender inequity behind him, Reverend Ipe, indeed the 'Blessed' Man – can smile his 'confident-ancestor's smile' while Ammachi has no choice but to look in the same direction as he does, even though with her heart, she looks away. Even the 'bison head' on either side of which are hung the portraits, suggests the binaries of the spousal relationship in its signification of the hunter and the hunted.

Mammachi and Pappachi's marriage too presents an assertion of the patriarchal male power within the marital bond and states the inanity and meaningless of the 'lovelessness' of this relationship. Their marriage exposes the falsehood of two myths, put forth and indicated by Friedan's *The Feminine Mystique*, the idea of togetherness and the concept of a happy housewife. As Friedan says, 'No one seemed to remember that women too have the capacity and vision of statesmen, poets and physicists. Few saw the big lie of togetherness' (Friedan, 1976: 42).

The enactment of this 'lie of togetherness' is what marks the marriage of Soshamma Ipe and Benaan John Ipe, noted entomologist – 17 years older than her. Their relationship is characterised by a mutual dislike, mostly on Pappachi's part, and in fact, his dislike for his wife even turns into bitter, lasting hatred which he nourishes carefully in his heart to his dying day. 'He had always been a jealous man' (47) and during their stay in Vienna, when Mammachi takes her first lessons in violin and her talent in music is praised by her teacher Launsky-Tieffenthal who calls her 'exceptionally talented' and 'potentially concert class' (50), Pappachi's jealous wrath makes him immediately discontinue the music lessons for his wife. A similar antipathy towards her creative ability comes to fore in Pappachi's relation to Mammachi's success in the pickles enterprise, after his retirement, Mammachi starts making pickles commercially and proves herself to be a great success in Ayemenem. She is busy throughout the year while he has 'trouble coping with the ignoring of retirement' accentuated by the realisation that comes like 'a shock' 'that he was an old man when his wife was still in her prime' (47). Pappachi refuses to help her in any way even though she is already practically blind, because 'he did not consider pickle-making a suitable job for a high ranking ex-government official' (47). He resents 'the attention his wife was suddenly getting' (47) and simply slouches sullenly around the compound, watching Mammachi at her business. But he does vent his suppressed rage when he breaks the bow of her violin – another symbol of her talent – and throws it into the river.

> Every night he beat her with a brass flower vase. (47)

When Chacko stops him from carrying on with this evening ritual, Pappachi is forced to confront opposition that he can't subdue so easily because it comes from his own son – young, strong and like him, a signifier of domination and power in the patriarchal hierarchy. The frustrated Pappachi, helpless in his son's grip, later smashes his favourite mahogany chair into bits and more importantly

> He never touched Mammachi again. But he never spoke to her either as long as he lived. (48)

Moreover, he buys a sky-blue Plymouth in which he allows none, not even Mammachi, to sit because 'the Plymouth was Pappachi's revenge' (48). Pappachi's photograph, reminiscent of Reverend Ipe's portrait, too becomes a signifier of patriarchal hegemony and male superiority. The photograph shows Pappachi in Vienna 'with his hair slicked down', in his usual 'dapper and carefully groomed' self; he is 'photogenic', with 'a little man's largish head' (51). His head's largeness is a too obvious signification of the arrogance and superciliousness that fills it. The overall 'watchful stillness' in the photograph exudes an 'underlying chill' (51) and even the ivory-handled riding crop, like the bison head between the older Ipe couple's portraits, is a continuation of the signification of cruelty. So much for togetherness!

And in all this, where is Mammachi and what does she do? Mammachi is the Indian *bhadramahila*, signifying middle-class respectability, the Friedanian 'happy housewife' who is anything but happy. The Indian society turns this idea literally into a religion (or may be the other way round!) when it prescribes the devoted wife and mother roles to be emulated from the Sita–Savitri tradition embodied in the ancient, classical canon. True to these images, Mammachi, despite 'the raised, crescent-shaped ridges' on her scalp, 'Scars of old beatings from an old marriage. Her brass vase scars' (166), is still the *bhadramahila* who proudly pastes on the family album *The Indian Express* clipping that reports her husband's death.

Mammachi's adoration of her son Chacko – which, being a typical product of patriarchy herself, she doesn't extend to her daughter – has an Oedipal signification. Understandably, Mammachi finds it difficult, rather impossible, to share her 'only love' with Margaret, the white woman who becomes Chacko's wife and whom he loves dearly. To the sophisticated, class conscious Mammachi, Margaret is simply a 'Shopkeeper's daughter' (168) who wears cheap perfume while Mammachi herself has 'a bottle of Dior in its soft green leather pouch locked away in her safe' (173).

However, Mammachi would have resented Margaret anyway 'even if she had been heir to the throne of England' because

> She hated Margaret Kochamma for being Chacko's wife. (168)

The silver framed black-and-white wedding picture of Chacko and Margaret tells a story of gender relations, different from those seen in other marriages in the text. Chacko and Margaret's marriage is an amalgamation and juxtaposition of two widely differing cultures – the (Anglicised) Indian and the characteristic western. Needless to say, the man–woman relationship is no longer defined by the patriarchal paradigm of the dominant and the subservient but by the historical, political hierarchy of the coloniser and the colonised. Chacko is not the typical, oppressive Indian male because Margaret is not an Indian woman, conditioned to social laws of subordination.

The wedding picture itself becomes a signifier of the strangeness, almost incongruity of such a match, as suggested by the man on his bicycle in the right hand corner of the photograph, who has turned to stare at the couple. The bride and the groom are dressed in a way that suggests the immaturity of youth: Chacko, dressed like Nehru (reminiscent of the child Estha dressed similarly at Ammu's birthday), seems to be 'laughing at himself and the way he was dressed. Like someone at a fancy dress party' (241) while Margaret's long, foaming gown is in stark contrast with her thick, dark eyebrows. The picture also draws attention to the position of Margaret and Chacko in the English social hierarchy. Margaret's 'cheap' tiara is a pointer towards her lower–middle-class status – she is, after all, working as a waitress, 'an only averagely desirable one' (243) and is the daughter of a baker and a milliner's assistant. And Chacko, though belonging to the elite, landowning Syrian Christian Community of South India, is simply reduced to a representative of a race that has been colonised by England. Indeed, Margaret's mother is 'looking away' out of the photograph, as though 'she would rather not have been there' (240) and her pursed up class-conscious morality, reflected in 'all the buttons done up on her long overcoat' (240), is in striking contrast to the giggling children present in the picture. Margaret's father's disapproval of Chacko, indicative of the pervasive attitude of the coloniser towards the colonised, is summed up in the sentence, 'He disliked Indians, he thought of them as sly dishonest people' (241). He can't believe his daughter is marrying one of such a race. Ironically, in the colonial paradigm, the aristocratic Indian landowner is not considered fit for an English waitress.

The marriage is bagged with uncertainty from the beginning: 'Until the day she (Margaret) married him she never believed that she would ever consent to be his wife' (244) and as for Chacko, 'he never knew till the last day whether or not she would marry him' (246). But the differences, though exciting at first, turn out to be strenuous and overwhelming, and Margaret's 'tiny, ordered life' (245), fascinated initially by the entry of 'the Rumpled Porcupine, a tortured Marxist', 'at war with an impossible, incurable Romantic' (245) finally cannot take his 'studently sloth' for too long (246). Margaret, unable to understand this aspect of her Indian husband, is drawn 'like a plant in a dark room towards a wedge of light' (248) to Joe, 'a biologist' (247) who is 'Steady, Solvent, Thin' (48) and is, in fact, everything that Chacko is not.

Chacko's attraction towards Margaret is also based on notions that later define the gender equation in their marriage. She is his first female friend, 'his first real companion' (245) even though she is not the first woman with whom he has been physically intimate. He loves her 'self-sufficiency' (246), which he contrasts with the dependence of Mammachi on him. He loves her

For not being his cloying mother (246)

The 'big lie of togetherness' is, hence, once again exposed in the text, this time in the marriage of Chacko and Margaret. But at one level of signification, this marriage is different. Unlike the silent distancing of the spouses in Revered Ipe–Aleyooti Ammachi's marriage and the bitter antipathy of Pappachi–Mammachi's, Chacko and Margaret continue to share 'a comfortable, committed friendship' (249). For Chacko, it is 'the only way of remaining in touch with the mother of his child and the only woman he had ever loved' (250) while for Margaret, after Joe's death, 'there was nobody (other than Chacko) in the world she would rather spend Christmas with' (250) and thus, a marriage begun in the first flush of infatuation and immaturity of youth ends at a not too discordant note.

The extremity of difference that culture brings to the structuring of gender relations of power and powerlessness within the marriage is illustrated in Ammu's relationship with her husband, her subsequent divorce and the parallels as well as the contrast of her experience as a divorced woman, with that of Margaret in London as well as at Ayemenem. In fact, 'the process of essentialisation, which uses the language of a "true woman" or "a real woman", is culture transcending, but the product, i.e. the actual content of this idea of "true" or "real" woman is culture specific' (Kelkar and Gangavane, 2003).

Ammu's marriage is the outcome of her desire to escape a life that suffocates her by not allowing her any avenues for growth. Margaret too seeks an escape from the 'small tight life' (241), she has at her parents' home and therefore she leaves London to work as a waitress at Oxford. However, there is a major difference: while Ammu seeks refuge in marriage, her only resort, Margaret defines her life in terms of a successful career. In Ammu's world, marriage is everything. Referring to the wedding customs of Syrian Christians, Susan Visvanathan says, 'In an odd rendering of passivity as power, the woman is seen to be constantly searching for the groom. Christ represents the completeness of virtue in a man, who is seen to be the sun, while the woman is the day' (194). Therefore, when the 25-year-old Bengali Hindu tea planter (known in the text only as 'Baba' – his name is irrelevant, only his patriarchal status matters) proposes to Ammu, she 'didn't pretend to be in love with him. She just weighed the odds and accepted' (39) because anything is preferable to returning to Ayemenem. Unlike Chacko, Ammu does inform her parents about her wedding but they do not respond. Like Margaret, Ammu too is disappointed in her husband who is an utter alcoholic. Yet, for a brief interlude, the 'beautiful young and cheeky' (40) Ammu becomes the toast of the Planter's Club. But there is no respite from her husband's drinking bouts and the breaking point in the marriage comes when he wants her to go to bed with his boss so that he can save his job. In Genesis 19: 8, there is a reference to a father offering his daughters to be raped: The men of Sodom gather around Lot's house, and ask him to bring his two guests out so that the men can 'know' them (This is frequently interpreted as a desire to gang rape the visitors, although open interpretations are possible). Lot, however, offers his two virgin daughters to be raped instead: 'I have two daughters which have not known man; let me, I pray you, bring them unto you, and do ye to them as is good in your eyes'. Yet, even after this despicable act, Lot is still regarded as an honourable man, worth saving from the destruction of the city. Allowing daughters (as Lot does) and wives (as Ammu's husband does) to be sexually assaulted appears to be a minor transgression, because of the powerless, inferior status of young women. The spirited Ammu, however, refuses and her husband's growing violence forces her to leave him and return to Ayemenem, the very place she had sought so hard to escape. Ammu has two young children and 'no more dreams' (42).

For herself she knew that there would be no more chances. There was only Ayemenem now. A front verandah and a back verandah. A hot river and a pickle factory. And in the background, the constant, high, whining mewl of local disapproval (5).

This 'disapproval' is the culture-specific factor that defines life for Ammu and differentiates it from that of Margaret. For Margaret, divorce is not loaded with a sense of shame and failure; she herself asks Chacko for divorce and moreover she leaves him for another man. Not surprisingly, Ayemenem has different parameters for a divorced, white woman. During Margaret's visit, Chacko flaunts her like a trophy, calling her his 'wife', omitting the 'ex'. In fact, despite the divorce, Chacko has always had 'a peculiar pride' (249) in her, 'As though he admired her for having divorced him', saying to Mammachi, 'She traded me in for a better man' (249).

For Ammu, however, the social reality is much more harsh and bitter. She knows, with a death-like finality,

Life had been lived. (38)

As Visvanathan points out, 'The sister Ammu is problematic because Syrian Christians have no place for the daughter once she is married off' (2002). And yet, what Ammu has done is no mere than what Margaret has: Margaret too married, and later divorced, a man of a different religion, community and in her case, even nationality. As far as Ammu is concerned, her divorce gives her a new edge of cynicism and insight into the reality of marriage, signified by her melting of the 'heavy' (44) wedding ring, suggesting the burden of domesticity in a biased gender relationship, into a thin bangle with snakeheads, signifying a primitive, archetypal fury of rebelliousness against tyranny.

An analysis of *Woman's Era* reveals the still dominant attitude towards divorce, considered the most unfortunate disaster that can befall an Indian woman (Tyagi and Uberoi, 1990). 'Adjustment' becomes a key word, a signifier of a woman's compromises that must be made to keep her marriage alive. The 'blissful' state of marriage, the result of a woman's perfect 'adjustment' in her marital life, is exemplified in the novel in the relationship of Kalyani with her husband Pillai. As a Communist leader, Pillai preaches equality of the comrades across caste and class lines but there is one boundary that his ideology refuses to cross – that of gender. So, Kalyani refers to him as '*addeham* which was the respectful form of "he" whereas "he" called her "edi" which was, approximately "Hey you P"' (270). Pillai has the 'easy authority of the Man of the House' and 'did not acknowledge the presence of his wife or his mother' (272). But the 'well-adjusted' Kalyani holds his dirty, sweat-soiled shirt 'as though it was a gift, a bouquet of flowers' (272). For Pillai, she is a slave to his desires, a sex object towards whom he feels sudden, intense urges of sexual craving. However, the marriage is functioning smoothly, as Kalyani has so thoroughly internalised the values of 'adjustment' to her wifely duties that the gender inequity in her marital relationship hardly ever occurs to her.

Ammu, however, is in stark contrast to Kalyani. She is conscious of her unfulfilled womanly desires which bring up the important issue of how 'Man's needs' (168), Chacko's needs – are absolutely comprehensible, whereas the needs of Ammu – a divorced mother of two children – are construed as preposterous, unimaginable, in other words, devastating for the honour of Reverend John Ipe's family. To the contrary, Chacko's sexual escapades with his Untouchable female factory workers have the tacit approval of Mammachi, Baby Kochamma and the societal norms, because as Mammachi says, 'He can't help having a Man's Needs' (168). Sexual exploitation of poor women is cited even in the scriptures. Genesis 16: 2 speaks of how Sarah gave permission to her husband Abraham to engage in a sexual relationship with her maid Hagar: 'Sarah said unto Abraham ... . I pray thee, go in unto my maid; it may be that I may obtain children by her'. Presumably, this was done without the consent of Hagar, who had such a low status in the society of the day that she was required to submit to multiple rapes at her owner's command. The idea of the importance of 'Man's Needs' cuts across religions and cultures. Nirmala Kulkarni points out that in *Satpatha Brahmana* (originating around third or fourth century B.C. and as such, one of the oldest Indian texts), there is a whole paragraph that cites various formulas to fulfil various wishes of man – if he wants to beget a child, if he does not want to beget from sexual intercourse, if he desires to destroy his wife's paramour, if he wants to beget a learned daughter, etc. Nowhere in the paragraph is there an indication of the fulfilment of the wishes of a woman (Kulkarni, 2003: 58). Also according to *Satpatha Brahmana*, a widower may remarry, but not a widow because a man 'needs' a wife to perform the religious rituals which are his prerogative. And since woman does not have an equal importance, after her husband's death, all the sacrificial instruments are burnt on the dead husband's pyre (Kulkarni, 2003: 54). In other words, 'Man's Needs', validated in the form of religious duty, are acknowledged, whereas a woman's fulfilment remains ignored in a status of widowhood or 'singlehood'.

Hence, Ammu's desire for Velutha, signifying her need for fulfilment as a woman, is interpreted from a completely unsympathetic perspective that refuses to acknowledge, what may be termed, 'Woman's Needs'. In her case, the transgression of the societal code is at two levels: (a) she seeks a gratification of her physical passion, outside the boundaries of marriage and (b) she dares to love a man from the forbidden margins of her caste and class-ridden society – an Untouchable. In her fury, Mammachi is unable to decide which is worse – Ammu ruining her virtue or Ammu ruining it for a Paravan. In the Doctrine of Purusartha, specifically the *Kama purusartha*, the purity of caste is maintained by strict rules of marriage. Lower-caste men are not allowed to marry upper-caste women:

> A strict dividing line was maintained between a woman inside the house respecting the boundaries of the four walls and a woman who stepped outside the boundaries. The former got respect not as an individual but because of her power of reproduction and her submissiveness. The latter was either condemned or was treated as an object of enjoyment. (Belsare, 2003: 168–169)

But to Ammu, with her 'Unsafe Edge' (44), the relationship with Velutha is a desperate attempt to escape 'the road to Age and Death' (233), to save herself from 'Fumes that wrinkled youth and pickled futures' (224). Punishment is severe: Velutha is killed by the police;

the children are intimidated into telling a dreadful lie and for 'Little' Ammu's family come the end of living. Why does all this happen? Because the 'Love Laws', lay down by history, are broken by Ammu and Velutha. One fact, however, stands out in surprising clarity in all this chaos: if 'togetherness' is found anywhere in the text it is not in the marital sphere, defined in accordance with the 'Love Laws' but in this socially and culturally blasphemous relationship of a divorced Touchable woman with the outcast, Untouchable Velutha.

Togetherness, outside the domain of marriage, becomes real also in the Estha–Rahel relationship, one that defies definition by its inability to categorise itself in the conventional norms. Interestingly, Rahel (like Ammu) fails to find togetherness in her marriage with Larry McCaslin who is always offended by her eyes that 'behaved as though they belonged to someone else' (19), even in the most passionate moments. For Estha, there is no question of togetherness with anyone as he lives a life of silence and solitude. Twenty-three years later, their reunion turns into another transgression of 'Love Laws'. Estha notes 'Their beautiful mother's mouth' (327) when Rahel speaks, while in the physical proximity with her twin, 'no watcher watched through Rahel's eyes' (328). What they share during that fateful night of physical and emotional togetherness is a culmination of grief – of what happened to them, Ammu and Velutha in the past, of the trauma of separation from each other, although 'They had known each other before life began' (327). Thus, what may seem incest to the conventional world is a sublimated form of togetherness for the twins, reliving the 'hideous grief' (328) of their wasted life:

> There is very little that anyone could say to clarify what happened next. Nothing that (in Mammachi's book) would separate Sex from Love or Needs from Feelings. (328)

The element of sexuality is suggested in the coming together of Estha and Rahel, 'Quietness and Emptiness fitted together like stacked spoons' (328) and '... it was a little cold. A little wet. But very quiet. The Air. But what was there to say?' (328) the same words define 'the Air' of Ammu's first passionate meeting with her lover. Togetherness and transgression hence merge into one experience for the twins because once again they break the laws of 'who should be loved. And how. And how much' (328).

Ammu's 'divorceehood' brings to fore another extremely relevant form of a woman's powerlessness: the question of her 'Locusts Stand I' (37). Though she does as much work in the factory as her brother Chacko (who, in fact, causes much financial loss), he still refers to it as his factory, his pineapples, his pickles. Legally, this is the case because

Ammu, as a daughter, has no claim to the property. Chacko tells Rahel and Estha that Ammu has no 'locus standi' and he can afford to say to his sister, 'What's yours is mine and what's mine is also mine' (57). Visvanathan points out that during the contesting of the inheritance act of the Travancore Christians by Mary Roy (Arundhati Roy's mother) and others, Mary Roy's argument that daughters must inherit an equal share of the father's property, was immediately countered by the writing of wills by a Syrian Christian patriarch. She adds that even the priests of many of the Syrian Christian churches came out against the Supreme Court judgment of 1984, saying that it would affect the patriarchal bases of Christianity (191–192). The scriptures again reveal the bias favouring men vis-à-vis inheritance. In Numbers 27: 8–11, 8–11, Moses describes the rules of inheritance that God has stated. If a man dies, his son inherits the estate and his daughter gets nothing, as in Ammu's case. Only if there is no son, will his daughter inherit. If there are no children, then the estate is given to the man's brothers; his sister (s) gets nothing. If he has no brother, the estate goes to his nearest male relative. '… If a man die and have no son, then ye shall cause his inheritance to pass unto his daughter. And if he has no daughter, then ye shall give his inheritance unto his brethren, and if she has no brother, then ye shall give his inheritance unto his father's brethren. And if his father has no brethren, then ye shall give his inheritance unto his kinsman that in next to him of his family …' Manu, the Hindu law giver, too affirms a similar subordination of woman: 'In childhood must a female be dependent on her father, in youth, on her husband, her Lord being dead, on her sons, if she has no sons, on the near kinsmen of her husband, if she be left with no kinsmen, on those of her father; if she has no parental kinsmen, on the sovereign, a woman must never seek independence' (*Manusmriti*, 68). No wonder, then, that Ammu has no 'locus standi', a phrase that becomes a signifier of her homelessness in general, in a society ridden with cultural and religious dogma on the inferiority of womanhood.

If the most complete form of 'love' in the text is signified in the Ammu–Velutha relationship that could never have turned into marriage, the bitterest signifier of 'lovelessness' too is presented in a relationship that does not materialise in matrimony, that of Baby Kochamma and Father Mulligan. The difference again lies in the 'togetherness' factor: while Ammu and Velutha find fulfilment, however fleeting, in each other, Baby Kochamma continues to live a lie – a togetherness that is never there. Baby Kochamma's powerlessness in her situation turns her into a tyrannical oppressor of her own sex, especially of Ammu, who fights with a fate that Baby Kochamma has herself 'graciously accepted':

The fate of the wretched Men-less woman. (45)

'The sad, Father Mulligan-less Baby Kochamma' (45) brings down the final curtain on the myth of togetherness; hers is a relationship that exists solely in her own imagination where she nurtures it with a deadly dedication.

Conclusion

The God of Small Things explicates the subtext of gender as the structuring principle of society, manifested in the institution of marriage which has its own dialectics of power. The binaries of this relationship, encoded in the social, historical, cultural and political paradigm, are signified in the 'powerful' male domination and the 'powerless' female subjugation. What happens when the female 'object' returns the masculine gaze, refusing to remain in the passive position, and questions/contests/debates the authority/dominance of the masculine position, is the crux of the gendered reading of the text in this chapter. As such, the making and breaking of female stereotypes has been analysed keeping in view the national as well as the universalised paradigm of male oppression and the corollary of the definition of female identity. 'The repressions of a patriarchal society create stances, things that cannot be said' (Madsen, 2000: 19) or as Roy would put it, only the small things are said while the big things ever lurk unsaid inside. The present reading of the text has been an effort to break such 'stances' and 'say' or interpret the 'Big Things' in their paradigmatic relation to the norms defined in the societal structures by the patriarchal order.

Notes

1. Arundhati Roy. *The God of Small Things*. New Delhi: India Ink, 1997, p. 57. All further references are from the same text and page numbers are duly given after each quotation in parenthesis.
2. All quotations from the Bible are cited from B.A. Robinson at http://www.religioustolerance.org

References

Allen, Paula Gunn. 1996. *The Sacred Hoop: Recovering the Feminine in American Indian Traditions*. Boston: Beacon Press.

Anzaldua, Gloria (ed.) 1990. *Making Face, Making Soul/Haciendo Caras: Creative and Critical Perspectives by Feminists of Color.* San Francisco: Aunt Lute Books.

Avasthi, Abha and Srivastava, A.K. (eds) 2001. *Modernity, Feminism and Women Empowerment.* Jaipur: Rawat.

Belsare, Vaijayanti Arun. 2003. 'The Doctrine of Purusartha: A Gender Perspective', in Meena Kelkar and Deepti Gangavani (eds), *Feminism in Search of an Identity: The Indian Context* (164–177). Jaipur: Rawat.

Brownmiller, Susan. 1975. *Against Our Will: Men, Women and Rape.* London: Secker and Warburg.

Chatterjee, Partha. 1986. *Nationalist Thought and the Colonial World: A Derivate Discourse?* Delhi: Oxford.

Chaudhuri, Maitrayee. 2001. 'The Woman's Question and Modernity: The Indian Story', in Abha Avasthi and A.K. Srivastava (eds), *Modernity, Feminism and Women Empowerment* (79–96). Jaipur: Rawat.

Davis, Angela. 1981. *Women, Race and Class*. London: The Women's Press.

de Beauvoir, Simone. 1949. *The Second Sex.* Trans. H.M. Parshley. Middlesex: Penguin.

Faludi, Susan. 1991, 1992. *Backlash: The Undeclared War Against American Women*. New York: Doubleday.

Friedan, Betty. 1976. *The Feminine Mystique.* Harmondsworth: Penguin.

Fuller, Margaret. 1845. *Women in the Nineteenth Century*. Oxford & New York: Oxford University Press.

hooks, bell. 1984. *Feminist Theory. From Margin to Center*. Boston: South End Press.

Kapur, Geeta. 1989. 'Ravi Varma: Representational Dilemmas of a Nineteenth Century Indian Painter'. *Journal of Arts and Ideas*, 17–18: 59–60.

Kelkar, Meena and Gangavane, Deepti (eds) 2003. *Feminism in Search of an Identity: The Indian Context.* Jaipur: Rawat.

Kelkar, Meena. 2003. 'Beeja-Ksetra-Nyaya: Some Considerations', in Meena Kelkar and Deepti Gangavane (eds), *Feminism in Search of an Identity: The Indian Context* (91–100). Jaipur: Rawat.

Kulkarni, Nirmala. 2003. 'The Satpatha Brahmans on Women', in Meena Kelkar and Deepti Gangavane (eds), *Feminism in Search of an Identity: The Indian Context* (50–60). Jaipur: Rawat.

Madsen, Deborah L. 2000. *Feminist Theory and Literary Practice.* London: Pluto.

Manusmriti. 1982. Vol. III. Trans and ed. Graves Chamnen Houghton. New Delhi: Cosmo.

Millett, Kate. 1970. *Sexual Politics.* London: Abacus.

Mohanty, Chandra Talpade. 1995. 'Under Western Eyes; Feminist Scholarship and Colonial Discourses', in Bill Ashcroft, Gareth Griffiths and Helen Tiffin (eds), *The Post-Colonial Reader* (259–268). New York: Routledge.

Moore, Henrietta L. 1988. *Feminism and Anthropology.* Minneapolis: University of Minnesota Press.

Robinson, B.A. 'The Status of Women in the Hebrew (Old Testament)'. 27 August 2004. 1–7. 12 August 2006. http://www.religoustotcrance.org/ofe_bibl.htm

——. 'The Status of Women in the Hebrew: Old Testament Passages Describing Women in Negative Terms; as Equal to Men; and as Leaders'. 27 August 2004, 1–5. 12 August 2006. http://www.religioustoterance.org/ofe _bibl.htm

——. 'The Status of Women in the Christian Gospel'. 27 August 2004. 1–5. 12 August 2006. http://wwwzeligioustoterance.org/cfe_bibl.htm

Roiphe, Katie. 1993. *The Morning After: Sex, Fear and Feminism*. London: Hamish Hamilton.

Rowbotham, Sheila. 1974. *Women, Resistance and Revolution: A History of Women in the Modern World*. New York: Vintage.

Roy, Arundhati. 1997. *The God of Small Things*. New Delhi: India Ink.

Sathe, Putul. 2001. 'Women in Literary Context', in Abha Avasthi and A.K. Srivastava (eds), *Modernity, Feminism and Women Empowerment* (238–253). Jaipur: Rawat.

Steinem, Gloria. 1983. *Outrageous Acts and Everyday Rebellions*. London: Jonathan Cape.

Thapan, Meenakshi. 1997. 'Introduction', in Meenakshi Thapan (ed.), *Embodiment: Essays on Gender and Identity*. Delhi: Oxford.

Tharu, Susie. 1989. 'Tracing Savitri's Pedigree: Victorian Racism and the Image of Women in Indo-Anglian Literature', in Kumkum Sangari and Sudesh Vaid (eds), *Recasting Women: Essays in Colonial History* (254–260). New Delhi: Kali for Women.

Tharu, Susie and Lalita, K. 1991. 'Introduction', in Susie Tharu and K. Lalita (eds), *Women Writing in India: 600 B.C. to the Present*. Vol. I. Delhi: Oxford.

Tyagi, Amita and Uberoi, Patricia. 1990. 'Adjustment is the Key: Postmarital Romance in Indian Popular Fiction'. *Manushi*, 61: 1–21.

Uberoi, Patricia. 1990. 'Feminine Identity and National Ethos in Indian Calendar Art'. *Economic and Political Weekly*, 28 April: 41–48.

Visvanathan, Susan. 2002. 'The Status of Christian Women in Kerala', in Arvind Sharma (ed.), *Women in Indian Religions* (189–200). New Delhi: Oxford.

3

Dalit Feminism

A Perspective on Bama's *Sangati*

Tanvir Likhari

The postmodern emphasis on identity and difference within feminism has broadened the scope of inclusion and made the articulation of new voices a reality. In the last decade or so Dalit feminism has challenged the threshold of Indian feminism by critiquing it as a politics of exclusion and branding it as Brahmanical. 'Brahmanical feminism is the possibility of occupying a feminist position outside caste: *the possibility of denying caste as a problem for gender*' (Rao, 1999: 208, emphasis original). Dalit feminism questions not only Indian feminism's hegemony in claiming to speak for all women but also the hegemony of Dalit men to speak on behalf of Dalit women. Gopal Guru (1995) in his path breaking essay, 'Dalit Women Talk Differently' described Dalit feminism as a 'discourse of discontent', 'a politics of difference' from mainstream Indian feminist thought. Western feminist theory of the early years of second wave had been critiqued as 'Eurocentric' focusing on the experience of white, middle-class women as representing all women, thereby marginalising women of colour, of the working class and of other ethnicities. A similar charge has been levied against mainstream Indian feminism by new and upcoming Dalit feminists for marginalising Dalit women from the mainstream. The leadership of the women's movement in India too has been dominated by upper-class women, although they have taken up cases and issues of women belonging to lower classes, low castes and minorities. In fact as Brazilian scholar Heleieth Saffioti, has emphasised that bourgeois feminism has always been 'fundamentally and unconsciously a feminism of the ruling class' (quoted in *hooks, 2000: 22).

Dalit feminist thought 'exposes the limits of feminism's capacity to represent women as somehow unmarked and disembodied from their caste or religious identity and stands to throw feminism (and its conceptions of gender identity) into crisis' (Rao, 2003: 3). Caste has become a very important factor not only in Indian feminism but also in Indian polity considering the post-Mandal, Right wing shift of the Indian political scenario. In the words of Rajeshwari Sundar Rajan, 'women *are* classed, caste and communal subjects, and both privilege and oppression may be grounded in identity recognised in those terms (in addition to being hierarchised in terms of gender)' (c.f. Rao, 2003: 3 emphasis original). A feminist theory to be authentic must link gender oppression to oppression of other hegemonies such as class, caste and nation. In this chapter I will examine the paradigms of gender and caste as they operate together in *Sangati* authored by Faustina Bama, one of the first Dalit women writers to be widely recognised and translated. The organisation of Dalit women both by the articulation of protest and agency is a subversion of centuries old neglect and a stubborn refusal to be considered as a subject. The 'subject' woman was produced in the nationalist discourse through exclusion of women of the lower classes, caste, of minorities or 'othered' communities. As Sangari and Vaid (1989) point out in *Recasting Women*, the early colonial constellation of the Aryan woman is a sternly elitist concept in class and caste terms. This elitist trend of the reformers is evident from Dayanand's advice to Aryan mothers to employ wet nurses to nurse their babies so that they may recover faster to procreate a strong race (Chakravarty, 1989). In fact the recognition of the existence of the Vedic *dasi* would have been an embarrassment to the Nationalists. Spivak (1996) in the essay 'Can the subaltern speak?' speaking in the colonial context says that 'the subaltern has no history and cannot speak, the subaltern as female is even more deeply in shadow' (325). But in the postcolonial, post-independence India, the subaltern as female does speak, though this act of speech or writing in the context of subaltern masses who are still illiterate might be taking them into channels of the literary elite. The gendered marginalised subaltern like Bama speaks for herself and others whom she represents, although it does raise the issue of heterogeneity among Dalit women – often educated and empowered ones representing the unlettered majority.

Sangati is to be analysed for the sheer fact of defiance by Dalit women and their apparent autonomy in the context of the contemporary historiography of the gendered, the marginal and the dispossessed. The marginalised no longer have to depend on what Spivak has called the 'exorbitation' of the postcolonial feminist critic to give 'the subaltern a voice in history'. It first appeared in Tamil in 1994, was translated into French in 2002 and into English in 2005, is written by Bama whose ancestors were landless peasants and had converted to Christianity to escape caste hatred in Tamil Nadu. In the words of Lakshmi Holmstrom (2005) 'is in a sense the autobiography of the community' of Dalit women (xv). It centres on the lives, culture, struggle, sorrows and resistance of a community of *paraiya* women, a neighbourhood group of friends and relations and their joint struggle. The conventional notions of the genre novel are flouted just as those of autobiography are flouted in *Karukku* (Bama, 2000). *Sangati* which means news or events in Tamil is a stringing together of interconnected anecdotes which happened in the lives of a series of protagonists. The presence of the narrator Pathima, who is a little girl at the beginning of the novel grown to a young adult towards the end, is the thread that binds all the events together. It teases out the way patriarchy works in the lives of Dalit women. Oppressed and ruled by multiple patriarchies, Dalit women are forced to break the structures of society in order to live. It expresses the multiple voices of strong and resilient Dalit women who had the courage to break the shackles of authority and dared to make fun of the class in power that oppressed them. The text is not only about the tears and sorrows of Dalit women, but also about their lively and rebellious culture, their eagerness not to let life crush them, their self-confidence and self-respect that enable them to leap over threatening adversaries by ridiculing them. It is also about the passion to live life with vitality and truth and about their hard labour. The collective voices of the community of Dalit women are to be heard through women – Pathima the narrator, Paatti her grandmother, her cousin Rendupalli and others.

Bama shares the aims of Dalit literature and other marginalised and subaltern groups worldwide in foregrounding caste, but goes further and brings together two historically marginalised paradigms of caste and gender. Tradition inaugurated by Phule, Ambedkar and Periyar is carried forward. The seeds of Dalit feminism are traced to the 14-year-old Muktabai's (1999) essay, 'The Griefs of Mangs and Mahars' where she links caste and gender. It is the experience of caste rather than gender alone which informs her mission of power and the resultant exploitation. The development of Dalit feminism can be traced to the movements of Ambedkar and Periyar and in the writings of women in the self-respect journal *Kudi Arsu*. Although Ambedkar foregrounded caste and untouchability rather than gender, yet his movement empowered Dalit women by encouraging their education, confidence and self-respect. Dalit women began to organise themselves on their own too within the ambit of the Dalit movement. Periyar went further to rework truly revolutionary notions of identity, sexuality and marriage within society, by questioning the monogamous marriage itself as well as the stringent codes of chastity forced upon women:

> The concept of husband-and-wife relationship has been seen as master slave relationship. The essential philosophy of marriage has been to insist on women as slaves ... why should human beings alone keep such contract of one man one-woman relationship ... until women are liberated from such marriages and from men, the country cannot attain independence. (Viduthalai quoted in Anandhi, 2003)

Periyar stipulated women to give in to the claims of a free self-validating desire, take on lovers, choose a life of economic self-sufficiency and abjure the responsibilities of motherhood – although these ideas could never fully find fruition in practice, it unchained a system of thought which few decades later gave rise to Dalit feminism.

It is with this tradition of revolt, anger and assertion of self-hood behind her that Bama writes, about the same time when Dalit women organised themselves in National Federation for Dalit Women (NFDW) – the first autonomous assertion of Dalit women's identity. In this context Dalit women's voicing their own stories, naming their difference becomes an important personal and political project. According to Rao (2005) the demands by the Dalits and other lower-caste women are not merely for inclusion, but for an analysis of gender relations as they are inflicted by multiple and overlapping patriarchies. It is such an analysis that is foregrounded. The text contributes both to the women's movement and to the Dalits' struggle by indicting both gender inequality and caste hatred equally as the cause of woman's oppression, seeped in anger and rebellion against both. Sharmila Rege, a Dalit feminist critic points out:

> The Dalit feminist standpoint is about historically locating how all our identities are not equally powerful, and about reviewing how in different historical practices similarities between women have been ignored in an effort to underline caste-class identities, or at other times differences ignored for the 'feminist cause'. (Rege, 2000: 5)

Dalit women have to face a double threshold of patriarchies – a 'discreet patriarchy' that is specific to caste and an 'overlapping patriarchy' of the upper caste, along with the paradigm of age-old caste oppression, written in the structures of society, in order to live a life of dignity. Rege (2004) also refers to 'two different kinds of patriarchal control: a dominant form of Brahmanical patriarchy that rests on conception of caste purity as well as patriarchal control within the community which sees them as sexual property of the male' (Rao,

2003: 94). Throughout history there has been a Brahmanical refusal to universalise a single patriarchal mode. Rege (2004) feels that the existence of multiple patriarchies is a result of Brahmanical conspiracy.

According to Lakshmi Holmstrom (2005), it is remarkable that, writing in the first half of the last decade, Bama was already formulating from the social political perspective of a Dalit and examining caste and gender oppressions together. Discreet patriarchy, among their own caste dictates that, power rests with men in the community in the institutions led by them – the caste courts, the Church and the panchayats. Bama touches the issues of domestic violence and economic inequality – violent treatment of women by fathers, husbands and brothers. Dalit women in *Sangati* are also wage earners like men, working as agricultural and building sites labourers, but earning less than men do. Rules for the sexual behaviour of men and women are very different. Whether it is the upper caste or the lower castes it is the men who draw the circumscribing line of the threshold.

> It is what men say that has become the rule of law … . Whatever happens must be according to their pleasure and their convenience. If anything is ever arranged for a woman's convenience, they will never stand it. They will leap between heaven and earth and prevent it. They will insist you must never cross the line they have drawn. (Bama, 2005: 110)

But a feminist point is made, 'what have we ever gained by never crossing that line all this time? (Bama: 110). Not only is the universality of women's oppression which cuts across lines of caste and class emphasised, but the difference of Dalit women is also focused on. Recent gender studies in India have pointed out the diversity of women's experience, questioning the usefulness of the homogeneous category 'women' in critical writing. Power imbalances that exist between different groups of women along with the universal fact of their oppression along the lines of gender are analysed. The lives of the Dalit women are in sharp contrast to the lives of luxury and ease of the upper-caste women They are different in their looks, dress, education, language and 'above all live a life of toil and hard labour'. The narrator's grandmother Paatti feels that they look like a 'Mahalakshmi, a goddess' wear fresh flowers every day and take 'a whole hour just to plait their hair'. Pathima, the narrator realises the privileges of the upper-caste woman but at the same time has the warmth and largeness of heart to recognise the upper-caste woman's oppression, her confinement within the four walls, her enslavement and dependence because of material conditions.

> If we are to live at all, we have to shout and shriek and keep ourselves sane. Upper caste women, though keep it all suppressed, they can neither chew nor swallow. They lose their nerve and many of them become unstable or mentally ill. (Bama: 68)

The resilience, strength and pride of Dalit women are foregrounded as they compare themselves to the upper-caste women. In their 'abundant will to survive' they 'find ways of coping' and 'work hard and earn their money and have a few coins in their hands. They don't hold out their palms to their husbands for every little expense like those others' (Bama: 68, 69). According to the narrator, the lives of the upper-caste women are without dignity and pride, 'They submit to their husbands like cobras that shrink back into their boxes' (Bama: 67). Their stifled lives of 'checks and rules' are further cramped by the practice of dowry which in no way guarantees their happiness as well as the 'life of death-in-life' for their widows. The low castes on the contrary have the traditional practice of bride price and do not have a word for widow in their language. The upper castes' humanity has to be redefined not only in terms of Dalit women but also for the upper castes' own subalterns, their widows and prostitutes. The Dalit social order gives a woman the freedom to leave or divorce their husbands or marry again. A woman, Pecchi we're told 'finished with her first fellow and then married Sudalai' (Bama: 92). Dalit girls also face ritual seclusion like their upper-caste counterparts on reaching puberty, but this seclusion is not coded with impurity, fear and anxiety about chastity, but is an occasion for celebration. According to O'Flaherty (1976), menstruation is a mark of a woman's innate impurity and at the same time her innate sexuality. When Dalit girls of the community come of age a little hut-like room was constructed with palmyra fronds and the young girl stays there for 16 days, while the relatives come with gifts and money. In the evening the women give her a ritual bath after rubbing her with turmeric, sing songs with choruses and grand ululations. Change and consumerism touch the lives of Dalit women too and the simple rituals are now accompanied with a show of gifts taken out in a procession. But for those who cannot afford this grand spectacle the women cannot be stopped from making joyous celebrations with their songs, chants and ululations. When Marriamma, the narrator's cousin comes of age the women gather together and sing:

> On Friday morning ...
> Shake her dry hair and comb with gold, Toss her hair dry and comb it with silver Comb her hair dry with a golden comb.
> And women, altogether raise kulavt. (Bama: 17)

The upper-caste woman on the contrary is an object of moral panic, fiercely controlled, secluded and guarded by upper-caste patriarchy (Chakravarty, 2000). The sexual politics of the low castes are characterised by a greater openness, equality and mobility for women – inured more by need than by social structure, where men work long and women to have to deal with society on their own. For many Dalit women the street, which is otherwise a highly gendered space, is the site of work where these women negotiate their spaces accordingly. Their marriage unlike the Hindus is not a religious sacrament that goes beyond life and death, but a human contract. Kancha Illaiah (2003) points out that it is governed by the rights guaranteed to women within the framework of the broad system of patriarchy. Violation of the other's rights can result in breaking the contract of marriage which may be renewed or formed with others. A Dalit wife need not treat her husband as God or address him as one. In case of a quarrel, a word for word and abuse for abuse is the norm. Their patriarchy thus is far more democratic than the upper caste.

Unlike the Hindus, the Dalit family prefers sons not for religious reasons that guarantee the Fathers' abode in heaven by ritual performance but for far more practical reasons of their being a more productive force. According to Illaiah (2003), Dalits are more open in the treatment of sexual desire. Among the Hindus the discourse of desire is a taboo at the personal or human level, but it is sublimated at the divine level with the amorous tales of Hindu gods and goddesses. Restriction on the mobility of upper-caste women further reduces the interaction between men and women. For the Dalits, on the other hand, sex is a human activity, an organic need of the body rather than a pleasure of the heart. Pathima calls upon the women of her community to celebrate their difference, have confidence in their own culture, pride in their beauty and strength. 'The way we wear our saris with the pleats at the back and the way we pull our hair back and knot to one side – all these have their own beauty' (Bama: 113). The same time they recognise the common thread of gender oppression of what bell hooks has called an 'absence of choices' in the lives of the women to whatever caste they belong. 'One way or another, it's all the same We suffer in one way, they suffer in another' (Bama: 12).

There is a strong sense of the unfairness of double-day among the women in *Sangati* which even Gail Omvedt's (2003) interview with a Dalit agricultural labourer reveals:

> We have to labour in the fields as hard as the men do, and then on top of that, struggle to bear and raise our children. As for the men, their work ends when they've finished in the fields. If you are born into this world, it is best you are born a man. We only toil in the fields and in the home until our vaginas shrivel. (Bama: 6)

The hard labour, the punishing schedules of the low-caste women is written on their bone-wearied bodies although both men and women perform hard labour outside, the men seldom or 'never give their wages to their women' thus inverting role of man as breadwinner (Bama: 6, 67). After a hard day's work in the fields at labour sites the men would go straight away to the bazaar or to while away their time, whereas the women would return home, wash vessels, clean the house, gather firewood, go to the shops to buy rice and provisions, cook, feed husband and children before they could eat what was left over and then go to bed.

Oppressed by their life of unending toil both inside and outside the house without any rest or respite, their stresses and strains, their lack of education gives rise to a culture of violence and belief in being possessed by spirits or *peys.* With no hope of peace, rest or happiness they vent their frustration by quarrels full of obscenities, 'direct and ugly', 'often dealing with sexual relations'. Their language with free use of obscenities and words relating to genital parts is in fact an act of subversion breaking established rules of decorum and decency. The voice of Bama coming through the narrator explains that 'because they have neither pleasure nor fulfillment in their own sexual lives, they derive a sort of bitter comfort by using these terms of abuse which are actually their body parts'. It is only by these cathartic fights that the women 'survive without going crazy. If we have to live at all, we have to shout and shriek to keep ourselves sane' (Bama: 68). Women who break down under the stresses and strains of their life come to believe that they are possessed by spirits. Iruluppan's wife, Manchi becomes possessed with a spirit of Esakki, who had died an unnatural death, having been murdered by her brothers in full-term pregnancy for marrying out of caste. Pathima, the narrator pertinently questions her grandmother about why only women and that too from the low castes get possessed. The stories of *peys* and spirits, Bama rationalises, are told to girls, 'to take away their freedom and control over movements. And we too become frightened, we gaze about us in terror, we're afraid of every little thing, they shiver we die' (Bama, 2005: 58). Just as the Sita–Sati–Savitri model is used to circumscribe the upper-caste women inside the thresholds, similarly fear of *peys* and spirits is evoked in Dalit girls to control them.

Michelle Barrett (1980) observes that sexual relationships are political because they are socially constructed and therefore could be different. 'This tension is played out between different generations of women – the narrator Pathima who feels that things could be different and her grandmother, who takes recourse to the argument that things have always been so'. Pathima blames the women themselves for the faulty socialisation of little girls:

> It's you folk who put butter in one eye and quicklime in the other ... . We aren't allowed to talk loudly or laugh noisily; even when they sleep they can't stretch out on our backs ... . We always have to walk with our heads bowed down, gazing get our toes. You tell us all this rubbish and keep us under your control. Even when our stomachs are screaming with hunger, we mustn't eat first ... . What, Paatti, aren't we also human beings? (Bama: 29)

The women internalise the patriarchal codes that have conditioned them and repeat the actions of discrimination with their daughters. They never let the baby boys cry, breast-feeding them much longer than the girls and nursing them with the greatest care. The little girls on the contrary are kept working all the time, cleaning utensils, drawing water, sweeping the house, gathering firewood, washing clothes and so on. When all is done they mind the younger siblings. Even when they play they mustn't join in the boys' games like *kabaddi* and marbles or they are chastised. The position of gender as a social construct whether among the upper castes or Dalits is established in the structure of society with women having internalised these values, and made their own narratives. They have built the oppression in the structures of their language, in their own narratives – their songs, heir tales and their riddles:

> Crab, O crab, my pretty little crab
> Who wandered through all the fields I planted
> I pulled off your claws and put you in the pot ...
> I waited and waited for him to come home
> And began to eat as he came through the door ...
> He pounced at me to kill me ...
> He almost crushed the baby in my womb. (Bama: 30)

Having remained silent themselves, they also cajole and advise the younger girls to remain silent in the face of oppression, 'It is better for women not to open their mouths. You just try speaking out about what you believe is right. You only get kicked and beaten and trampled upon-for your pains. And it isn't just here that it happens. It's the same throughout the world. Women are not given that kind of respect'. Vrinda Nabar (1995) says that the dependence of one generation of women upon an earlier one has perpetuated forms of oppression by turning them into categories which define what it means to be *Caste* as a Woman. Most Indian women are taught by other women that they have no choices, that the oppressive condition incorporates both stri-jati and stri-dharma.

Barrett (1980) points out that feminism has given a central place to sexual abuse of women. It has insisted on the political character of sexuality, on the unequal power of those involved in sexual relationships. Sexual politics is established as a significant area of struggle. As sexual property of the low-caste male, they have no control over their sexuality and often live in abusive and brutally violent relationships. The narrator's aunt is brutally killed by her husband:

> The man was crazy with lust. Because he wanted her every single day. How could she agree to his frenzy after she worked all parts of the day and night, inside the house and out? He is an animal, that fellow. When she refused, he practically broke her in half. Once in my very presence he hit her with the rice pounder. May his hand be bitten with a snake. (Bama, 2005: 10)

When her husband is beating her to death, no relative or passerby comes to help for she is the sexual property of her husband to use, abuse or to kill if he wants. The logic of the wife as property of the husband runs even in upper-class patriarchy and can be seen in the patriarchal bias of the police and judiciary in hesitating to interfere in cases of dowry harassment regarding it as a strictly private affair. Domestic violence is the routine lot of most Dalit women. Thaayi, a neighbour who 'looked like Nayakkar women is routinely dragged along the street by her husband and flogged like an animal with a stick or belt'. Feminists have opposed the sexual abuse of women, their de-personification into objects for male satisfaction and the reduction of women to breeding machines. In the words of Barrett (1980), 'many aspects of sexual relations are simply irreducible to questions of class. Engles' analysis for the enforced monogamy of bourgeois wives leaves us with an analysis that is incapable of explaining how or why male control over women's fertility should exist among the proletariat where the inheritance of property is not an issue. The lack of power of the low-caste male comes into conflict with the myth of male supremacy. As workers they are dominated by the upper-caste patriarchy and controlled by the economic needs of hegemonic castes and classes. According to hooks (2000) unlike working women, working men are fed daily the fantasy diet of male supremacy and power. In actuality they have very little power. Yet they cannot rebel against the economic order. They are socialised by ruling powers to accept their dehumanisation and exploitation in the public world of work, and they are taught to expect that the private world, the world of home and intimate relationships, will restore to them their sense of power, which they equate with masculinity.

Robbed of power in the private sphere, the men rely more on the use of violence to establish and maintain a sex role hierarchy in which they are in a dominant position. Man suppresses the violence that begins with psychological abuse in the public world, where he is powerless to retort and releases it in what hooks calls a 'control' situation – where he has no fear of retaliation, the home is his control situation and the target of his abuse is usually the woman. This violence stems from his emotional pain, which when released on the female results in a feeling of 'relief, even pleasure' for him. 'The psychology of masculinity in sexist societies teaches men that great knowledge and express pain negates masculinity and is symbolic of Castration, causing pain rather than expressing it restores man's sense of completeness, of wholeness, of masculinity' (hooks, 2000: 122). The loss of pride and confidence in social relations of power makes him wreck vengeance on the only subject over whom society gives him unbridled control. Bama's voice filtering through, Pathima the narrator also analyses this culture of violence:

> I wonder whether all that violence was because there was nowhere else for them to exert the male pride or show off their authority. All that suppressed anger was vented when they came home and beat their wives to a pulp. Even though they are male, because they are Dalits, they have to be like dogs with their tails rolled up when they are in the fields, and dealing with the landlords. There is no way they can show their strength in those circumstances. So they show it at home on their wives and children. (Bama: 65)

It is not just the oppression of discreet patriarchies that Dalit women have to face but sexual harassment at sites of work and threat of rape from overlapping patriarchies of upper castes as well. According to Kannabiran and Kannabiran (2003):

> Gendered space has dimensions of caste and class which crucially structure the way in which women of different caste and class experienced gender ... when women especially those belonging to the lower castes confront their being policed by upper-caste men, rape is the ultimate punishment – for the women certainly, but more importantly for the men. (255)

Paatti the narrator's grandmother warns the narrator of rape by upper-caste men, 'Women should never come on their own to these parts. If upper caste fellows clap eyes on you, you're finished. They'll drag you off and rape you, that's for sure' (Bama: 8). The shaming of Dalit women is marked with judgments by overlapping patriarchies. The upper-caste patriarchy maintains a strong sense of gendered spaces into public and private spheres, where it circumscribes its women into the interior. It is the barrier between the public and private which defines respectable and non-respectable women, the legacy of the culture of *purdah* that ensured women's safety only within doors and made them fair prey in public spaces. The habitual visibility of Dalit women in public spaces, which they inhabit the sites of work, signals her transgression of the private spheres as well as her availability. It becomes a comment on their character, as well as the character of caste, women being the flag bearers of honour, purity and tradition. Furthermore, the bodies of low-caste women have traditionally been inscribed as lustful, whose sexuality cannot be controlled by the low-caste male. This construct is a legacy of the nationalist discourse, which marked the Dalit women, the stage actress as women of loose and low character primarily because their social relations and manners were different from the mainstream upper caste. But the Brahmanical centre judged the marginalised women with its own hegemonic vision, thus labelling them as debauched women. This foregrounds the failure of the upper-caste male/patriarchy to acknowledge and respect difference, hybridity of the low castes with their different social order.

Dalit women, the subaltern among subalterns, bear the brunt of multiple patriarchies as well as caste discrimination – a fact which becomes apparent in the case of Marriamma, the narrator's cousin. The upper-caste landlord Kumarasani Ayya's son drags Marriamma inside a pump shed and tries to molest her as she stops to have a drink of water from his pump. Her friends, who advise her to keep quiet, 'It's you who'll get the blame; it's you who'll be called a whore' are aware that all paradigms of class, caste and gender will work against them. 'The landlord is an evil man fat with money. He's an upper caste as well' (Bama: 20). The landlord in turn accuses and implicates Marriamma and another Dalit boy in an indecent scandal launching the complaint with the patriarchal Dalit elders. Even as both plead innocent, it is Marriamma who is made a badge of the community honour and turned into a scapegoat in order to conceal the inadequacy and sense of powerlessness of the Dalit men to confront the powerful hegemonic upper-class patriarchy and protect their women. It is she who is fined heavily and made to prostrate herself and beg forgiveness. The women of the community murmur in protest: 'its only to us they'll brag. Ask them just to stand up to the Mudalaali. Not a bit, they will cover their mouths and their backsides and run'. But they are also aware of the precariousness of the situation of their community vis-à-vis the nexus of hegemonic powers of the administration, the police and the upper castes. Not only can the upper castes 'set the police on them', but they themselves 'have to go crawling to them tomorrow and beg for work' (Bama: 24–25). Kannabiran and Kannabiran (2003) say:

> The social relations of caste and gender are based on the exercise of power through the use of force. This power could have many dimensions: it can be simple (or) ... complex in not permitting the space for the raising of issues ... but the most absolute exercise of power is that

> grievance or dissent is not even articulated. To articulate grievance indicates a degree of political awareness of a wrong, which the absolute exercise of power does not permit. (253)

In fact what is evident today is the weakening of an absolute power that did not allow or permit the space for the articulation or even the awareness of grievance or a sense of wrong and the consequent blurring of carefully drawn lines of demarcation.

The Church as an overarching patriarchy, guilty both of sexism and casteism has curtailed the freedom of Dalit women particularly their right to divorce. Bama (2000) in *Karukku* had foregrounded casteism rather patriarchy within the Church but in *Sangati* the hegemonies both of caste and patriarchy are deconstructed and Church rules forbidding divorce are exposed as traps to keep women under control. The parish priests are not sympathetic towards women's individual choice of life partners' especially inter-caste ones. In *Sangati* a young girl battered by her father and brothers for wanting to marry inter-caste appeals to the parish priest who instead of helping her 'broadcasts it to all and sundry, speaks about her as if is a whore cast suspicion on her morals, met her in a room all alone and leered at her, made false promises to her and kept her running between the Church and home like a dog, but never organised a wedding or anything' (Bama: 108). The Dalit women are made to perform menial tasks in the Church, but are not allowed to sing in the chorus or perform in the Church dramas. Even little girls who are fair enough to 'play baby Sesu' are debarred from doing so.

Sexual liberation, of the kind that western feminists talk about as articulating desire or 'expression of the individual's need', as 'the raw impulse life' 'does not deconstruct the power relations between men and women, as women are still exploited by old sexual paradigms' (hooks, 2000: 151). For Dalit women still trapped in the paradigms of sexual oppression and violence it would be as much expression of sexual freedom to have a choice not to participate in sexual activity as it is to choose to do so. Bama presents her women's sexuality as oppressed, and nowhere foregrounds any relationships of pleasure or gratification. She analyses representations of Dalit female sexuality only in terms of sexual oppression with the aim of raising political awareness, but not in terms of agency. In fact, it is *Viramma* an oral reminiscence of a Dalit woman revealed to Racine and Racine (1997) over nearly a decade that there is a free and frank treatment of conjugal sexual relations. In fact, Bama's representations of brutality and oppression are less sexual in nature but relate more to domestic violence and wife battering. According to Carol Vance (1989: 324), 'to speak only of violence and oppression ignores women's experience with sexual agency and choice and unwittingly increases the sexual terror and despair in which women live'. After a hard days toil in the fields or on labour sites they return to work at home their bodies 'wracked with pain' get no respite, and are claimed for sexual gratification by their men. In fact as Kancha Illaiah (2003) states, sex for them is not a leisure bound activity but one that is need based.

The sophisticated French notions of women writing their bodies, in 'white ink and milk' is brought to an ironic expose, as Bama tells of the abuse of Dalit women's bodies always bone-weary and tired rather than any pleasurable sexual libido. When the low-caste woman writes her body it is not with 'white ink and milk' but with blood and sweat of her labour and the violence that is unleashed upon her. This aspect is further exposed in Mahasweta Devi's (1995) *Doulti* the bonded prostitute whose body lies wasted and ridden with disease at the age of 27. Their need is the positive presence of social and psychological conditions that foster satisfying sexual relations (Willis, 1982). Bama (2005) explores the issues of Dalit women's loss of control over their bodies (health hazards) in their innumerable pregnancies, lack of awareness and availability for healthcare. Women rarely go to hospitals, but deliver their children in a makeshift way, many times at work in the fields. Birth control particularly for the rural Dalit women is difficult to achieve and the sterilisation available is only of a haphazard, untrained variety. A woman, pregnant full term cuts grass for her cow in the fields, narrates the grandmother:

> She went into labour there and then, and delivered the child straightway. She cut off the umbilical cord with the sickle ... dug a whole and buried the placenta, and then walked home carrying her baby and her bundle of grass. (Bama: 6)

In strong contrast is the seclusion of the upper-caste women and their 13 days ritual impurity which the Dalit women can ill afford as most have to return to work the very next day.

In the midst of circumstances multiple patriarchies, that seek to oppress all aspects of their lives there is evidence of the creation of a distinct feminist space, a celebration of life itself in the very language that they use – in their folk songs, dances and proverbs. In India, where literacy in itself is a milestone yet to be achieved, the oral tradition in itself is a sign of breaking of silence of one half of humanity that was condemned to invisibility. The spoken word in this context resumes the significance of writing one's body, as women play out their lives in it. These narrative express voices that are ambivalent giving expression to women's consent, as well as protest and some collectively become the agent of strength and liveliness in their dull and dreary lives. 'Laughing and chatting, women make up their songs and chants as they please each other and go about their work weeding, transplanting rice, harvesting or grinding masalas at home They sing all the time at work, too, so that the woods rang out to the sound of their laughter as they make up words to tease each other' (Bama: 76). They sing lullabies to their babies, choruses and ululations on coming of age rites, *oppaaris*, and of man and woman relationships and create songs on the spur of the moment to tease one another. Their language with its closeness vile abuse and songs, chants and proverbs is expressive both of their pain and suffering as well as the quality of strength and 'rebounding like a ball'.

Facing multifarious oppression, the women find ways of coping, resisting, protesting and somehow surviving. Whether it is the patriarchy discreet or overlapping, the state or the church, caste oppression or poverty, *peys* or spirits they must somehow devise strategies of coping by resorting to vile abuse, acrimonious fights, sheer strength of will or empowerment through education. Pathima's rebellion against the structures of Oppression is close to Bama's own and it is author's voice that seeps into the text:

> 'I decided that it is up to us to be aware of our situation, and not fool ourselves that we have been possessed by peys ... I told myself that she must never allow our minds to be worn out, damaged, and broken in the belief that this is our fate. Just as we work hard so long as there is strength in our bodies, so too, must we strengthen our hearts and minds in order to survive. (Bama: 59)

She seethes in anger and protest at the treatment meted out to her cousin Marriamma, who is humiliated both by the upper-caste landlords and by their own community of elders, the women of her neighbourhood who faced brutal violence at the hands of their husbands as well as the caste oppression that their women have to face. 'If we continue to be frightened, everyone will take advantage of us. If we stand up for ourselves without caring whether we die or survive, they creep away with their tails between their legs'. 'But they are not going to think of giving up all this easily ... . It's we who must uphold our rights. We must stand up for ourselves ... . If we believe that someone else is going to come and uplift us, then we're doomed to remain where we are forever' (Bama: 66–67). Other women of the community too evolve their own strategies to deal with their oppressions. Raakamma a woman who gives it back to her husband 'word for word' when he turns abusive uses strategies of subversion – rails and rants, spits on him, asks him to drink his son's urine, 'her motherly blood', effeminates and challenges his masculinity 'Let's see if you're a real man. You only know how to go for a woman's parts. Go and fight with a man who is your equal, and you see. You'll get your balls burnt for your pains' (Bama: 61). She even lifts her sari in front of the entire crowd, as a deliberate tactic to shame her husband and prevent him from using violence on her.

In the postcolonial, post independence India Dalits no longer share the dominant ideology of *Karma* handed out to them by the Brahmanical hegemony, but in the changing scenario of electoral politics they have become aggressive and confident. Bama gives vent to her frustration and anger. Sammuga Kizhavi, one of the women of her Dalit community links caste and gender in her strategies of defiance and ridicule of the upper-caste hegemony. Caught red-handed having a bath in one of his high-caste wells, she defiantly spits out a mouthful of water into the well saying that his water was not good at all but salty. In another gesture of ultimate subversion she urinates in the landlord's pot of drinking water after he thrashes Dalit children for touching his pot by mistake.

To break the structures of oppression hierarchies of both caste and gender have to be ruptured. Despite the toil, the 'hellish torment', the 'domestic violence' which leaves them beaten 'to half or quarter life' runs a subtext of strength, resistance and resilience (Bama: 67). An issue is taken up in each chapter, of discrimination, of sexual harassment, of domestic violence, of possession, of domination by the church and along with these oppressions voices of strong note, of dissent and the need for change:

> A woman's body, mind, feelings, words and deeds and her entire life are all under his [man's] control and domination. And the two had accepted ... that, – our happiness lies in being enslaved to man. But if only we were to realise that we too have our self-worth, honour and self-respect, we could manage our own lives in our own way. (Bama: 68)

A strong plea is made for Dalit women themselves becoming the agency of control and change in their lives, 'even the ocean will support us, if only we dare' (Bama: 67). According to Lakshmi Holmstrom (2005), 'The ideals that Bama admires and applauds in Dalit women are not the traditional Tamil feminine ideals of *accham* (fear), *nanam* (shyness), *madam* (simplicity, innocence), *payirppu* (modesty), but rather courage, fearlessness, independence and self-esteem' (xix). Pathima, the narrator expresses her admiration for the little girl Maikkanni, who not only takes up the role of a bread-winner for her household but along with other children stands up to take collective action against an incident of atrocity which takes place at the factory – all the children collectively rise up in rebellion, shouting words of abuse, threatening to go home in protest.

Dalit women's oppression lies in the structures of ignorance and lack of education, so female agricultural labourers in *Sangati* resolve to educate their children. But the empowerment of Dalit women in particular is an issue fraught with tension and subversion of dominant hegemonic ideologies. Towards the end of the text Pathima is an ultimate subversive position – the position of an educated, unmarried Dalit woman living alone, a position she shares with the author. Bama admits that even empowered with *education one has to face many difficulties, the biggest of which is being a* Dalit. 'My people are punished constantly for the simple fact of having been born as Dalits'. Being a Dalit woman, she says makes it even more difficult and the ultimate subversive position is 'trying to live alone as an unmarried Dalit woman'. Being an unmarried single woman, people assume that she has known many men as a prostitute, gossip about her, hesitate to let a house to her. The common Indian belief that 'unmarried woman is signed, sealed and delivered to one man' 'otherwise she is the common property of many fellows' is subverted by Bama asking, 'why should a woman belong to no one but herself?' (Bama: 121–122). Pathima's grandmother warns her that things will not change just by learning 'a few letters of the alphabet', but it is in the letters of the alphabet that the promise of deliverance and empowerment lies. Bama (2005) hoped that Dalits women who read *Sangati* will rise up in fervour and walk towards victory as they pick in their struggle as pioneers of a new society.

Bama (2005) improvises strategies of subversion not only to counter oppression of gender and caste but like other Dalit writing is non-conformist in content and form, and challenges received literary norms of a conventional plot. According to Raj Gauthaman (1995) Dalit literature describes the world differently from a Dalit perspective and should therefore outrage and even repel the guardians of caste and class into asking if this indeed is literature. It seeks to disrupt the propriety and taste of upper class and accordingly the language of the Dalits is marginalised as vulgar and obscene. Bama brings into Tamil literature subject matter hitherto considered inappropriate; it uses a language hitherto considered unprintable. Language of these women makes frequent use of folklore, proverbs and folksongs just like the writings of upper class women fall back on the received myths and mythical figures that they have internalised. Language is also used by certain women in her community to lampoon and ridicule authority figures. In *Kisumbukaaran* which literally means making mischief of playing pranks, she foregrounds this aspect. In a subversion of cannons Bama bridges the gaps between autobiography, fiction, polemics and also a call for action. She moves between these forms weaving them together with the novelty, strength and resilience of a Dalit writer.

Bama (2005) urges Dalit women themselves to take on the agential role of their empowerment and not to depend on any outside agencies whether it be the State or the Church. The political fact of a Dalit intellectual like Bama herself taking on the task of making visible the experiences of hurt and humiliation of Dalit women and exposing the mainstream structures of forgetting cannot be undermined. Dalits feminism has added the paradigm of caste to the analysis of gender and called for linking all oppressed and marginalised groups thereby enlarging the scope of Indian feminism. This stance originating from the works of Dalit feminist intellectuals becomes emancipatory. Rege (2004) says that it places emphasis on individual experiences within socially constructed groups and focuses on the hierarchical, multiple, changing structural power relations of caste, class, ethnic, which constructs such a group (Rege, 2004). However, the Dalit feminist standpoint must link itself to other marginalised groups, even the upper-caste women, as Bama also at various points connects the oppression of women of different classes. At the same time it must allow for the possibility of non-Dalit women to 'speak for' though not 'speak as' Dalit women thus opening up the narrow gauge of identity politics based on experience, while at the same time enlarging their own humanity by embracing the other. It calls, as Rege (2004) has pointed out for a re-visioning of the voice that Indian feminism had gained in the 1980s by transforming 'their cause' to 'our cause' and repositioning subjectivities to open up possibilities for non-Dalit feminists to reinvent themselves.

References

Anandhi, S. 2003. 'The Women's Question in the Dravidian Movement c. 1925–1948', in Anupama Rao (ed.), *Gender and Caste*. New Delhi: Kali for Women.

Bama, Faustina. 2000. *Karukku*. Trans. Lakshmi Holmstrom. Chennai: Macmillan.

——. 2005. *Sangati: Events*. Trans. Lakshmi Holmstrom. New Delhi: Oxford University Press.

Barrett, Michelle. 1980. *Women's Oppression Today: The Marxist/Feminist Encounter*. London: Verso.

Chakravarty, Uma. 1989. 'Whatever Happened to the Vedic Dasi? Orientalism, Nationalism and a Script for the Past', in Kumkum Sangari and Sudesh Vaid (eds), *Recasting Women: Essays in Colonial History*. New Delhi: Kali for Women.

——. 2000. 'Conceptualising Brahamanical Patriarchy in Early India: Gender, Class, Caste and State'. *Economic and Political Weekly*, February 5–11.

Devi, Mahasweta. 1995. 'Doulti'. *Imaginary Maps*. Trans. and ed. Gayatri Chakravorty Spivak. London: Routledge.

Gauthaman, Raj. 1995. 'We Have No Need for Haloes'. *India Today Annual*: 96–98.

Guru, Gopal. 1995. 'Dalit Women Talk Differently'. *Economic and Political Weekly*, XXX(41–42): 2548–2550.

Holmstrom, Lakshmi. 2005. 'Introduction'. *Sangati*. Faustina Bama. New Delhi: Oxford University Press.

hooks, bell. 2000. *Feminist Theory: From Margin to Centre* (2nd ed). London: Pluto Press. *Gloria Watkins, a black feminist writer has assumed the pen name 'bell hooks' (written lower case) and written numerous critically acclaimed books on the politics of race, gender, class and culture under this name.

Illaiah, Kancha. 2003. 'Why I Am Not a Hindu', in Anupama Rao (ed.), *Gender and Caste.* New Delhi: Kali for Women.

Kannabiran, Vasanth and Kannabiran, Kalpana. 2003. 'Understanding Dynamics of Power and Violence', in Anupama Rao (ed.), *Gender and Caste.* New Delhi: Kali for Women.

Muktabai. 1999. 'The Griefs of Mangs and Mahars', in Susie Tharu and K. Lalita (eds), *Women Writing in India 600 BC to the Present*. Vol. 1. Delhi: Oxford University Press.

Nabar, Vrinda. 1995. *Caste as Women*. New Delhi: Penguin.

O'Flaherty, Wendy D. 1976. *The Origins of Evil in Hindu Mythology*. Berkeley: California University Press.

Omvedt, Gail. 2003. 'The Downtrodden among the Downtrodden: An Interview with a Dalit Agricultural Labourer', in Anupama Rao (ed.), *Gender and Caste.* Delhi: Kali for Women.

Racine, Josine and Racine, Jean-Luc. 1997. *Viramma: Life of a Dalit*. London: Verso and New Delhi: Social Science Press (2000).

Rajan, Rajeshwari Sunder (ed.) 1999. *Signposts: Gender Issues in Post-Independence India*. New Delhi: Kali for Women.

Rao, Anupam. 1999. 'Understanding Sirasgaon: Notes Towards Conceptualising the Role of Law, Caste, and Gender in Post-Independence India', in Rajeshwari Sunder Rajan (ed.), *Signposts: Gender Issues in Post-Independence India*. New Delhi: Kali for Women.

Rao, Anupama (ed.) 2003. 'Issues in Contemporary Indian Feminism', in Rajeshwari Sunder Rajan (ed.), *Gender and Caste*. New Delhi: Kali for Women.

Rege, Sharmila. 2000. '"Real Feminism" and Dalit Women'. *Economic and Political Weekly*, February 5–11.

——. 2004. 'A Dalit Feminist Standpoint', in Maitrayee Chaudhuri (ed.), *Feminism in India: Issues in Contemporary Indian Feminism*. Vol. 2. New Delhi: Kali for Women.

Sangari, Kumkum and Vaid, Sudesh. 1989. *Recasting Women: Essays in Colonial History.* New Delhi: Kali for Women.

Spivak, Gayatri Chander. 1996. 'Can the Subalterns Speak?', in Lawrence Cahoone (ed.), *From Modernism to Postmodernism.* Oxford: Blackwell.

Vance, Carol. 1989. 'More Danger, More Pressure: A Decade after the Bernard Sexuality Conference', in Carol Vance (ed.), *Pressure and Danger: Exploring Female Sexuality.* Ontario: Pandora Press.

Willis, Ellen. 1982. 'Towards a Feminist Sexual Revolution', *Social Text*, Fall: 3–21.

Part Two

Work, Employment and Entrepreneurship

The meaning of work has been undergoing change over the time, as new meanings and dimensions have been added to it. Even the meaning of work tends to change from one society to another at a time. What is work and what is not work is socially defined. It is not a quality inherent in any particular act. People's orientations to work tend to be dynamic. Initially orientation may be instrumental when people take up work to satisfy their material needs, but many times, usually at the advanced stage of work, one's orientation becomes expressive and then people may be working to satisfy their social and psychological needs. There are gender differences in work orientations. Studies have shown that women are more likely than men to value social relationships at their workplace. Women do not generally desire jobs that are highly paid, male centred, strenuous and more time involving as their gender role socialisation encourages them to place more value on social relationships in the family, community and on the job (Krahn and Lowe, 1993).

The beginning of women's work may be traced back to the world wars. World War I drew women into paid work but their participation remained limited. It is with World War II that women were recruited actively to fill non-traditional men's jobs and they successfully performed these jobs. In a way, women's working was treated as a war obligation and hence patriotic. Their participation in workforce did not decline with the end of war, rather their participation continued to rise. Kemp (1994: 173) writes that 'women desired to participate and companies desired to utilize their cheaper labour'.

Challenging the traditional view, women's work participation increased dramatically after the Second World War all through the world.

Certain kinds of work are valued differently by different people. We ask a woman 'Do you work'? We always mean paid employment. But we know that a great deal of women's work is unpaid. It means work as a concept has a gender bias built into it. Novarra (1980) argues that for men work is indeed a paid employment and activities outside the job are hobbies or sports. But we cannot make such a neat division in case of women. Women's household work is not considered to be work as it is not productive which earns her income.

Women have been contributing to the family income in variety of ways. Some of the common types of work are defined (Omvedt, 1992) as 'petty commodity production' in the unorganised sector or the informal sector. It includes work done for wages in a direct form, work that may be called 'disguised wage work', that is home production in which the worker is given the raw material and paid piece rates for the finished product, for example agricultural crops, gathered forest produce or sale of artisan products. It also includes 'subsistence production', that is work done for home consumption in order to reproduce the household without involving any cash income. Even in present times a large number of women both in rural and urban areas have been working for earning besides performing household tasks. The production of the factories is also being carried out through putting-out system. Women are mainly engaged as home workers and paid on piece rate basis. They may be called as self-employed. Rural women through various welfare schemes of the government, NGOs, self-help groups, helped with Microfinancing schemes, and mahila mandals have started petty and small enterprises, which they are operating from the house. These petty or small women entrepreneurs are contributing to the economy in a big way. Their artisanal products and ethnic goods are in great demand in the international market. Unfortunately, their work remained unrecognised, undervalued and invisible falling in the vast sea of unorganised sector where majority of the women are engaged. The organised sector is concentrated almost entirely in the cities, though cities also have their unorganised sector, but by and large, the unorganised sector is concentrated in the villages.

The Census of India has been playing with the definition of women's work and over the decades this proportion of women's work participation in India has just increased from 20 per cent in 1981 to 28 per cent in 2011. Recent survey of National Sample Survey Organisation (NSSO) shows that female workforce participation rate for urban areas is 20.50 per cent and in rural areas this proportion is 35.80 per cent. Why do we have such a low work participation of women? There is found to be regional variation in India with regard to women's work participation as well as recognition of their work. Tribal areas have higher rate of women's participation; in fact, all the agriculturally backward states have higher rate of women's work participation. As the states developed agriculturally, the women's participation in work dropped. The case of Punjab and Haryana reveals an inverse relationship between economic development and work participation of the women. The significant point is that the upper-caste/class women were withdrawn from the agricultural activity as the income of the family increased. Majority of the women who are engaged in the agricultural activities in developed states belong to the scheduled castes or the scheduled tribes, who face discrimination, wage differentials and even sexual exploitation. The problem in all these decades has remained that as the status of family improved, the women were withdrawn from work. Women's working outside for income generation has been regarded as insult for the family. Women have been working only at the time of dire need of the family. Her work was taken with sympathy and carried no social value. For instance, many of the Hindi movies till 1980s showed Nirupama Roy stitching clothes day and night to run the house in the absence of the male member. Woman working outside the house was never valued high in our society, even though the woman was educated. It is only when the women from upper-middle-class families with high status started going for higher education and on the basis of their education they entered the job market largely in the organised sector, the value of work for women started getting social acceptance. Still women remained concentrated in certain types of occupations such as teaching, medical and other government jobs.

The significant changes started occurring in our society with regard to women's work due to globalisation process, which Indian economy started experiencing after the grand summer of 1991. There is no denying the fact that it has generated variety of occupations for women. The aspirations of girls as well as their families are undergoing change in a big way. The number of working women has increased significantly during the last two decade or so. Still many of the girls stop working once their marriage is fixed. They drop out particularly in urban areas where the trend has set in to take up work as more jobs are available in the service sector. Marriage decreases the participation of urban women in the workforce. A survey shows that 19.4 per cent married women were working in 2012 in urban areas, while in the same year the proportion of unmarried women was 22.9 per cent (Rukmini, 2014), whereas in Japan it makes an M-shaped curve, means women withdraw from workforce due to child birth and then again start working, initially part-time and then to be employed full time for rest of the period (Custers, 1997). Even in the West the birth of the child is usually associated with women dropping out of workforce, but in India marriage is one of the most important factors. An International Labour Organisation (ILO) study shows that women with primary or secondary education were less likely to be in the workforce than do women at the two ends of the education spectrum – illiterate women and those with tertiary education. Thus, economic development in urban areas has created work opportunities for highly educated women in contemporary times.

Pandey (2014) in her study found that globalisation has brought many sectors of employment in India, such as BPO (Business Process Outsourcing) and IT (Information Technology) sectors brought work opportunities for women due to increase in demand for unskilled, semi-skilled and skilled labour. The advent of BPO sector has substantially increased the employability of English-speaking women into the workforce and their participation is continuously increasing from 25 per cent of the total workforce in 2006 to 45 per cent in 2010. Though most of these jobs are contractual, informal and are peripheral, but the salaries offered are good as per the Indian standards and the work culture is also driven by the Western corporate world. For example, a call centre employee with a graduation degree is offered ₹ 15,000 to 30,000 per month when they are in their early 20s, when most of them are unmarried.

In this broader framework is located the second part of the book comprising seven chapters and all these are empirical studies covering the states such as Gujarat, Maharashtra and Karnataka. Some serious theoretical issues have been raised regarding women's work in the chapter by Kalpana Shah. She argues that in spite of the involvement of women in various activities which may or may not be income generating, proper recognition has not been given to their work. This is largely due to the ideology of patriarchy in which gender roles are defined and provides for the domination of man over woman at all levels of hierarchy. This ideology has become so hegemonic that the existing dominant mode tends to consider women's work as secondary and thus we have concepts such as working mothers, ideal mother and so on. It is argued that women's status is linked with social structure which needs to be altered to bring change.

The next chapter by renowned economist Vibhuti Patel brings out that the development process has pushed women away from the work. Their lower position in the economy is an indicator of women's sociocultural oppression. It is not only the existing separation between the domestic work and gainful employment in the case of women's work, but also the marginalisation of women and their work in the socioeconomic environment which is the focus of the chapter. She quotes that women constitute half of the World's Population, two-third of World's Workforce but in return they get one-tenth of World's Income and own one-hundredth of World's Wealth (United Nations, 1985).

Jari industry, an exclusive monopoly of Surat city, India, entails certain interesting features as described in the chapter by Jayshree Soni. Most of the women workers belong to one caste and the work has become hereditary. The discussion focuses on present position of women workers, and their conditions vis-à-vis men workers, status of women workers and the attitude of owners of Jari industries towards them. One of the major findings of the study is that Rana women's position has remained unchanged for decades.

Sericulture has been considered a household agro-husbandry in Karnataka. Women constitute the most important workforce in sericulture. The study conducted by E.N. Ashok Kumar in Chitradurqa district brings out the facts relating to the high degree of women's involvement in the whole process of production of sericulture and shows that gender inequalities affect the whole process.

The chapter by Anuradha Ghandy and Geetha Thachil is a case study of Bidi Workers' Cooperative in Bhandara district, Maharashtra and describes the struggle of women workers to gain control over it. It has been argued that the state policy of development from above has pitfalls. Cooperativisation and development can only go together if the masses are involved at equal footing with the so called local elites.

Suguna Pathy in her chapter examines the conditions of the female migrant workers from Andhra Pradesh in the Jari industry of Surat. The process of globalisation, which is more a threat than a challenge to this industry, has constructed a different discourse on women's work. Women are already burdened with social and biological reproduction. With the help of data, the study shows how women's groups are raising the consciousness of women migrant workers as a result of which they have got organised and have started negotiating for better wages.

All the empirical studies included in this part of the book deals with the time of 1980s that is up to 1990 when the concern for women and work was central and a number of terms and concepts with regard to work came under focus. Some of the issues on women and work have either been resolved or disappeared over the time, yet some new concerns such as sexual harassment at workplace, glass ceiling and so on have become more serious. The last chapter included in this part by Gail Omvedt and Chetna Gala, much ahead of its time, published in 1993 has argued that the new economic policy is going to affect positively the women, particularly the rural women. Rather than having nothing the policy outcomes would at least provide them something. They are already an exploited lot in the unorganised sector. The new developments at least would provide them some kind of employment even though it is in the informal sector. Their concern seems to be founded well by the turn of the century. The issues which were central in 1980s lost their significance in the contemporary times. The globalisation changed the availability and nature of women's work. Though the enumerated data for 2011 census show a marginal increase in the participation rate of women in work but many other non-governmental sources show much increased rate of women's participation in work.

References

Custers, Peter. 1997. *Capital Accumulation and Women's Labour in Asian Economies*. New Delhi: Sage.

Kemp, Alice Abel. 1994. *Women's Work: Degraded and Devalued*. New Jersey: Prentice Hall.

Krahn, Harvey J. and Lowe, Graham S. 1993. *Work, Industry and Canadian Society*. Ontario: Nelson Canada.

Novarra, Virginia. 1980. *Women's Work, Men's Work: The Ambivalence of Equality*. London: Marion Boyars.

Omvedt, Gail. 1992. 'The Unorganized Sector and Women Workers'. *Guru Nanak Journal of Sociology*, 13(1): 19–61.

Pandey, Shelly. 2014. 'Consumer Agency of Urban Women in India', in Nita Mathur (ed.), *Consumer Culture, Modernity and Identity*. New Delhi: Sage.

Rukmini, S. 2014. 'Marriage Driving Urban Women Out of Jobs'. *The Hindu*, August 11: 9.

4

Women, Work and Ideology

Kalpana Shah

The National Commission on Self-Employed Women in its voluminous report points out that the vast majority of rural women in the unorganised sector work in the farms, they look after the animals, they are actively involved in food production, food processing, forestry and rural industry. They also participate in construction work, labour in the factories, work in mines and engage in trade and fending. In addition, they have the burden of bearing and rearing children, collecting and fetching water, gathering firewood, cooking and cleaning activities, which consume much time and energy.

The Seventh Five Year Plan Document recognising the plight of working women records that women play an important role in agricultural production, animal husbandry and other related activities such as storage, marketing of produce and food processing. Apart from these they spend almost 10–12 hours per day doing household chores, including fetching of water and gathering of fuel. Large number of female labourers are engaged in marginal occupations in order to supplement the family income by collection of fish, small game, firewood and cow dung; maintenance of kitchen gardens; tailoring; weaving and teaching. Quantification of these activities in terms of work hours contributed or its income-generating equivalent was not attempted or recorded.

The National Commission on Self-Employed Women further notes: 'Although women work for longer hours and contribute substantially to the family income, they are not perceived as workers by either the women themselves or the data collecting agencies and the government, as all of them do not recognize the multidimensional functions of women which include their productive and reproductive labour. Women are quite often the major earners for their families. This also goes unrecognized'.

A woman works hard from dawn to dusk. She earns small income out of it. But in 'man-power' planning statistics this is not considered as employment and she does not get a status as a worker. The income of the poor households is generally increased by women, but according to statistics, she is not working. Even though women work harder than men, society is not ready to accept the fact. Why does women's work go unrecognised, unaccounted and unaccepted? The explanation given by economists, statisticians, planners and policy makers is, because many of the economic activities usually performed by women (such as subsistence agriculture, handicrafts, petty trading, family chores and other informal activities) lack official visibility in statistics. Women overwhelmingly dominate the informal sector. But many activities in the informal sector are not quantified because they are considered to be an extension of family and domestic functions (Patel, 1989).

The explanation is not sufficient for an answer to the question raised above. It further leads to a question why is there non-visibility? The non-visibility on the part of data collection agencies and the government suggests an attitude towards women prevailing in the society. These are prejudices against women. These prejudices induce a lower status for women and are responsible for the low-self-esteem women have. The secondary status of women in turn becomes a justification for giving them work lower in status and hence wages lower than their male counterparts.

In many cases women are economically active, but there is no acknowledgement of their status as workers. 'Even when women work in the outer economy, their work is seen as an extension of housework and they are treated as supplementary earners' (Patel, 1989). Underenumeration of women in population or workforce has been attributed mainly to the prejudices of the respondents and enumerators. Social and cultural biases of the heads of households, both when they are males and females, prompt them to underreport economic activities of the females. Such an attitude is attributed to an ideology which governs the patriarchal society.

The failure of women to achieve equal status despite their participation in the process of production indicates that a Marxist or materialistic analysis of the problem is not sufficient to explain the persistent inequality between the sexes, and suggests that an ideological dimension must be added and thereby the gender specificity of the problem be explained.

This specific ideology not only influences the values and beliefs of the enumerators but also influences women's own perception of their role in the household production, saving activities and drudgery involved in it. Afshar (1985) rightly observes 'the apparent invisibility of women's worth, as well as their work, is widespread and persistent. Women's work has, on the whole, been severely devalued by universal ideological framework that regards them as inferior bearers of labour and generally defines their work as the property of men. This perception appears to be at its strongest in many rural areas in under-developed countries, where a coincidence of interests between capital and male policy makers has resulted in the creation of a female domain in subsistence agriculture responsible for reproducing and nurturing a large reserve army of cheap labour'.

What is this ideology and how does it operate and influence norms and values of the people in the society? We commonly know it as an ideology of patriarchy, which has a strong influence over cultural values and norms. The gender-specific division of labour which persists in the society is a product of this ideology. It is not the theme of this article to discuss who precedes what, but a patriarchal culture which is carried over from one historical period to another to protect the sexual hierarchy of society, suggests its strong historical roots. Even capitalist society operates with the presumption of gender-specific division of labour. The nature of patriarchal society, however, is not the same everywhere. Regional variations are found within and across the country. In a country like India where the factor of caste is influential in determining the work status, it works at different levels. In a caste ideology, the women of Hindu high castes are usually not free to sell their labour, except within ideologically acceptable boundaries. On the other hand, the women of middle and lower castes, untouchable, tribal and of all farming communities have a long tradition of work. Work is associated with low social standing in a caste hierarchy. However, industrialisation, planned development and women's growing education have changed the traditional norms regarding work. The women who had barriers to work started working with the change in cultural norms of the society. On the other hand, women who used to work without any barrier have stopped working either because they are withdrawn as economic status of the family has reached the desired level or poorer women, because of their own constraints, do not have an access to work. Ideology of male dominance (formulated as a result of historical forces) plays an active role not only in deciding whether to allow women to work or not but also in determining the nature and status of work done by men and women in the society, whether the society is caste oriented or class oriented. It very much reflects in the definition of work and the division of work between men and women. An analysis of occupational structure suggests that generally jobs that offer promotion prospects go to men, while women remain in dead-end, low-wage and presumably unskilled jobs. 'One well-known theory which purports to explain this pattern of employment is that of dual or segmented labour market' (Afshar, 1985). The parameter of ideology favours menfolk for opportunities to move up leaving behind women at bottom. The sex division of labour in the household is extended in the labour market for its own interest and defines people's activity, purposes, goals, desires and dreams according to their sex. The laws of all social institutions work according to gender relations and thereby power relations. And, therefore, we find that labour market not only excludes women from skilled jobs but also downgrade jobs or does not consider them as work when they are performed by women. Plan/policy makers, enumerators and also male as well as female respondents operate within this ideology of power relations of gender.

Work is divided into paid and unpaid, main or primary and secondary. Unpaid workers and those who are engaged in secondary work are not considered as economically active or 'workers'. Even 1971 census has followed these criteria. This grossly underestimates the number of women workers. The Census of India, 1981 did not include domestic work and unpaid economic work of women as work in its definition. Work is defined as (1) participation in any economically productive activity and (2) productive activity only for sale or wages. Here work done for domestic consumption is not 'work' (Patel, 1989). The census definition of worker excludes women's domestic work and unpaid family work.

The nature of work of women in India is of two types: (1) income producing and (2) income saving. Thus the work of women is divided into (1) home-based unpaid labour for family subsistence or unpaid work in the family farm and (2) outside the home, which can be wage work, self-employment or services. If the same job of home-based worker done by paid workers, only male paid workers are accounted and reported as workers. Even though in case of household workers, both men and women, are equally unqualified for any other jobs and are equally unskilled, the works of 'higher status' are always performed by men. The internalisation of cultural values is so strong that both the genders do not see any discrimination in it and work as if they are naturally carved out for such type of differentiations in work and thereby wages.

The range of income-saving economic activities of women is very wide. From sweeping and cleaning to run family shop or work in family farm, women of poorer and lower-middle-class households work hard and for long period in a day. Their work, however, is extremely important for the survival of their family. But because of the unpaid nature of their work, it is not considered worth at societal value. The intricacies of social and cultural ideology work both ways; on the one hand it keeps women busy all the time and on the other hand conveniently ignores them as an active participant in the national production.

In addition to income-saving economic activities, these women are engaged in innumerable types of wage work outside their home. They have to carry the double burden of domestic work and child care on the one hand and waged work on the other. Women have to stretch the working day infinitely which makes them totally exhausted. Thousands of women have narrated this to the committee for the status of women in 1974 and again to the National Commission on Self-Employed Women in 1988. An average working woman generally suffers from overexhaustion due to too much work for the family survival and their desperation for wage work. Instead of challenging women's overburden and easing out their work, the general tendency of the people who are in power is to make women's work subsidiary and supplementary and to establish the status of women as part-time workers. The internalisation of social and cultural values that the prime work and responsibility of women are the household duties and to look after children, operate at all levels. The recent scheme of part-time work for women of Maharashtra Government provides a good example here. The scheme realises the recent increasing compulsion for women to seek employment due to economic necessity. Women have to spend longer day outside home to work. The thrust of the scheme is: 'This has increased the problem at home, the crucial problem being the care of young children. There are no suitable and adequate facilities for children. The alternative to this situation is half-time employment for women. This would make it possible for women both to earn an income and also fulfill their responsibilities towards their children and family. Women may be free to choose between full-time and part time employment depending upon their situation at home' (Gothoskar, 1989). The sexual division of labour and society remains intact even with women in the paid economy. Ideology adjusts to this by defining women as working mothers. And the two jobs get done for less than the price of one.

It is assumed that women give birth to children and, therefore, they are ones who should do cooking, cleaning and washing. The social division of work is considered as natural. Even though menfolk directly benefit out of women's work, societal values do not allow them to accept their share in the household work. Women also provide certain specific free services such as child rearing, but they hardly receive any kind of benefit in exchange. The sexual definition of woman as mother either keep her in the home doing unpaid labour or enables her to be hired at a lower wage because of her defined sexual inferiority. And because women are not defined as workers within the ruling ideology, women are not paid for their labour or are paid less than men. Eisenstein (1979) sharply shows how the process involved in domestic work in turn help in the perpetuation of existing society. According to her (1) women stabilise patriarchal structures (the family, housewife, mother, etc.) by fulfilling these roles; (2) simultaneously, women are reproducing new workers, for the paid and unpaid labour force; (3) they work as well in the labour force for lesser wages and (4) they stabilise the economy through their roles as consumers.

The ideology adjusts further with the changing economic and social structure remarkably. With the advent of industrialisation and with the new economic structure, the concepts such as beautiful home, ideal mother and the educated housewife have been institutionalised. In pre-industrial society, men, women and children worked together in the home, the farm or on the land to produce goods necessary for their consumption. Women were procreators and child-rearers. But the nature of the organisation of work was such that it had a limited impact of sex role distinction. With the rise of industrial society, men were brought out of the home and into the wage-labour economy. Women were left behind, confined to home. They were viewed by the society as non-productive, even though many of them work in the industries. They came to be seen solely in terms of sex roles.

The rise of nuclear family with industrialisation forced women further towards confinement at home. Now, it becomes necessary to create a conducive atmosphere around home. A new role for women emerged. However, it is a case of old wine in a new bottle. Education as an effective instrument successfully disseminated widely the ideology of ideal housewife. A course on home science has been evolved to train women specifically for this ideal. It means sophisticated and time-consuming workload for women for which they do not gain anything except 'vah vah' (praise) from family members. Even those women, who are engaged in white-collar jobs and are overburdened with double work, are valued through their success at home front.

Thus, it is the prevailing ideology of the society which needs to be examined carefully to be attacked. It operates everywhere at all levels and at all times. Unless and until it is challenged, women's work is not going to get the due recognition and worth. However, I am aware that ideology does not work in vacuum. It is related with the structure of the society. But at the same time it has its own autonomy and capability to reproduce its norms and values in society even if the structure changes. The continuation of degraded position of women in feudal, capitalist and socialist societies highlights the strength of ideology and necessity to attack it.

References

Afshar, Haleh (ed.) 1985. *Women, Work and Ideology in the Third World*. London: Tavistock Publications.

Eisenstein, Zillah. 1979. *Capitalist Patriarchy and the Case for Socialist Feminism*. New York: Monthly Review Press.

Gothoskar, Sujata. 1989. 'Part-Time Work for Women'. *Economic and Political Weekly*, XXIV(46). 2537–2538.

Government of India. 1974. *Towards Equity*. Report of the Committee on Status of Women in India, New Delhi: Delhi: Department of Social Welfare, Ministry of Education and Social Welfare.

—— 1989. Shramshakti: Report of the National Commission on Self-Employed Women and Women in the Informal Sector. New Delhi: Ministry of Women and Child Welfare.

Patel, Vibhuti. 1989. 'Visibility of Women in Statistics and Indicators: Changing Perspective'. Paper Presented at National Workshop, SNDT, Bombay.

5

Perspective on Indian Women's Work and Status

Vibhuti Patel

One of the fallouts from the development debates of the 1970s has been a keen interest in women's economic roles. Women's work in the economy is not sufficiently recorded, recognised and rewarded. Economic development has made women's economic condition increasingly precarious. Debates around concept and definition of work, time-allocation studies, visibility of women's statistics and indicators, housework, economics of unpaid family work in rural households for both household consumption and household production, women's work for family's survival need such as fetching water; collection of fodder, fuelwood and fruits; livestock raising and kitchen gardening that involve hours of backbreaking and strenuous work have challenged basic premises of mainstream economics, sociology and development planning.

Workforce Participation Rate of Women

Working-class women in India have been the pioneers of textile, mine and plantation workforce. But with economic development women's job opportunities have reduced. Women are treated as an auxiliary force to be hired last in the period of economic expansion and to be fired first in the period of economic crisis, rationalisation and automation. Except in the tertiary sector and in the most exploitative informal sector, participation of women in the social production is declining. During the last three decades women workers have lost their ground both in the primary and the secondary sectors.

Table 5.1 *Participation of Women in the Labour Force and the Workforce.*

Year	*Percentage of Women in the Labour Force*	*Percentage of Women Workers to the Total Female Population*
1911	34.44	33.73
1961	31.53	27.96
1971	17.35	11.86
1981	28.60	14.44
1991	42.00	22.69

Source: Census of India, Provisional Population Totals, series-1, 1971, 1981, 1991.

* Processed from Table 2.5 of the Sixth Five-Year Plan, 1980–1985, Planning Commission, Government of India (GOI).

Important definitional changes took place in the concept of 'Workers' used in the 1971 census. These definitional changes resulted in changing the economic status of many female unpaid family workers mainly in the rural areas. Table 5.1 reveals that those who were 'workers' in 1961 census became 'dependents' in the 1971 census, as the latter did not take into account the interchangeable role of women as housewives and gainful workers; 2.3 million women who were doing unpaid but economically productive work were classified as non-workers. But, we must also be aware that the fall in the female work participation rate shown in the census is also reflective of the actual trend.

In the organised sector, many of the traditionally women-dominated industries such as textiles, jute, mining and manufacturing industries, the percentage of women workers has declined drastically over past 30 years due to rationalisation, mechanisation and automation. Women workers are not given training for skill upgradation so whenever there is mechanisation, women workers are the first to be eased out. Earlier in these industries retired women workers were replaced by their daughters or daughters-in-law, later on, this practice stopped; instead they are replaced by their sons or sons-in-law. The trade union leadership also connives with the management that retrenches women workers first by using patriarchal ideology that women are 'supplementary earners', women 'work for pin money', 'primary role of women is domestic duties' and so on. In the statutory sector, number of 'crèches' has declined drastically. In the agrarian sector also shift from subsistence crops to commercial crops, new land reforms and agricultural mechanisations have marginalised women.

We all harbour a notion that women in the child-bearing age are too engrossed in domestic responsibilities of cooking, cleaning and caring to find time for wage work. That is not true as per Table 5.2, which denotes work participation of women in different age groups. We can see that the majority of women workers are in the age group of 15 to 34 years when they may also be expected to have the care of small children.

Table 5.2 gives the percentage distribution of men and women workers by industrial classification as well as occupational classification. All workers are classified as coming under nine broad industrial classifications. Within that classification, the description of the actual work that the person is doing is termed as the occupational classification.

Regional Disparity Among States

Except for predominantly tribal areas, the work participation rate of women is very low in our country. In the economically developed areas the work participation rate for women is lower as compared to their less developed counterparts. The lowest work participation rates for females are in Punjab, Lakshadweep, Delhi, Chandigarh and Haryana. Can these be attributed to technological changes? Economic prosperity, higher agricultural productivity, immigrant labour, influx of remittances, decline of traditional handicraft and cottage industries and changes in cropping pattern (71% sown area in Punjab is now under wheat and maize cultivation) are factors that have influenced the decline of women's participation in the labour force in Punjab and Haryana. All findings in India appear to show that economic development and work participation of women have a negative relationship (Patel, 1982). As per 1991 census, women constituted only 14 per cent in 1981 and 16.43 per cent in 1991 of the main workers (Census of India, 1991, Series-1, Paper-3, workers and their distribution, p. 323).

Work participation rates for women in Maharashtra and Gujarat are 33.02 and 27.08, respectively as per the 1991 census (10th Rank for Maharashtra and 14th Rank for Gujarat among all states and Union Territories). In Greater Bombay, 11.37 per cent of total women are 'Economically active' that is they are employed as wage workers or salary earners.

Sectoral Distribution of Employed Women: Problems and Prospects

Among the total women workers, 94 per cent are employed in the unorganised sector and only 6 per cent are engaged in the organised sector. Nineteen per cent of the female labour force is engaged in the unpaid family work as per the 1991 census.

Table 5.2 *Percentage Distribution of Men and Women: Industrial Classification as Well as Occupational Classification*

India/States	Total Rural Urban	All ages	Age Group									
			0–14	15–19	20–24	25–29	30–34	35–39	40–49	50–59	60+	15–59
1	2	3	4	5	6	7	8	9	10	11	12	13
INDIA	T	13.99	2.95	18.46	20.39	22.59	24.59	26.13	25.99	21.53	10.15	22.61
	R	16.00	3.52	22.74	24.36	26.20	27.76	29.37	28.92	23.90	11.27	26.07
	U	7.28	0.91	6.21	9.32	12.26	14.45	15.52	15.39	12.40	5.63	11.71
Andhra Pradesh	T	27.02	7.21	36.71	38.90	41.72	45.08	45.44	46.34	40.27	19.75	41.94
	R	31.94	8.79	47.12	48.62	50.44	52.48	52.60	52.39	45.38	22.16	49.90
	U	10.49	1.79	9.64	12.51	1.6.27	19.30	20.61	22.55	19.22	9.39	16.47
Bihar	T	9.06	1.56	12.34	13.38	14.66	16.21	17.26	17.81	15.20	7.26	15.23
	R	9.70	1.71	13.84	14.55	15.70	17.29	18.35	18.76	15.87	7.54	16.32
	U	4.17	0.45	2.69	5.07	7.34	8.32	9.37	9.98	8.61	4.50	7.08
Gujarat	T	11.03	2.22	16.98	17.59	17.55	18.82	19.53	18.86	14.56	6.38	17.70
	R	13.46	2.95	22.76	23.10	21.99	22.51	23.04	21.66	16.52	7.30	21.83
	U	5.49	0.41	4.53	6.82	9.09	10.95	12.04	12.24	9.59	3.98	8.86
Haryana	T	4.69	1.08	7.24	8.27	8.85	9.47	9.10	7.60	5.01	2.15	7.90
	R	4.89	1.29	8.61	8.94	9.02	9.14	8.73	7.62	5.12'	2.11	8.25
	U	3.99	0.20	2.52	6.30	8.34	10.55	10.12	7.52	4.59	2.30	6.75

Cont'd...

...Cont'd

Himachal Pradesh	T	18.71	4.25	28.14	31.47	31.87	32.96	31.74	29.96	25.50	11.72	30.16
	R	19.38	4.49	29.91	33.46	33.17	33.68	32.51	30.80	26.32	12.07	31.39
	U	9.59	0.63	5.20	11.46	18.42	24.70	22.04	18.42	12.19	5.17	15.23
Karnataka	T	18.95	4.87	26.12	28.36	30.99	34.11	34.98	34.27	26.71	11.51	30.52
	R	22.28	6.02	33.20	35.17	37.02	39.38	40.20	38.82	30.47	12.98	36.23
	U	10.53	1.79	10.69	19.29	17.75	21.11	21.83	21.63	16.03	7.23	16.95
Kerala	T	12.77	1.89	12.18	17.83	21.85	25.98	28.58	26.63	18.65	6.96	20.68
	R	13.47	0.77	13.44	19.46	23.41	27.27	29.77	27.78	19.61	7.44	21.89
	U	9.67	1.12	6.75	10.93	15.48	20.91	23.41	21.79	14.73	4.88	15.13
Madhya Pradesh	T	22.35	5.27	31.20	32.75	35.52	38.73	40.29	42.05	36.29	18.56	36.49
	R	25.78	6.30	39.54	39.52	41.80	44.46	45.92	46.93	40.09	20.38	42.42
	U	8.31	0.92	6.57	10.00	13.04	16.06	18.38	20.13	17.30	8.77	13.70
Maharashtra	T	23.98	4.90	30.46	35.15	37.68	42.32	44.53	45.00	36.33	15.45	38.59
	R	31.39	6.36	44.45	49.50	51.69	55.43	51.08	56.29	44.78	18.64	51.30
	U	9.11	0.76	6.82	12.34	15.48	18.09	19.29	19.47	15.73	6.94	14.80
Orissa	T	10.70	2.45	14.88	14.83	16.85	18.80	20.24	20.12	16.03	7.19	17.30
	R	11.07	2.60	15.84	15.55	17.44	19.49	20.87	20.44	16.12	7.22	17.90
	U	7.65	1.21	7.65	9.86	12.72	13.69	15.25	17.01	15.14	7.22	12.52
Punjab	T	2.27	0.27	1.92	3.29	4.74	5.82	5.30	3.89	2.76	1.26	3.74
	R	1.72	0.31	1.94	2.49	3.31	4.06	3.55	2.83	2.14	1.07	2.78
	U	3.71	0.18	1.87	5.06	7.84	10.23	9.61	6.71	4.62	1.91	6.14

Cont'd...

...Cont'd

Rajasthan	T	9.32	2.73	15.38	15.33	15.82	16.30	16.63	15.91	12.14	4.80	15.40
	R	10.58	3.27	18.93	18.18	18.00	17.97	18.28	17.31	13.09	5.07	17.51
	U	4.45	0.52	3.74	6.05	8.22	9.82	10.21	10.07	7.95	3.59	7.60
Tamil Nadu	T	22.36	4.52	28.05	29.77	32.29	36.33	38.86	38.80	32.45	16.47	33.57
	R	27.85	5.76	36.92	39.04	46.87	44.29	46.58	46.45	39.36	20.70	41.88
	U	11.01	1.94	11.65	13.73	16.52	20.04	21.50	20.67	15.88	7.09	16.68
Uttar Pradesh	T	5.39	0.91	6.68	7.50	8.59	9.61	10.38	10.69	9.57	5.63	8.95
	R	5.90	1.04	7.90	8.42	9.38	10.36	11.18	11.39	10.12	5.98	9.81
	U	2.99	0.27	2.12	3.79	5.21	6.08	6.51	6.99	6.42	3.46	5.04
West Bengal	T	5.81	0.91	7.26	8.79	10.23	11.44	11.82	11.20	8.39	3.48	10.04
	R	6.19	0.93	8.65	10.34	11.45	12.31	12.47	11.90	8.72	3.65	10.70
	U	4.66	0.86	3.51	12.07	7.14	9.31	10.18	9.32	7.39	3.00	8.28

Women in the Unorganised Sector

Among the women employed in the unorganised informal sector 80.1 per cent are employed in the agricultural occupations and 19.9 per cent are working in the non-agricultural sector.

Table 5.3 *Percentage Distribution of Total Workers by Industrial Classification*

Industrial Classification	*Percentage of Total Workers by Main Activity*			
	1971		*1981*	
	Males	*Females*	*Males*	*Females*
Cultivators	45.90	29.84	43.70	33.20
Agricultural labourers	21.54	50.86	19.56	46.17
Division-0: Agriculture, hunting, forestry and fishing	2.24	1.91	2.37	1.84
Division-1: Mining and quarrying	0.54	0.40	0.63	0.35
Divisions-2 and 3: Manufacturing and repair	10.13	7.01	12.09	8.19
Division-4: Electricity, gas and water	0.35	0.03	0.54	0.05
Division-5: Construction	1.36	0.65	1.88	0.87
Division-6: Wholesale and retail trade: restaurants and hotels	5.57	1.67	6.46	1.80
Division-7: Transport, storage and communications	2.86	0.47	3.36	0.37
Division-8: Financing, insurance, real estate and business services	0.80	0.11	0.95	0.24
Division-9: Community, social and personal services	8.71	7.05	8.46	6.92

Women working in the unorganised sector (Table 5.3) do not come within the purview of the protective labour laws and policies that are for welfare of these women. They receive low wages, work for very long hours and many times are sexually harassed by their employers and their agents; invisibility and insensitivity concerning these women are brought out succinctly by Shramshakti report (1988). Women in the unorganised sector are in the land-based occupations (Table 5.4) such as agricultural and forestry, dairying, small animal husbandry, fisheries, sericulture and mining; tobacco and *bidi* industries; home-based occupations such as handloom weaving and spinning handicrafts, garments, food processing, vending and hawking; construction; domestic work and contract work for the manufacturing industry. None of the labour laws are applied in this sector. Virtually, the law of jungle prevails. Women workers do not get equal remuneration for their backbreaking work, minimum wages act is mercilessly flouted, and there is no social security or workers education programme. This section of the working-class women is deprived of land and water resources, fuel, fodder, toilets, space, easy access to raw material, market, credit, licensing, identity cards, safe transport, housing, crèche, ration card, better tools and health and safety provisions.

Table 5.4 *Percentage Distribution of Total Workers by Occupational Classification*

Occupational Classification	*Percentage of Total Workers by Main Activity*			
	1971		*1981*	
	Males	*Females*	*Males*	*Females*
Cultivators	45.90	29.84	43.70	33.20
Agricultural labourers	21.54	50.66	19.56	46.17
Division-0–1: Professional, technical and related workers	2.71	2.84	3.16	3.21
Division-2: Administrative, executive and managerial workers	1.12	0.07	1.30	0.12
Division-3: Clerical and related workers	3.40	0.68	3.86	1.05
Division-4: Sales workers	4.74	1.46	5.36	1.51
Division-5: Service workers	3.36	3.13	3.12	2.69
Division-6: Farmers, fishermen, hunters, loggers and related workers	2.35	1.97	2.24	1.81
Division-7–9: Production and related workers, transport equipment operators and labourers	14.40	8.94	16.56	9.58
Division-X: Workers not classified by occupations	0.46	0.21	1.14	0.65

Workforce participation of women is declining among certain occupations in the agrarian sector as a result of increasing pauperisation leading to loss of land and insufficient growth of employment opportunities on family farms, technological displacement in agriculture and so on. The drastic increase in the percentage of landless women agricultural labourers has increased from 1961 to 1991 (As per the 1991 census 16.18% of total women are main workers). Among the women employed in the non-agricultural sectors, there had been a serious decline in the workforce, during 1970s 'in some sectors such as horticulture, livestock breeding, food-processing, dairy products' (The Draft Five-Year Plan, 1978–1983). But in the 1980s this trend is reverted and we find slight increase. In the household industry, women's employment opportunities have increased slightly (from 4.59% to 4.63% of total women main workers). Women were the greatest victims of the process of industrialisation in the post-independence period because these household industries were the largest source of women's employment in agriculture.

Many household industries such as rice pounding, tobacco, leather, handweaving and oil processing lost their economic viability because of factory production. But in the latest census we see women being economically active mainly in the occupation such as weaving, handicraft, tailoring, forestry and sale of fish.

Table 5.5 *Women in Different Types of Profession*

Profession	*Year*	*Male*	*Female*
IAS	1987	4,209	339
IPS	1987	2,418	21
Indian Foreign Service	1987	480	53
Indian Customs and Central Excise	1987	1,053	59
Income Tax Services	1987	2,244	195
Indian Audit and Accounts Services	1987	530	59
Indian Postal Services	1987	454	52
Indian Economic Service	1987	481	71
Indian Statistical Service	1987	645	32
Indian Forest Service	1987	1,733	10
Central Information Commission	1987	770	69
Central Secretariat Service	1987	976	34
Indian Railways	1987	15,72,666	42,974
Judges in the Supreme Court	1990	16	1
Judges in the High Court	1987	380	11
Advocates	1985	180/83	10,493
Chartered Accountants Apprenticeship Trainees	1987	43,700	934
(a) Engineering graduates	1987	3,796	308
(b) Diploma holders	1987	11,714	830
ITI trainees	1983	1,78,554	13,486

Source: Women in India – Statistical Profile-1988.

Women in the Organised Sector

Out of 6 per cent of the total female workforce that is employed in the organised sector, 2.7 per cent is engaged in the industrial sector and 3.3 per cent is with services and profession (Table 5.5). The female workforce has faced joblessness in some industries such as cotton textiles, mining, coal, iron, jute and food processing, but at the same time, in many modern industries such as manufacture of machinery, pharmaceuticals, medical and scientific instruments, electrical appliances and among services and profession, the employment of women has risen. There are complaints that in the railways, LIC, Bank and other offices, the new recruitment has stopped due to computerisation. Number of women in the echelons of state administrative machinery is increasing gradually. Number of female doctors, engineers and entrepreneurs has been increasing.

Recently, a debate has started on the issue of part-time work for female employees. The argument in favour of this is that the working women have to shoulder double burden of domestic duties as well as office work so reduction of working hours will give them some relief; majority of employed women have refused this offer as they feel that this will be used as a bogey to deprive them of career promotion, responsible assignments and it will further strengthen the belief that women are 'supplementary earners'. Moreover, the most strenuous part of doing the job is commuting, and part-time work will involve the same consumption of time and energy for commuting. They feel that part-time job does not question the existing sexual division of labour in the family. It is a negative solution as far as women's development is concerned. The best way to reduce the burden of working women can be to inculcate the ethos of sharing of housework by both men and women in the family, cheap eating facilities, cheap and safe child-care facilities, transport and so on.

These days many large-scale manufacturing units are retrenching the regular women employees and branching out their work at piece-rate wages, through ancillarisation or home-based work. It is known as 'putting-out system' of production process. It saves women of factory; they work in their homes and sometimes whole family does the work for hours together to maximise the wages. With the New Economic Policy (NEP) women's employment will increase in the informal sector but at an unfavourable terms and conditions. Rise in the interest rate due to NEP will affect poor self-employed women drastically as they will find it prohibitive to borrow from the banks and they will have to either stop their petty business or be trapped in the hands of private money lenders.

Women and Unemployment

All findings have shown that women are greater victims of unemployment and women of all age groups are affected more than their male counterparts. This fact shatters the myth that for sociocultural reasons, Indian women do not wish to participate in the workforce. Various data-gathering agencies such as National Sample Survey Organisation (NSSO), Rural Labour Industry and Agricultural Labour Inquiry (Table 5.6) have also proved the same. Number of educated women job seekers has also risen drastically. But the work participation rate among the educated women is also not satisfactory enough.

Table 5.6 *Daily Status Unemployment Rate (DSUR) of Indian Women*

Year	*Rural*	*Urban*
1972/73	11.2	13.7
1977/78	9.2	14.5
1983	9.0	11.0
1987/88	6.7	12.0

Source: Sarvekshana (*Journal of NSSO*), Vol. IX, No. 4, April 1988 and Special Number, September 1990.

General antipathy towards women's employment, familial responsibilities, traditional forum of discrimination against employment of women, huge unemployment even among men, women's work and earning being treated as supplementary to that of men's and absence of cheap eating facilities and child-care centres are the major factors hindering the gainful utilisation of female labour force.

Economic Development and Employment: Status of Women

'In order to ensure women the right to work it is especially necessary to eliminate unemployment and under-employment and all forms of discrimination, enable them to have access to every profession, assure them of general and vocational training and to eliminate illiteracy through the establishment of functional literacy', states the panel document adopted at the IV World Trade Union Conference on the problems of working women.

While describing factors affecting women's employment status the National Perspective Plan for Women (1988–2000 AD) states, a combination of social and economic factors is responsible for the low work participation rate for women. The most critical are:

(i) Segmentation in the labour market which works against women.
(ii) Adverse implications of technological growth for women.
(iii) Lack of unionisation of female workers.
(iv) Absence of purposeful human resource development policy aimed at improving women's employability and productivity through training.
(v) Conceptual ambiguities and lack of a National Labour Policy encompassing workers in the unorganised sector.

Many well-intentioned plans and programmes have been evolved, but they have hardly changed the employment status of women. The schemes such as Employment Guarantee Scheme, Food for Work Programme and Women's Cooperativism have not helped to make much dent in the problems as many researchers have shown

(Sharma, 1986; Kelkar, 1981). Even in the training programmes, the biases of the officials and administrators come in the way of women beneficiaries.

Conclusion

The main reason for women's subordinate economic status is the fact that they are not only economically exploited but also socioculturally oppressed. Subordination of women in all walks of life, burden of housework and men being seen as masters, all these myths marginalise women. Women's work and economic worth remain invisible to the planners and the data systems. Women's income plays crucial role for the survival of the household among the poorer strata. One-third of the rural households are women-headed households, which also happen to be the poorest of the poor households. New international division of labour relies on the cheap labour of Third World women. In the era of decolonisation of the Third World countries, their women are colonised for superprofits of the world capitalism. What does our drive towards 21st century mean? To cater to just 5 per cent of the male labour force that is highly skilled and technologically advanced and throw the rest of the labour force in the insecurity of the 'Informal sector', that does not enable millions of women to get even two decent meals a day? To enhance the status of women in the employment market, we need to fundamentally change the course of economic development that bypasses women.

References

Government of India. 1988. 'Women in India: A Statistical Profile'. Department of Women and Child Development, Ministry of Human Resource Development, New Delhi.

Kelkar, Govind. 1981. 'Rural Development and Underdevelopment of Women Perception of Roles'. Paper Presented at the National Conference on Women's Studies, SNDT University, Bombay.

National Perspective Plan for Women 1988–2000 AD. 'Employment and Training'. Chapter II (19–48). Department of Women and Child Development, Ministry of Human Resource Development, New Delhi.

Patel, Vibhuti. 1982. 'Women and Work', in Neera Desai and Maithreyi Krishnaraj (eds), *Current Information Series*. Bombay: Research Centre for Women's Studies, SNDT Women's University.

Sharma, Kumud. 1986. *Policies for Employment Generation: Impact on Women*. Delhi: ICSSR.

Shramshakti. 1988. Report of the National Commission on Self-Employed Women and Women in the Informal Sector. New Delhi: Ministry of Women and Child Welfare, Government of India.

The Draft Five-Year Plan 1978–1983. New Delhi: Planning Commission, Government of India, p. 85.

6

Jari Industry and Women Workers

Jayshree Soni

Several studies have been and are being carried out on workers and industries, but an important aspect that remains ignored or dealt only scantily in most of these studies is related to the problems of women workers in specific industries. In addition to the usual problems faced by a worker the women workers have to face certain special problems within the immediate context of their work. This article is aimed at examining their problems within the jari industry in Surat.

Of course, now-a-days a lot of debates are going on about awareness among the women and their problems. Special laws are enacted for protection of their interest; articles and books are written on the problems of women workers. But still all this is not in a significant degree. Industry may be the same, but the problems of male and female workers may be different. But as it happens in other spheres of life in our country, the problems of workers are seen only from the male point of view. That is to say, the problems of working hours, wage rates, leave and so on concerning only the male workers are thought about and the activities regarding these are undertaken.

On the other hand, a women worker of today has to perform two roles – those of a woman as well as a worker. The efforts made by her to strike a balance between these two roles and the part of her personality which is spent in striking this balance demand a very careful analysis. A beginning has been made in thinking and studying about this aspect, but its extent is quite limited. This study just indicates towards this direction.

A research project on 'The Women Workers of Jari and Embroidery Industry' was undertaken by the Centre for Social Studies, Surat. As I worked as a Research Officer for this project, I had an occasion to come into close contact with the women workers of this industry, during the fieldwork. As per the target of the project, we interviewed 500 female jari workers through questionnaires, and took in-depth interviews of 100 female workers. In addition to this, I came into contact with many jari merchants, Akhadedars, and workers. But it was these women workers who drew my special attention.

The jari industry is about a century old and provides employment to around one and a half to two lakh workers. The patronage provided by the Mughals helped the growth of this industry in the city. The industry was also given special protection by the emperor. Moreover, as Surat was an important port during that time, and enjoyed trade relations with parts of the world, many travellers and traders from various countries and also the Muslims going for pilgrimage used to visit Surat frequently and purchased artistic items of jari.

In terms of their present day location the industry is concentrated in the areas such as Golwad, Kotasfil Road, Begampura and Sayedpura, which form the central as well as the old city area of Surat. Production remains primarily located at the residences which is a main characteristic feature of this industry. The production is organised around three main actors, viz. (i) the factory owner or the trader; (ii) Akhadedar and (iii) worker.

The Factory Owner or the Trader

He owns on an average of 10 to 15 machines for different types of processing on different machines. If number of workers is around 50 to 60, the owner is called as 'Karkhanadar' or the factory owner.

The processed jari is sold by the trader to other traders. This subgroup is called the class of traders.

Another class of 'traders' who purchases the raw materials and also owns the factory premises and machines, does not come into direct contact with the workers. These traders give their own factory and machines to others on hire and get their own goods processed. They pay the labour charges and retain finished goods. The persons taking the factory and machines on rent hire labourers from outside and make finished goods and thus come in to direct contact with the workers. The traders do not have to worry about wage rate, working hours and casual leave of the workers. Thus, the trading class consists of these three subgroups of traders. This group is very prosperous, but in terms of their numerical strength they only form about 5 per cent in the entire industry.

The Akhadedar

Persons who purchase raw materials from the traders and manufacture and prepare finished goods are called the Akhadedars. The entire family takes part in the production process. The Akhadedar hires outside workers only if it is found necessary. An almost equal proportion of men and women are found among the Akhadedars. This does not mean that the women become Akhadedars and bring raw material from the traders and give back the finished goods, but similar to the other workers they start working on their machines from 7 or 8 o'clock in the morning. For them, however, cooking of meals and looking after the machines go on simultaneously. We find large number of women working in this manner, for whom it is just a routine matter.

Workers

The third group in the industry is that of the workers. They come to the factory between 7 and 8 A.M. and work up to 7 P.M. A worker is paid only for the days on which he has worked and the payment is made at the end of the each month. On Sunday he is not supposed to work but remains unpaid for the day. Similarly, there are holidays on some festivals for which he is not paid. Seventy per cent of the people engaged in this industry belong to this category.

The types of work done by these workers are as follows:

Pavatha Section

Pavatha is a type of equipment which has a die of holes of various sizes fitted at one end, through which upper line passed and pulled for about 10 to 12 feet. Subsequently, the wire is again passed through a die of smaller holes and the process turned the wire into thin thread. An electric machine has now made this job much simpler. The task has been and still is done only by men alone.

Gifting Process

The process of gifting the thin threads of copper by silver or gold is called the gifting process. Only the male workers are engaged in this work.

Spindle Machine

The third process is done on the spindle machine. The processing on the spindle machine makes the gifting thread more and more thin which previously was done by only male workers. Now the task is also performed by female workers. However, the proportion of female workers in this job is quite less compared to that of the male workers.

Patia

The fourth stage of processing is called 'patia' in which the thread that has passed through the spindle machine is turned on a reel. In this task too the proportion of male worker is more, though the number of female workers is increasing day by day.

Thread Flattering

In the fifth stage of processing, the thread is flattered by arranging the reel of thread on one side of the machine and by taking it out on the other side. In between, the thread gets flattened. There is a predominance of female workers in this work.

Pechak

The sixth stage is called 'pechak' (twisting). There is a 10- to 12-feet-long machine with a height of about 3 feet. The flattened thread is kept in a reel on the upper portion of the machine. There is one more reel either of yarn or silk thread. These two threads are mixed and they come out in the form of jari. Work on this machine ensures that no thread is shaped and if it happens, the worker has to rearrange the thread on the reel. This work requires a lot of diligence and good eye sight. This work is exclusively done by women. The presence of male workers on this machine is considered ridiculous.

Reel Filling

The seventh and the last stage of processing is that of filling the reels with the processed jari threads. This work is entirely done by females. One notable thing is that this work is mainly done by girls of 10 to 15 years of age.

As the fifth and the sixth stages of processing (flattering and twisting) require more skill and good eye sight, the unskilled women are employed in the last stage of processing. The work of filling the reels is considered inferior and insignificant compared to the fifth and sixth stages. So the women workers working on flattening have a higher status than those who work in the seventh stage.

Another notable fact is that most of the work in this industry is done by the women workers, that is 70 per cent of the total workforce are females. Looking at such a large number of women workers in this industry, one starts thinking as to how could all these women enter this industry? How was it possible to have a large number of women workers who belong to the same caste in the same industry? And how did this come about? Let us examine this in greater detail.

Having described all the seven stages of processing let us now see as to in which stages of processing men and women are employed in larger number. First three jobs are exclusively done by male workers. Women have started working in the fourth stage of processing but the last three stages are exclusively performed by women. The jobs in which the male workers are employed apparently require more physical labour. So from the very beginning they are dominated by male workers. But today the conditions are different. Because of the invention of various machines, the physical labour involved has decreased considerably. When we examined the wage rates of the workers, we found that they were paid eight *annas* a day when the work was done manually in the first stage of processing. Now they work with a machine and are paid ₹ 35 to 40 per day.

In the job usually performed by women, one finds that the flattening machine has not been improved, except for a motor which is used instead of hands. Similarly, as far as the twisting machines are concerned, they were earlier arranging 30 to 35 reels on a machine and now arrange about 70 reels. So the workers have to look after 70 reels at a time. When a worker had to look after 35 reels, the wage rate was four *annas* and now it is ₹ 12 and 13 per day.

The leaders of this industry claim that additions of new machinery and industrial progress has reduced the physical labour of the workers, but they overlook the fact that this is true only for the workers who work in the first to the fourth stages of processing. But it is not true for the workers engaged in the fifth, sixth and seventh stages of processing. Thus actually such mechanisation has gone in favour of the male workers.

Caste Structure of Jari Industry

It is believed that traditionally this trade has been the exclusive domain of the Ranas. However, our study of 500 families in the city revealed the following distribution.

Caste	*Number of Families*
Rana	482
Khatri	6
Darji	1
Marathi	1
Kanbi	8
Kansarel	2
Total	500

An interesting feature of this industry is that whomsoever I met during the study belonged to the same caste. In the prevailing social conditions and according to widely held belief, there is no dominance of a particular caste in a particular industry or trade in the Indian economy. This has been so because of industrialisation and modernisation. The link between 'caste' and 'occupation' is thought to be broken. But one finds exactly opposite situation here. There may be dominance of a particular caste in a particular occupation, but here one industry is completely dominated by one particular caste.

Jari Industry and Women Workers

As mentioned earlier, about 70 per cent of the workforce in this industry consists of female workers. In this context, following questions seem relevant here:

(1) What is the present position of these female workers who started to work in the industry to help their menfolk in their work?

(2) What are their conditions vis-à-vis the male workers?

(3) What is the status of these female workers who actually form the basis of this industry?

(4) What is the attitude of industry owners towards the female labour?

In order to provide answer to these questions, we tried to know the domestic, social and economic conditions of these women workers. We had detailed interviews with them specifically on the aspects related to traditional occupation of the family, its economic condition, their social customs and so on. Whatever information we gathered from these interviews is given here in their own words.

Compulsory economic activity is not a new thing for these women. It is natural that poor economic condition of the family, social backwardness, lack of education and indifference towards education lead them to this compulsory work. Compulsory work has become a motto of the women of this caste. It is natural for them to join this work at the age of 8 to 10 years. When they are asked about the occupation of their grandfathers or grandmothers, father-in-law or mother-in-law, the answer has been uniform. 'They were doing this same work. What else they could do?' When they were asked whether they started 'doing this work voluntarily or under somebody's pressure', the women replied, 'where is the question of our own wish? We started the work in our childhood. When everybody in the family did this work, we also joined it'.

It is quite natural that the domestic conditions prevailing at the parental as well as that of the husband's homes affect these women. They are affected if the family is a joint or a nuclear family. We have discussed the types of family. We found neither joint nor nuclear. We feel that the joint family system is the best for these women workers. The problem of taking care of children is solved in the joint family system, while in the nuclear families these problems exist. In this connection we found that even a joint family is not very useful for the women workers, because all the female members of the family are engaged in working outside or inside the house. So the problem of rearing children remains. Moreover, the domestic work creates problem in a joint family which ultimately results in creating tension for the whole family and unhappiness for the women workers. Finding the unhappiness of women in a joint family system, one likes to examine the position of women workers in a nuclear family. The family may be joint or nuclear but the problem of children and other problems resulting in family tension seem to be routine.

As mentioned earlier the women workers are affected both by the father's house and by the husband's house. A woman starts working right from her childhood when she is at her parental home. She has to work compulsorily in order to help her father in his financial responsibilities and for contributing to the expenses for her marriage. Not only this, but also for becoming eligible for marriage, a girl had to learn jari work. The reaction of the women workers, traders and factory owners in this respect are interesting:

1. We do not want a girl who does not know this work.
2. We do not want a girl who knows only cooking. We want a girl who can also work on a machine.
3 If my father-in-law gives me a scooter, I may reject it, but instead if he gives me two machines, I will never return them.
4. When a boy is to be engaged, we must ask whether the girl knows jari work or not. If she does not know it, she is useless for us, even if she is a beauty queen.

It is not surprising that the eligibility condition for marriage for a girl is skill at jari work. We came across many women workers in various age groups during our field investigation. We did not find a single woman worker who could tell us clearly when and why she accepted this work.

Since their birth, they are economically self-sufficient. The women shoulder more than half of the economic burden of the family either voluntarily or compulsorily.

At a broader level, one finds that the position of woman as an individual in the family and the society is considered to be inferior. Many studies on the status of women conclude that the women are treated like slaves as they are not economically self-sufficient. So if they become economically self-sufficient, they can live an independent life with self-respect. This, however, seems far from reality.

We should now examine how much economic independence and self-respect women could have as a result of their economic self-sufficiency. To do this we had detailed discussions with the female workers, which included questions such as, What use do they make of their own earnings? How much do they spend on themselves from their earnings at their parental and husband's home? Does she save anything? Can she use the savings according to her own wish? If married, whether she is able to use her earnings according to her wish? We found from the discussions that whether or not a woman is economically independent she has a secondary position as far as economic matters are concerned, that is even though she is shouldering more than half of the financial burden; there is not a single case where economic self-sufficiency has provided them with economic independence. On the contrary there is a double burden. They have to carry the economic burden and they cannot get freedom from the family responsibilities, social customs, child care and so on. The males who have shifted a part of their own economic burden on the women do not make an attempt to make them free from or themselves share family responsibilities. The woman has to keep her child in a cradle kept in between two machines. Only one-hour lunch break does not give her sufficient time to eat. She has to make provision for the dinner during that time. To do both the jobs simultaneously – cooking and arranging on the machines seem to them as natural as breathing. In short as a woman she has to do the household work, child care and so on, but economic self-sufficiency has not relieved her from the family responsibilities.

We see all these as exploitation of women. But what do these women themselves believe? Are they aware about their double burden and exploitation? Through discussion with them, we found that they see this as their duty. This reflects lack of education, lack of outside contact and lack of awareness among them.

Women Workers and Protection of Interests

The rights and benefits of protection given to the workers employed in all types of occupations and industries are in a sense debatable. The government has enacted many laws related to the duration of working hours; wages and other benefits such as provident fund, casual leave, accident compensation, sick leave, medical reimbursement and bonus. But it is a debatable point whether the workers actually get these benefits or not. In some industries and processing houses these laws are implemented to some extent and benefits given to some workers. When the workers do not get these benefits, they use instruments such as strike to protect their interests.

Though jari industry is called a household industry, but it is not above the labour laws. So we tried to get information on this aspect by asking questions to them during our discussion, whether they get the benefits such as fixed working hours, weekly holidays, provident fund, bonus and so on. In the interviews all the women workers expressed surprise when they were told about these laws. Only 3 per cent of the women workers were aware of such laws. Of course, some women workers were aware of the law regarding working hours. But even this awareness was expressed in the following words, 'Yes ... when the staff of the municipality wants to make some money, they come to the owner and start asking questions, since what time the factory started working, whether a register is kept or not, whether the names of workers are written or not, etc. But the owner simply gives them tea with snacks and puts something in their pockets and they go away' When the women were asked, 'why don't you complain about the working hours when the officers of the municipality visit your factory?' They replied, 'The employer is not an employer as such. He belongs to our caste, he is our relative, and should we speak something against our relative? We also need a job. If he removes us from the job, who else will give us job? The municipality and the officer do not have any other work, so they come just to collect money. The owner has given us jobs, not the government' Continuing this discussion, they were asked, 'then why don't you ask for wages for Sunday?' They replied, 'We should get wages only for the days on which we work, we are not educated or salaried employees who get wages for Sundays also. We are workers. We get wages in proportion to the work done by us'. The women workers, who expressed such opinion, do not get all the benefits. Moreover, they are not even aware of these benefits. But if the benefits are given, all of them are ready to accept them.

So it is clear from the opinions expressed by the women that they in fact desire to get the benefits, but they do not speak out. Perhaps there are some constrain on them. Jari industry is a small-scale industry. The number of outside workers is kept at the minimum. Even these outside workers are from the same caste and often relatives. So it is not surprising that the kinship and caste serve as obstacles in the path of awareness.

Even the social conditions too become obstacles. The women have to follow many types of social customs. Occasions such as marriage, death, sickness and so on arise frequently. At such times, the women have to go to the concerned houses. Since they work at the places of their relatives, they can take part on such occasions without any problem. Only the condition is they have to finish their incomplete work on the next day. Apart from such occasions, the customs prevailing in their own families also contribute in keeping their mouth shut. The occasions such as marriage, death and so on incurs high expenses. The total earning of the husband and wife is hardly sufficient, and hence, on such an occasion they have to depend on loans from the employers. This obligation from the employer prevents them from raising a voice against them. The expenses are not always made directly from the earning of the women workers. Sometimes the father or the husband takes the advance from the employer and if the time and his wages are not sufficient to make repayment, then women in the family are asked to work in the same factory, so that the repayment can be done on time. The women also have to do this work without raising any voice as the loan is taken for an occasion in the family. There was one shocking case in which the married woman had to work in her father's factory in order to make the repayment of the loan taken by her in-laws.

Sometimes a loan is taken from the factory owner. Then if the father or husband or father-in-law gets more loans from the other factory, he leaves his first job. The cases of the women workers doing the job in jari industry for making repayment of loans are quite common. This condition of compulsory debt does not create any dislike in the minds of the women workers.

The lack of organisation also is an obstacle in creating awareness about their rights even though a large number of women workers are working in the same industry, they are not organised and also do not wish to be organised. The idea about organisation of these women who are indifferent to the needs of an organisation fighting for their demands, are as under.

Why do we need an association? We get our wages. Why should we get organised? Who will organise us? We do not have time for this organisation; it is the job of men, who will listen to us? We have to accept the reality of the women workers who express such opinions about the association.

Apart from these obstacles, one more obstacle in the way of achieving the rights of women workers is the problem of security from sexual offences. They have to think about their security as women. They think that they are safe when they work in the places of their relatives. If they go out and work in the place of someone else, they have to worry about their security. So when they decide about the place of work, they see whether it is located in the neighbourhood or whether the factory owner is their relative. The women workers who are ignorant about all other things are very conscious about their safety. The mother will check whether a place is safe before sending her young daughter for a job when a woman wants to change her place of work, the men in her family first check whether a new place is safe or not and then only the woman worker is allowed to go there.

Conclusions

(1) Jari industry and the Rana caste are mutually dependent. But the type and degree of this dependence makes one think, whether in

future this caste will join any other occupation or not? The way the industry and caste have been integrated today, we do not see any likelihood of their going for any other occupation. It is not that this caste is unhappy about its having only one occupation. On the contrary, it can be said without any doubt that since jari industry is a handy occupation for them, it has played an important role in keeping them free from worry of finding work for them and their future generations.

(2) The base of the industry is the participation of women. The industry maintains its existence because of the self-sacrifice and co-operation of the women workers; if the women workers withdraw themselves from the industry, it will be more than sufficient to completely destroy the roots of the industry. In spite of this the leaders of the industry are indifferent to payment of proper remuneration, raising their problems in public and drawing attention of the concerned authorities towards their problems. This is in spite of the fact that there are several women's associations, women workers and women political leaders in such a large city as Surat. No one is able to see the exploitation of the women workers working in the areas which are so near to Bhagal area, the heart of the city. What do the women organisations think about these women and their work? The picture is really disturbing. According to the workers of Mahila Mandel which is established with the objectives of liberation and equality for women, 'the members of our organization are from well-to-do families of upper castes. The women of low-castes will not even join our organization. Our job is to bring awareness among the women. The workers' unions should think about the women workers of the jari industry, it is not our job'.

(3) The trade unions are also equally indifferent. 'We are ready to solve their problems, if they come to us and present their case'. On the other hand the absence of trade union is helplessness of the jari workers leave alone the membership of any leading trade union of the industry, even if an Akhad :dar or worker is found to be 'union minded', no businessman will be ready to give work to him. So no one even thinks about forming an association. The women workers cannot remain aloof to such traditions. If the so called strong and vocal class of male workers abstains from forming an association, naturally the women workers have no courage or capacity to do it.

(4) The compulsion of work is not a phenomenon of today alone. It is a tradition dating back to several years. The women believe that they have to work.

But this also does not mean that the women dislike the compulsory work. In a way the work takes them outside the home for a few hours. While working alone with other women they feel more relaxed. They are in an unhappy condition not because of compulsion of work because of the double burden of work. A woman worker is aware of her difficulties and her position but the social customs emerge as obstacles. If awareness is created among the women workers, they can be brought out by removing such obstacle. The first reason for lack of awareness seems to be the lack of education. But the condition of even educated women is no better. The educated women also have failed to become aware of social evils, problems of women, exploitation of women and so on. The educated women do not think differently than other women. They have obtained knowledge through formal education but not an awareness of their own situations.

(5) The theory that economic self-sufficiency gives equality and independence to women also withers out here. The women workers in this industry who work along with the male workers are not even aware of equality and independence, leave alone about getting them.

In the end one can say that jari industry, which has majority of the workers from the women of Rana caste will remain in their hands for years to come.

7

Women in Sericulture

Some Preliminary Observations

E.N. Ashok Kumar

Karnataka state is called as 'Silk Bowl' of India accounting for 60 per cent of total raw silk production. Presently, in Karnataka sericulture is being practiced in about 50 per cent of the villages covering almost all the districts of the state. During 1987 to 1988, the total production of mulberry silk in the state was 4970 tonnes,[1] the highest among the silk-producing states of India. Thus, sericulture is emerging as an important commercial farming in the rural areas of Karnataka.

Sericulture is a household agro-husbandry. The production process of sericulture is highly labour intensive, and women constitute a large portion of the workforce (more than 60%). The women members of the sericulture practicing households contributed a significant amount of labour in silkworm rearing and production of cocoons. Since the major portion of the workforce consists of women, there is a need for understanding in what ways the productive labour of women is utilised in sericulture practice. This chapter is an attempt to answer certain very pertinent questions such as which section of the women are engaged in sericulture? Is there any division of work based on the skills between men and women? In case there are divisions, what are the factors associated with it?

This chapter has three parts. Part I deals with the context of the village in which fieldwork was conducted. Part II is devoted to the activities carried out by the male and female members in various stages of sericulture cocoon production. Part III gives the summary view.

I

Thekalavatti (hereafter TK), a drought-prone village in Holalkere block of Chitradurga district (Central Karnataka) is taken for our field study.

It is an interior village situated 30 km away from any town including the block headquarter. The transport facilities are very poor. There are only two buses plying across the village, connecting Chitradurga and Davanagere, the important market centres in the district. As the village is prone to perennial droughts, the water resources are limited. The farmers grow food crops, viz., Ragi, Jowar, Millets and Maize in large scale depending on the favourable monsoons. Sunflower, Sesame and Groundnut are the major cash crops grown in relatively small quantities in the village. A small proportion of large farmers have dug wells which has helped them to raise horticulture crops. The vast tracts of the village lands remain barren for several seasons due to inadequate monsoons. Majority of the small and marginal farmers including the landless migrate to neighbouring districts as wage labourers. The village was electrified in 1980 facilitating many farmers to make use of electricity for agricultural operations.

In the recent year that is in 1980s village TK is emerging as a prominent sericulture village in Holalkere block. After the advent of electricity in 1950s, many farmers have deepened their dug wells, fixed electric motors and increased their land area under well irrigation. They have started cultivating mulberry leaves and rearing of silkworms. In TK at present there are 23 households (out of 140) rearing silkworms regularly. Around 17 acres of land area is under the cultivation of mulberry leaves used for feeding silkworms. With this background, an attempt is made in this chapter to describe the participation of women in sericulture – rearing silkworms and how their work is different from the male members.

Farming households in the village are divided broadly into three groups:

1. Upper Strata – Farmers holding above 15 acres of land
2. Middle Strata – Farmers holding 5–15 acres of land
3. Low Strata – Farmers holding less than 5 acres of land

In upper strata, there are 16 households and all of them belong to Lingayat caste. Middle strata consist of 61 households consisting of Lingayats, Gollas and a few Nayak and Madiga households. The lower strata consist of 63 households and large number of them belongs to Madiga and Nayak castes, who are also, scheduled castes.

The village TK has 23 sericulture households. Sixteen of them belong to upper strata and remaining seven are middle strata farmers. By caste, two households belong to Golla, two Nayaks, one Madiga and remaining eighteen are Lingayats. This clearly indicates that sericulture practice in this village is confined only to upper and middle strata households, mostly Lingayats. Sericulture is more viable for the upper segment farmers than the small and marginal farmers. At the first instance it requires land and water resources to cultivate mulberry leaves to ensure the feeding requirements of the silkworms. It requires implements and bullocks for the tillage of land. Frequent manuring of both farmyard and chemical fertilisers is necessary to raise good-quality mulberry leaves.

On the other hand, cocoon rearing is carried out in houses as it requires constant supervision and care. To rear cocoons also requires separate space inside the house to keep wooden stands and large-size bamboo baskets to carry out rearing activities. This implies that the sericulturists require spacious houses for cocoon rearing. Sericulture practicing also involves investment on sericulture implements such as 'Thatte', 'Chandrike' and 'Mosquito Nets'. In spite of all this, there is a popular belief that 'cocoon rearing is a highly sensitive process involving risks and uncertainty', which is one of the inhibiting factors for small and marginal farmers to take up sericulture in TK.

II

There is a notion that since women has the experience and knowledge of rearing children, it would be more appropriate if they take up the job of rearing silkworms which need to be handled with delicacy and care.

In the village TK the women's involvement in sericulture is more than that of men at the household level. Hanumanthappa is a sericulturist. In his house six women and two men assist in sericulture. Rudrappa is another sericulturist with four women and one man carrying out silkworm rearing in the house.

In sericulture, cocoon rearing is considered to be a household agro-husbandry practice. More than 60 per cent of the labour requirement for cocoon rearing is said to be coming from the women members of the household. What type of work women are allocated in sericulture? In what ways their participation in sericulture differ from the male members of the household? Answer to this question is vital for in-depth understanding about the position of women in the sericulture practice.

Sericulture involves various stages[2] starting from hatching of silkworms until the development of 'pupa', that is the formation of silk cocoons. We shall describe the process stage after stage.

Silkworm rearing is carried out in ordinary rearing trays made of bamboo or wood called 'thattes', before the beginning of rearing, women clean the 'thattes', dry them and also keep them ready. Rearing stand on which thattes are placed would also be cleaned by the women. The rearing room needs to have good ventilation and be free from dust. In case of mud floor, women clean it with cow dung. In case of stone or cemented floor, it is cleaned with water and sometimes with diluted formalin solution.

Male member, generally head of the household, takes the decision from where the silkworm eggs to be procured. In the village TK, the sericulturists normally procure eggs from the government recognised grainage in Chitradurga. Also there are instances of buying eggs from Hiriyur and Ramanagaram. Ramanagaram is an important place (in Bangalore district) to market silk cocoons. Buying good-quality eggs requires skill and expertise. The male members while buying eggs observe bold and plump looking eggs containing greater amount of yolk material. After procuring eggs, they take precaution to preserve them properly. The sheets of paper containing eggs are spread out in rearing trays and covered with paraffin paper or ordinary newspaper. In order to obtain uniform hatching of eggs, the egg sheets are placed in a card board box and wrapped up in black piece of paper or black sheet of paper. Uniformity in hatching assures good harvest. It requires skill and care to achieve uniformity and thus is carried out by the male members.

On the expected date of hatching, the women go to the field to pluck the mulberry leaves. In the initial stage, the women are instructed by the male members regarding the type of leaves required. Since the worms are tender, leaves are expected to be tender, succulent and dark green in colour. However, the experienced women pluck this quality of leaves on their own. As the worms grow, less and less tender leaves are used for feeding. Women chop the leaves into smaller pieces when the worms are young.

When the worms hatch out, the male member recognised as the skilled person in the household watches whether more than 90 per cent of the eggs are hatched out or not. These members have learnt about sericulture through relatives and neighbours taken to sericulture much earlier. In the recent years, several farmers are taught about silkworm rearing by the Sericulture Assistants.[3] These skilled persons brush the newly hatched worms on to the rearing beds (trays) carefully with the help of a chicken feather.

Women have the job of sprinkling minutely chopped mulberry leaves all over the rearing trays. The worms start feeding over the leaves. From this stage onwards, women start involving more and more in cutting leaves and feeding worms. They visit field two times a day to bring mulberry stock to the rearing house. These leaves have to be plucked before 9 A.M. and after 4 P.M. which is considered to be an appropriate time. Both young and middle-aged females go to the fields to carry leaves. They carry gunny bags on their heads filled with mulberry leaves. As the worms grow, the feeding requirement also increases. Women have to walk to the distant fields (2–3 km) and bring large quantities of leaves. In some cases they bring leaves more than two times a day depending on the situation. However, men also do this work whenever women are not available. This apart, women have to clean the rearing trays once in a day or two. They remove dry and eaten leaves and the worm's excreta. They put this waste into compost or feed the same to the cattle in case they have any. These activities require less skill and are generally allocated to the females.

Spacing of the worms in the trays is also an important aspect which requires care and attention. When the worms begin to grow, the space becomes crowded leading to under nourishment and uneven development of the worms. During this stage, the male member takes decision to increase the number of trays to facilitate more space. He suggests the female members to increase the trays and distribute the worms. Women do it. This will continue until the worms grow to a maximum size.

In the regular cocoon-rearing practice women look after all the feeding requirements of the worms. If the worms are overcrowded in spots (on rearing trays) they are removed and redistributed uniformly. Women arrange the worms such that they have equal access to the green leaves. The precautions promote the worms to go for moulting[4] uniformly.

During the process of cocoon development, the worms take four moults and each moult is a crucial phase which requires optimum care. Most of the failures in harvest are due to the lack of proper care during moulting. Handling the works during moults requires skill and expertise. That is one of the reasons why the male members take care of the worms during moulting. They regulate feeding in such a way that the worms go for moulting uniformly. As the signs of moulting are observed, they take every effort in drying the rearing bed gradually to facilitate moulting. They give reduced quantities of feeding until more than 90 per cent of the worms settle for moulting. They have to confirm this proportion accurately. They stop feeding during moults which take around 20 hours. After 20 to 24 hours, the worms begin to come out of moulting. They decide about re-feeding only after ensuring that the required per cent of worms come out of moult. Then they suggest women to start feeding.

Mounting is the last stage in the silkworm rearing. On completion of 6 or 7 days after passing fourth moult, the worms stop feeding. They become ripe for spinning cocoons. The women clean the 'Chandrikes'[5] and keep ready for mounting worms for spinning. The male members identify the worms which are ripe enough to spin cocoon. They look for ripe worms possessing translucent body colour and rising heads actively. Such worms are grouped together and mounted on 'Chandrikes' with appropriate spacing. The mounting is done by both males and females, since this is not a highly skilful one. Women harvest the cocoons spun on Chandrike.

The market activities are solely done by the male members. They collect cocoons and weigh. Cocoons are packed in gunny bags or in the bags made of cloth. The sericulturists of TK sell their cocoons in Ramnagar Cocoon Market.

In the preceding description, it is clearly revealed that the participation of men and women in sericulture is not alike. Women are allocated certain activities which are relatively low skilled. They have taken up mechanical activities such as plucking leaves, feeding worms and cleaning the rearing beds. Most of the sensitive and skilled jobs such as maintaining uniformity in hatching eggs, regulation of feeding during and after moulting and spacing of worms are carried out by the male members. All these amount to thinking that why there is such a division of work between men and women, notwithstanding the fact that the women are also equally capable of handling skilled works competently.

However, several factors have been associated with such divisions of work in sericulture. Firstly, the sericulture began in TK by Rudrappa, a school teacher belonging to Lingayat caste. He learnt it through one of his relatives in Hosadurga Taluk who had been practicing sericulture for many years. After seeing Rudrappa's success, Hanumanthappa took interest in sericulture. He sent his son Nagendra to receive training in sericulture. Only in mid-1980s the extension officials from the Department of Sericulture started visiting the village TK. In most of the cases, the extension workers meet the male members of the household and impart technical knowledge about sericulture. Therefore, it is worth noting that the knowledge of sericulture is first acquired by the men and later on by the women. Perhaps this would be one of the reasons why the women are allocated relatively less skilled works compared to their male counterparts.

Women like Sharadamma and Gowramma have been involved in sericulture for the past 5 years. They raise three to four harvests in a year and are familiar with the skills involved in various stages of sericulture. Though they are confident of their skills, but never take decisions without consulting the male members. As Gowramma said 'I can decide independently when to stop and begin feeding while the worms go for moulting. But I don't do it. Because in case anything goes wrong they (male members) will put blame upon me'.

There are also beliefs and rituals associated with sericulture practice, which regulate the total participation of women in silkworms rearing. For instance, during menstrual cycle women are not allowed inside the rearing house for 5 days. It is believed that the silkworms which resemble Basavanhula are the incarnations of Lord Shiva. Any such violation related to purity and sanctity would lead to silkworm diseases resulting in the failure of harvest. In the village TK, the women in prenatal and postnatal periods are prohibited to enter the rearing house (room). They are kept away from all rearing activities. Because they believe that silkworm generate excess of heat which would affect their health. There are several instances of farmers giving up the sericulture for a few months in case prenatal or postnatal women at home. These farmers do not have spacious houses or the separate rearing houses.

What do the women feel about their work in sericulture? It seems that they never distinguish anything like skilled or unskilled work in sericulture. They do what their male members assign to them. However, they have their own perceptions about the participation in sericulture as a whole. One group of women feels that the advent of sericulture to their homes has doubled their workload. In addition to sericulture work, they have to attend domestic work such as cooking, cleaning, maintaining cattle and usual farming work. In many cases, women are asked to look after feeding during night shifts. This they have to do by foregoing their night's sleep especially during peak rearing activities. They feel sericulture work as strenuous and burdensome particularly, when they do not get good harvest. These women belong to the upper strata of TK and have some acres of garden lands. Another group of women are quite satisfied with their new roles as sericulture workers. These women belong to the middle strata of TK. Before taking to sericulture, these women used to have lot of leisure time without any productive work. Seasonally, they used to work as wage labourers or mutual labourers on the fields of large farmers of TK. The coming of sericulture has given them an opportunity to work at home. They need not have to request large farmers for labour. Moreover, the advent of sericulture has brought a new hope for these members to improve their living conditions.

III

Sericulture has entered as a new farm technology to TK, a drought-prone village. Characteristically, sericulture practice is managed by women who constitute the major segment of the workforce. Notably, men are also involved in sericulture, in relatively small proportion, but they play vital role in the sensitive phases of sericulture which requires skill and expertise. In other words, there is a division of work between men and women in carrying out sericulture activities, though this division is not a hard and fast rule of practice or to follow. There are notions among the administrators and the social scientists that the participation of women in sericulture is at par with their male counterparts which need to be re-examined. Our study offers several vital clues indicating division of work between men and women in sericulture. It is evident from our description that the work participation of men and women is not similar in various stages of sericulture. It is observed that the men assume highly skill-oriented work, whereas semi-skilled and less skilled works are allocated to women. In spite of their small proportion, the men take major decisions in carrying out silkworm rearing. As referred to earlier, women are restrained from carrying out sericulture during menstrual cycles, prenatal and postnatal periods. This is due to societal taboos and beliefs associated with purity and pollution which have restricted the participation of women in rearing silkworms. Though the basis of such beliefs is not known, yet the sericulture in TK follows these norms strictly.

In the light of our observations, this chapter offers some suggestions. Since the major segment of the workforce constitutes women, there is a need to utilise women labour equally in both skilled and unskilled sectors of sericulture. In order to achieve this, the concerned agencies have to give special attention to women sericulturists in reducing division of work between men and women based on skills. Sericulture extensions have to give priority to women in training and imparting skills of sericulture in order to inculcate confidence among them. Women should take up skilled work, and make decisions, independent of men. Sericulture has all potentials to be treated as an activity exclusively of women and for women. Organising co-operatives of women sericulturists would be one such step in achieving this objective. However, it is to be seen, whether the sericulture would improve the social status of women at large needs special attention, careful thinking and consideration by social science researchers. Such area of issues and problems highlights the need for further empirical research.

Notes

1. Silkman's Companion, Central Silk Board, Bangalore, 1989, p. 41.
2. Hatching of silkworms from eggs, feeding silkworms, cleaning the rearing bed, spacing the worms and so on.
3. Sericulture Assistants are the village level extension workers deputed by the Department of Sericulture. There are also female sericulture assistants.
4. Moulting phase is an important stage in the growth of silkworms and requires skill and expertise to maintain the uniformity in moulting. Before the development of cocoon, the silkworm undergoes moulting four times. During moulting silkworms stop feeding for a day and develop new skin.
5. Chandrikes are the bamboo stands with concentric grooves used for moulting silkworms to spin the cocoons.

8

Women Bidi Workers and the Cooperative Movement

A Study of the Struggle in the Bhandara District Bidi Workers' Cooperative

Anuradha Ghandy and Geetha Thachil

The very fact that a National Commission on Self-Employed Women and Women Workers in the Informal Sector was appointed by the Central Government in 1987 proves that the problem of poor women workers in the unorganised sector has become serious. In spite of a professed policy of poverty eradication, the fact is that poor women have not gained access to developmental resources. Instead the growth of modern industry has either pushed out women from many jobs in the organised sector or prevented their absorption into that sector. They have been left to fend for themselves in the informal, poorly paid sector. These women are at a disadvantage when confronted with the complex modern laws and administration. This advantage is evident even when they are involved in the process of cooperativisation, a pronounced state policy to fight capitalist exploitation. In reality can the process of cooperativisation in its existing form fulfil this aim merits investigation?

The present chapter is a case study of a bidi workers' cooperative in Bhandara district. It is an account of the struggle of the women workers to gain control of this cooperative and the response of the state to their attempts. In this case study we seek to highlight not unique features of the attempt instead we seek to show that it is representative of the nature of the state-sponsored cooperative movement in India and its relation to the strategy of development adopted by the states in India.

The first section deals briefly with the background of Bhandara district; the second section covers the condition of bidi workers in the district. The third section deals with the struggle of bidi workers in the district. The next section gives details of the district-level cooperative of bidi workers that was set up. The fifth section is an account of the struggle of the women workers to control the society, and the sixth section analyses the response of the bureaucracy and government to the struggle. The conclusion relates this struggle to wider economic processes.

Background of Bhandara District

Bhandara district is located in Vidarbha region. At the Eastern extreme of Maharashtra it is in the rice-producing tract of Vidarbha. It consists of 13 tehsils. An agriculturally backward district, only 50 per cent of its land is cultivated. More than one fourth of the land is under forest cover. The per hectare yield of rice, wheat, jowar and maize are lower than the state average. The district has been industrially backward with primarily some agriculture – and forest-based industries such as rice mills, oil mills and bidi industry. Recently an ultra-modern steel plant has been set up near the district headquarters, Bhandara.

The district ranks second in the state with reference to overall work participation and stands first in female work participation rate in the state (*Bhandara District Census Handbook*, 1981) This high work participation and especially female work participation rate is primarily due to (1) the district being a rice growing area and (2) widespread bidi production both in rural and urban areas of the district.

According to the 1981 census of Bhandara district, there are 2.17 lakh male and 1.63 lakh female cultivators among the main workers. The number of female agricultural workers is more than that of male agricultural workers, female being 1.20 lakhs and male being 1.06 lakhs. In household industry too, the number of women workers (50,333) is more than that of male workers (39.334). The number of female marginal workers is much high than that of male marginal workers, female being 69,058 and male being 19,457.

Of the total female workers (main and marginal), the proportion of cultivators is 45.01 per cent which is much higher than the state average (38–48%). The percentage of female agricultural labourers (33.92%) is significantly lower than the state average (45.61). Their percentage in household industry (41.1) is higher than the state average of 2.4. This is clear because of the large proportion of women involved in bidi rolling.

The total number of bidi workers in the district is estimated to be 89,667 of which women constitute 50,333. While the overall number of bidi workers continued to increase up to 1971, the number has come down in 1981. It has been widely noted that this is due to the bidi manufacturers shifting to other states where labour is cheaper.

The proportion of the Scheduled Castes (SC) population in the district is 18.24 per cent of the total population. This figure has been arrived at by adding the Buddhist population to the SC population. Statistics on the number of SC population does not include the Buddhists who are in fact Mahars converted after 1956 of the total population. Of this an overwhelming majority of 90 per cent are Mahars/Buddhists. A majority of bidi workers in the district are SC, especially Mahars. In fact initially the bidi industry consisted of only SC workers, and it is only in the past few decades that non-SC women are also entering this industry.

Conditions in Bidi Industry

The exploitative conditions of work and the general plight of the bidi workers have been documented as far back as 1929 by the Royal Commission of Labour. Many recent studies have also highlighted these facts (Bhatty, 1981; Prasad and Prasad, 1985). The salient features are mentioned below:

1. *Shift in production process:* When the bidi industry began around 1910 the workers congregated in the sadars (workshops) for production. But sometime in between 1931 and 1951 the mode of production shifted to the contract-based home production. The main reason for this shift was the application of the Factories Act of 1923 to the bidi establishments with 20 or more workers after 1930. This resultant atomisation has led to flagrant violation of labour laws and exploitation of workers. It seems at that stage the workers too did not oppose this shift in the production process as they were unaware of its consequences. They were attracted by convenience in working from their own houses in their villages.
2. *Marginalisation of bidi workers:* With the contractor, home-based system of production the bidi production reached remote villages of the district. As a result the number of bidi workers, particularly women, increased. But the contract system helped to keep the wages low, even depress them further. As a result bidi making can no longer be a source of livelihood, and it has been relegated to a secondary position. The practice of parallel or 'business' bidi production by unknown and unregistered establishments has also brought down the wages. Study conducted by the National Labour Institute in 1985 showed that the workers were paid between ₹ 3.50 and ₹ 4.00 for 1000 bidis instead of the then

prevailing minimum wage rate of ₹ 9. At present in Bhandara town also, the prevailing rate in business bidis is ₹ 6.00 for 1000 bidis as against the minimum wage rate of ₹ 12.

3. *Increase in the proportion of female workers:* Since 1961 there has been an increase in the proportion of female workers the main reason for which could be the extremely low wages paid, as a result of which male wage earners are seeking other better paid forms of labour. Also the general inflation has forced women to supplement the family earnings and the home-based nature of the bidi production is convenient for women even if the wage rate is low.

4. *Forms of exploitation:* The exploitation of bidi workers has been well documented. There are many ways in which the women are exploited by contractors and industrialists: (a) they are paid low wages on a piece rate basis. (b) They are supplied with less tobacco and leaves than required for making 1000 bidis. To make up the shortfall in order to avoid a wage cut, the women have to buy the tobacco or leaves from the contractor at the price set by him. (c) The contractor wets the tobacco before distributing it in order to increase its weight, and supply defective leaves so that the women are forced to buy fresh leaves. (d) As high as 20 per cent of the bidis rolled in a day are set aside as rejected and sold subsequently under another brand name. Lack of proper procedure for rejecting bidis has led to this form of exploitation. (e) Bidi rolling being a seasonal job the work pattern is very irregular. Because of the informal nature of production and the lack of proper records most of the workers depend upon the contractor to give them work and are therefore unable to protest against his arbitrary style of functioning. (f) None of the labour legislation was applicable to the workers; for example whether the provisions of Bidi and Cigar Workers' Act, which binds the contractors to maintain proper registers, give the workers an identity card and wage book; and the Maternity Benefit Act, the Provident Fund Act and the Bonus Act are not implemented for the home-based workers. Constant inhalation of tobacco dust leads to bronchial problems including TB. The companies have no responsibility to maintain the health of their workers. Many of the older women workers felt that after years of bidi rolling their bodies accustomed to this sort of work are incapable of any other forms of physical labour.

This rampant exploitation has led to the bidi workers getting organised. The setting up of cooperative societies was seen an answer to their existing problems.

Mobilisation and Organisation of Bidi Workers in Bhandara

The formation of the district-level cooperative of bidi workers in Bhandara in 1981 was preceded by struggle of the workers over the closures of several centres by big bidi manufacturers and over the issue of raising the minimum wage rate.

The bidi workers of the Bhandara have had a long history of struggle. This is because of a concentration of bidi workers in the district and the fact that most of them belonged to one caste. Though no documented account of the struggle of the bidi workers in the area is available, the narrations of older workers points out that even in the early 1950s there had been militant struggles of bidi workers with a high participation of women workers, especially around Gondia. Though a section of them had been organised by a communist group that called itself Bolshevik Party, most of the workers in the area were organised by the followers of Dr B.R. Ambedkar. The most dynamic and successful of them was Advocate Dadasaheb Kumbhare. The enactment of special legislation for bidi workers namely the Bidi & Cigar Workers Act, 1966 and the extension of the other protective benefits such as maternity benefits, provident fund and bonus for bidi workers were primarily due to the agitations led by and efforts of Advocate Kumbhare.

The agitations of the bidi workers have had a political and social impact in Vidarbha. This has been possible due to a significance of bidi industry to the economic life of Bhandara district coupled with the large proportion of Scheduled Caste workers in the industry especially Mahar/Buddhist and the strong and articulate political organisation among them.

But each time certain provisions were made applicable to bidi workers; the bidi manufacturers have responded to set the gains to naught. When the Factories Act was made applicable to the dingy, unventilated, overcrowded sheds, they dismantled the sadar system and introduced the contractor-mediated home-based system of production (Report of the Royal Commission on Labour in India, 1931). The minimum wage rate is rarely applicable due to the prevalence of the dispersed, irregular contractor system; when the Maternity Benefit Act was extended to cover the women bidi workers, the bidi kings struck off the names of the women from the rolls and introduced the names of their male family members. So women became the benami producer for their brothers, husbands or sons. When the PF was made compulsory, they deducted from the workers' wages but did not deposit the money with the PF Commissioner nor did they contribute their own share. Thus the workers' deducted wages was appropriated as capital for their business. Only 10 years later, after a Vidarbha-wide agitation, the workers are now gradually getting their PF back. When these manoeuvres were not successful enough, they shifted their manufacturers to other states where labour was less organised and therefore more easily exploited.

Every time many centres of these bidi manufacturers close down rendering thousands unemployed; agitations have been launched. One of the important and spontaneous responses to closures has been to set up workers' cooperatives. Hence several cooperative of bidi workers were started in the late 1950s, and again in the early 1970s. But none of these cooperatives have been successful, most of them wound up after some years. The only exception in the whole of Vidarbha has been the one started by Advocate Kumbhare in 1960 in Kamptee (Nagpur District). The Kamptee-based Majdoor Bidi Sahakari Sanstha Pvt. Ltd., which began without any government financial aid, is still running profitably with 361 women workers.

In 1980 when one more wave of closures of bidi production centres, of big manufacturers like C.J. Patel & Co. and Mohanlal Hargovinddas occurred whereby thousands of workers were thrown out of jobs, Bhandara Zilla Bidi Kamgar Sahakari Sanstha was set up.

Formation of the Society to its Collapse

In 1980 manufacturing firms in Bhandara and Nagpur districts closed their centres and fled to other states such as Bihar, MP and AP where the minimum wage rates were much lower. As a result of this a total of 11,842 bidi workers in Bhandara district became unemployed almost overnight. A tehsilwise breakdown of these workers who lost their jobs in 1980 is given in the Table 8.1:

Table 8.1 *Tehsilwise Number of Workers became Unemployed*

Taluka	*No. of Workers Employed*
Bhandara	1,639
Mohadi	1,700
Tiroda	835
Gondia	350
Pauni	1,650
Sakoli	1,790
Tumsar	1,125
Total	11,842

Source: Progress Annual Report of the Bhandara Zilla Bidi Kamgar Sahakari Sanstha, 1985.

Table 8.2 *Centre wise distribution of workers and period of production*

Tehsil	*No. of members*	*Centre*	*No. of workers*	*Period of production*	
				Opening	*Closing*
Bhandara	512	Bhandara	110	September 1981	October 1986
Mohadi	576	—			
Tiroda	441	Paraswada	64	November 1981	April 1984
Gondia	977	—			
Pauni	725	Adyal	193	September 1981	April 1984
—	323	Konda	78	March 1982	April 1984
Sakoli	861	Lakhni	84	November 1982	July 1986
Total	4,850		529		

Spontaneously these workers decided to start local-level cooperative societies to generate employment. At that time Haribhau Naik, the state minister for Labour in Antulay's cabinet, an INTUC leader of Vidarbha, intervened to provide government finance. It was decided that instead of several smaller societies, a district-level cooperative would be set up, one in Nagpur and other in Bhandara. A total of 4850 unemployed bidi workers became members of this society by buying shares of ₹ 11 each. A taluka wise distribution of these members is given in Table 8.2. To the amount of ₹ 55,000 collected as share capital from the workers the government granted ₹ 23.6 lakhs as share capital. Some additional funds were granted towards the cost of advertisements, for purchase of vehicles and so on. The society started production in September 1981 with its headquarters in a rented building in Bhandara town.

The society started off on an extremely sound financial footing with a capital stock of more than ₹ 25 Lakhs. Thus the Bhandara Zilla Bidi Kamgar Sahakari Sanstha was born. The bidi rolled by the society were sold under the brand name of Zhopdi bidi.

Five centres were started in the quick succession generating employment for 529 workers. Most of the 84 workers in Lakhni were women and all except two belonged to the Scheduled Caste. This centre functioned for three and a half years. Lakhni being a big village with a population almost 9000, there were several rice and oil mills and agricultural work in the surrounding area. But the bidi workers, having rolled bidis for decades found it difficult to find alternate employment.

The Paraswada centre which functioned for two and a half years gave employment to 64 workers of which 54 were women. All the workers were from the SC. This village located 25 km from Tiroda, is a small village with a population, of less than 2000. It is an extremely backward village; it has no industries and single crop cultivation predominates. The people of the village have tended to migrate in search of employment.

The Adyal centre was the first to start production. A large number of workers lost their sources of livelihood when Mohanlal Hargovinddas & Co. closed its centres here. The centre, employing 193 workers, half of whom are women, was the first to close after functioning for two and a half years. Adyal too is a village with a population of more than 9000, and it is a commercial centre in the area and has a few saw mills, rice mills and so on. Many of the workers from the Adyal migrated to Madhya Pradesh when the Zhopdi Bidi Centre closed down.

Konda, located 11 km from Adyal was subcentre of Adyal. Here too, of 78 members only half were women and all belonged to the SC.

At the Bhandara centre a total of 110 workers were provided with work of which 108 were women. Though a majority of them belonged to the Mahar community a sizeable number of Hindu women, belonging to the Teli and Kumbi caste were also members. The Bhandara centre was the last to close down. The women worked in the sadar in the head office of the society till October 1986.

The management of the society was entrusted to a managing committee fully nominated by the State Government. The committee was to function under the supervision of the District Deputy Registrar (DDR) of Cooperatives. The Assistant Commissioner of Labour based in the Gondia was the President of the Society and the Assistant Registrar (Coop) was the Vice-President. A Grade I officer of the Cooperative Department was on deputation as a Managing Director of the society. Apart from these high-ranking bureaucrats in the committee there were seven representatives of the members of the society who were also nominated. All of them without exception were private contractors of bidi manufacturers. Not one of the ordinary workers and not a single woman was nominated to the managing committee, although a majority of the members were women. The expectation of the State Government that the contractors who had so far exploited the workers would suddenly transform and fight the monopoly of the bidi kings to whom their interests were tied, was nothing short of utopia!

According to the cooperative officials the reasons for the failure of this cooperative venture were several. According to them the cooperative was started at too short a notice because of which no proper ground work could be done. They also said that their cost of production was too high because they paid wages according to the Minimum Wages Act, while private manufacturers did not. Also private firms evaded payment of excise duty while the society did not. Thus their cost of production exceeded the prevailing market price. Thus they concluded that bidis could not be manufactured on a cooperative basis profitably and labelled the whole attempt a failure.

The failure of the cooperative venture was not only in the reason given above but in the very structure of the cooperative that was set up. The managing committee consisting of bureaucrats and contractors could hardly be expected to have the interests or spare the time necessary to make such a venture successful in the face of the competition of the bidi kings. Not merely was there indifference but also open corruption, allegations regarding which have been made by employees and women workers and which were never denied. The society became a private fief of the officer of the cooperative department on deputation. It is little wonder that the cost of producing 1000 bidis was shown to work out to ₹ 35 when the market price for selling did not exceed ₹ 25 per thousand! No efforts were made to cut down the production cost.

There was no planning before the society was launched and no proper marketing facilities developed that led to stockpiling within two years of the society's birth was true. By 1984 there were 1.75 crores of bidis left unsold in the society's godowns. With special permission of the government they were finally sold at one-third the cost of production. But the managing committee was chosen from the cooperative department precisely because of 'expertise' to handle such problems and their total lack of interest in the success of the society is reflected in the indiscriminate opening of centres. Centres were opened to appease political and other leaders rather than help the society grow slowly and soundly. Marketing has been the main problem of every cooperative society in any sector, but bidi is an item for which the market has not contracted. Notwithstanding all these problems, the employees built up a market for the Zhopdi bidi, but the committee managing the society made no systematic efforts to help the society to become viable.

As a result, the financial crises deepened by late 1984. Out of a total more than ₹ 25 lakhs share capital with which the society started, the society was left with hardly 5 lakhs.

It is significant to note that during this entire period the ordinary members had no say whatsoever in the running of the society. It was only when the news about the mismanagement and imminent closure of production became known that the employees and the members of the society stirred themselves into action. They knew that the only way the society could survive and be rehabilitated was to get rid of the corrupt bureaucrats in management and wrest control of the society themselves. Thus confrontation between the cooperative department and the bureaucrats on one hand and the women workers and the employees on the other hand began.

The Women and Their Struggle

'The Society Belongs to Us, the Loan Was Given to Us'

These women from poor families, with little or no formal education, and whose lives had revolved around their homes were trying to face up to the might of the bureaucracy. With hardly any experience of any struggles they were at a disadvantage. Barsanbai, an elderly woman, widowed soon after her marriage, from Lakhni was one of the few exceptions. She had earlier participated in an unsuccessful attempt to start a cooperative of bidi workers. With her 30 years of experience in various bidi workers' agitations she was undoubtedly the leader of the Lakhni workers whom she mobilised very effectively.

Malanbai from Bhandara a widow of about 45 years was yet another leader who had participated in an earlier struggle. She is well known for the 10-day hunger strike she had set on, in 1980 when her company had closed down. It was with great pride she said, 'I broke my fast only when the Collector himself assured me that he would look into the matter'. Needless to say she had a hang in the initial stirrings among the women which began in October 1984.

As news about the rapid erosion of the capital stock of the society came into the open the women started getting restless. Already the women were contributing 50 bidis a day free to help the society tide over its losses. The women's anger knew no bounds when the misuse of the society's finance became more and more blatant. For the first time a group of 30 women workers of Bhandara mustered enough courage to question the managing committee. Chitra, an orthopaedically handicapped young woman, the only matriculate among them was their spokesperson. She drafted a letter demanding an explanation for the alleged losses and the expenditure incurred. The letter also questioned the need to remain certain employees in service. This letter signed by 30 women and handed to the managing committee at the annual General Body meeting held in October 1984 was the first jolt the committee received. The Vice-president finding himself on a sticky wicket adjourned the meeting. All those years these women who had only been workers and had been kept that way by the managing committee had now begun to assert themselves as member of the cooperative society.

When no information was forthcoming the employees of the society mooted the idea of forming a union of the bidi workers and paid staff of the society. A well known local labour lawyer, long associated with the struggle of the bidi workers, was made president. The inherent inequality of our traditional social structure which views women as incapable and inefficient to handle any position of power was reflected in the appointment of the union's office bearers. Not a single woman was made the office bearer of the union. Yet it was these very same women, who later participated actively in the demonstrations, morchas, gheraos and hunger strike and even went to jail for the brief period.

Initially the union submitted a detailed memorandum to senior officials of the cooperative department and the state Minister for the cooperation. Facts about the callous mismanagement of the society, the nepotism and corruption by the cooperative department officials running the society were submitted. They pleaded for an enquiry and intervention to help the society get reorganised. These charges were detailed out for the Chief Minister as well. The union even submitted various suggestions on how to cut losses and improve sales. In spite of the question being raised in the DPDC meeting and special meeting being called by the District Collector of the workers' representatives and the managing committee nothing came of the suggestions and proposals, except that a special audit of the accounts was ordered.

The women workers of Bhandara and Lakhni centres got activated when their centres closed in July 1986. From then onwards they were in the forefront of the struggle to save the society from closure, and to demand control over the society.

One of the main demands of the workers was that the existing managing committee should be dissolved as its terms had ended and elections should be held so that the workers members of the society could choose their own representatives. The other important demand of the women was for government help to rehabilitate this society.

With these two main demands for six months the women continuously agitated, sometime demonstrating outside the office of the Asst. Labour Commissioner, the President of the society, sometimes shouting slogans in front of the cars of the visiting ministers in order to attract their attention and even *gheraoing* the officials of the cooperative departments. For all the women this was a tremendous experience, and they completely overcame their fears and hesitations; mild mannered Ahilabai, from a protected lower-middle-class background, spontaneously learnt to argue vehemently with the management, for example.

A morcha to the Vidhan Sabha, several delegations and meetings with ministers and officials yielded nothing more than well – sounding but vague assurances. Finally when all the assurances given by the divisional and district-level cooperative department officials and the managing committee were exposed as being totally false and misleading that the women decided to sit on a relay hunger strike-cum-dharna.

It was lack of knowledge of the formal rules and complicated procedures of the cooperative laws that the women could be fooled all these days but the bureaucracy ultimately exposed itself. Yet through this process the women learnt the complex structure of the bureaucracy, and its devious ways. They learnt to identify the various ministers so that Anubai's high school going children could gasp with surprise at their mother's newly learnt ability to casually identify the ministers who were touring the town.

At the end of January 1987 the relay hunger strike-cum-dharna was launched in front of the DDR's (coops) office. The pandal for the dharna was colourful with poster exposing the deeds of the corrupt officials. A handbill explaining their misdeeds was distributed all over town. Many local people came forward to give support and even funds for the agitation. Every day the women gathered at the gate and demonstrated, while four of them sat on the 24-hour fast. Several times workers from Paraswada and Lakhni too joined the hunger fast. A militant demonstration even led to 30 of them being arrested and sent to jail for two days. Even the bravest among them were terrified when they heard they too had to go to jail. Women who had been married for over 20 years dissolved in tears at the thought of what their husbands were likely to do when they were released. Nursing mothers had to get their relatives to bring their infants to the jail to be kept with them. Yet their fears of the life behind the huge stonewall disappeared and they could recount with pride later about their trip to jail. In fact when plans for reopening of society appeared to be finalised they insisted that those who had been to jail should be the first to be given work. Contrary to the women's fears, all of them were welcomed back to their homes. This was because at this time there was support from the localities in which the women were concentrated since the struggle was viewed as a just struggle against the usurper bureaucrats. The dharna continued through the arrest and after their release.

All this had an effect and the local MLA intervened through the district palak (patron) minister. A high-level meeting with senior state-level officials of the cooperative department in the presence of the Minister and MLAs was held in Bombay in the Mantralaya. A concrete sounding decision about transferring the management of the society to a committee of local MLAs and representatives of the member Chosen by the union was agreed. A proposal for the rehabilitation of the society was to be submitted to the government on behalf of the worker-members by the union.

The 25-day long dharna was finally lifted after these decisions with the hope that the society would restart production within a couple of months.

Many of the women who had been diffident to voice their opinions in meetings, felt inhibited to come out into the streets and shouts slogans, but the momentum of the struggle had brought about a lasting change in these women so that two years after the agitation had ended, some of them have still got the jest to fight. Kisanbai Sakore, a 55-year-old Teli widow said, 'just let me know when and where the next demonstration is. I shall come even if it is in Bombay'. Women who had never gone beyond their small villages were willing to go up to Bombay to get their society restarted. Long-lasting friendship between women of the SC and non-SC developed.

Most of the women who took initiative and came forward as activists and organisers were widowed or separated. Hence they were free from the pressure of the home to some extent. The more militant ones were those who lived off this income and hence needed and valued the earnings from the society.

Determination with which these women fought deserves mention. Participation in the agitation meant a disruption of their schedules. They would do their household work, roll 'business' bidis in the night or work on somebody else's land to earn a few pennies as well as rush for meetings and demonstrations. Indu Dhurve, a young Teli widow, brimming with enthusiasm and initiative leaving her three children behind, would go from house to house gathering the women for meetings, bringing tea for the women in jail, helping to organise the necessary papers for releasing them on bail. All this with education up to mere standard four!

The agitation ended after six months of continuous effort but the reopening of the society was struck in the tangle of the bureaucratic maze, and the whims of ministers. When several months passed without any sign of the society reopening the union managed to organise a delegation of the 15 MLAs to approach the concerned Cooperative Minister to approve the proposal. He passed the proposal for rehabilitation, approved the new committee and agreed that the government would stand guarantee for bank loan. The papers went to the Chief Minister for his signature, and several months later when a delegation of the union met the Chief Minister it was informed that the CM disapproved of such a scheme of rehabilitation with such limited funds. He wanted a bigger, more comprehensive scheme applicable not merely to this society but to others as well. To pursue this further a delegation of Ministers, MLAs and a few others went on a trip to Kerala to study the success story of bidi cooperatives there. Several more proposals were sent to the CM. But then the Chief Minister and his entire cabinet had to resign and a new CM appointed. With that any plan for the revival of the society was shelved

Work in the society had been prized among bidi workers. They worked together in the Sadar; they were free from the petty harassment and exploitative tactics of contractors. They desperately wanted it to restart. While waiting for the reopening of the society the women were forced to go back to rolling bidis for private companies. They had to bear the brunt of the taunts of the contractors who hesitated to give work to these 'Zhopdi' bidi women. Some of the younger ones, like Ambar took to work on construction sites where the rate is better than for bidis, old Deolabai went picking guavas in nearby orchards and Kisbabai and Tulsabai went for work as agricultural labourers in the season. As the months passed and more and more other private companies closed down production, the women have been desperate to earn from all sorts of odd sources. While just a few managed to get permanent jobs (in the place of their dead husbands), for most life has been depressing. Kamalabai got out of the drudgery of bidi rolling. She was married off to an old railway worker who died within two months of her marriage. He has left her well provided. She lives with his college going son off his pension. All the women felt that she was lucky. Jenabai, separated from her husband many years ago, had lived with her married sister's family earning her sustenance through bidis. With Zhopdi bidi closing she rolled bidis for private companies. But when even that stopped and she found it impossible to fend for herself with the rate of ₹ 5 to 6 that business bidi rolling fetched her. She was forced to leave Bhandara and go back to her parents in some remote village. Anubai's husband, a class IV employee in the ZP died. Now she and her almost blind mother-in-law sit all day long rolling bidis in a mechanically desperate fashion to supplement the meagre pension. Kisnabai's eye sight has deteriorated. She complained that she did not get work on construction sites because they said she was too old. So she now works in fields when she can get work and rolls business bidis in the night for a contractor who lives in another village. Chitra, the educated, handicapped one, who cannot do other work but roll bidis looks bleakly at her future. The house she and her old mother built on encroached land had collapsed in the rains and they were back to a small rented room looking for contractors who would supply with enough work to sustain themselves. None of them can use the CG dispensary for bidi workers since their cards have been cancelled. These women, dispersed and tied to the exploitative grind of daily work, are no longer in a position to present their case afresh to the new CM and his ministers. The proposal lies on the shelves of the secretariat, while the hopes of the women recede with each passing month, nay year.

Response of the State to the Struggle

> 'The need for a simple and unified cooperative legislation cannot be overemphasized. The question of removing the restrictive provisions in the cooperative societies Act and giving them a democratic character has been stressed in a number of conferences including the conference of State Chief Minister held in 1968 in Madras. My feeling is that steps taken so far have not produced the desired result make the movement really democratic – with equal opportunities for all, particularly the weak and the downtrodden. There has been very little representation for the weaker sections on the committees of management even in the village based societies. On the other hand some of the state governments have enacted certain legislation which might tend to weaken the democratic character of the cooperatives'.
>
> Annasaheb Shinde,
> Minister of State for Cooperatives, January, 1973.

The manner in which the society was set up, the structure and functioning of the managing committee and the response of the government and the bureaucracy to this cooperative and to struggle of the women reveals both the undemocratic structure of the cooperative legislation and the resistance of the state to any democratisation initiated by the people.

The officials of the cooperative department in charge of the society were not particularly concerned whether this venture failed or not; it made no difference to either their jobs or their salaries. It is more enterprising among them who saw the society as a source of income for their relatives and themselves. The very spirit behind the cooperative movement, the challenge of taking on capitalist enterprises and succeeding in competition with them was lacking. To place the society under the management of those who lack time, experience and above all any interest in such a challenge shows the indifference of the state to such an attempt. Worse still, private contractors whose material interests are tied to the continuation of capitalist enterprise; in whose interest it is that such a venture should fail were the representatives of the workers in the managing committee. The government preferred to entrust ₹ 25 lakhs to such a nominated committee rather than trust the women and other worker members. The record of such nominated committee is not unknown to the state. In fact as far back as 1965 the Committee on Cooperation stated in its report, 'This practice of nomination has been going on for a long time but it cannot be said that it has been successful always. We received a number of complaints that the nominated persons did not contribute to the proper functioning of the societies on whose committees of management they served, many of them did not even attend the meetings regularly. Some of the most unsuccessful societies to which our attention was drawn has a majority of nominated directors and some even had some senior officer of the chairman'.

More revealing was the response of the state when the women workers whose interests, future and self-dignity were tied to the success of the cooperative got organised to take control of the society.

Lacking a detailed knowledge of the formal procedures in running of the cooperative, the questions raised by them at the Annual General Body Meeting could be brushed aside with impunity. The District Collector could cow down a delegation of the women workers by blaming them for not keeping a check on the managing committee over the year. The very nature of the Cooperative Act places the cooperative movement out of reach of those sections of the people who lack formal training and information about rules and procedures.

The Cooperative Act concentrates power with the Registrar and his assistants. They have the power to dissolve the managing committee or extend its term. They can remove a member or co-opt one; they can convene meetings and even convene elections; they can investigate the functioning of a society or the accounts of a society. Their wide-ranging powers can be used to serve certain interests and to suppress others.

As a result when the five-year term of the government-nominated managing committee was coming to an end in September 1986, the DDR extended the term of the managing committee. This happened in spite of the fact that concrete allegations regarding mismanagement and corruption had been raised by the employees and the MLAs. Also this was in spite of the fact that the women members had made a written application to the DDR demanding that elections be held.

Not only was the term extended but was done secretly without consulting or informing the members. Every time a delegation of the women workers went to meet the DDR regarding the holding of elections he informed them that he had written to the State Government for permission to hold elections. He said that he had no power to call for election. But finally when confronted by the women in a gherao he said that district-level elections are an expensive process, which the society with its financial crisis could ill-afford. Six months later when a compromise formula of handing over the society to another nominated committee consisting of representatives suggested by the worker members through their union and local MLAs was worked out before the guardian minister, the society had no funds left to restart!

The managing committee, the DDR and the Joint Registrar assured the women workers in the presence of the District Collector, the Cooperative and the Labour Ministers and the Commissioner of Cooperatives that they were trying for a bank loan to rehabilitate this society. But finally it was revealed through a letter of the Divisional Head – the Jt. Registrar – that there was no possibility of trying for a bank loan because they had already overdrawn ₹ 2 lakhs which had to be returned to the State Government. Obviously the managing committee, the DDR and the Jt. Registrar had colluded to hoodwink the women. For six months, through meetings, through gheraos and in deliberations with ministers the assurances about getting a bank loan had been false.

The attempt of bureaucrats was to close down the society so that all proofs of corruption would die with it. The society had been looted as long as the capital lasted. The special audit ordered by the DDR did not get far because the managing committee informed the auditors that the records had been eaten up by white ants! The indignation of the women knew no bounds. The society was theirs, the ₹ 25 lakhs had been theirs and these officials and contractors had squandered the money. It was not merely the question of losing employment, but this indignation was due to the feeling of being cheated and looted of what was theirs by right that pushed them to try to rehabilitate the society by taking it out of the control of the cooperative department officials.

Most significant of all, it was not the deviousness of the local bureaucrats taking recourse behind the book of rules to shield the corrupt that beat down the women, but the centralisation of decision-making and power with the State Cabinet that was the final blow. With centralisation comes inaccessibility. Combined with inaccessibility are the whims of those who occupy the chair. The power to decide about a government guarantee loan of less than 1 lakh for a district-level society was vested with one person, the Chief Minister. The Cooperative Minister was convinced, but he failed to convince the Chief Minister whose signature was essential. The Chief Minister wanted a grandiose scheme, but he did not last in power to see the scheme into operation. The grander the scheme got, the more it went beyond the control of the women workers and their union based in a remote corner of the state. The larger the government help proposed, the more Ministers and MLAs and other such power brokers who frequent the corridors of the Secretariat were involved and the further removed the poor unemployed women workers rolling bidis in their mud houses.

The MLAs lost interest as soon as it became evident that government money would not be forthcoming so easily. For them the needs of the private traders and big sugar cooperatives' bosses were most important. These were after all only poor women bidi workers without any influence, whose votes could be garnered through deals with the heads of their community.

The bureaucratisation of cooperative movement is a failure of democratic institutions. It is reflective of entire development strategy adopted by India in which the people have no role as participants. The women bidi workers were at the best passive recipients of state patronage. When they sought to become active they faced resistance. For the polity the lakhs of rupees squandered by callous government officials did not merit attention, but to give several thousand rupees to the women needed deliberation from the Chief Minister himself. When the women attempted to gain control over their society, they were trapped in the maze of bureaucratic procedures and suppressed by bureaucracy that utilised authoritarian powers to hide their corrupt practices. Thus they were marginalised, not merely in economic terms but also politically by a centralised policy.

Conclusions

From the experience of this cooperative bidi worker in a backward district of Maharashtra, several important conclusions can be drawn.

State policy with regard to the growth of cooperatives among the unorganised, piece-rated bidi workers has a dual character. On the one hand the state encourages the growth of cooperatives and has even given financial aid to such societies. On the other hand it leaves the societies exposed to unrestrained market forces, and they are expected to compete with well-organised private enterprises and succeed.

More important the approach of the state has been the formation of cooperatives from above through state intervention and regulation of these cooperatives by the administration. Instead of emphasising the need to mobilise from below, of involving the poor in the process of formation and management the state becomes the main agent thereby marginalising the people from this process. The 'bureaucratic stranglehold', that 'kills the cooperative spirit' (Shramshakti, 1988: 123) due to anti-cooperative laws are a result of this approach. Authority is concentrated with bureaucrats and ministers.

This approach is not an isolated phenomenon but is a part of the overall strategy of development adopted by the state in India.

Emphasis has been placed on development through capital-intensive industrialisation. But this type of industrialisation which is based on sophisticated technology has meant heavy capital investments and dependence on import of technology, which only a handful with extensive contacts and access to capital can participate in. The modernisation theory that has found favour advocates dependence on the more industrialised countries rather than encouragement to and the generation of resources – human, technical and capital – from within the country itself. It is a development from above, without mobilisation of the people.

This strategy of development has meant the growth of islands of concentrated industrialisation, the displacement of less skilled labour, of which women are an important part, on a large scale, and an inability of the modern industrial economy to absorb the lakhs who need work. Thus these lakhs remain marginalised from the mainstream of economic development and are left to fend for themselves in insecure, poorly paid unorganised sector or forced to lead a semi-proletarian existence as self-employed.

The development policies of the various Five Year Plans have emphasised the need for schemes for the upliftment of women, SC and scheduled tribes. But in fact scant attention has been paid to the problem of how the lakhs, who in fact come from these three sections, who are forced to continue in the informal sector, will be assured secure sources of livelihood. Women have been given importance in state policy primarily in their reproductive role. Therefore, focus has been on family planning and child care and marginal attention has been paid to socio-economic programmes.

While the state has enacted labour laws to guarantee a minimum wage, and other protective measures such as Maternity Benefit, the machinery set up to ensure implementation is toothless and ineffective. Violation of these laws is rampant not only in the private sector but also in the state sector. The largest employer of workers on a contract and piece-rated basis is the government departments and the public sector. Workers in the informal sector, contract and piece-rate are a source of high profits. The system has a vested interest in keeping this mass of women and men workers in this state. Women workers are the most vulnerable section.

All organised attempts to get these laws implemented have been dealt with ruthlessly by the very state that has enacted them. Therefore policies for development of workers in the informal sector notwithstanding, women workers in the unorganised sector are a neglected force, exposed to the bondage and exploitation of contractors, money lenders and the market forces.

The existing policy expects that within the framework of this strategy of development, in the midst of capitalist forces and in spite of the grip of contractors, cooperatives of unorganised women workers will thrive through bureaucratic initiative and intervention.

References

Bhandara District Census Handbook. 1981. Progress Annual Report of the Bhandara Zilla Bidi Kamgar Sahakari Sanstha. Government of Maharashtra (1985).

Bhatty, Zarina. 1981. *The Economic Role and Status of Women in the Beedi Industry in Allahabad, India*. Geneva: ILO.

Government of India. 1977. *Towards Equality*. Report of the Committee on the Status of Women in India, New Delhi: Department of Social Welfare, Ministry of Education and Social Welfare.

Prasad, E.K.V. and Prasad, Anuradha. 1985. *Bidi Workers of Central India: A Study of Production Process and Working and Living Conditions*. New Delhi: National Labour Institute.

Report of the Royal Commission on Labour in India. 1931. Calcutta: Central Publication Branch, Government of India.

Shramshakti. 1988. Report of the National Commission on Self-Employed Women and Women in the Informal Sector. New Delhi: Ministry of Women and Child Welfare, Government of India.

9

Political Economy of Female Migrant Labour

The Case of Jari Workers in Surat

Suguna Pathy

Seventeenth-century direction of progress with regard to science and technology indeed has become a hurdle, as modern science views fact in isolation of values. The apparent reductionist perception fragments the sphere of study reflecting the colonial path of development even after political independence. The emergence of monolithic concept of nation-state is one such historical condition. The transition to democracy became a narrative of the *exclusion of women* without space. However, as a result of various struggles of women across the world the last decade witnessed a space of global conferences on concerned issues such as environment (Rio), human rights (Vienna), social development (Copenhagen) and population (Cairo) culminating in the Fourth World Conference on Women in Beijing on the theme of empowerment of women. World nations agreed for Common Action in Beijing to address the burning issues affecting women. In this context, the UN Secretary General's report on the status of women in 1999 observed that women are placed at the lower end in policy-making agencies with little influence on overall planned programmes, while gender insensitivity and inherent *a priori* notions, lack of financial access and information, and so on block the entry for women. Millennium Declaration at the UN Millennium Summit was unanimously adopted by about 189 countries (India is one among them) to create global partnership in development. The fact, however, is that we are complacent with paradoxes, idiosyncrasies and contradictions. Despite unparallel success in science and technology, we have collectively failed in the field of human relations and social justice. Today, the social fabric is fragmented more than ever before with mounting inequalities between and among states, classes, communities and men and women. At the outset, it implies social injustice marked by unequal power equation terminating into marginalisation augmenting the very survival and dignity of the people. While the achievements in economic growth and human development have been significant, the gaps in social security with regard to poverty, malnutrition, gender concerns, child survival, increasing old-age population, widows, and child labour, more so, are alarming contradictions of capitalism in South Asia. Worse is, this region is fast emerging as the poorest, the most illiterate, the most malnourished and the least gender sensitive in the world (Haq, 1997). Currently globalism is marked by unprecedented movement of goods and services, capital and labour between and among regions – a clear road map of corporate capitalism, a techno-economic and politico-ideological project.

In the ensuing pages, we make an effort to understand the issues central to female migration in the unorganised sector from the wider matrix spelled above. This is only a brief note of a larger part of our study of female migrant jari workers in the unorganised powerloom industry of Surat in which a sample of 500 Telugu female workers engaged in jari textile work and domestic labour, that is both paid and unpaid were interviewed randomly. We collected data through personal interview schedule comprising general information on household census, demographic composition and social background of the female workers. Besides, qualitative data are collected through personal interviews, informal group as well as individual discussions with the women workers. We also used participant observation and other related anthropological techniques for data collection. On sensitive issues pertaining to very private, special confidence generating efforts were made to share their experiences. The entire process of field work was carried out in 6 months and we wish to clarify that the methodology we adopted is largely qualitative than quantitative. In this connection, it is essential to mention at the very outset that we did not face otherwise usual problems in data collection as the author has the privilege of working with the workers in general and women workers in particular on related social concerns. Indeed, I humbly acknowledge the larger effects of people's struggles on my world view and priorities in life. However, the exercise invariably suffers from the alienation of the author from the masses and, hence, the apparent shortfalls in the present chapter.

In due course of history, Surat embraced ongoing changes in economy, polity and culture to its fold manifesting a composite configuration to the city. The demographic profile of Surat subsequently has undergone considerable changes. There has been a continuous flow of migrant labour to the silk city as Surat is known (as well as city of diamonds where child labour is the predominant ingredient) since decades on. The estimated population of Surat according to 2001 census is 30 lakhs, out of which migrant labour constitute 12 lakhs. It has the fastest growth rate of population in the country. The migrants in Surat hail largely from different states such as Orissa, Andhra Pradesh, Uttar Pradesh, Maharashtra and Bihar. Steady pace of industrialisation and the industrial policy of the state recorded an increasing number of industries attracting a large workforce from various states. In the entire process of labour movement, family is used to reproduce and socialise labour, while the wages are used for family's needs.

The Problem

Women constitute 50 per cent of the total humankind and a major share of workforce. Despite their total involvement in production, their work is undervalued and unnoticed overall and also in researches. More often women are perceived as for household not only by men but also by women due to patriarchal internalisation processes.

Though there are several studies on women and migration in general and in South Asia in particular, the trend does not tally with the increasing extent of migration of women particularly since the last decades. Barring a few exceptions, migration phenomenon in South Asia has been researched largely from the male notion with the result female migration has largely been ignored, or treated as uninteresting because much of this movement, given the practice of village exogamy is considered as 'marriage migration' (Schenk-Sandbergen, 1995: 10). Thus, the female side of migration is left out of analysis, which is central to the process of articulation of unorganised labour with capitalism. Accordingly, large number of migration studies centre the research confining to male rural–urban labour movement, assuming women as appendages. Needless to point the apparent negligence of gender dimension in the concerned works. In the final analysis, gender scope on migration and arrangements of men and women eventually imply the changes in political economy at large.

Be that as it may we seek to understand the pattern of articulation of unorganised sector with the domestic work of women of the migrant households. Exactly as the production and reproduction of labour power takes place within the family through the labour of women and thus her labour is a vital generator of surplus value as our study of Telugu female jari workers of the migrant households reveal. In this connection, it may be mentioned that female migration to Surat like any other place is coordinated by social arrangements of marriage. Therefore, we argue that not just the male labour moves but equally so female labour as both husband and wife move out of their native place. Perhaps due to inherent bias some might argue this as male migration – primarily. However, we reiterate that the present study clearly indicates that it is equally female migration along with men in the household. The changes in different modes of production influence the pattern of kinship structures, which ultimately define the position of women in the whole process of production and reproduction. The dynamics of household organisation in conjunction with the formal (paid) and informal (unpaid) economies and social relations in production ultimately determine kinship pattern. Labour is reproduced through the institution of family and monogamous marriage. Here, patriarchal system controls fertility and the sexuality of women, while social relations of production are reproduced through religion as well as religious fundamentalism, educational system (re-writing of history), family and mass media. The emergence of market economy and the subsequent changes in the organisation of production has direct bearings on the organisation of households and family structures. In pre-capitalist societies kinship system serve as both economic and cultural determinant and the link between agrarian and industrial structures continues under such conditions. The advent of market exchange ultimately determine the structural process of household in terms of politico-economic and intra- and inter-households within the community. Who does what in the family is regulated by tradition and by class position as distribution of work within the family depends on labour market. Thus, social reproduction becomes household activity involving entire network of kin relations (Goody, 1972). We submit that housework generates and augments surplus value in capitalism (Rapp, 1978; Vogel, 1979; Zaretsky, 1976). In most of the Third World countries, age and sex constitute prime categories of division of labour enforcing interdependence of family labour, which is legitimised and perpetuated by specific set of norms in turn ensuring gender identities. Accordingly gender-based works incorporate assessment of their social value, legitimising the unequal distribution of the products of labour in the household (Roberts, 1981). In this process, the question of women's right for self-determination of her sexuality is completely ignored by lending social explanations. No wonder barring a few migration researches assume that the world consists wholly of men and that women are extras. Indeed in cultural representation of gender diversities in the society, only one gender seems to represent both part and whole. Everyday language usage amply reflects this contents; for instance 'man' and 'humanity' become synonymous, while women never become general, never universal, but are only particular, only located in relation to men (Pathy, 2000). By and large, social scientists analyse women as objects in the process of social transformation.

The Dynamics of Female Migrant Labour

As we notice from our data that migrant women participate in paid employment since in unorganised sector male wages are insufficient to ensure the survival, which necessitates pooling of resources from the other family members to support the household economy. In this connection, we noticed that by the very nature of better wages, men dominates in the family, while low female wages subordinate them, although if counted unpaid domestic labour of women by far exceeds (Table 9.1).

The table reveals that 66 per cent of the female workforce from the sample suffers from severe back pain, dwindling eye sight and mental and physical strain besides other routine health disorders such as cold and fevers, headache, jaundice, gastroenteritis, anaemia and so on, not only due to improper imbalance of food intake but also because of their own negligence of their health due to lack of time and long hours of work. Meanwhile it is a fact that by and large all women particularly in the Third World countries neglect their own health and other personal concerns vis-à-vis the rest in the family. Perhaps this may be due to the very socialisation process of women that 'others first than self' and second, due to the strong hold of pre-capitalist relations of production. In this connection, it may be mentioned that domestic work by and large has four attached assumptions dividing both the sexes: (i) economic dependence through marriage a common stereotype; (ii) exclusive allocation of work to women; (iii) its subsequent status as unproductive work and (iv) primacy to women only, that is priority over other roles (Oakley, 1974). Accordingly domestic work carries cultural and social dimensions that are assumed of having sacrificial and pleasure dimension socially and survival culturally (Benston, 1969). By the very notion, the domestic work denotes irrationality and its cultural importance as the whole domestic work stands in violent contrast to the rest of the occupations (Caplan, 1954). Domestic work contributes to surplus value as it is part of social production (Table 9.2).

Table 9.1 *Distribution of Female Workforce in the Sample*

S. No.	Work Category	Number of Workers	% of Workers	Work Hazards
1.	Home-based production (Paid labour + domestic work*) Jari work, making plastic bags Lace bags and bidi rolling	330	66	Poor eye sight Back pain + stress and strain
2.	Market production (Paid labour + domestic work*) Winding (textiles)	150	30	Back pain + strain
3.	Only domestic work* (Unpaid labour) Cooking, cleaning, washing, fetching water, rationing from PDS, nursing the sick, etc.	20	04	Back pain + strain
	Total	500	100	

*Domestic work refers to cooking; cleaning; utensil washing; washing clothes; sweeping; fetching water; caring the sick, children and the aged; daily marketing and so on.

Table 9.2 *Wages, Economic Participation and Allocation of Time*

Work	Wages in ₹ P/D	Nature of Production	Time in Hours
Jari work + DW	15	Home based	3–5+5 DW
Winding + DW	35–50	Factory based	8+5 DW
Making of plastic and lace bags, bidis, etc. + DW	15–20	Home based	3–5+5 DW
Only domestic work	Unpaid labour	Home based without exchange value	7–9

Note: DW denotes domestic work (unpaid labour).

The table reveals the co-existence of paid labour and unpaid labour in the household unit in capitalism, which in turn reflects the social relations and production and reproduction and how it is being reproduced. Besides it also implies, the existence of unorganised and that too female workforce with cheap production cost for the advantage of capitalism, as all the economic activities excluding winding job in the sample take place at home. During the fieldwork, we noticed that there is no leisure time for the female workers who are with home-based production, which means only work all day. This necessarily means low wages, unspecified long hours and tedious work in tandem with unending domestic drudgery for women. In this context, we argue that the unpaid domestic labour of women generates the paid labour force (both men and women) that is necessary for the maintenance of capitalism. Our data also show that an average woman work more than 10 hours per day. It needs to be mentioned that several qualitative tasks performed by them could not be quantified. If we include these works on crude estimates, the number of work hours would go beyond 15 hours schedule per day.

The analysis of labour supply to the market by way of the theory of demand for leisure time and hours of work in the market constitutes an exhaustive dichotomy. Accordingly the logical compliment to leisure time is work broadly construed, whether it includes remunerative production in the market or work that is currently unpaid. The latter includes various forms of investments in oneself, the production of goods and services for home and family. Work at home is an activity to which women on an average denote the larger part of their married life and thus it becomes an exclusive work of many women. We observed in our study that the total amount of work performed both at home and outside is an outcome of family demand. Meanwhile, we also noticed that increased family income does not mean decrease of total hours of work at home.

Regardless of the differences on the question of domestic labour, there are some important concerns where we can come to an agreement. Often it is assumed that the payment made by capital to labour is based on the existence of certain value of domestic work and state services. The influence of capital is such that in the presence of domestic labour, the wage is lower than it would have been: if the working-class family would depend on purchased commodities. Thus, the surplus labour is extracted from the domestic work and ultimately transformed into surplus value (Humphries, 1971). However, we should not over generalise the role of capital exclusively without relations of production and class antagonisms theoretically or else we would trip on technological determinism (Tables 9.3A and 9.3B).

Tables 9.3A and 9.3B point out the bifurcation of different essential household activities that are necessary for daily survival and maintenance of the family. We wish to state clearly that unpaid labour tasks are exclusively performed by women largely. The time required for each work only shows approximation and this we deduced through umpteen talks, observations and through cross-checking during data collection. Nonetheless, we admit the apparent arbitrariness in calculating time due to the sensitive nature of work, internationalisation process and the limitation of time from the respondents. Second, we did not include child care and nursing the sick, exclusively personal works related to health, aesthetics, leisure and other activities, which are qualitative in nature and certainly cannot be quantified mechanistically. We see from Table 9.3-B that though all women work in all types, the major tasks have been cooking (95%) followed by the most tedious job of getting rations (80%) particularly kerosene oil, sugar and rice. More often women have to stand in long queue irrespective of whether only in vain, as the shopkeeper does not give proper time. Besides the shopkeeper carries the ration distribution slowly and often many women after standing several hours have to return with empty cans with bitter feelings. During this standing session, they exchange and share their concerns, pains and pleasures on several issues ranging from dowry-related murders particularly among the Telugu migrants, besides various forms of prevalent domestic violence, the conflicts in the household, the happenings in their native place and so on to other issues such as movies, festival preparations, chit fund activities, buying ornaments or consumer items and so on. Furthermore, we also notice that the labour-intensive but cheap production cost work based on home production (66%) exploits female workforce as the readily available cheap unorganised labour gets integrated to the capitalist market locally and globally. At the face of it, the most labour-intensive and time- and health-consuming domestic work does not seem to have exchange value directly. However, it enters indirectly through the relations of reproduction. Meanwhile, it is worth to note the role of home-based production, which is threefold: (i) restriction of women's mobility, a sort of segregation at work, (ii) increase in the rate of domestic work almost without any time for self and above all resulting in deterioration of women's health and (iii) finally, inducing in the minds that it is not an important economic activity and creating and enhancing notion, of dependency on the men. Precisely, as many as 66 per cent of the women interviewed are engaged in this poorly paid home-based economic activity stated that they 'do no work' but perform only housework. Besides this 'only housework' is so internalised by the women that they do not consider it work at all and on the contrary they see it as a part of womanhood. *Ergo* home-based production not only strengthens patriarchy but also reinforces on the one hand and integrates these home-based female workers to capitalist mode on the other hand. This clearly specifies that patriarchy is not autonomous as some would make us think.

Table 9.3A *Bifurcation of Domestic Work*

Work	*Approximate Time (in hours)*
Cooking	1
Cleaning (sweeping, mopping and washing utensils)	1½
Washing clothes	1½
Fetching water	1½
Fetching rations from PDS (Fair Price Shop)	2½
Child care and nursing the sick*	Varies and unlimited as the work involved is qualitative
Total	8

* Excluded from the total amount of time

Table 9.3B *Distribution of the Sample According to the Bifurcation of Work*

I			*II*			*III*		
Domestic Work/Unpaid Labour Respondents	*Number of Respondents*	*%*	*Home-based Production Paid Labour*	*Number of Respondents*	*%*	*Market Production Paid Labour*	*Number of Respondents*	*%*
1. Cooking	450	95	Jari work	180	36	Winding	150	30
2. Cleaning (sweeping, mopping & washing utensils)	300	60	Making plastic and lace bags and rolling 'bidis'	150	30			
3. Washing clothes	300	60						
4. Fetching water	350	67						
5. Fetching ration	400	80						
6. Care of the child and sick	cannot quantify							

Note: (a) The sample distribution with regard to domestic work invariably overlaps.
(b) Only domestic work category of work (20-see Table 9.1) is covered under Category I.

Market Value of Female Labour

It is a fact that some labour is necessary to safeguard the survival of the family to which the individual belongs as Marx aptly calls as 'the ensemble of the social relations' (Marx, 1967: 7). Accordingly it implies that labour has to relate to the maintenance and reproduction of the individual in certain definite relationships. This requires some surplus labour over and above necessary labour, which is present in all modes of production. This way domestic labour has use value encompassing the socially necessary labour time to secure the conditions of reproduction in all social formation. But in capitalism the domestic labour becomes isolated and this separation renders it invisible and valueless. Thus, the unequal relations between men and women reinforce the differences between sexual division of labour in the market. And therefore the productivity of wage labour rises in relative terms with domestic work by strengthening the unequal relations among the skilled and semi-skilled workers, which is further pushed by the domestic work (Humphries, 1971). Therefore, proletarianisation of some family members becomes imperative for survival. As is evident from Tables 9.3-A and 9.3-B, both wage workers and domestic workers participate in the exchange of activities and services. As mentioned, domestic labour is separated from the means of exchange and therefore becomes invisible and distinct from the wages work.

Relations of dominance and subordination pertaining to age, sex and division of labour exist within the family. This by no means denotes either glorification or idealisation of family. Meanwhile the gender-based works such as cooking, cleaning, washing, child care, and so on incorporate cultural assessment of their social value resulting in legitimisation of unequal distribution of the products of labour in the household.

Table 9.4 *Exchange of Labour in the Market (P/M)*

Wages in ₹	*Winding Work*	*%*	*Jari Works*	*%*	*Making Bags and Bidis*	*%*
400–600	–	–	40	22.22	80	53.33
600–800	20	13.33	120	66.67	60	40.0
800–1,000	35	23.33	20	11.11	10	6.67
1,000–1,200	80	53.33	–	–	–	–
1,200–1,400	15	10.0	–		–	–
>1,400	–	–	–	–	–	–
Total	150	100.0	180	100.0	150	100.0

Note: Out of 500 sample 20 respondents perform only domestic work which cannot be exchanged in the market.

Table 9.4 points out that even in paid labour category, direct market-related labour has favourable exchange value than those who enter the labour via households. Thus, 80 workers earn between ₹ 1,000 and 1,200 per month, while 55 of them earn ranging from ₹ 600 to 1,000 per month prove the market value of the labour. On the contrary, the home-based worker's earnings start from only ₹ 400 and reach below ₹ 800 per month. Only about 30 workers manage to earn between ₹ 800 and 1,000 rarely. We reiterate that these home-based works are not only labour intensive but also time consuming. The complex part of these works is their adjustment or combining with the domestic work as more often women jointly perform both the works at the same time. For instance, while cooking or waiting to fetch water or standing in the queue for ration before the public distribution shop they do lace works and other related works that have exchange value. So we argue that money value for the paid work is derived from the time value of the unpaid work. Second, we also hold that this kind of labour process deprive the people of thinking and reflecting and divert their objectives to market direction. Both the arguments hold true for the direct market labour too. Thus,

Exchange value for market and home production	=	Non-exchange value of domestic labour + exchange value of market labour.
Therefore, paid labour value	=	Unpaid labour time + paid labour time

Accordingly, domestic labour is socially reproductive labour expended in the context of domestic unit. Hence, it is essential to understand the mechanism of articulation of domestic labour with different modes of production (Caplan and Bujra, 1978). Here lies the context of domestic labour and its articulation with the mode of production and it may be argued that domestic labour is socially productive as paid labour value is derived from the combination of unpaid labour time and paid labour time. At the very outset, it is daily labour expended in cooking, cleaning, washing, child care and so on. Besides through existing ideologies children are socialised in such a way as to articulate domestic labour to the relations of production.

Thus, women's labour particularly in working-class family serves in two ways by producing and generating socially necessary labour force and corresponding relations of capitalism. The correlation between the wage level and working class living conditions depends on purchased commodities and on household activity. For, wages have to be transformed into the use values consumed in the home, a transformation embodying a considerable time. It may be recalled once again that our sample of female workers hail from the Telugu-speaking industrial labour who have migrated from Andhra Pradesh. As many as 350 respondents' husband or father/brother (70%) own below two acres of dry land with poor remuneration, while 150 (30%) do not own any agricultural land. They were supplementing their income through available agricultural labour before their migration to Surat.

It may be noted here that none of the women in our sample own any land as the property ownership rights are male based largely. However, widows do inherit ownership rights, but we do not have any widows in our sample.

Indebtedness and Migration

The family has social relations network based on genealogical relationships that needs to be produced and sustained by social practices reinforcing reciprocal kinship relations. In this context, we come across studies holding that 'lines of class division and conflict run between but not through families' and that 'the position of the family as a whole within the system of stratification ... deprives from that of the family "head" the separation of sex roles within the family ... being itself the expression of a major form of inequality existing between the sexes' (Goldthorpe, 1983: 468–469). Family is not an organic whole, but a hierarchical system. Kinship and parenthood are not natural but are essentially social institutions. Therefore, in actuality it is not possible to analyse sexuality without relating to the political economy within which it is embedded. In other words, we cannot understand sexuality as a concept without contextualising as sexual practices do not exist in a vacuum and thus cannot escape the cultural set. Precisely as 'what people want and what they are made to want and allowed to do' (Caplan, 1954: 25). Sexual identities are culturally and historically specific and are relational and are about our relationships to ourselves, precarious unities of conflicting desires and social commitments 'composed of heterogeneous fragments of fossilized cultures' (Gramsci, 1975: 213). Identity is historically contingent, seemingly inevitable, potentially limiting and politically essential. To reiterate, sexual identities are encoded in a complex web of social practices – legal, pedagogic and personal. In a world of widening inequalities and injustice, there exists unequal relations between men and women and any imagination sans inequality is next to impossible under the given conditions of political economy.

More often the spouses of the migrants supplement the survival and the other household requirements in order to meet the escalating urban cost of living. It is essential to note here that without women's work (paid) it is difficult to manage the household in urban areas and therefore women's paid labour besides unpaid labour forms an important factor in the reproduction of industrial capital. Besides, other family members of the migrants also work to ensure the survival of the household. Besides, the textile industry is shrinking since recently resulting in closure of sick units and also reduction in work days due to frequent strikes by the owners and the workers and power cuts. Thus, the approximate number of paid work days would be between 20 and 22 days per month. Therefore, women's contribution is all the more crucial for the family survival in Surat and hence we argue for equal weightage for women's labour, although their earnings are at low level than the earning of the men in the family. Besides as mentioned earlier, not only their paid work but also the unpaid domestic labour jointly forms an integral part of industrial capitalism. Meanwhile about hundred respondents invest on chit fund through which they buy necessary items for the family such as consumer goods, furniture and also clear their debts both in Surat and in the village. We found that as many as 450 of the respondents (90%) spend their earnings for the maintenance of the family unit in different ways.

Our data reveal that 450 households in the sample are indebted ranging from ₹ 3,000 to ₹ 18,000 to the moneylender in the village in Andhra Pradesh (Table 9.5), while 50 households do not have any debts in the village and are creditors to friends and relatives in Surat. Main reasons for debt are survival and dowry as most of the respondents hail from small peasant and agricultural labouring classes. More often they mortgage small pieces of land to the village landlord-cum-moneylender. We found that one of the major factors of migration to Surat is indebtedness followed by less work opportunities and irregular and low income.

Table 9.5 *Debt Pattern of the Households in the Sample*

Reasons	*Amount (in ₹)*							
	<5,000		*5,001–10,000*		*10,001–20,000*		*Total*	
	No.	*%*	*No.*	*%*	*No.*	*%*	*No.*	*%*
Food	150	33.33	–	–	–	–	150	33.33
Marriage	20	4.44	50	11.11	60	13.33	130	28.88
House repair/construction	–	–	20	4.44	70	15.55	90	19.99
Social obligations	50	11.11	–	–	–	–	50	11.11
Health	5	1.11	5	1.11	10	2.22	20	4.44
Others	2	0.44	8	1.77	–	–	10	2.22
Total	227	50.43	83	18.43	140	31.10	450	99.96

The table shows that about 50 per cent of the sample households are in debt of below 5,000 largely for food and social customs associated with post-marriage customs, birth and death besides sickness of relatives and friends while the maximum debt range indicates that about 31 per cent are in debt of below ₹ 20,000 towards marriage expenses, mostly involving dowry followed by house repair or construction, respectively. The data also show that only two households took loan below 5,000 for sending their children to college education to a nearby town, in Andhra Pradesh, while eight took loan to purchase two-wheeler (Luna) and to open a petty grocery shop in the village. Largely, the continuous debt trap compels the people to migrate to industrial cities such as Surat. Here it may be noted that women migrated to Surat through marriage, as men migrate first and after securing regular job as weavers in the textile sector would bring their spouse to the city. And it is here women's labour needs to be recognised as her contribution is a determining factor in the production of capital. Therefore, we reiterate that although women are not prime migrants as men *per se*, their participation as *indirect working class, but are migrants* like their men as our data reveal, is an essential feature of capitalism in Third World societies. We term indirect because the women workers as in our sample are related to the production process indirectly through their unpaid domestic labour and directly through paid labour to the market, while their male counterparts have direct relations of production. Precisely chores such as cleaning, cooking, washing, nurturing, and so on are generally understood to be the part and parcel of female work. Domestic work is more intertwined, inseparable and invisible from the paid work in the household. Sexual division of labour within a class in the sexual division of resources, changes in the sex resource base affects either increasing or decreasing of resources in the class (Leacock, 1979). Therefore, it is necessary to understand the interrelations between production and reproduction as part of a single process and it is essential to explore relationship of family with the socio-economic and political processes under capitalism.

Closely related to the structural mechanism of women's labour in the market and family is the violence against women both within the household and at workplace. Our qualitative data reveal that nearly all the respondents are subjected to various types of violence ranging from verbal abuse, humiliation of the person and her family (parental if married), restricting her movements and so on, resulting in physical abuse. The reasons for the violence at the outset are broadly economic and social. The former relates to the oppressive system of exploitation of working class by capitalism where the workers are alienated from the means of production. The latter reflects the unequal relations between men and women and are constantly reproduced culminating in the perpetual subordination of women in society. In other words violence is the extreme manifestation of extreme inequality that serves the system in different ways. In the family, the very social fabric of male domination denies equal access to women. However, we argue that trans-historical subordination of women varies according to specific historical conjunctions. For, the reproduction of labour power revolves around sexual division of labour within specific modes of production. The family reproduces relations of ideology and relations of production because in the family property relations become the historical expression between men and women.

The regulation of female sexuality is carried with utmost social legitimacy. The informal discussions with the respondents and our observation during investigation reveal that the women who have internalised social mores like to be passive, obedient and tolerant of the violence (physical and other forms such as abuse and humiliation) to be stoical and bear all kinds of discrimination. It may be mentioned that the women's body invariably forms the content and form of the abuse, whether the contradiction is between men and women or between and among men. Sexual abuses are collective and receive social sanctions. Women have been butt of male ridicule in proverbs and myths alike in insulting women's bodies, mocking their mental capacities. Thus, she is not spared even in abuses!

Conclusion

To wind up the foregoing analysis, we hold that women as domestic labourers perform the double task of reproduction, viz., social and biological; however, this reproduction is not necessarily oppressive uniformly. The structuring of social relations inhibits or slows or blurs the collective consciousness and finally contributes to the oppression of women. In an oppressive and class-ridden society, objective consciousness of domestic labour does not necessarily transform into subjective consciousness because domestic labour is not specific to the reproduction of one class but to the reproduction of opposing classes. Historically, gender-based subordination has curtailed women's access and control to resources and labour power and imposed sexual division of labour. However, the subordination of women varies across region, classes and castes in time and space. In the ultimate analysis, women have to struggle.

In this context, local women's group is relentlessly working since a decade to unite and organise the women migrant workers through *conscientisation* process. With the result there is a considerable political and social awareness among the women today; a renewed confidence to address and negotiate their issues with the traders (*sethias*) in jari work. They organise systematically during protests for demanding better wages or demonstration against sexual harassment or any type of violence on women including domestic violence, dowry and divorce-related matters. The emergence of local leadership from among them is a matter of satiety for the women's group, a *small-big* step in the larger women's movement towards transformation. Interestingly, most of the migrant labourers from Andhra Pradesh hail from politically conscious region with the experience of mass organisation. Therefore, it is not surprising to hear their perceptions on political concerns, unequal relations between men and women, exploitation of working class, communalism and terms such as imperialism and feudalism and so on, though 95 per cent of them are illiterates. The author is grateful to these women, the symbols of struggle and commitment for enlightening and clearing middle-class conceptions. The tenor in the present outline reiterates the power of women in liberation. The urgent need is to restructure the policies and reconstitute governance towards justice and social equity to humankind. In this context it is essential to probe the effects of globalisation on the social fabric as a whole. We hold that globalisation is a political, economic and cultural package. In this process transnational corporations not only cause irreversible damage to the environment but also generate social conflicts within the communities. For instance, the adverse effects on the ecosystem results in shortage of drinking water, food, fuel and loss of common property. It has far-reaching implications for the underprivileged especially women, particularly in the agricultural sector as women comprise a large chunk of agricultural workforce. In addition, cuts in food subsidies aggravate unequal allocation of food for women and girls, shrinking livelihood patterns due to tailored globalisation scheme not only intensifies gendered and andro-centric notions of female labour but also accentuates prostitution and trafficking of women ending at the gates of HIV. Thus, it sounds that the prevailing trend of globalisation and marketisation of governance is far from sustainable. This is a challenge to the women's movement and various progressive organisations to reassert governance for social transformation.

References

Benston, T. 1969. 'The Political Economy of Women's Liberation'. *Monthly Review*, 21(4), September: 13–27, reprinted in Ellen Malos (ed.) 1980. *The Politics of Housework*. London: Allison and Busby.

Caplan, P. and Bujra, J.M. (eds) 1978. *Women United and Women Divided*. London: Tavistock.

Caplan, T. 1954. *The Sociology of Work*. New York: McGraw Hill.

Goldthorpe, J.H. 1983. 'Women and Class Analysis: In Defence of the Conventional View'. *Sociology*, 17(4): 465–488.

Goody, J. 1972. 'Domestic Groups'. *Addison-Wesley Modules in Anthropology*, 28: 1–32.

Gramsci, A. 1975. *Selections from the Prison Notebook*. London: International Publishers.

Haq, M. Ul 1997. *Reflections on Human Development*. London: Longman.

Humphries, J. 1971. 'Class Struggle and the Persistence of the Working Class Family'. *Cambridge Journal of Economics*, 1(3): 241–258.

Leacock, E. 1979. 'Women's Development and Anthropological Facts and Fictions', in C.D. Deere (ed.), *Women in Latin America*. Riverside: Latin American Press.

Marx, K. 1967. *Capital*. Vol. 1. New York: Internal Publishers.

Oakley, A. 1974. *The Sociology of Housework*. New York: Pantheon Books.

Pathy, Suguna. 2000. *Sexual Division of Labour: The Engendered Labour Dynamics in the Textile Industry of Surat* (Mimeo). Surat: South Gujarat University.

Rapp, Rayna. 1978. 'Family and Class in Contemporary America: Notes Towards Understanding and Ideology'. *Science and Society*, 42 (3): 278–300.

Roberts, P. 1981. 'The Sexual Politics of Labour in Western Nigeria and Hausa Nigeria', in K. Young (ed.), *Serving Two Masters: Third World Women in Development*. New Delhi: Allied Publishers.

Schenk-Sandbergen, Loes (ed.) 1995. *Women and Seasonal Labour Migration*. New Delhi: Sage.

Vogel, L. 1979. 'Questions on the Women's Question'. *Monthly Review*, 31(2): 39–59.

Zaretsky, E. 1976. *Capitalism, the Family and Personal Life*. New York: Harper & Row.

10

The New Economic Policy and Women

A Rural Perspective

Gail Omvedt and Chetna Gala

Introduction: Hopes and Fears

The proclamation of a 'new economic policy' (NEP) by the Narasimha Rao Government in 1991 sent shock waves throughout the country. After a gruelling election campaign dominated by slogans of 'Mandir, Mandal and Stability', this turn to a market-oriented economic policy took the nation by surprise. Since then, an increasing wave of 'reforms' has continued to produce a feeling of being buffeted by unexplainable forces. Quite understandably, many have seen the World Bank and International Monetary Fund (IMF) as the source of change. There has been much anxiety, many promises, even more predictions of dire gloom; informed debate has been at a minimum. This is especially true in the women's movement.

Both hopes and fears are raised in discussions on economic policy. Those who see hope stress the openness of the situation, the removal of the oppression and corruption represented by the 'license-permit Raj'. The Indian economy is said to be a 'caged tiger', held down for so long by bureaucratic inefficiencies, a plaything for politicians and bureaucrats; free it from these and it can surge forward in the world like the tigers of Southeast Asia (and now China). An admittedly painful period of adjustment may be needed to introduce efficiency and market capability in the economy, but basically its healthy growth can come only from being released from bureaucratic fetters. Even if the overstaffed pampered organised sector employees suffer, export-oriented growth will aid employment in informal sector and rural-based industries, including agriculture. India and its poor can only benefit from being integrated in the global economy.

But voices expressing fears have been louder. The spectre of price rise, unemployment and increased MNC takeover is held up. Export oriented agriculture, it is argued, will lead to a loss of 'food security' and an increase in malnutrition with 'cash crops' displacing 'food crops'. Women, it is said, will suffer the most since they are at the bottom anyway. Even if some growth of employment takes place in small industries and commercial agriculture, this will aid rich farmers and men will displace women in more lucrative jobs. Overall, a picture of an increasingly disabled economy is projected, indebted, impoverished, dependent and polarised.

Beyond their specific critiques of the NEP, opponents seem trapped in the crash of hopes of self-reliant socialist development. In the context of bewildering changes in the heartlands of socialism, the turn towards a market economy is interpreted to mean that the capitalist market is taking over completely, that this means the end of the state. And the state in countries like India has been projected as a liberating force. Metaphors of we are losing control of things 'abound, with the feeling that either foreign imperialism or an impersonal market economy, giving priority to profit over human values, is completely dominating events'. According to political commentators such as Rajni Kothari, nothing is left but a 'yawning vacuum'.

These fears (and the hopes) cannot be simply dismissed; they have to be thoroughly and soberly examined. Much of the extreme pessimism about a turn to a market economy strikes us as the fears of an upper class, urban-centred elite, which has controlled the Indian state and the Indian economy for so long that it cannot imagine anything else, an elite for which recognition of the laws of the market represents a loss of the power, which was masked under the veils of 'socialist' and 'anti-poverty' rhetoric. Nevertheless, there is no reason to put faith in the present power holders promoting the NEP in the monopoly money makers (foreign or Indian) looking to move in. There is a need not only to look at specific aspects of economic policy, but also to reexamine the nature of 'market' and 'state' (and possible alternatives to both). This chapter is a small effort to do that.

We would like to take the perspective of rural women, and especially agricultural labourer, peasant, low caste, Dalit women. Much of the critique of the NEP given by women's movement activists (whether feminist or party linked) is really from the perspective of middle-class urban women. For example, the talk about unemployment almost always looks at loss of employment in the urban and organised sector: it is said that women will lose these jobs and be forced into the unorganised sector. Movement of industry out of Bombay is seen as a loss, with arguments that this means exploitation of cheap labour. However, from the perspective of rural poor women, the question is not that of an organised sector job, as there were hardly any of these jobs in any case; the question is whether the economy will expand to provide some kind of employment at all, even if it is low paid and insecure by Bombay organised sector standards; and the question is whether markets and employment will grow in the village or nearby towns.

Similarly, most of the talk about food security looks at the issue only in terms of the availability of PDS rations, and there is a constant invocation of 'cash crops' replacing 'food crops' that ignores agricultural realities. Rural women would see the issue in terms of how much food is actually being grown, what are prices and weather conditions, and how much role they can have in producing the food. The urban bias in the discussions on PDS is also shown when people argue that it is too costly and complex to 'target' PDS to the poor; these are the same people, generally, who have always argued for excluding the 'creamy layer' from the Mandal Commission and excluding objections to targeting. There seems to be an element of self-interest involved here, along with a perhaps wilful ignorance of what it has meant to maintain a policy of providing cheap food for all sections of the population.

Examining the NEP from the perspective of the rural poor means asking specific kind of questions. In terms of employment, for example, we are not only interested in whether companies are retrenching – male workers to hire female workers at lower pay, but also interested in whether there will be a creation of new jobs in the economy, particularly in the rural areas. In looking at the issue of economic self-reliance, we will ask not only whether India can grow enough food to feed itself, but also whether it can establish a form of agricultural production – and an overall production system – which minimises fossil fuel and costly industrial inputs and thus can minimise the imports. We do not care much about whether people are driving Bajaj or Vespa scooters, but we do care about whether we can minimise the development of a road/automobile economy. We are not concerned about whether people will be drinking Pepsi or Thums Up, using Colgate or Vicco toothpaste; we want to focus instead on the strengthening of an economy based on local products and local markets and a production system that relies primarily on renewable energy sources. We are not only concerned to give a critique of the government's NEP; we want to think in terms of an alternate NEP.

It has to be remembered that an NEP is not simply what the Indian Government is trying to do, or what IMF-World Bank Structural adjustment programs are imposing. There are socialist forms of

NEP as well. In fact, the first NEP was that of the Soviet Union in the 1920s, which broke the domination of the top-down 'war economy' to give more freedom to producers. Nikolai Bukharin, its chief proponent, even told peasants to 'get rich' and emphasised the spontaneous growth of cooperatives. The Russian NEP was overturned by Stalin, and millions were murdered in processes of forced collectivisation, including Bukharin himself. But NEP type reforms have emerged again and again in socialist societies. The most recent case is that of China, whose 'economic reforms' that begun in 1978 broke down collectives and gave higher prices to peasants, resulting in a spurge of production and investment that, among other things, resulted in 21 million rural enterprises employing 100 million people by 1990, producing nearly one-third of the country's gross domestic product (GDP). The saga of China's current economic development is not yet finished; it has perhaps many negative aspects and countervailing trends, but it seems clear that it has been leading China away from its position as the world's largest 'low income' country.

Everywhere today movements towards a market-oriented economy have resulted from the crisis of state-dominated production systems. In India also, the NEP has been generated by the crisis of the economic development path followed since independence, what is called by many the 'Nehru-Mahalanobis model of state-dominated heavy industrial development'. As long as the government's NEP remains dominated by industrial capitalist and bureaucratic interests, it cannot offer a true way out. Nevertheless, the situation offers an opening for an alternative basis of development and a chance to restructure radically the relations of state and market in a way that can benefit the communities of the poor. In the words of Devaki Jain, we see the possibilities of 'converting the crisis into an opportunity'.

Economic Trends of the 1980s

First, we believe that liberalisation itself is not necessarily the disaster its opponents picture; rather it is a necessary component of an economic alternative (although not the whole of that alternative). The opponents of the NEP talk about the beginnings of liberalisation in the 1980s, since the NEP is too new to give a real assessment of effects, economists turn to the beginning of liberalisation under Indira and Rajiv Gandhi. Left economists, in fact, trace the downfall from the 1981 IMF loan, and implicitly or explicitly defend the Nehru model of development, which had guided India's economic policy before this.

But if we take this as a criterion, evidence seems to show that the rather modest liberalisation of the 1980s had favourable effects in increasing the growth rate and reducing the incidence of poverty. In fact, as Tables 10.1 and 10.2 show in the 1980s for the first time the economy had broken out of what economists used to call the 'Hindu rate of growth', 3.5 per cent. The improvement has not been very dramatic, but it has been significant.

Table 10.1 *Growth Rates in India*

	Percentage Annual Growth Rates of					
	GNP	Agricultural GNP	Industrial GNP	Population	Exports	Imports
1965–1980	3.6	2.5	4.2	2.3	3.0	1.2
1980–1990	5.3	3.1	6.6	2.1	6.5	4.2

Source: World Development Report (1992).

Table 10.2 *Poverty Ratios*

	Percentage Below the Poverty Line		
	1977–1978	1984–1985	1989–1990
Rural	51.2	39.9	26.2
Urban	38.2	17.7	19.3
Total	48.3	36.9	25.8

Source: CMIE Basic Statistics on the Indian Economy, 1990, Table 9:12.

India still remains a terribly poor country: according to the World Bank (World Development Report, 1990: Poverty), it has the largest poor population in the world, over one-third of the world total, with 420 million poor people and 250 million, 'extremely poor' or 55 per cent and 33 per cent by the 'headcount index'. Another survey: *Hunger* 1992 shows 28 per cent in urban areas and 40 per cent in rural areas living below the poverty line. What this meant can be shown by some other statistics on human development. The average lifespan has risen to 58 for women and 50 for men in 1990, a significant gain from 44 and 46 in 1965 and from the drastic situation of the colonial period when life expectancies did not reach 30 until 1941. But it is a stunted and undernourished population surviving on an average of 2,229 calories per day (much less, perhaps half of that, for the really poor sections). Between 1980 and 1990, 41 per cent of children below four years of age were classified as underweight, and 30 per cent of babies were born with low-birth weights; 20 per cent of population were without access to health facilities, 24 per cent of urban and 50 per cent of the rural population were without access to safe water (*Hunger*, Tables 10.2 and 10.3).

The situation is thus quite bad, but the grinding poverty and malnutrition is a consequence, not so much of liberalisation, but of the developmental inadequacies of the previous Nehru model. As the South Commission has put it:

> Growth was not high enough to trickle down ... In India, growth in the first three postwar decades was much slower than the average for the developing countries. The rise in India's per capita income, of the order of about 1.5 per cent per year was too small to secure a significant improvement in the living standards of the masses of the people. (*Challenge to the South,* 84–85)

In contrast, there has been a modest economic improvement since the late 1970s. The reduction in the poverty ratio shown in Table 10.2 came after years of high level of stagnation, and is backed by other sources, such as the World Bank's 1990 report *Poverty* and a world survey on *The State of the World's Hunger*. Both of these sources (one a progressive NGO and the other very symbol of international capitalism) also agree in linking this decline in poverty to growth in agricultural production and agricultural incomes. The World Development Report argues that 'Econometric analysis confirms that rural poverty in India has a strong negative link to farm incomes' (49), while the *Hunger* survey sees Green Revolution-induced agricultural growth (while admitting its negative aspects) as the main factor in the proportion of the rural population under the poverty line falling by more than half in the Punjab, Haryana, Gujarat and Andhra. It links agricultural growth to all-around rural employment growth:

> tapping the vast potential for developing rural enterprises is the key ... farmers spent 40 per cent of their increased income on goods and services produced in local, labor-intensive nonfarm enterprises, and 20 per cent on labor-intensive agricultural commodities such as fruits, vegetables and livestock products. (42–46)

Very frequently the choice of economic strategies is put in terms of an 'import-substitution' development (linked to state-dominated economies) versus an 'export-oriented' one (linked to a more open market orientation. Both are inadequate. Rather, Left economists have traditionally spoken of the need to 'develop the home market', that is, raise the incomes of the vast majority of the toiling people, as key to both growth and poverty alleviation, and we agree with this perspective. In India, this means that raising farm incomes is central. The vast majority of the population are still workers in agriculture or in areas dependent on agricultural prosperity, and women even more than men are bound here (partly this is underestimated because of census undercounting of women workers). Cultivators and agricultural labourers, as statistics of the CMIE show, are poorer than any other section of the population. The raising of their incomes, accompanied by measures ensuring that the poorest sections among them (landless, Dalits, women) have a share of the gains, is the key to poverty alleviation.

Table 10.3 *Income of Workers, 1981*

		Workforce (000s)	*Average Annual Income per Worker (₹)*
1.	Wage and salary earners	965	4,468
A.	Organised sector	229	10,851
	(Public)	155	10,643
	(Private)	74	11,289
B.	Unorganised sector	736	2,482
	(Agricultural workers)	555	1,703
	(Nonagricultural)	181	4,871
2.	Self-employed	1,260	3,549
A.	Cultivators	925	3,000
B.	Non-cultivators	335	5,066

Source: Centre for Monitoring the Indian Economy, Basic Statistics 1985, Volume I, Table 10.1.

It is also the key to economic growth, as increased farm income lead to increased local purchase and local investment, that is, the development of the small rural industries that are labour intensive rather than capital intensive. In this sense, the long-time slogan of the farmers' movement ('remunerative prices for agricultural productions') and the slogan of the Left ('land reform' – interpreted to mean an access of the poor to resources of all kinds, including water and forests) go together.

The growth of agriculture, the agricultural-based home market and agricultural-linked rural industries is the key to any viable economic policy that seeks to link welfare and growth. This requires a discussion of the role of market and state in this growth, as well as a discussion of ecological issues underlying both forms of growth.

Market and State

India's NEP is part of a broad swing to 'liberalisation' in practically every country in the world. These have many variations. In particular, some policy changes are internally propelled (e.g. China, and the earlier development policies in Southeast Asia's 'four tigers'), while others clearly have an element of IMF – imposed 'structural adjustment'. The variations and specificities mean that each has to be evaluated separately; they also mean that supporting liberalisation in general is not the same as supporting a specific set of policies and not at all the same as endorsing IMF structural adjustment. Still there is a common factor, and that is to lessen the role of the state in the economy and give more scope to the market.

What does the market mean to women? This is not such a simple question. Markets have existed in all societies beyond the simplest tribal bands, and in most of them women have played a major role. In traditional Indian economies, the sale of vegetables, fish, fruits, milk and eggs was primarily in the hands of women. In many cases, women also controlled the production of these, as well as playing crucial agricultural roles such as the preservation and selection of seeds. In the pastoral economies of much of Maharashtra, for example, while men controlled the sales of bullocks, women controlled that of cows, buffalos, sheep and goats, with whose products they were most concerned. In other words, not only the agricultural production but also a good deal of processing and marketing was in the hands of women. Even today in India, this is true in many areas.

The development of large-scale capitalism has eroded women's economic power, including women's market power. It has created large-scale monopolised markets dominated by men. However, where many argue that this is due to the fact that capitalism makes the market the dominant, unchecked controlling institution of society, we believe instead that it is a result of state intervention in the market. From the time of Columbus to the wars over oil, markets, their prices, the modes of participation and access have always been dominated by states, force and violence.

State intervention has built monopolies; it has also helped to turn markets into male-dominated institutions. For instance, Ester Boserup's famous *Women's Role in Economic Development* showed the effects of government's discrimination against women in giving training and resources in 'modern' agricultural and industrial production. More recently, Viji Srinivasan has shown the role of the state and World Bank-influenced programmes in setting up 'fishermen's cooperatives' and depriving women as well as many traditional fisher castes of their share in an expanding export market. This male bias has been consistent throughout in the structuring of markets and requires coordinated state programmes to overcome it, but it cannot be attributed to an inherent flaw of 'markets' as such.

The Marxist-dominated Left has, however, consistently seen the 'market as such' as an enemy force. It has been thought to be the core of capitalist-exploitation, and state control of the market, or even replacement of markets, has been seen as the solution to exploitation. In India, hostility to *banias* comes not only from lower castes but also from a Brahmanic claim to superiority, to the fact that the state bureaucracy in particular has been under control of the higher castes. The market as enslaving and the state as libratory have been part of a larger and still not fully examined discourse in India.

The women's movement, dominated by urban feminists and party-linked women, has by and large taken over this image of the market as enslaving. It has added the critique that production for the market involves greed, individualism and selfishness. Conversely, while, the state is viewed as an enemy many women activists feel more comfortable in relating to the state bureaucracy. The women's movement over the last 20 years has been focused on making demands of the state – demands for more laws, more vigorous enforcement of existing laws, more welfare spending and so on. The total effect is to strengthen the state.

There has also been a disregard of some elementary economic rules: that everything has to be paid for, in nature, and in the economy. That is, a society cannot go on extracting timber or minerals from the earth without costs; people cannot extract subsidies, pensions, wages, bonuses, welfare and other benefits from the state or from enterprises without a clear conception of how it will be financed. *Somebody has to pay.* If this is not to be done by the enterprise as such (self-financing or the 'user pays' principle), then it has to be done publicly, that is, through state monies collected by taxes or other forms from the citizens. Now we do not mind paying collectively for the welfare (including health and education) of the poor, the aged, the sick and the young, those who cannot support themselves. *But what has been happening in the development progress in India is that subsidies have been going not to the weak but to the strong, and they are often being paid for disproportionately by the weak.* Thus, we find that the state is asked to subsidise the continuing operation of organised sector companies with employees making far higher incomes more than the rural poor we are concerned with. We find that PDS is being subsidised to a much larger extent by the farmers who receive low prices (and even the rich farmers of Punjab are on average have lower incomes than even the lowest of organised sector employees) than it is by the government. In other words, the collective is supporting its richer elements; the weak are paying for the welfare of the strong. This is not only objectionable, but also it has brought economy to a point of crisis.

This is why, though talking of 'profitability' or 'economic viability' sounds individualistic and brutal, the issue of cost recovery has to be dealt with. The tragedy is, however, that the working-class movement has shown little concern for the issues of productivity and cost recovery. The industrial working class, far from being a vanguard for building a more equalitarian society, has become a powerful interest group struggling only for its own higher incomes and welfare. We do not, however, blame the workers, but rather the left leadership that led them on to cease worrying about the nature of production itself.

In the large-scale, sophisticated, intricately interlinked economies of today, the market, for all its imperfections, is a much more efficient allocator of goods than the state can ever hope to be. It seems only logical then to say that the state should not try to 'run' the economy, but rather serve as a regulator, watchdog, filling welfare role and infrastructural functions. (And even much of infrastructure state spending should be minimised and replaced by a user pays principle; since otherwise state spending allows industries to 'externalise' their costs and in the process encourages waste). It can do this best in taking a realistic account of the objective constraints of the market. This is why the Chinese concept of a 'socialist market economy' or 'socialist commodity economy' makes sense. It is not a question of the market replacing the state or vice versa, but of each performing its role. In fact there is no sign, historically, of the state withering away either in 'market capitalist' any more than in socialist societies. The role of governments has increased even under such marketers as Reagan and Thatcher. Those who talk of the 'vanishing state' are under an illusion.

There are dangers in both the state and the market. The state, like the economy, can be said to have a dual nature. On the one hand, it is an expression of the society organised as a collective of the 'public will', the political realm. On the other hand, it is also an instrument of violence and domination. In recent years, in particular, we have seen not only special interest groups able to dominate the functioning of the 'public', but also a growing state-related violence: *goondaism*, criminality, brutality and corruption seem to be on the rise, irrevocably tied up with the political life.

This is perhaps a sufficient reason itself to speak of weakening the state. But it is not only a matter of the state 'withdrawing' from the economy. We should talk not only of structural adjustment in the economy but also of *restructuring the state*: there should be a movement towards *decentralisation of powers, autonomy for local units and community control of resources such as land and forests and not central state control.* Here is where the Panchayati Raj slogan is important to the toiling poor and to women if it means real local power and not just eye-wash.

Finally, beyond state and market, we can draw an insight from the Green movement and from Gandhism to remember that an industrial, fossil fuel-based economy tends to become ecologically unsustainable, whether it is under state domination or market management. This brings us to the question of sustainable development and the 'ecological imperative'.

The Ecological Imperative: Sustainable and Regenerative Production

Along with the shift away from state-dominated economies, the great transformation of our time is expressed in the issue of ecological sustainability. Both state and market seem guilty here. On the one hand, the rapid growth and lack of sufficient regulation linked to market economies leads to horrors such as Bhopal Three Mile Island; state-dominated, nonmarket economies have been as ecologically destructive as the pure capitalist ones, for example, Chernobyl the drying up of the Aral Sea. Even massive irrigation projects such as Narmada and Three Gorges seem more linked to bureaucratic and political interests than to real capitalist cost-effectiveness.

The environmental problem is not one of simple 'conservation' or something that can be handled by a few 'cleanup' measures. It is a question of a fundamental reorientation of production itself. Specifically, we have to move away from an economy based upon nonrenewable fossil fuel energy sources to other sources that are more energy efficient and use an increased percentage of renewable energy (solar, wind, biogas, hydro, etc.). This ecological imperative has a different meaning for developed and developing countries. Developed countries use energy voraciously (and use military power and financial manipulation to keep energy, specifically oil prices low); theirs is the main responsibility for environmental destruction. Developing countries, however, start from such a low initial fossil fuel energy base that there is no way they can achieve the levels of the developed country without a fundamental reorientation to renewable energy sources (wind, solar, biomass). For example, in 1989 India consumed 231 kg oil-equivalent energy per capita China 598 compared to 7,822 the United States, according to the CMIE's report on energy. For its own developmental needs, as well as to prevent environmental pollution, India needs to make the energy transition. This is also linked to self-reliance, since petroleum products are a major chunk of import bills.

This reorientation seems to require both market and state measures. As important as state regulation may be the simple question of pricing: fossil fuel energy, first coal and now oil, has traditionally been underpriced or subsidised by many countries, with the United States and developing countries such as India being the worst (India reportedly has energy prices at 40% of world level). These energy subsidies were meant to encourage heavy industrial production, but their overall result has been a wasteful use of energy. Ecological economists argue that energy prices should be high, and many propose that the basic tax base of governments be shifted to levying taxes on energy (or on carbon dioxide emissions), which would encourage development of technologies for efficient energy use and renewable sources of energy. Higher fossil fuel energy prices would have many overall economic implications: higher prices for transport, for instance, would mean that locally produced goods have a much bigger advantage over those carried from long distances; higher prices for plastics and oil-based materials would mean that natural fibres would again become more economical than polyesters and so on. This shift would also require a fundamental rethinking about movement demands, since Left and progressive movements fighting against 'price rise' have unthinkingly opposed rising transport costs and so on.

Such ecological restructuring would have crucial implications for women, since it will aid the development of a more decentralised economic system, with locally produced and controlled energy production (i.e. community controlled or even individually owned gasifiers, cogeneration systems, producing energy fed into a central grid) serving as a material basis for genuine community autonomy.

It is rural and urban poor women who experience the worst blows of drought, deforestation, pollution and degradation of the environment. But women are not only victims of environmental destruction, as it has been argued. Because of their historically developed social roles, women have an orientation to a more regenerative, nurturing form of production. But this does not automatically get expressed in movements and policies that have the real, material effect of nurturing the earth. Uninformed action even when motivated by good intentions can help to maintain a destructive, wasteful, elite-dominated economy. Now, there is a need for the women's movement to develop a more advanced conscious understanding of the material base of a sustainable development – a regenerative economy.

Ecological restructuring should be a fundamental element in any NEP. Both market measures and state regulatory and directive measures will have to be oriented in this direction. In the long run, a regenerative economy will move away from both market and state, with local self-reliance in production and fulfilment of basic needs providing the material basis for autonomous communities, a pluralistic and equalitarian culture, and a federal political system. Even in the short run, development of a local subsistence base for the rural poor is crucial to allow them to stand up in a society dominated by large-scale markets and states.

Specific Concerns: Unemployment, Food Security and MNCs

From a general and theoretical point of view, therefore, liberalisation or moving towards a greater market orientation can be beneficial. But what about more specific fears that have been expressed?

1. *Unemployment:* Both proponents and opponents of the NEP seem to agree that liberalisation leads to organised sector unemployment, but growing employment opportunities in the unorganised sector. While opponents argue that this will mean only low-paid, insecure and exploitative jobs, supporters of liberalisation have argued that it is changing the relationship between capital and labour to the advantage of world labour – because liberalisation will give an impetus to labour-intensive production, and growth of employment will be disproportionately for workers in the Third World and the 'informal' sectors. If this is true, then from the perspective of rural women – the uneducated rural poor, or the partly educated girl (even matriculate) from agricultural labourer or peasant families who is looking for some kind of income outside of agriculture – the rise of this 'flexible' employment will be a gain.

   Clearly small-scale, rural nonagricultural employment will grow most healthily and with most safeguards for worker when it is oriented to a local market for goods, whether produced by self-employed or by those working in small rural factories. But it also appears to be true that an 'export-oriented development' as opposed to an import-substitution development generally leads to wider employment. This is because import-substitution (Nehru model) development is focused on heavy industries that are capital intensive and employ a relatively smaller proportion of the population, whereas the exports of any developing country are initially those of the primary sector (agriculture, etc.) and light manufactures, which are much more labour intensive. Only gradually does a country 'move up' into export of more sophisticated manufactured goods. This means for India, exports of agricultural products and of primary processed goods, of textiles, of handicrafts of all kinds, of leather goods, and so on – precisely the products of the rural poor, Dalits, artisans and other low castes – will move up. An increased export orientation offers the possibility of helping these sections, rather than the middle and higher castes and urban working-class groups employed in the more sophisticated and heavy industries.
2. *Food security:* Two major objections are made to the NEP in this regard: first, it will mean the destruction of PDS and second, cash

crops will grow at the expense of food crops. Both are baseless. We feel that there should be no objection to restructuring the PDS to provide rationed food only to the poor; for too long the better off sections of the urban (and rural) populations have profited from cheap food financed by low peasant incomes. More crucially, food security is not simply a matter of rations, it is a matter of whether a country, or a region, produces enough to feed its people, and not only at a bare biological minimum but also at a growing standard of living. In other words, while a PDS system should continue to provide a 'safety-net' for the very poor, in the long run food security can only be assured by the fact that enough food is grown locally and people have incomes high enough to buy it.

As for cash crops versus food crops, the very terminology is surprising. On one hand, wheat and rice or any food grains are obviously cash crops and will continue to be as long as nonagricultural populations exist and grow. On the other hand, vegetables and fruits are just as clearly food – unless one is ready to argue that the poor should eat only grain! And the two types of crops are not mutually exclusive; many countries that have increased vegetable/fruit production in recent years have also increased food grain production. In most countries (for instance in Africa), cash crops have developed at the cost of food production, but these are cases where food grain prices are so low that farmers neglect them. This is again a state policy and not the market that can be held responsible.

Ironically, women's role in vegetable/fruit production is often greater than it is in grain production. In many of the ex-socialist countries, for example, women have been particularly concerned with the 'family plots' or the 'sidelines' (vegetable, fruit, poultry, animal raising) production and have benefited when encouragement has been given to these. Women have a greater chance of controlling horticultural crops and in nonplough-based farming where they simply tend to be field labourers.

Even more, when such crops are grown ecologically, with only minimum amounts of external chemical and industrial inputs, on the basis of what is now being called LEISA (low external input sustainable agriculture), women have an opportunity to play a major role in programmes for increased and healthy production on very small plots of land. Similarly, women do play a major role in primary processing of agricultural products and can play even more important roles with some access to resources and training.

Many feminists, who are saying that women are oriented to 'subsistence' production and that the market is an enemy, act as if they want to perpetuate a situation in which states and other large-scale institutions help men to take advantage of the market. It is true that women have a concern to feed the family first, to take care of basic human subsistence, but this does not mean they have nothing to do with a cash economy. *Our goal is to empower women in the market and political institutions, not to keep them alienated from these within the four walls of the house*. It makes sense to begin with those sectors where women have traditionally played a major economic role (vegetable and fruit production, milk, processing, weaving, textiles, etc.) and support policies that strengthen these sectors within the total economy and that provide training, skills and resources to help their modernisation and the participation of women in these.

(Similarly, we can argue that Dalits, balutedars and other low castes should have the opportunities to reach to the heights of state power and the distances of the 'world market' and not be enclosed within the village. *Globalisation is in the interests of the poor, the low castes and women.* Care must be taken to ensure that the artisan and other specialised castes are not sidelined by richer higher castes when the occupations they are linked with gain markets and profitability. Special training and aid programmes as well as the general spread of education in these castes through reservations are important here).

3. *Multinationals* are the focus for many fears: the main objection raised to liberalisation is usually that 'MNCs will come and take over'. A process of recolonisation is said to be at the heart of the process, and we are told there is a need for a new Swadeshi movement, of 'Azadi Bachao'.

Here we want to say clearly that if the choice is between a high-caste capitalist Indian company with a highly privileged all-male workforce (perhaps employing women in the cafeteria) producing steel or automobiles, and a relatively labour-intensive multinational-linked company in a rural area employing women, then we will prefer the multinational. We don't feel that 'swadeshi' by itself is necessarily better. After all, Manu is swadeshi, Chaturvarnya is swadeshi and sari is swadeshi. So many patriarchal and oppressive customs have been part of Indian tradition. We welcome globalisation that allows entry into a modern world where prosperity, liberty and equality become realisable ideals – because these are the values expressed by the real traditions of the Indian masses. While we want to maintain and develop the genuine equalitarian traditions of the people, we do not want to go backward to the precapitalist Indian village where caste and patriarchy reigned. And we do not want a saffron swadeshi.

In any case, the belief that a freer market will mean the automatic dominance of foreign companies neglects some modern realities. In the last decades, Europe and Japan have increased their share of world GDP compared with the United States, and they have also increased their share of MNCs (of the top 200 industrial corporations), the United States share went down from 127 in 1960 to 68 in 1990; Japan's and Europe's increased; even small South Korea now has six companies in the top 200, and one in the top 10. World economic realities show a dispersal of MNC dominance and contemporary economic trends towards decentralisation, flexible production, autonomy for local units of larger corporations and so on. We are not very concerned about whether Indian giant corporations join the list of the world's top 200 MNCs, but we do want small and medium Indian companies to grow, and we see no reason why they cannot grow under a more open market. As the *Economist* has recently argued,

> Far from presenting the world's biggest companies with new opportunities, falling trade barriers are opening them to attack ... Few small firms could afford to tailor their produce to the standards of foreign markets, employ people overseas, or cope with the legal and tax complexities of international business. The opening of markets is removing many of these barriers and making it easier for smaller firms to sell their products all over the world ... . The era of corporate empire building is over. An age of broader, fiercer global competition, with all its risks and uncertainties, has begun. (17 April 1993: 11–12)

Those who argue that MNCs will simply take over under an open market want to maintain the state bureaucracy, which supervises a closed economy, are not only picturing Indian producers as 'weak', but also seem to be speaking in the name of bureaucrats and those big corporations that have benefited by their political connections. We would like to know why the Chinese can feel confident that they can gain from market liberalisation and joining GATT, and why the Indian elite feels so weak. We would also like an explanation of the curious phenomenon that the Indian Left is taking a position regarding the opening up of international trade (i.e. towards GATT and all) that is the same as the BJP, but opposite that of the Chinese Communist Party.

This is not to say there are no danger of unemployment, undermining of food security and corporate domination under the name of liberalisation. There will be a struggle between farmers and small producers, including local cooperatives, and the monopoly sector. If the government gives unlimited access to land, subsidies and other 'facilities' to big corporations that claim to be doing export agriculture – rather than supporting small farmers or other small producers, then both the poor and the economy as a whole may suffer. Or, if the government goes on importing food grains and other 'dumped' Western agricultural products (this year it accepted 40,000 tons of soybean as a US 'gift') to hold down prices to placate the urban middle class, then food security will be undermined. There is a need to ensure training and skills to women, Dalits and low castes, not only to upgrade their production but also that people from these sections can lead in the entrepreneurship and technical skills that link the producers to the market (this is another important part of the Mandal Commission report). Agricultural extension facilities that support ecological agriculture must be fought for, and access to resources (land, water, and rights over products of the land) for the landless, resource-poor, women, Dalits and adivasis must be ensured. And it has to be remembered that whether it uses the language of liberalisation or 'welfarism' the state has been and will continue to give subsidies and facilities to corporations, bureaucracies and the upper castes, unless it is checked by active people's movements and unless power is continuously devolved to local governments.

The Indian Government's NEP

We have been arguing that there is a need for a 'new economic policy, in which both market liberalisation and ecological restructuring have a significant part. While there are many types of NEP, unfortunately the only one we have to deal with in India is the NEP of Manmohan Singh and the Narasimha Rao, since the Left and opposition parties have not put forward a coherent economic policy of their own, but have contented themselves with predictions of disaster. What then can we say about the NEP of the Indian state?

We may note that even in rhetoric, the government has been quite timid, insisting that it is still following the Nehru model. And in fact this is quite true; there are enough indications that the interests of bureaucrats and big industrialists are those that are sought to be served through the promised liberalisation.

- Deregulation and delicensing have been primarily for industry; there have been very little lifting restrictions on agriculture (zoning, monopoly purchasing schemes, regulations against farmers doing their own processing of products, etc.). A major battle was fought over the last two years on food grain prices, when the government ended by purchasing 3 million tonnes of wheat from the United States, Australia and Canada at prices of more than ₹ 500 per quintal after refusing to pay ₹ 300 to Indian farmers. This year 40,000 tonnes of soybean oil has been accepted as a US PL. 480 gift, again driving down local prices. In other words, the state is continuing to compromise India's food security.

- Liberalisation and deregulation should mean the cutting down of bloated government bureaucracies, but there has been no sign of this. 'Exit policies' are not even being talked of for government employment.
- The government's talk is all of 'export orientation' and 'foreign investment', that is, it is clear that the economy is sought to be built up in the world economy not through developing the home market and giving scope to the countless small producers and toilers, but rather through encouraging monopoly production. Even in regard to agricultural and agro-industrial export, for instance, the state seems to assume that it is large corporations, aided by government concessions and subsidies, that will be most effective at doing this. The state continues to take over land from fisher communities and others at low prices and turning it over at bargain rates to Indian monopolies and multinationals.
- There is clearly no conception of the ecological imperative. In spite of some government's talk of renewable energy, watershed management, environmental clearance and others, this is not linked to overall economic planning. Rather it is simply argued that economic growth will lead to funds to cope with environmental cleanup. Though petroleum and petroleum products represent the biggest part of the import bill, there is no real strategy for cutting down on these.
- Similarly, welfare programmes such as health and education continue to be cut, even though the strongest defenders of the market economy argue that a healthy and educated population is necessary to compete in the world market.
- We might therefore argue that if India continues to follow an NEP based on a fossil fuel-centred, industry-focused, export-oriented development, running after foreign markets and foreign investment rather than giving priority to developing home markets, it will result in increasing environmental destructiveness, immiseration for many of the poor (including women) and increasing indebtedness and dependence. A fundamentally reoriented NEP is needed instead.

Our Suggestions: For a People's NEP

1. *Political restructuring is essential:* government administration and bureaucracy must be reduced at all levels, especially in the rural areas. Genuine autonomy should be given to states. Local district

bureaucracies and bureaucracies controlling the cooperative sector should be drastically reduced and powers be given to local elected bodies (Panchayati Raj). At all levels, popular participation in economic management should be developed. Irrigation bureaucracies can be vastly reduced, for example, and costs cut down, by turning over water distribution to water users' societies (as the Vaidyanathan committee on irrigation pricing has proposed). Cooperatives and other rural industrial and agricultural enterprises should be deregulated.

2. The guiding theme of the NEP should be neither a saffron swadeshi import-substitution (capital-intensive industries producing luxury for a small national elite) or export orientation (producing for an overseas market) but rather building the home market by increasing incomes of farmers, agricultural labourers, the self-employed and other rural labourers. This will lead to increased demand and increased rural industrial, small industrial growth. There is no harm in export as such (particularly when it involves labour-intensive industries leading to increased employment and thus a broadening home market), or in producing some luxury consumer goods (particularly when these are products of labour-intensive traditional crafts), but the focus must be an economy built around a mass home market.
3. The NEP should not be based on a chase after foreign investment. Investment should come primarily from internal sources, especially from the savings of peasant and small producer/worker households generated by their higher incomes. There is also the question of using savings productively and efficiently, for which the Indian record has been quite bad. This however does not require a blocking of foreign investment. MNC competition will be useful for transferring technology and heightening efficiency among Indian producers; in any case hopes (and fears) of a massive inflow of investment are overdone. Control over MNC domination can come by minimising the corruption-creating regulations of the 'license-permit raj' and rigorously implementing the environmental and health standards and, above all, by refusing special privileges and facilities to monopoly firms (such as land provided at low cost, etc.).
4. Petroleum prices should be allowed to rise to world market levels. This will lead to increased efficiency of energy use and development of substitutes for fossil fuels as well as increasing demand for natural substitutes produced by the low castes and rural poor, that is, cotton and silk cloth, natural rope, baskets, jute and so on.

5. On the other hand, prices of communication and information technologies should fall, for example, computers can be made cheaply and easily available by cutting down all customs duties and letting software manufactures and computer users (small entrepreneurs, small businesses, cooperatives) afford modern equipment. This will aid in building the networking and market information needed to help small rural-based enterprises become viable. The spread of modern information and communications technologies will help substitute for transportation, make rural life more viable and attractive and reduce the flow to the cities. Training in such modern skills should be given to all the Dalits, 'backward castes' and women.
6. Governments should not be allowed to confiscate land except for public necessities with the required approval of local populations (gram sabhas, etc.), and even then the market price for the land must be paid. Local governments rather than the state or central government should have control of land, including wastelands, pastures and forests.
7. There should be programmes for giving access to resources (including land, water, etc.) to women and the landless. These may be part of a collective development project for the village as a whole and may involve use of part of 'common property resources' of the village.
8. The national focus should be on building a railway economy and not an automobile economy. Bicycles could be subsidised. Public transportation in cities also can be upgraded and urban roads banned to all but public transportation and bicycles.
9. PDS should be restructured; organised sector workers, the urban middle classes and the rural middle classes and rich should pay market prices for food. Food grains provided on PDS should be traditional foods of the toiling people of an area, that is, jawar and bajra in Maharashtra, rather than only wheat and rice. We may consider restructuring PDS on Mandal Commission lines, that is, exclude the upper castes and the creamy layer from OBCs. This will simply be a matter of administration since it can be built on already issued cards of identification and will be fair and socially realistic under Indian conditions.
10. Extension services for agriculture should focus on ecologically sustainable alternatives to high-input chemical agriculture. Fertiliser subsidies must be phased out. Development of biofertilisers and integrated pest management can be supported, not so much by the state providing these cheaply as by provision of technical

expertise and support to groups and companies developing these locally. A patent regime that encourages improvement and use of local seed varieties and local technologies should be developed. Large dam projects should be reexamined and the irrigation focus should be on watershed development, rainwater harvesting and judicious combinations of local and external water sources based on principles of equitable water distribution. Renewable energy sources (solar, wind, cogeneration with biomass, etc.) should be promoted.

11. Handloom cloth and handicrafts should be promoted. But this should not be done by attempting to subsidise these as items for mass consumption; rather production can be for a high-quality market. We must recognise that handlooms and other traditional Indian crafts are products of high skill, even luxuries. Thus, weavers (and other craftsmen) can find their place by producing fine silk and cotton items both for overseas and an internal market. There should be, concurrently, special training for children of weavers and other craftsmen to help in marketing, skills and technology development.
12. In any promotion of rural schemes or industries, women must be specifically included and not as low paid workers in these enterprises. Special training and a promotional effort is needed to overcome the history of state discrimination as well as social barriers.
13. Military and all related spending should be reduced. This by itself will allow the stepping up of government spending on 'human infrastructure', that is, health, education and other welfare measures. There may be some debate and discussion about whether private bodies can also play a role in providing some services, about whether local level or state and national governments should take the bulk of responsibility, but there has to be a reaffirmed national commitment to health and education for the masses.

psychology, which [illegible] stratification systems. [illegible] which led to po[illegible] stratifi-cation is [illegible]. It began [illegible] role of [illegible], women [illegible]

Domination [illegible] of some[illegible] the bluepri[illegible] the economy [illegible] to dom[illegible] is bad, bo[illegible] must go. Bo[illegible] system is [illegible] attack[illegible] all other[illegible] nated [illegible]

Th[illegible] slave[illegible] free wo[illegible] artific[illegible] develo[illegible] du[illegible] happen[illegible]

br[illegible] man[illegible] pract[illegible] physica[illegible] th[illegible] mor[illegible] w[illegible] lie[illegible]

Part Three

Equality, Status and Empowerment

Women in India are not homogeneous; rather their diversity and differences are central to the understanding of their status in the society. All women do not experience the same amount and kind of subordination; their experiences tend to vary according to their placement in the social hierarchy, location in class and ethnic and religious categories. Ganguly-Scrase (2000: 85), while analysing the status of women in India, writes, 'Since the heydays of the women's liberation movement in the 1970s, when there was a sense of women's solidarity and sisterhood, feminist theorists have shifted their attention to the study of difference among women'. Therefore, to imagine the Indian women as a homogeneous category is impossible, and in terms of their diversity and disparity, two significant issues emerge. One is government initiatives from above targeting the rural poor women. Various policies and programmes were launched by the Indian Government to improve the earning power and status of women. Second, through the constitutional amendments certain provisions were given to women to empower them with decision-making ability and giving them formal political equality. Two issues of women's economic and political empowerment have been examined in this part of the book through seven chapters based on empirical studies.

To understand the issues theoretically, a review of governmental initiatives is significant, though all through the years nongovernmental and women's organisations have also been working for the development of women. Initially for the first few Five Year Plans, the focus of the government remained on launching various schemes for the welfare of women. The most common model was Mahila Mandal and Mahila Samiti delivering various services and helping in income-generating activities. This approach viewed women as beneficiaries or recipients of benefits, services and concessions. It was later taken over by the developmental approach. Karlekar (2004) informs that there has been coexistence of three models for women's development. From 1980s onwards these are: Women in Development (WID) explains the reasons for women being treated as beneficiaries; later on, Women and Development (WAD) integrates women in development work as active change agents; and then Gender and Development (GAD) emphasises the understanding of gender relations and empowering the weak. By the turn of the century, policy makers realised that women themselves need to be independent in all aspects of their lives and hence empowerment approach got prominence. It focuses on self-development of women, that is, capacity building; it involves women learning some new skills that they can utilise to have economic empowerment, which further would enhance their self-worth. Empowerment literally means 'to give power', 'to delegate authority' and 'to give legal rights'. The process of empowerment can be both at individual level and at collective level. In the process of empowerment, a number of NGOs and women's organisations are attempting to make women aware, particularly at the grassroots, of their situation and suggesting the ways to gain a sense of autonomy. Desai and Krishnaraj (2004) are hopeful of the development that has occurred during the last two decades in the form of the emergence of women's movement, wherein women have started raising their voices against inequality, patriarchal values and the inegalitarian social structure. In addition, changes that have taken place in the last one and half decades, particularly the Indian Government's efforts to further liberalise the economy and constitutional amendments, such as to reserve quotas for women in self-government, will crack the gendered public activities. With the globalisation, middle-class urban working women have experienced more autonomy and freedom than their other counterparts. At the same time, the women from working class, due to statutory reservation and availability of variety of low-level unskilled jobs in the highly competitive market, have enhanced their earning capacity resulting in improvement in their quality of life. The benefits of the initiatives of the state from above along with the role of women's organisations and NGOs have served the non-identical interests of women with differences differently.

The chapters included in this part bring forth the efforts of Indian Government to uplift the status of women through various schemes. The empirical studies have shown the efficacy of these programmes as to what extent they have remained successful to bring about change in the status of women. The first chapter by J.P. Singh describes the extent of gender inequality and discrimination in the recent times in Indian society. He argues that the study of gender has remained largely a neglected area of research in sociology of most developing countries. Sociologists have generally identified problems or issues in sociology more in terms of male concerns and on the basis of male prejudice. Feminist ideas as anywhere else were introduced in sociology only at the margins of the discipline. During the last century, urbanisation, rise in female education, democratisation of political system, spread of media of mass communication and modernisation have brought far-reaching changes in the life of women across the world. The author makes a fresh assessment of status of women in India with a special focus on developing countries. In the planning process, under the trickle-down theory, it was expected that women will equally benefit along with men. This has been belied by actual developments. Neerja Ahlawat in her chapter argues that women in the social structure of Haryana occupy a low and secondary place. It seeks to analyse various demographic and socio-economic variables such as gender imbalance, incidence of female mortality, maternal mortality and health status and educational level of women. Further, women as workers and their participation in various income-generating activities have been assessed.

The status of women in India over the time has undergone a lot of change. Women enjoyed equal status to men prior to the dictum laid by Manu, the law maker of the second century. The degraded position of women continued and was reinforced during the medieval period in India. The status of Hindu women further deteriorated due to various reasons under the British Rule. But, postindependent India has witnessed a great transformation in the lives of women. Indian women have been given equal rights in the Constitution. As a result, a number of women welfare programmes were initiated and women started breaking sociocultural barriers of the society to regain equal status. The studies on the subject reveal that despite various efforts, a large number of women still suffer from a number of hardships and are being discriminated. The chapter by Raj Singh and Nishi Batra based upon the primary data collected from 400 respondents examines the impact of selected women welfare programmes in improving the status of rural women. It was noted that the level of participation in decision -making was significantly associated with participation in women welfare programmes. Similarly, the respondents who participated in these programmes had deviated considerably from the observance of traditional customs, which were responsible for lowering their status. These programmes, however, did not succeed in bringing about any radical improvements and most women are still being discriminated. The authors reiterate that structural transformations are imperative for enhancing their status in the rural society.

An in-depth analysis of the Adult Education Centres, Mahila Mandals and other vocational programmes conducted for the education of women has been made by Raj Mohini Sethi in her study of Dharampur block of district Solan in Himachal Pradesh. It also tries to learn the relative importance of each in urging the women to march on to the path of achieving equality and in making them responsible citizens. The chapter concludes that mass literacy cannot be achieved in a specified period of time and it fails to make women responsible and aware citizens. The functional education through nonformal education schemes is more useful in the empowerment of women, in urging them to achieve women's equality and also instil among them a self-confidence and independence through sustained interaction and exposure.

Various welfare schemes launched by the central government and state governments are actually conceived to give succour to the needy women and uplift them socially and economically. It is in this context that Bindu Duggal has made an attempt to assess the impact of these schemes on the status of women in Punjab. The assessment of various parameters has been studied at the grassroots level by conducting a survey of 935 women beneficiaries from 45 villages. Such a comprehensive review of the schemes brings forth that schemes have succeeded in bringing a limited change in the status of women.

According to them, empowering women means more power, authority, autonomy, voice, representation and participation with the aim to raise their socio-economic status, build confidence and nurture strengths so that they are able to challenge the prevalent discriminatory practices. The chapter by Swinder Singh and Sumita Bakshi examines the impact of 73rd Constitutional Amendment Act on women empowerment, especially in the context/background of other measures adopted by the government. The sample of the study included 156 randomly selected respondents drawn from four blocks of Punjab and Haryana. The data were gathered by administering specially designed interview schedule in order to find out the impact of the new Panchayati Raj system on women at the grassroots level. The study reveals that while the number of elected women members has gone up, the awareness level and participation of the women in decision-making process has hardly changed. Hardly any discernible change has been observed in leadership pattern. As a positive sign, a number of respondents have shown their willingness to benefit from government-aided orientation cum training programmes. However, such programmes need to be organised. Also consistent efforts are needed to uplift the position of women and to make a dent in the male-dominated society. Policy makers, bureaucracy, NGOs, women's organisations and the women themselves all need to join hands in a positive way if the rural women are to be really empowered.

Finally, S. Gohilavani examines the most debated concept and elaborately discussed issue of women's empowerment. Seminars, conferences, workshops and a number of meetings are organised to discuss in-depth on the strategies and modus operandi towards achieving women's empowerment more than clarifying it conceptually. Women's empowerment is considered a goal and, hence, necessary aspects of such a goal are investigated at all levels especially in the context of policy making and project formulation in view of developing women in the country. The latest attempt of the Government of India to introduce Women's Empowerment Bill of 2001 reflects undoubtedly the necessity of achieving it as a goal. A 19 paged policy document contains all issues pertaining to women, all possible strategies are fixed and targets are determined, with a belief that such measures would ultimately 'empower', that is, facilitate women empowerment in the country.

References

Desai, Neera and Krishnaraj, M. 2004. 'An Overview of the Status of Women in India', in Manoranjan Mohanty (ed.), *Class, Caste, Gender: Readings in Indian Government and Politics* (296–319). New Delhi: Sage.

Ganguly-Scrase, R. 2000. 'Diversity and Status of Women: The Indian Experience', in Louise Edwards and Mina Roces (eds), *Women in Asia: Tradition, Modernity and Globalization* (85–111). Ann Arbor: The University of Michigan Press.

Karlekar, Malavika. 2004. 'A Note on the Empowerment of Women'. *Indian Journal of Gender Studies*, 11(2): 145–155.

11

Sociology of Gender Inequality and Discrimination

J.P. Singh

In the present day world, the women are spotted in many different roles. Women, besides being wives and mothers, do cooking, mending, sewing and washing. They also take care of men but are commonly subordinate to male authority. These facts characterise almost all societies. The most basic division of labour appears to be founded on sex. With the rise of Women's Liberation Movement, the reasons for sex-based division of labour and for the inequality between sexes have been fiercely debated in the academic circles as well as political fora. This has led to the emergence of sociology of women as a subject area in its own right. It has been largely developed by women, by radical feminists, by a new generation of female sociologists and anthropologists and also by established ones. Consequently by now a whole lot of facts and ideas have developed in the arena of gender studies.

With the beginning of a new century of a new millennium, the world, especially the developing countries, is faced with a new era of globalisation and therefore there is a need to make an assessment of women's position in a changing world as people who are just as important as men from a sociological angle against the backdrop of different theoretical perspectives. Effort is also made to evaluate different theoretical perspectives in the light of recent facts and figures. Let us begin with the way the women are treated as members of family at the micro level and as members of society at the macro level in a broader global perspective. A discussion of this type would also throw light on the nature of changes that are going to surface with respect to the women as a whole, as development and globalisation continue to sweep the developing world. In the course of this discussion, it would be obvious that changes, which are occurring in the life of women generally, are not always socially intended and warranted; some of the changes are also unwarranted and dysfunctional for the sustenance of society in general.

The feminist scholars, in general, expediently offer subjective and exaggerated views about the plight and predicament of women in relation to men. In their view, the situation has come to such a passé that it has indeed become very difficult for women to live any longer comfortably with men. But had the feminists been correct in their exposition of reality of gender discrimination, the relationship between men and women would have been surely severed a long time back, giving a final blow to the perpetuation of human civilisation. They seldom bring the fact to a focus that women are also duly loved, cared and respected as mother, daughter-in-law, grandmother, daughter, sister, wife, girlfriend, colleague and professional. It is not true that women are always relegated to an inferior position or second-class citizenship. Some women in real life in all ages have been more influential than men to govern the destiny of their family or even the entire nation. Queen Elizabeth and Queen Victoria, in England, Mrs Sirimavo R.D. Bandaranaike in Sri Lanka and Mrs Indira Gandhi in India, for instance, are a few glaring cases in point.

Over the last several decades, women around the world have made significant advancement in such vital arenas of social life as education, health and work. This progress is due, in part, to a growing awareness that continuing social and economic development depends on improving women's lives and on allowing women to participate fully in society. International conferences, notably the 1994 UN International Conference on Population and Development (ICPD) held in Cairo, the 1995 UN Fourth World Conference on Women held in Beijing and the 1995 UN Social Summit Conference in Copenhagen, have called for a greater push for women's progress and equality. Such efforts are genuinely necessitated, because women throughout the life cycle are often at a disadvantage relative to men, which has ramifications beyond individual women's experiences. The disadvantages are quite conspicuous in the field of education, health, work and exercise of authority within the family. Here these disadvantages are briefly dealt with.

Concept of Gender

Before we begin the discussion it is important that the term 'gender' is defined at the outset, for it means different things to different people. Scholars of different academic persuasions have defined the term in their own ways, creating further confusions. Confusions are also because it is often mixed with sex. Though gender and sex are interrelated, both convey two different meanings. A detailed discussion on issues relating to the conceptual aspects of gender can be seen in Lorber's (1994) work.

Anyway, gender is commonly described as the way a society is organised rather than just as an attribute of individuals. Here, whether the differences between men and women are biologically or socially governed is less important than the way the society is generally organised around those differences. Within this perspective gender is viewed as a set of social and cultural practices that affects the life of men and women in every society. Because culture helps to construct gender and it differs greatly from one society to another.

Some social scientists have tried to separate physical attributes (sex) and cultural or social elements (gender) quite clearly, but in reality these are not easily separable. Gender includes aspects of sex; expectations and meanings of gender are often based on real or perceived observations about the physical bodies or minds of men and women. Although individual researchers may focus on particular aspects of gender or sex-biologists might study physical differences, between men and women, economists might be interested in labour force roles that women and men play, and anthropologists might study how culture constructs the social meanings of sex differences – these researchers can learn much more by studying the definitions and elements of gender used in allied disciplines. Keeping the above perspectives in view, Riley (1997) has tried to explain gender as a social institution, as a cultural construct and in terms of differences in power. Drawing a clear distinction between sex and gender both from sociological and anthropological viewpoint, Giddens (1998: 91) has observed: 'While sex refers to physical differences of the body, gender concerns the psychological, social and cultural differences between males and females'. The chapter has tried to address the issues relating to gender keeping this conception in view.

Theoretical Perspectives

Women are biologically different from men. So their participation in society is also different from that of men. But there is disagreement among social scientists regarding the exact nature of consequences of this difference. Such differences in opinion have given rise to several theories. They are a part of new scholarship on women. All these theories are women centred and a majority of contemporary feminist theorists are oppression theorists.

> All theories of gender oppression describe women's situation as a consequence of a direct power relationship between men and women

in which men, who have fundamental and concrete interests in controlling, using, subjugating, and oppressing women, effectively implement those interests. (Ritzer, 1992: 470)

These theories are not necessarily sociological theories. They differ from sociological theories in many ways. They are the work of an interdisciplinary community, which includes not only sociologists but also scholars from other disciplines, such as anthropology, biology, history, law, literature, philosophy, economics, political science, psychology and theology. By and large the scientific credentials of these theories are poor. Most of the theorists are closer to political activism, seeking to produce a better world for women. However, feminists' ideas continue to be on the margins of sociology, and in fact it is true for most developing than developed countries.

The feminist writers have made seminal contributions to the present day sociology. The work of feminist scholars gradually pushed the 'founding fathers' of sociology to the periphery of the discipline on gender issues. The men who assumed central position in sociology till the days of Talcott Parsons and R.K. Merton could not be able to respond in a critical way to issues of gender differences and inequality. Therefore, women's studies have developed as an independent female-dominated subject. But like sociology, it does not have 'founding fathers'; rather it is discipline with 'founding mothers'. Important perspectives relating to gender are quite briefly dealt with here. This would help us understand the issues associated with gender discrimination, as addressed herein.

Biological Viewpoint

Social scientists believe that human beings generally behave in accordance with their culture. Differences in behaviour patterns between men and women reflect the culture they represent. Contrary to this view, biosociologists Tiger and Fox (1972) have argued that behaviour of the human beings is determined essentially by 'biogrammar' and not so much by culture, it is genetically based programme that predisposes humans to behave in certain ways.

It is not to be mixed up with instinct. It is inherited from one generation to another. Biogrammars of men and women are similar in many ways, but they are not exactly the same. Biogrammars of men are such that they are more aggressive and dominant than women. These characters are generally based on and result from differences between men and women hormones. Women are programmed by their biogrammars to reproduce and care for children.

Though anthropologist G.P. Murdock's approach is different from that of Tiger and Fox, he – on the basis of cross-cultural studies of 224 societies – has observed that the sexual division of labour is present in all the societies. Men with superior physical strength are more capable than women to undertake strenuous tasks. Because of their biological function of reproduction and child rearing and nursing, they are more tied to the home base. Talcott Parsons expresses a similar view when he states that biological differences between the sexes provide the foundation on which the sexual division of labour hinges. He has clearly emphasised the 'expressive' role that a woman in nuclear family plays in the process of socialisation of children. Such expressive role as warmth, security and emotional support is also necessary for the bread winners of the family.

Cultural Viewpoint

On the other hand, there are social scientists who contend that human behaviour is largely determined by culture. Norms, values and roles are culturally determined and socially transmitted. From this perspective gender roles are a product of culture rather than of biology. It has been argued that unlike those biological differences that are anatomical and genetic in character, gender is an acquired identity One, such, protagonist of this view is British sociologist Ann Oakley. Using the ethnographic materials of G.P. Murdock, she has exploded the myth that sexual division of labour is universal. She has argued that Murdock has looked other cultures through both western and male eyes.

Oakley (1974) has examined a number of societies in which biology appears to have little or no influence on women's role. She is also critical of Parsons' view of the family and the role of the expressive woman within it. The expressive housewife role is not essential for the functioning of the family unit. It merely exists for the convenience of men. Parson's explanation of gender roles is simply a validating myth for the domestic oppression of women.

Oakley (1974) suggests that gender roles are neither inevitable nor a particular task is universally assigned exclusively to one sex or the other. But she has not offered adequate explanation for the existence of a clear-cut division of labour in practically all societies. Nor does she explain why the tasks of women are similar in most societies and why men generally have power and authority over women. Friedle (1975), however, has tried to offer explanations to these problems. Answers to these questions are from both biology and culture. According to her, male dominance and gender roles are culturally determined. The fact that women bear children forms a central part of her explanations for the sexual division of labour.

Ortner (1974) claims that it is not biology as such that ascribes the women to their status in society, but the way in which every culture defines and evaluates female biology. Thus, if this universal evaluation changed, then the basis for female subordination would be removed. Ortner has argued that in every society a higher value is placed on culture than on nature. Culture is the means by which man controls and regulates nature. The universal evaluation of culture as superior to nature is the basic reason for the devaluation of women. Ortner fails to show conclusively that in all societies culture is evaluated more highly than nature. It should be recognised by the protagonists of cultural perspective that gender identity is not entirely free from biological differences. Biological differences have been a crucial determinant of cultural contour of gender identity. Culture has not been developed in a planned manner; rather, it has evolved of its own in course of time resulting from orthogenetic and heterogenetic encounter and experience of humans.

Marxian Views

Marxian feminism brings together Marxian class analysis and feminist protest. This theory does not produce an intensified theory of oppression; rather, it is merely a muted statement of gender inequality. The foundation of this theory was laid by Karl Marx and Friedrich Engels. Engels argued that progressively greater restrictions were placed on sexual relationships and reproduction of children throughout man's history. He speculated that the present system of monogamous nuclear family evolved through a series of stages including promiscuous horde life and polygamy. Each successive stage of marriage and family placed greater restriction on the number of mates available to the individual. The monogamous nuclear developed with the emergence of private ownership of the forces of production and the advent of the state. The state instituted laws to protect the system of private property and to enforce the rules of monogamous marriage. This form of marriage and the family developed to solve the problem of the inheritance of private property. Property was owned by men and in order to pass it on to their heirs, they must be certain of the legitimacy of those heirs. They, therefore, needed greater control over women so that there would be no doubt about the paternity of their offspring. The monogamous family provided the most efficient device for this purpose.

Engels speculative explanation was largely based on *Ancient Society* – a book by the nineteenth-century American anthropologist, Lewis Henry Morgan. Modern research has proved that Morgan's interpretation was erroneous. The evidence reveals that many of its details compiled by him are incorrect. For example, monogamous marriage and the nuclear family are often found in hunting and gathering bands. Both Engels and Marx have offered inadequate and lopsided interpretation of the position of women in society.

According to Engels, female subordination, as stated before, is an outcome of the emergence of private property, in particular the private ownership of the forces of production. Monogamous marriage developed to shield the institution of private property.

Men needed control over women to ensure the 'undisputed paternity' of their offspring and heirs. Male-dominated monogamous marriage involved the economic dependence of the wife upon her husband. These, however, are basically speculative and over-generalised views.

Marxists believe that women are unequal to men not because of any direct conflict of interests between genders, but because of the working out of class oppression. Women in all classes often remain more disadvantaged than men. The prevailing disadvantages of women are nothing but a historic carry over from the collapse of primitive communism. Consequently, the solution for gender inequality lies in the destruction of class oppression. This destruction will come through revolutionary action by a united wage-earning class, including women and men. But any direct mobilisation of women against men is counter-revolutionary because it divides the potentially revolutionary working class.

Neo-Marxism Views

Marxian analysis of the family in capitalist society developed in late 1960s and 1970s, when several feminist writers employed Marxian concepts in their criticism of the family. From this perspective, the family is seen as a unit that produces one of the basic commodities of capitalism, labour. Many feminist writers are dissatisfied with such a simplistic interpretation of Marx and Engels. They argue that Marxian theory fails to provide an adequate explanation for sexual inequality. They are rightly disillusioned with the promise that socialism will liberate women. Radical feminist Firestone (1972) in her book, *The Dialectic of Sex*, attempts to do just this. Firestone has argued that the sexual division of labour and the 'sexual class system' pre-dates and is more basic than the specialised division of labour, which differentiates all members of society and the economic class system that divides both men and women. She claims that the sexual inequality is rooted in biological differences. She argues that unlike economic class, sex class sprang directly from a biological reality; men and women were created different and not equally privileged. Because women bore children they were dependent on men for their survival. Dependence on men produced unequal power relationships and 'power psychology', which formed the basis for all future stratification systems. Men derived pleasure from their power over women, which led to power psychology, the desire to dominate others. Thus, stratification is based ultimately on biology rather than on economics. It began not with private property, but with the different reproductive role of men and women.

Domination of men over women was extended to domination of some men over other men. The sexual class system provided the blueprint and the prototype for the economic class system. The economic class system provided the means by which some men came to dominate other men. Since, in Firestone's view, all domination is bad, both the sexual class system and the economic class system must go. Both men and women must be liberated. Since the sexual class system is the primary form of stratification, it is the main target for attack. In Firestone's views, the sexual class system is the model for all other exploitive systems and thus the tapeworm that must be eliminated first by any true revolution.

The sexual class system can only end when women cease to be slaves to their biology. Reliable birth control techniques have begun to free women but true freedom will only be realised by means of artificial reproduction. Only when babies can be conceived and developed outside the womb will women be freed from their reproductive role. But the moot question is that – is it really going to happen on a large scale?

Radical feminists have defined violence against women very broadly with a view to covering up the natural differences between man and woman. According to them, patriarchy is a kind of violence practiced by men against women. It does not always signify overt physical cruelty. It can be hidden in more complex practices of exploitation and control such as standards of fashion, ideals of motherhood, monogamy, chastity, heterosexuality and sexual harassment at the workplace, practice of gynaecology, unpaid household drudgery and unpaid wage work. But the theme of violence as overt physical cruelty lies at the heart of radical feminism's linking of patriarchy to violence: rape, sexual abuse, prostitution, spouse abuse, incest, molestation of children, witch burning, persecution of lesbians, female infanticide, forced suicide of Hindu widows, dowry-related violence and the practice of circumcision of female genitals among Muslims. Physical violence by men is believed to be the last line of defence of patriarchy. Men create and maintain patriarchy because women are a uniquely effective means of satisfying male sexual desire. Their bodies are essential for reproduction of children. These arguments are, however, quite controversial. This fact is also not free from dispute that women can also be ornamental signs of male status and power, for men's status too can be a symbol of status and power for women.

Many feminist writers advocate the abolition of gender roles with the mother-housewife role being selected as the prime target. In order to liberate women, Ann Oakley (1974) suggests following steps: First, the housewife role must be abolished. Second, the family as it now stands must be abolished. On the other hand, Susan Brownmiller suggests that husband and wife should split their traditional roles down the middle. Each should work for half a day and spend the rest of the time taking care of the children. Jessie Bernard has also supported this idea. But such a solution is hardly viable from economic angle.

All these ideas, which have developed against the established men and women relationship, suggest that the root cause of discrimination and inequality relating to gender seems to be heterosexuality, resulting in monogamous family. According to the feminists, men's inherent desire for dominance over women is the root cause of all problems faced by women. Men are so biased against women that they often become inimical to women's interests and that attitude is well reflected in their violent behaviour. This is one of the important reasons why many feminists prefer to lead the life of spinsters or have formed households independent of their boyfriends. Children are born out of wedlock. God alone knows about the future of such children. It appears from the arguments of radical feminists that the women liberation would be accomplished in a true sense only when all women become completely lesbians and live independent of men. But the inherent danger with such a state of affairs is that it would mark the end of human civilisation very shortly.

Socialism or communism based on promiscuous life is not a real solution since there is bound to be struggle for dominance by men over women and among men themselves for privatisation of women. This should be obvious from the fact that men always try to privatise their girlfriends or sometimes even prostitutes of their choices and in a similar vein women also try to exercise monopoly over their boyfriends or male prostitutes. Personal choice is never constant, as human beings always try to go for the best as per their choice. So long as both men and women live and work at the same place, there cannot be complete gender equality. Some dissensions and discrimination are an inevitable social reality. No known society, small or large, has really ever existed without any kind of differentiation or hierarchy.

The available facts and arguments suggest that all theories are based on half-truth. They have developed out of intellectual craze of leisure-class women from the affluent world, who are unhappy with their life for one reason or the other. So long as the human beings have a lack of satisfaction with what they have, they are bound to be discontent with what they have achieved. Quest for a better life or greater pleasure in life makes people unhappy with their past and present and encourages them to dream a better future. All these theories are a mere reflection of what little they have achieved and what more they dream or aspire for in future.

No single perspective on gender is really able to offer an objective and holistic view of the dynamics of gender relationship. Therefore, there is need to consider the gender issues independent of any rigid theoretical framework to arrive at a scientifically tenable conclusion. Herein the discussion is carried forward from sociology-of-gender-standpoint rather than from the women-centred standpoint, as commonly pursued by feminists.

Gender Discrimination: Some Empirical Realities

Now we highlight the major areas of gender discrimination and inequality across the world. At the outset, let us begin with the issue of education, which is one of the most vital areas of social development. The value of education in life is so enormous that it can drastically change the face of women both inside and outside the home. But the women continue to be discriminated in matters of education for one reason or the other.

In nearly all developing countries, women are more likely to be illiterate and to have completed fewer years of education than men. Although literacy rates have climbed in recent years, women record a larger proportion of the illiterate population in developing countries, especially in South Asia and Africa. But since the 1970s, literacy rates for women have gone up from 54 per cent to 64 per cent. And since the 1980s, the gap between girls and boys enrolled in secondary schools has lessened, from 80 girls to 90 girls enrolled per 100 boys (PRB, 1998). Although the education gap between men and women is narrowing in many countries, worldwide more men than women are literate (80% compared with 64%). The difference is greatest in less developed regions where overall literacy rates are low. In more developed regions, nearly all boys and girls are enrolled in both primary and secondary schools. In less developed regions, however, girls are less likely to attend school than are boys.

This disparity is more pronounced at the secondary school level than at the primary school level. In the less developed world, more particularly in south Asian countries such as Bangladesh, India and Pakistan, lower enrolment levels of girls in secondary school are largely due to social, cultural and economic factors. These factors include early marriage and childbearing, household duties, parents' perception that secondary school is more beneficial for their sons than for their daughters, worries about girls' safety outside the village environment and limited job opportunities for women in sectors that require higher education (see the report on *Human Development in South Asia* for detailed discussion) (MHHDC, 2000).

The World Bank rightly calls women's education the single most influential investment that can be made in the developing world. Many governments now support women's education not only to foster economic growth, but also to promote smaller families, increase modern contraceptive use and improve child health. Greater female education is associated with smaller family size throughout the world. In a number of less developed countries, women with no education have about twice the number of children as women with 10 or more years of schooling (United Nations, 1997: 12).

Health

With respect to health condition, there has been significant improvement in the health of women's life. Since the 1950s, women's life expectancy at birth has increased from 49 years to 68 years. But the incidence of maternal mortality continues to be very high. Most maternal deaths occur in the less developed world, particularly Asia and Africa. The ratio of maternal deaths to live births varies enormously throughout the world. A women's lifetime risk of dying from pregnancy-related complications or during childbirth is 1 in 48 in the less developed world, versus only 1 in 1,800 in the developed world. About 80 per cent of maternal deaths are due to causes directly related to pregnancy and childbirth – unsafe abortion and obstetric complications such as severe bleeding, infection, hypertensive disorders and obstructed labour. The environment in which women live influences maternal health. Maternal deaths are strongly associated with substandard health services and the lack of medical supplies at the time of labour, delivery and immediately after birth. Women may also delay or fail to seek treatment because of logistical, social or cultural barriers.

In 1997, almost 6,000 women around the world were infected with HIV every day. Globally, women account for 41 per cent of adults who are living with HIV/AIDS. But the proportion of HIV-infected adults who are women varies by region. HIV is sexually transmitted at least four times more efficiently from men to women than from women to men. Societal norms of acceptable sexual behaviour for men and women increase women's susceptibility to HIV. Their risk of HIV stems more from their partner's behaviour than from their own. Women are susceptible to HIV also because they often lack the power to avoid sexual coercion or to negotiate safe sex with their partners.

Female genital cutting (circumcision), yet another form of gender-based violence, is practiced in most Islamic states – 28 African countries and in about a dozen Middle Eastern and Asian nations. Some 130 million women and girls have been subjected to the practice, which is fundamentally about controlling women's sexuality. The effects of gender violence can be devastating and long lasting. Such violence is a particular danger to a woman's reproductive health and can scar the survivor psychologically, cognitively and interpersonally. Since girls are more often subjected to sexual violence, they run the risk of becoming infected with HIV at a much younger age than are boys. Forced and unprotected sex also leads to unintended pregnancies, abortions and unwanted children.

Work

With regard to participation in work, women's position is also not good. Since the 1960s, women's participation in the labour force has increased from 33 per cent to 54 per cent in 1998. But throughout the world they face a dual responsibility: doing a larger share of work in the home than men – cooking, cleaning and child rearing – and working outside the home. Worldwide, women are far less likely to work in the formal labour force than are men (54% for women as against 82% for men) and are likely to be employed primarily in the agricultural and service sectors (PRB, 1998). Women in nonagricultural jobs are paid less than men. Where employment in the formal sector is limited, women and men in less developed countries work in the informal sector, selling goods in the local market or working for themselves or for family members in cottage industries. Women make up more than one-third of the informal labour force in many countries. Many low-income women work for themselves in small businesses, although their ability to start and expand such businesses is often restricted by limited access in credit.

Female heads of households are a special group of women in society. With no spouse present, they are solely responsible for home and family. Women head approximately one-quarter or more of households in Eastern Africa, the Caribbean, North America and parts of Europe. Globally, the percentages of female-headed households are 27 per cent for developed and 14 per cent for developing countries and they are rising because of increased levels of marital dissolution (through abandonment, separation, divorce or death), migration and nonmarital childbearing (PRB, 1998). Available data suggest that households headed by women are poorer than those headed by men. In many countries, women who head households with young children are limited in their employment opportunities, in part due to the absence of a spouse to share family responsibilities. Also, in many countries a large proportion of female-headed households consist of elderly women living alone.

Gender Violence

The term 'violence against women' refers to many types of harmful behaviour directed at women and girls because of their sex. In 1993, the United Nations offered the first official definition of such violence when the General Assembly adopted the Declaration on the Elimination of Violence against Women. According to Article 1 of the declaration, violence against women includes (United Nations, 1993). 'Any act of gender-based violence that results in, or is likely to result in, physical, sexual or psychological harm or suffering to women, including threats of such acts, coercion or arbitrary deprivations of liberty, whether occurring in public or private life'.

Violence against women is different from interpersonal violence in general. The nature and patterns of violence against men, for example, typically differ from those against women. Men are more likely than women to be victimised by a stranger or casual acquaintance. Women are more likely than men to be victimised by a family member or intimate partner (Butchart and Brown, 1991; Crowell and Burgess, 1996: 225; Heise et al., 1994: 72; Koss et al., 1994: 344; Tjaden and Thoennes, 1998: 16). The fact that women are often emotionally involved with and financially dependent upon those who abuse them has profound implications for how women experience violence and how best to intervene.

Violence against women and girls comprises physical, sexual, psychological and economic abuse. It is often known as 'gender-based' violence because it originates in part from women's subordinate social position. Many cultures have beliefs, norms and social institutions that legitimise and therefore perpetuate violence against women. The same acts that would be punished if directed at an employer, a neighbour, or an acquaintance often go unchallenged when men direct them at women, especially within the family. Two of the most common forms of violence against women are abuse by intimate male partners and coerced sex, whether it takes place in childhood, adolescence or adulthood. Intimate partner abused – also known as domestic violence, wife beating and battering – is almost always accompanied by psychological abuse and in one-quarter to one-half of cases by forced sex as well. The majority of women who are abused by their partners are abused many times. In fact, an atmosphere of terror often permeates abusive relationships.

Worldwide, one of the most common forms of violence against women is abuse by their husbands or other intimate male partners. Partner violence occurs in all countries and transcends social, economic, religious and cultural groups. Although women can also be violent and abuse exists in some same-sex relationships, the vast majority of partner abuse is perpetrated by men against their female partners.

While research into intimate partner abuse is in its early stages, there is growing agreement about its nature and the various factors that cause it. Often referred to as 'wife beating', 'battering', or 'domestic violence', intimate partner abuse is generally a part of the patterns of abusive behaviour and control rather than an isolated act of physical aggression. Partners' abuse can take a variety of forms including physical assault such as hits, slaps, kicks and beating, psychological abuse, such as constant belittling, intimidation and humiliation; and coercive sex. It frequently includes controlling behaviour such as isolating a woman from family and friends, monitoring her movements and restricting her access to resources.

Women are vulnerable to violence at all stages of their life. They are threatened by female infanticide, incest, child prostitution, rape, partner violence, dowry death, psychological abuse, sexual harassment, wartime violence and harmful traditional practices such as child marriage, female genital cutting and widow burning (Singh, 2001). It has been reported in the Population Reports (JHU, 2000: 1) that 'around the world at least one woman in every three has been beaten, coerced into sex, or otherwise abused in her lifetime. Most often the abuser is a member of her own family'.

Evidence exists to show that violence against women, especially domestic violence occurs in all parts of the world and is largely unpoliced (domestic violence is defined by the United Nations as violence occurring within the private sphere, generally between individuals who are related through personal intimacy, blood or law). The extent of domestic violence worldwide is difficult to measure because country-level studies are scarce and vary in methodology. According to the UN Human Rights Commission, most domestic violence is perpetrated by men against women.

Though gender violence is widespread, information is fragmented and anecdotal. A culture of silence surrounds cases of violence against women in most countries, particularly in developing countries, making it difficult to get a true picture of its extent. Part of the difficulty is that gender violence mostly occurs in what is thought of as the private sphere – within families, inside homes and out of sight. This type of violence is under-reported and even deliberately covered up by both the survivors and the societies in which they live. The reliability of crime and health statistics varies among countries and refusal to recognise the problem is a barrier to its solution.

Domestic violence, which typically occurs when a man beats his female partner, is the most prevalent form of gender violence. In the United States, more than a million and a half women are battered by partners each year (Straus and Geller, 1986). In the 1995 Egypt Demographic and Health Survey, 35 per cent of the women reported being battered by their husbands during marriage (El-Zanaty et al., 1996). It is, therefore, hard to imagine that with the rise in development and education, relationships between men and women would be more comfortable and congenial.

Domestic violence against a woman affects her mental, physical, economic and social well-being. Many women tolerate such abuse because they fear retaliation by their spouse or extended family, or both, if they protest. Women's vulnerability to domestic violence is reinforced by their economic dependence on men, widespread cultural acceptance of domestic violence and a lack of laws and enforcement to combat it. Boys who witness battering of their mothers or sisters are more likely to become batterers themselves, while girls are more likely to become victims of battering.

Rape, a pervasive form of gender violence, has long symbolised a man's ability to have his way with a woman. Around the world, most rapists are known by those they attack and are often the victim's father, partner, some other household figures or the neighbour. Statistics on rape suggest that 40 per cent to 60 per cent of those raped are 15 years old or younger. In some societies, the rape of the girl or woman is thought to bring shame on her family. The girl may consider committing suicide or the family may consider marrying the girl to her rapist as the only way to recover her honour. In some cases, the girl is condemned to prostitution.

Multilateral institutions have begun to address gender violence, and the problem was placed high on the agenda of recent UN world conferences. The 1995 Fourth World Conference on Women in Beijing adopted a Platform for Action, which declared, 'Violence against women is an obstacle to the achievement of the objective of equality, development, and peace'. Ending physical and sexual violence requires long-term commitment and strategies involving all parts of society. Many governments have committed themselves to overcoming violence against women by passing and enforcing laws that ensure women's legal rights and punish abusers. In addition, community-based strategies can focus on empowering women, reaching out to men, and changing the beliefs and attitudes that permit abusive behaviour. Only when women gain their place as equal members of society will violence against women no longer be an invisible norm, but instead a shocking aberration. This fact has to be realised that the men often behave outrageously with women because they are endowed with superior 'bio-power'. This is true not only of humans but also of animals.

In general, the feminists tend to make men solely responsible for all acts of violence against women and present their ilk as innocent. Women's role in provocation behind the perpetration of violence is always concealed or underplayed. Quite recently Laura Schlessinger's *The Surrendered Wife* has globally agitated the mind of feminist intellectuals to review their contention concerning gender discrimination. She has argued that the women are happiest when they obey their husbands.

Gender Equality and Development

Studies of development have almost neglected women until recently. Development planning has been both by men and for men. Women have usually only appeared in the context of 'women and children' as a dependent group. Prior to 1975, less than 1 per cent of all writing on development had specifically referred to women (Ware, 1981: 3). From 1980s onward, the issues relating to women and development started to draw increasingly greater attention of various multilateral institutions such as UNDP, UNFPA, World Bank, ILO and other such organisations and fora of the UN, IUSSP, IPPF and other organisations. Woman, gender equality and development are stated to go hand in hand. The countries with smaller gaps between men and women achieve higher economic performance, as it has been reported by the World Bank. The societies that discriminate on the basis of gender pay a significant price in the form of greatest poverty, slower economic growth, weaker governance and lower quality of life. Evidence has shown that gender issues are crucial to development and poverty reduction. Gender inequalities in basic rights, education, access to resources and participation in public life affect development, and they tend to be largest in low-income countries and further these inequalities are greatest among the poor.

Countries where only 50 per cent of the girls are likely to go to school have 21 more infant deaths per 1,000 live births than countries with little gender gap in schooling. In Sub-Saharan Africa, if the ratio of female-to-male years of schooling had been near parity in 1990, its under-five child mortality would have been 25 per cent lower. It is widely acknowledged that gender inequalities in education and access to other productive resources create inefficiencies that reduce countries prospects for economic growth. It appears from some studies in Sub-Saharan Africa that improving gender equality in access to productive resources could increase agricultural productivity by as much as one-fifth. Much of the recent debate about gender and development has highlighted growth-oriented approaches more than rights-oriented approaches. But the available evidence suggests the economic development and institutional changes are complementary and that both are necessary. Cross-country evidence on the impact of gender inequalities in education in Sub-Saharan Africa, South Asia, the Middle East and North Africa supports these findings. In no region do women experience full equality with men in social, economic and legal rights. In a number of countries, women still lack independent rights to own land, manage property, undertake outside employment, or even travel, without their husband's consent. In parts of Africa, women obtain land rights chiefly through their husbands, as long as the marriage endures, and they lose these rights when they are divorced or widowed.

The UN Development Fund for Women (UNIFEM) has observed that while globalisation has spurred women's participation in the market economy, the process has also contributed to widening inequality among and within countries that women are increasingly forced to take up insecure and low-paying jobs, and that child labour is rampant. At the special session of the UN General Assembly on poverty for the first time countries made a time-bound commitment for addressing poverty. They set a 2015 deadline for freeing some 600 million people from absolute poverty, which is defined as income of one dollar a day or less. But the plan falls short on key details on how to get the job done.

Nonetheless there has been much improvement in the absolute status of women and in gender equality in most developing countries during the last three to four decades. With a few exceptions, women's education levels improved considerably. The primary enrolment rates of girls have nearly doubled in the Middle East, South Asia and Sub-Saharan Africa, rising much faster than boys, and substantially reducing large gender gaps in schooling. The last 50 years have seen women's life expectancy increase by 15–20 years in developing countries. With greater investments in girls and women and better access to health care, the expected relationship between female and male longevity has emerged in all developing regions. In the 1990s, women in South Asia, on an average, are living longer than men.

In politics, women continue to be vastly under-represented in national and sub-national assemblies accounting for less than 10 per cent of the seats in parliament, except in East Asia. It has been reported recently by Angela King, the UN Assistant Secretary General and Special Advisor on gender issue and advancement of women, that there had actually been a decrease in the number of women serving in parliament. In order to ensure greater participation of women in development, cultural values restricting individualism of women need to be redefined through educational means. As individualism does not constitute a significant ideology in Islamic society, parental and conjugal roles have a high degree of primacy, adversely affecting the role of women in developmental activities. The neighbouring country of Pakistan, similar to some other tradition-bound Islamic states, is a case in point (Shah, 1986: 5–40).

The Beijing Platform, a 150-page document, has become a key tool in the struggle for respect for the human rights of women and girls. It identifies 12 critical areas of concern, ranging from women's health to their absence in decision-making areas. Yet, seven years after its adoption, the lives of millions of women have either remained the same or have worsened – often in the face of poor economic conditions. A World Bank report, *Global Economic Prospects: 2000*, indicates that the number of the world's poor has increased and predicts that the trend is likely to persist still further. The meeting, titled 'Women 2000 – Gender Equality, Development and Peace', held at New York in June at the time of special session of the UN General Assembly acknowledged that little had been achieved to increase women's participation in economic decision-making and in political parties and parliaments.

As a matter of fact, women in most developing countries have gone ahead of their western counterparts, as at the comparable stage of economic development the western women were far worse than what the women in the developing world are today. In most developed countries, the women did not exercise even voting right till the end of nineteenth century. Voting right was granted in the United Kingdom in 1918, only women older than 30 years were eligible. In the United States, women's suffrage was granted two years later. Until the end of World War II, it was rare to see a woman as the head of a large organisation and institution. That is however, but natural, because when the now-developed countries were developing there was no developed country to inspire them. Therefore, the women in developing countries, despite many disadvantage and discrimination of various kinds, are really much better off than what they should have been. Social gains seem to have gone ahead of economic development through the process of globalisation and acculturation. The educated women in cities of developing countries are, therefore, no less restless that the western women in matters of gender discrimination and violence. Here India can be cited as an important case in point (Singh, 2000, 2001). It is all in the larger interests of the nation as well the female members of the civil society.

Conclusions

With the rise in the tempo of economic development, modernisation and consequential social change women's icon at the societal level might have improved, but at the familial level ensuing patterns of gender relationship do not seem to sugar so well for the society as a whole. With the lapse of time, relations between men and women – predominantly in the developed as well as in metropolitan societies of the developing world – are getting tenser and increasingly discordant in many significant ways. The new unfolding scenario does not appear to chip in well with the sustenance of the family system generally. Hence, the sociologists, both men and women, own enough responsibility not only to look into the new contours of gender inequality and discrimination but also to explicate and spell out the rising critical issues concerning the redefinition of men–women relationship in the larger interests of society. It is recognised that other social analysts and activists, too, can perform no less a significant role towards the understanding of impending changes and challenges of the new millennium in the arena of gender relationships.

Urbanisation, rise in female education, democratisation of political system, spread of media of mass communication and modernisation have brought epoch-making changes in man–woman relationships on a societal canvass. Gender issues have brought many more changes in the role of women in diverse capacity. Through the process of globalisation, gender has become an important social and political issue even in developing countries, which are way behind the developed world with respect to the level of female education, expectancy of life at birth, urban and industrial development, political awareness, spread of media of mass communication and modernisation.

References

Butchart, A. and Brown, D. 1991. 'Non-fatal Injuries due to Interpersonal Violence in Johannesburg-Soweto: Incidence, Determinants and Consequences'. *Forensic Science International*, 52: 35–51.

Crowell, N. and Burgess, A.W. (eds) 1996. *Understanding Violence against Women*. Washington, D.C.: National Academy Press.

El Zanaty, F. et al. 1996. *Egypt Demographic and Health Survey*. Cairo: National Population Council and Calverton, MD: Macro International.

Firestone, R. 1972. *The Dialectic of Sex*. London: Paladin.

Friedle, E. 1975. *Women and Men: An Anthropological View*. New York: Holt, Rinehart & Winston.

Giddens, Anthony. 1998. *Sociology*. Oxford: Polity Press.

Heise, L. et al. 1994. 'Violence against Women: The Hidden Health Burden'. Discussion Paper 255, Washington, D.C.: World Bank.

JHU. *Population Reports 2000*. Series L, No. 11, Population Information Program, Johns Hopkins University, Baltimore, August.

Koss, M.P. et al. 1994. *No Safe Haven: Male Violence against Women at Home, at Work, and in the Community*. Washington, D.C.: American Psychological Association.

Lorber, Judith. 1994. *Paradoxes of Gender*. New Haven, CT: Yale University Press.

MHHDC. 2000. *Human Development in South Asia*. Karachi: Oxford University Press.

Oakley, A. 1974. *Housewife*. London: Allen Lane.

Ortner, S.B. 1974. 'Is Female to Male as Nature is to Culture?', in M.Z. Rosaldo and L. Lamphere (eds), *Women, Culture and Society*. Stanford: Stanford University Press.

PRB. 1998. *Women of Our World* (Data sheet). Washington, D.C.: Population Reference Bureau.

Riley, Nancy E. 1997. 'Gender, Power and Population Change'. *Population Bulletin*, 52(1).

Ritzer, George. 1992. *Sociological Theory*. Singapore: McGraw Hill, Inc.

Shah, Nasra M. 1986. *Pakistani Women: A Socio-economic and Demographic Profile*. Islamabad: Pakistan Institute of Development Economics and Hawaii East: West Population Institute.

Singh, J.P. 2000. 'Indian Democracy and Empowerment of Women'. *Indian Journal of Public Administration*, XL(4): 617–630.

——. 2001. 'Social and Cultural Aspects of Gender Inequality and Discrimination in India'. Paper Presented at the 6th Conference on Women in Asia, Canberra: Department of Anthropology, The Australian National University.

Straus, M. and Geller, R. 1986. 'Societal Change and Change in Family Violence from 1975 to 1985 as Revealed by Two National Surveys'. *Journal of Marriage and Family*, 4: 465–479.

Tiger, L. and Fox, R. 1972. *The Imperial Animal.* London: Secker & Warburg.

Tjaden, P. and Thoennes, N. 1998. *Prevalence Incidence and Consequences of Violence against Women: Findings from the National Violence against Women Survey*. Washington, D.C.: National Institute of Justice, Centre for Disease Control and Prevention.

United Nations (UN). 1993. *United Nations General Assembly Declaration on the Elimination of Violence against Women*. Proceedings of the 85th Plenary Meeting, Geneva, December 20.

——. 1997. *Linkage between Population and Education*. Department of Economic and Social Affairs, Population Division, New York.

Ware, Helen. 1981. *Women, Demography and Development*. Canberra: The Australian National University.

12

Status of Women in Haryana

Neerja Ahlawat

While writing the preface for the 'Report of the National Commission on Self-employed Women and Women in the Informal Sector', its chairperson Ela R. Bhatt has recommended to the government to actively help initiate and maintain a network of grass-roots-level organisations such as village 'Mahila Mandals'. The Commission strongly pleads for entrusting the village Mahila Mandals with the responsibility: one, of implementation of poverty alleviation programmes, and, two, block-level planning, monitoring and setting targets for women's development at the local level. To fight the wrath of nature – drought and floods, it is believed that the village Mahila Mandal is the best vehicle (Shramshakti: 1988). This chapter addresses itself to clarify various demographic and socio-economic variables, viz., (i) gender imbalance, (ii) incidence of female mortality, (iii) maternal mortality and health status, (iv) educational level, (v) socio-economic aspect: women as workers, (vi) women's contribution to the family income and (vii) women in dairying, which are responsible for making women in a disadvantageous position in Haryana and also pinpoints certain roles women and women's organisations should play in initiating the process of social change.

In the planning processes, under the trickle-down theory it was expected that women will equally benefit along with men. This has been belied by actual developments. The Seventh Plan document recognises that 'in spite of the development measures the constitutional legal guarantees; women have lagged behind in almost all sectors' (Seventh Five-Year Plan, 1985). In the past decades, there have been various forces and pressures which are more dominant than those which have tried to push women towards growth and development. This chapter seeks to analyse the various forces and pressures, which have reduced women to a low and secondary place in the social structure.

Methodology

The study is confined to two women's non-government organisations committed to work for the women's empowerment programme in Haryana. The Janvadi Mahila Samiti, Rohtak, is committed to enhance the position of women in the society. It seeks to make women self-reliant socially and economically and encourage their participation in decision-making in the urban areas of Rohtak district, and the Akhil Bharatiya Mahila Parishad, Rewari, claims its involvement in encouraging rural women in Rewari district. Their activities involve creating awareness among rural women, motivating them to participate in dairy and marketing, cooperatives, handicrafts and skills acquisition for income generation.

Exploratory type of research design was used for the present study. It helped us to seek and analyse women NGO's developmental activities at the grassroots level, as well as mobilisation process for women's empowerment, creating awareness and developing inter-linkages on issues related to women and gender concern. Apart from this, secondary data have also been used to interpret women's position in the society.

Gender Imbalances (Sex Ratio)

The first instance of gender imbalance is the sex ratio itself. The sex ratio continues to be highly unfavourable to women. In the 1991 census, the overall sex ratio of the country as a whole works out to 929 per 1,000 males. On the sex ratio front, some trends are puzzling. Haryana is the second richest state in India in per capita income but the sex ratio in Haryana is 874 females per 1,000 males, which are lower than the country as a whole (exact inverse relationship in rank). To this kind of trend, Amartya Sen et al. (1987) call as 'the missing women'. The 'missing women' phenomenon is more in the urban areas of Haryana, where the sex ratio is 849 females per 1,000 males in comparison to rural areas where the sex ratio is 876 females per 1,000 males (Table 12.1). The existence of a very low sex ratio in the rural areas of Haryana on account of the incidence of male migration to urban areas and also due to sharp fall in death rates in urban areas clearly indicates relatively less access of women to urban areas. It is a pointer to their weak position in taking advantage of modernisation and development which is concentrated in the urban area.

It is disturbing to note that the age-specific sex ratio declined with the increase in the age group. Table 12.1 suggests that the sex ratio in the age group 0–4 years is 921. It declined to 873 in the age group 5–9 and to 865 in the 10–14 years.

Table 12.1 *Sex Ratio by Broad Age Group 1991: Females per 1,000 Males*

Age Group	*Haryana*		*Total*	*India*		*Total*
	Rural	*Urban*		*Rural*	*Urban*	
0–4	920	924	921	977	967	975
5–9	868	896	873	939	945	940
10–14	861	883	865	893	907	896
15–19	798	818	803	896	972	890
20–24	910	851	894	1028	861	979
25–29	911	787	876	1006	883	971
30–34	965	782	915	1019	825	965
35–39	965	819	925	997	830	952
42–49	942	782	902	940	770	897
50–50	1000	866	971	900	786	897
60+	767	801	774	955	988	961

Source: Based on the Census of India, 1991 Haryana Part-11, Special.

The adverse sex ratio in these age groups is mainly because of the high incidence of mortality among women. It can be attributed mainly to social discrimination and neglect of women in the matter of health care. The phenomenon of adverse sex ratio is peculiar to Haryana, unlike India. It is evident from Table 12.1 that a highly pronounced rural-urban disparity in the sex ratio points to the differential attitudes and treatment to which women are subjected to. They are more confined to rural areas than the males. Rural-urban gender disparities get more pronounced in the upper age groups.

The 1991 census has recorded a population sex ratio of 929 females per 1,000 males, which is five points lower than the 1981 census ratio of 934 in India (Population Projections of the Registrar General's Office, India, 1991). Rohtak district in Haryana has an abysmally low sex ratio. Rohtak has now become a fulcrum for female foeticide which, in all probability, accounts for the alarming decline in sex ratio in the district. If the overall sex ratio in the country has dipped from 934 to 929, in Rohtak district the situation is far worse, the decline being as substantial as 13 points (879–866) from 1981 to 1991 (Table 12.2.).

Bose (1991) feels that it is of considerable concern, since the factors responsible seem to be neither out migration of women nor the migration of men into the district. That leaves only female foeticide as a major cause. 'It is not entirely unpredictable, since the Jats are not known to accord a high status to their women (Lewis, 1958), and the sex-ratio was lowest among this caste even as early as 1931. Moreover, sex pre-selection is not illegal in the state of Haryana as it is in Maharashtra'.

Table 12.2 *Sex Ratio and the Population Growth (1981–1991)*

District/State	Females per 1000 Males		Decennial Growth Rate of Population	
	1981	1991	1971–1981	1981–1991
Ambala	885	899	+26.23	+29.19
Yamunanagar	885	883	+31.50	+26.72
Kurukshetra	873	889	+32.23	+22.21
Kaithal	848	853	+27.58	+20.44
Karnal	856	874	+30.62	+33.22
Panipat	851	854	+30.62	+33.22
Sonepat	860	854	+26.32	+25.40
Rohtak	876	866	+20.99	+17.41
Faridabad	811	832	+40.32	+48.71
Gurgaon	880	887	+29.12	+30.68
Rewari	926	927	+24.58	+25.49
Mohindergarh	939	950	+25.79	+24.83
Bhiwani	899	897	+30.84	+21.05
Jind	856	846	+23.35	+22.47
Hissar	867	867	+28.93	+23.23
Sirsa	877	866	+32.51	+27.58
Haryana	870	874	+28.75	+26.28

Source: Calculated from the Census provisional figures; Haryana 1981–1991.

Incidence of Female Mortality

The discrimination against women is clearly borne out by the fact that though females are universally acknowledge to be biologically stronger than men, yet in India as a whole and also in Haryana, female mortality rates are generally higher than the mortality rates of males. The infant mortality rate for country is 115 for females and 113 for males. The figures for urban areas are 142 for females and 130 for males and in rural areas, 71 for females and 69 for males (Survey on Infant and Child Mortality, 1987).

As a UNICEF study observes 'If female infants die at a faster rate than male infants, despite their biological superior strength, the inference is that social neglect of female health is deeply entrenched'

(UNICEF, 1984: 75). A study conducted by the Indian Council of Medical Research on the 'Women accessibility to health and family planning' prevalent in Haryana lends support to this observation. It was found that the percentage of male children receiving treatment was 76.8 per cent as against 23.2 per cent in the case of female children (ICMR, 1983: 69).

It was observed during our field visit that often in the case of daughters, parents avoided taking medicines and visiting dispensaries as they commonly believed that their daughters would recover on their own; if she dies the father would save at least ₹ 20,000. A doctor poignantly commented, 'People neglect daughter's treatment. For son, people take loan, sell land and spend thousands of rupees to save his life. But for a daughter even ₹ 50 becomes too much'. During the field survey, it was observed that nearly one-sixth of the total female deaths occur in the age group of one year or less in the rural areas of district Rewari. The high incidence of infant mortality is attributed, inter alia, to factors like low rates of female literacy and early marriages.

One heartening feature, however, is the high degree of awareness among doctors, women's rights activists and government officials about the need to curb the practice of female foeticide. When we discussed it with Dr K.B. Kanwal, Chief Medical Officer of Rohtak, and Dr B.D. Kalra, the District Family Welfare Officer, they stressed that the absence of legal constraints leave them helpless. Dr Kanwal himself spared no efforts (in vain, however) to persuade the state government to pass a law banning pre-natal sex selection. As many as 100 doctors, including activists of the Vigyan Manch and the Janvadi Mahila Samiti, also petitioned the then Chief Minister Ch. Devi Lal to pass the bill 'We were unsuccessful, but we at least managed to increase social awareness through our campaigns', says, Nirmala, Secretary of the Samiti. But changing the attitudes of people is a slow process, she acknowledges. Given such a regressive social situation, it is no wonder that practices such as pre-natal sex-determination are being accepted even by the victims – women, themselves. 'In fact', discloses Nirmala, 'One of my female colleagues and member of the Janvadi Mahila Samiti herself went in for an ultrasound and aborted the foetus on finding it to be a girl. If this is so among the educated sections, how can you expect anything better from the uneducated rural populace?' There are about 10–15 ultrasound clinics operating in Rohtak city and 7–10 were operating in Rewari district. Dr Kambhoj, 'the pioneer of this technique in the state' has his mobile ultrasound service to cater to the needs of 40–45 patients on an average in the rural as well as in urban areas of Haryana. The Narula's X-Ray and Ultrasound Clinic, for instance, had earlier put up a board outside announcing '*Ladka hai ya Ladki Janch Karoo*' (find out whether it is a girl or a boy), but following demonstrations by the Janvadi Mahila Samiti, it was withdrawn and now occupies pride of place in the waiting room, the prefix 'Swasth' (healthy) having been added for legitimacy.

So effective is Dr Kambhoj's publicity network (he employs both printed pamphlets and word of mouth, and unlike other doctors, claims 100% accuracy in diagnosis) that he has now extended his area of operation well beyond Haryana, to include Meerut and even Delhi. A pamphlet handed out to visitors to the clinic unabashedly proclaims him to be the ultrasound expert, '*Jinhe shayad Bharat me is test ki sahi report likhne ka sab se jyada tajurba hein*' (who possibly has more experience in this field than anyone else in the country).

Unfortunately, Haryana's women have allowed themselves to be decimated to an alarming degree despite their immeasurable capacity for hard work and contribution to the economic prosperity of the state. But, Janvadi Mahila Samiti members asserted, 'There is no need to wallow in despair, instead we would intensify our campaign to spread awareness of this practice among the people and get the powerful state apparatus to treat it not merely as a medical problem but a social evil'.

Maternal Mortality and Health Status

Notwithstanding the sizeable expansion in health facilities in the country, particularly during the last two decades, the maternal mortality rate continues to be as high as 418 per lakh live births (UNICEF, 1984). In the rural areas of Haryana, more than 70 per cent births are attended by untrained *dais* (Sarin, 1986). In the field situation, this figure is as high as 19.6 per cent in Rewari district and 17.3 per cent in Rohtak district of the Haryana state. The crude birth rate is still as high as 31.3 per cent in rural areas and 23.4 per cent in urban areas of Haryana (Sample Registration Scheme, Haryana, 1988). Other factors responsible for high incidence of maternal mortality include maternal ill health, malnutrition, anaemia and frequent births. A study conducted by the Department of Social and Preventive Medicines, Medical College, Rohtak, revealed that more than 40 per cent women are suffering from malnutrition in Haryana. The incidence of anaemia among rural women is as high as 69 per cent in the district of Rewari and 65 per cent in the Rohtak district, leading to the low-birth weight of babies (SPM, Monograph on Health and Malnutrition, 1988). It is estimated that on an average a rural female in Haryana gets pregnant about six to eight times in her lifetime, spends about 16 years in pregnancies and lactation and gives birth to more than six children of whom about four survive. About 68 per cent of the births in rural Haryana take place in the age group of 20–29 years. The general fertility rate continues to be as high as 149.1 births (per 1,000 women in the age group 15–59) in rural areas and 116.2 births in urban areas (SPM, Monograph on Health and Malnutrition, 1988: 105).

Educational Level

The high incidence of illiteracy among women constitutes one of the greatest barriers to their development. It limits their scope of employment, training utilisation of health facilities and exercise of legal and constitutional rights. There are scores of studies, which show the positive correlation of female literacy with socio-economic indices. In a recent study of the census data, Sharma and Retherford (1987) have listed several such positive correlations. Some of these are (i) female literacy is strongly and positively related with mean age at marriage; (ii) female literacy rate is moderately and positively related with female employment in nonagricultural and nonhousehold industry; (iii) female literacy is strongly and negatively related with (a) infant mortality rate, (b) percentage of married females aged 14–44, (c) crude birth rate and (d) total fertility rate (Occasional Paper No. 1, 1987: 44). Despite high priority attached to education in our plans, the study observes that the increase in literacy rate has not been 'fast enough to keep illiterates from increasing in absolute number'. The number of female illiterates has been increasing at a faster pace than that of the males (Sharma and Retherford, 1987). The Seventh Plan document observes that nearly 73 per cent total nonenrolled children in the 6–11 years age group were girls (Seventh Five-Year Plan, 1985). In Haryana, female literacy rate according to the 1991 census is barely 33.61 per cent as against 55.97 per cent for males (Table 12.3); the female literacy rate in Haryana is less than the female literacy rate (39.41%) in the country as a whole.

Table 12.3 *Literacy Rate among Males and Females 1991*

District/State	*Male*	*Female*	*Total*
Rohtak	61.98	44.08	53.67
Rewari	67.03	37.92	53.03
Haryana	55.97	33.61	45.54

Sources: Census of Haryana 1991, Provisional figures.

Table 12.4 *Literacy Rate and Enrolment Ratio 1988–1989*

Educational level/	*Rohtak District **		*Rewari District***	
Age Group	*Male*	*Female*	*Male*	*Female*
Literacy rate	61.5	44.8	67.2	36.0
Percentage of school going children age group 5–9	75.2	44.5	68.5	38.5
Age group 10–14	77.7	48.1	73.3	42.2

Source: * Director Public Instructions (School) Haryana, Chandigarh.
** Estimates for Rewari District Education office Rewari, Haryana.

In the field situation (Table 12.4), gender disparities in the literacy rates are greater in Rewari district than in Rohtak district. In the rural areas of Rewari district adjoining Rajasthan, it was observed that the female literacy rates were ranging from 26.6 per cent in Jatusana village to 18.8 per cent in Mandola village.

The slow growth of literacy rate particularly among females is a highly disturbing phenomenon. Sharma and Retherford (1987) have projected that at the existing rate, it may take about seven decades or more in the country to reach the goal of full literacy or universalisation of education in the age group of 5–14 years. Some states such as Kerala have already reached this goal, while other states such as Haryana may require more than a century to come up to this rate.

Socio-economic Aspect: Women as Workers

The economic profile of the socially unprotected women workers forms the weakest link in labour statistics. The conventional classification of workers and their contribution to the national economy reduces them into total invisibility.

Broadly speaking, the unprotected workers include all those, who are outside the pale of the organised sector. By the nature of their activities, they can be classified under the following broad categories:

(i) Home-based producers including artisans and piece rate workers, paid and unpaid family labourers
(ii) Petty vendors and hawkers who do not hire labour but take the assistance of family members
(iii) Contract labour and subcontract labour
(iv) Providers of services such as washer women, scavengers, domestic helpers
(v) Women engaged in processing work in traditional and nontraditional areas

(vi) Those doing manual work such as construction labour and those working in agriculture and other primary sectors

On the basis of employment status, the aforesaid groups can be classified under three broad categories, namely:

(i) Self-employed
(ii) Wage earners working outside homes (agricultural workers, construction workers, contract and subcontract workers etc.) and inside homes (home-based workers working on putting out basis) and
(iii) Unpaid family helpers

Both the major official sources of data, the Census of India and the NSSO, differ in their approach in measuring the workforce. In the census enquiries of 1971 and 1981, a person who has worked for major part of the year (not less than 183 days) is regarded as the main worker, and if the person has worked for a fewer number of days, he or she is regarded as a marginal worker. The NSSO, on the other hand, has an elaborate categorisation. It defines three distinct working status, namely, usual status, current weekly status and current daily status comprising 22 activity categories (from 01 to 99), where 01–71 are for workers (01–51 for usual status and 61–71 for current status), 81 and 82 are for and/or available for work (unemployed), and 91–99 are for those not in labour force.

The accounting of women as workers in the census and the NSSO suffers from serious enumeration and reporting drawbacks. According to Mitra (1981), the under reporting of female workforce participation rates in the census varies from 30 per cent to 40 per cent. He estimates that the participation of the women in the informal sector is as high as 49 per cent as against 15 per cent to 17 per cent in the case of men. In the context of Haryana, Ahlawat (1988) found that the measurement of female labour force participation suffers from gross 'under enumeration, inadequate attention to unpaid family labour, own production and household work and relationship between them'.

In the 1991 census, the workforce participation rate among women was barely 26.71 per cent in district Rohtak and 28.35 in Rewari district (main workers). The 38th round of NSSO (1983) records female workforce participation rate on a higher side, that is, 21.9 per cent in the case of main workers and 29.6 per cent of main and marginal workers. The workforce participation rate among females in Haryana was only 10.58 per cent (main workers as against 69.42 per cent for males, Census of India, 1991).

Another interesting feature which is neglected by census as well as NSSO officials is duration of work in a day for women. In the context of Haryana, number of studies show that women work for longer hours and contribute more than men in terms of total labour energy spent by household members (Jain and Chand, 1987; Ahlawat, 1988; Sarin, 1986).

On account of deeply entrenched social customs, taboos and prejudices, women's work in Haryana continues to be invisible and confined more to non-monetary activities. It was observed during the field work that the average hours of unpaid work done by married women outside the home in the Rohtak town varied from 6.13 to 7.43 hours per day. The situation in the rural areas of Rewari district for the unpaid work done by married women outside the home (mainly agricultural activities) was worse. On an average, a woman has to work for 10.21 to 11.30 hours per day.

Women's Contribution to Family Income

In Haryana, women are mainly engaged as self-employed workers largely in home-based activities where their work at home intermixes with their household duties. Therefore, the productivity of their work as well as their status as workers remains invisible. Though there are a host of conceptual and methodological problems involved in measuring the economic contribution of women, yet an attempt was made during the intensive field work in this regard. It was observed that the women are undoubtedly engaged in several activities which add to household income but are totally outside the sphere of the market economy. There are several activities such as free collection of fodder and fuel, maintaining of dairy, looking after cattle, food processing, sewing and weaving, in which women are engaged in rural Haryana and increase the 'household's command over the necessities'. The household would have to spend a lot of money in procuring these services, if they are not rendered by women. The 87.3 per cent of women engaged in Rewari district (under our survey) in the activities include domestic duties along with free collection of goods and vegetables, roots, firewood and cattle feed, sewing, tailoring, weaving for household use and fetching water. It is clear that the high proportion of women engaged in these activities is mainly because these activities provide the opportunity for combining household duties with productive work. Under the present sociocultural pressure in Haryana, women are burdened with heavy domestic duties and child care. A large majority, nearly 73 per cent of our respondents from Rohtak city was engaged to add something to the family's real income by engaging themselves in market-oriented or nonmarket-oriented household activities. The quantitative contribution of women to the family income is not only highly significant but the qualitative contribution is also of immense value to their families. Unlike the men who spend a portion of their earnings on themselves, the female workers were hardly spending anything on themselves. The entire earnings are spent on the upbringing and betterment of the family members.

Some prominent activities in which women attend household activities (Table 12.5) in the rural areas of Rewari district include (i) fetching water from outside household premises (84%), (ii) preparation of cow dung cakes for use as fuel (52.5%), (iii) grinding of food grains (38.6%), (iv) household dairy (62.3%), (v) fodder cutting (40.6%) and (vi) sewing and tailoring (10.4%). In Rohtak city, corresponding figures are (i) bringing water from outside household premises (32.5%), (ii) preparation of cow dung cakes for use as fuel (16.21%), (iii) sewing and tailoring (29.7%) and tutoring of children (24.6%).

Table 12.5 *Percentage of Females Engaged in Household Duties and also Participated in Specific Activities to Total Females Engaged in Household Duties*

S. N.	*Activities*	*Rewari District* (Rural)*	*Rohtak** (Urban)*
1.	Work in household dairy	62.3	18.2
2.	Fetching water from outside the household premise	84.0	32.5
3.	Preparing of cow dung cakes to use as fuel	52.5	16.21
4.	Grinding of food grains	38.6	1.9
5.	Husking paddy/Bajra	34.7	0.2
6.	Preparation of Gur	1.2	–
7.	Sewing, tailoring	10.4	29.7
8.	Free collection of firewood, cattle, food, etc.	40.6	10.5
9.	Spinning	17.2	13.5
10.	Tutoring of children	8.2	24.6
11.	Maintenance of kitchen garden, Orchards, etc.	8.51	3.5
12.	Cattle rearing	36.2	1.2
13.	Percentage of females engaged in household duties to total person	48.2	46.5

Source: Rewari District* (Rural) data pertains to our sample for the study.
**Rohtak District (urban) data pertains to our sample of Rohtak city. Percentages calculated for each activity from the total sample.

The proportion of women engaged in domestic duties along with the free collection of goods (vegetables, fodder, firewood, cattle dung cakes), sewing, tailoring and weaving is several times more than males. In the rural areas of Rewari district, it was observed that women attending domestic duties account for more than 48.2 per cent, whereas in the urban segment of Rohtak city the proportion of women participating in the domestic duties is 46.5 per cent.

As per 32nd round of NSSO (1977–1978), there were 16.8 lakh female domestic workers as against 6.2 lakh male domestic workers in the country as a whole. The proportion of female domestic workers is two and a half times more than the male domestic workers. In the rural segment of Rewari district, it was observed that the incidence of female as domestic workers was less as compared to the Rohtak city. In the urban area of Rohtak, it was 12.5 per cent, whereas in Rewari district only 0.8 per cent was engaged in as domestic workers. It is also observed that the domestic workers have no specific terms of employment, no rigid job description, no social security benefits, no provision for paid leave and so on. Often if a female worker takes leave for more than a few days, she is expected to provide a substitute or she is dismissed on the spot, or she may come back only to find that she has been replaced permanently. A unique feature observed is that the domestic workers are isolated from each other and the problem of organising them is almost insurmountable. It becomes difficult for them to discuss their problems and develop a common identity (Ahlawat, 1992).

The female domestic workers are subjected to the worst kind of exploitation. It is not only that they work on casual and temporary basis, suffer from total casualisation of work and are devoid of legal protection, particularly in terms of payment of wages and hours of work, but in majority of the cases it was reported that they are often suspected for thefts and abused by the employers as well. In a few cases, even sexual harassment was done by the employers. The members of Janvadi Mahila Samiti, Rohtak, when interviewed, stated that the domestic workers urgently need recognition of their status as workers.

Women in Dairying

Haryana is known for dairying and dairy products. Women's contribution to dairying ranges from collection of fodder, to milching of animals, cleaning and taking care of animals. Not only this, they are the last to go to bed, but they are the first to rise as early as around 2.30 A.M. for preparing animals for milching. Yet in the field study analysis, it was observed that women hardly have any say, in owning the animals, or the cash income obtained from the sale of milk. In both the districts, Rohtak and Rewari, women are not included as members in the milk cooperative society, though there are some success stories of the dairy cooperatives which show that women can manage the cooperatives equally well and use their income for the betterment of the family (Mitra, 1981). It was observed that being outside the cooperatives women do not get fair price of milk, or proper marketing outlets and were found to be selling milk to the local procurers of milk. According to a study done by Rajgopalan (1987), much of the failure of the milk cooperatives, Gujarat being exception in India is due to the fact that the cooperative laws do not encourage the spirit of voluntarism and cooperation.

During the field visits, it was observed that there is a lack of proper leadership in the existing milk cooperatives. Akhil Bharatiya Mahila Parishad has not been able to organise women to take care of the milk cooperatives in the rural areas of Rewari district. However, due to lack of leadership training and development of the females, their role in decision-making remains minimal. Since milk cooperative is a good means by which women in Haryana can improve their socio-economic well-being and gain confidence and self-esteem, therefore, existing scheme of milk cooperatives should be given impetus at all levels.

Thus, the analysis pertaining to demographic and socio-economic variables in Haryana's social structure described the women in a highly disadvantageous situation. The broad trends show that the economic development process for the last 40 years has not yet brought any desired changes in their socio-economic milieu. What is required at this crucial juncture is the fact that unless the vulnerable sections of women are organised, the fruits of development will not reach them. So mobilisation and organisation of women through voluntary organisations seem to be the only way out through which women not only become aware about their subordinate position in the society but also gain confidence to change their status in the social milieu.

Note

The scanty data available on the unprotected workers is mainly drawn from the census, the National Sample Survey Organisation, central and state government departments, various Boards/Commissions, the Handloom and Handicraft Board, the Khadi and Village Industries Commission.

References

Ahlawat, Neerja. 1992. *Social Networks: A Study of Two Women's Organizations in the State of Haryana*. Ph.D. Thesis (unpublished), Chandigarh: Department of Sociology, Punjab University.

Ahlawat, S.R. 1988. *Green Revolution and Agricultural Labour*. New Delhi: Deep and Deep Publications.

Bose, Ashish. 1991. 'Analysis on 1991 Census'. *The Times of India*, April 14.

Census of India. 1981. Series I, Part-2, Special, New Delhi: Office of the Registrar General and Census Commissioner, India.

——. 1991. Series I, Special, Census of Haryana, New Delhi: Office of the Registrar General and Census Commissioner, India.

ICMR. 1983. *Project on Infant Mortality in Haryana* (Memo). Rohtak: Department of Social and Preventive Medicine, Medical College.

Jain, Devaki and Chand, Malini. 1987. Report on a Time Allocation Study: Its Methodological Implications. New Delhi: Institute of Social Studies Trust.

Lewis, Oscar. 1958. *Village Life in Northern India*. Urbana: University of Illinois Press.

Mitra, Ashok. 1981. *Implications of the Declining Sex-Ratio in India's Population*. Bombay: Allied Publishers.

Occasional Paper No. 1 of 1987. New Delhi: Office of the Registrar General and Census Commissioner, India.

Rajgopalan, Shashi. 1987. *Cooperative Legislation and Self-employed Women*. Sanakhya, NCSEW.

Sample Registration Scheme. 1988. Haryana: Office of the Registrar General of India.

Sarin, Madhu. 1986. 'Some Insights into Rural Women's Lives: A Study of Village Projects in Haryana'. *Manushi*, 35.

Sen, Amartya et al. 1987. 'Malnutrition of Rural Children and the "Sex Bias"', in Devaki Jain and Nirmala Banerjee (eds), *Women and Poverty*. New Delhi: Vikas.

Seventh Five-Year Plan. 1985. New Delhi: Planning Commission, Government of India, p. 221.

Sharma, O.P. and Retherford, R.D. 1987. Recent Literacy Trends in India. Census of India, Occasional Paper No. 1, New Delhi: Office of the Registrar General and Census Commissioner, India p. 52.

Shramshakti. 1988. Report of the National Commission on Self-employed Women and Women in the Informal Sector. New Delhi: Ministry of Women and Child Welfare, Government of India.

Survey on Infant and Child Mortality. 1987. Census of India, Occasional Paper No. 5, New Delhi: Office of the Registrar General of India, p. 22.

UNICEF. 1984. *An Analysis of the Situation of Children in India*. New Delhi, p. 75.

13

Changing Status of Women in Rural Haryana

A Sociological Interpretation

Raj Singh and Nishi Batra

The prosperity and growth of a nation depends on the status and development of its women folk as they are not only important in themselves but also more important from the point of view of creating reactions in the public. Also, they are the mothers of the next generation. A woman is the foundation stone of a family in particular and the society in general. She shares a number of duties and responsibilities of maintaining the daily life of its family more than on equal terms with its menfolk, hence, requires greater attention and status.

The status of women has undergone lot of changes right from the primitive societies. Role and position of women in hunting and agricultural societies was more dependent on the sexual division of labour. In hunting stage, man was the food gatherer while woman had to stay in her dwelling cave protecting her children (Baig, 1976). But with the advent of cultivation, it had become compulsory on the part of women to participate in the outdoor work. She used to take part in some of the agricultural operations such as weeding, transplanting and harvesting in the fields and also in many other types of work that she could and, hence, had equal status to man. Indian women from 1500 B.C. onwards enjoyed freedom to great extent along with men. She participated in religious ceremonies and social activities in the Vedic period. She was husband's companion in weal and woe, mistress of the household and partner in all his activities, temporal and spiritual. However, patriarchal family system emerged a little later during this time which resulted in the deterioration of position of women. Their position further degraded by the dictum laid by Manu, the law maker of second century. This degraded position of women continued and was reinforced by the Muslims in India. With the advent of foreign ruler, the status of Hindu women further deteriorated due to various reasons.

The Hindu law gave unequal and indifferent treatment to women. They were discriminated in marriage, marital status, divorce, widowhood and inheritance. Women had to lead a cloistered life. They moved within the narrow sphere of their kitchen. Cooking, childbearing and rearing and catering to the relatives and husband, comprised her work, life and activity. She was treated as an appendage of man with distinct and meekly accepted conception of her family duties and obligations. The Britishers first followed a policy of noninterference in the social and religious life of the Indian people to win their cooperation in the administration of country. But, when they observed some strange and cruel traditions, and after being persuaded by social reformers, they passed certain acts to upgrade the status of women. The intermixing of western and eastern cultures enabled women to realise their subordinate position and persuaded them to regain their legitimate status. Women played an active and important role in India's freedom struggle. Post-independent India has witnessed a great change in the lives of women. Indian women have been given equal rights in the Constitution. As a result, women started breaking the socio-psychological barriers of the society to regain equal status they enjoyed in the Vedic period (Kripalani, 1975). Government and several public as well private institutions tried to change and improve social conditions and gradually elevate the low status of women. Accordingly, the government provided policy guidelines on women in successive Five Year Plans and many welfare schemes were launched. The Central Social Welfare Board started welfare extension projects in 1954–1955 to cover a number of activities.

National Commission on Self-employed Women (1987) noted that despite various efforts in improving the conditions of women, a large number of women workers particularly in the unorganised sector suffered from various disadvantages relating to their working lives as well as their homes. Dixit (1985) stated that several projects by the government have been launched for improving women's health, education, employment, general awareness and political participation but a very small segment of them have been benefited. Joshi (1985) concluded that nonformal education for women is expected to help women to raise their status, become economically independent and politically aware. Bansal and Chamola (1986) reported that women got maximum benefit under the programme of animal husbandry for which loan is provided by the bank for the purchase of animals and an outright subsidy is provided by the DRDA. Chamola et al. (1986) reported the impact of TRYSEM (Training for Rural Youth for Self Employment) on income of women of Hissar district and found that it is greater in first 3 or 4 years after training and it starts declining afterwards. Verma (1986) noticed a notable change among women before and after taking up the Integrated Rural Development Programme (IRDP) activities in Rajasthan. Decision-making power was shifted from husband and parents to respondent herself. Singh (1988) states that benefits of any rural development programme are reaped by rural rich at the cost of rural poor. In brief, benefits by and large do not reach those who need them the most. Bhat (1989) reports that number of voluntary organisations have helped the state in fighting social injustice, economic inequality and in mitigating the sufferings of poor and downtrodden. Vermani (1989) revealed in a study of Haryana on TRYSEM that none of the pass out trainees started his or her own self-unit. Lack of finance to purchase instrument or machines, lack of marketing prospects, nonavailability of credit facilities and lack of personal interest contributed for not starting their own production units. It may be concluded that most of these so-called welfare programmes had not succeeded in bringing desired improvement in the status of rural women.

A lot of research studies have been conducted on general status of women in the country, but there is scarcity of researches pertaining to the impact of women welfare programmes in changing their status in rural Haryana. In order to bridge this gap, present empirical study was undertaken with the specific objective of studying the impact of salient women welfare programmes in enhancing their decision-making status within the family.

Methodology

This chapter is based upon the data collected for the study conducted in four purposively selected districts of the Haryana state. Literacy-cum-employment status of rural women was the basis for selecting the respondents. A cluster of two to three villages from each of the selected district was drawn purposively for gathering primary data from married women of the sampled villages in the age group of 15–45 years. Comprehensive lists of all such women from the sampled villages were prepared keeping in view four broad criteria, that is, literate employed, literate nonemployed, illiterate employed and illiterate nonemployed. From each selected cluster, a sample of 25 respondents from the aforesaid lists was drawn through simple random sampling technique. This way a sample of 400 respondents was obtained for gathering primary data for the present study. The primary data for the study were collected with the help of an interview schedule, which was specially developed for this purpose during 1988. To measure respondents participating in decision-making, a three-point scale was developed and used. Percentages were calculated and chi-square test with Yates correction was applied for understanding association between dependent and independent variables.

Results and Discussion

In India, around three-fourths of the women population resides in rural areas. So, it is essential to accord due recognition to the contribution of women in various spheres. Inferiority of women's status and position is one of the basic characteristics of the underdeveloped economies (Leibenstein, 1957). Development, both economic and metamorphosis, is, therefore, unimaginable without improving the women's status and position in the underdeveloped countries. India is committed to a steady improvement in the status of women; bring them in the mainstream of national development (Planning Commission, 1978). So, basic approach of the development seeks to inculcate confidence among women and bring about awareness of their potential for development and also of their rights and privileges.

The last five decades have seen ceaseless efforts to bring about a desired transformation through various programmes. Here, an attempt has been made to find out the difference in the status of beneficiaries and the nonbeneficiaries of women welfare programmes functioning in the selected villages. Change in the social status would be assumed, if by joining these programmes, there is a change in their traditional behaviour pattern, and increased level of participation in decision-making within the family. Deviation from the observation of traditional behaviour pattern was noticed on the basis of three point scale and their level of deviance was associated with the participation and nonparticipation in developmental programmes. Similarly, level of participation in decision-making was also associated with participation in welfare programmes. Mahila Mandals, craft centres and adult education centres were the prominent welfare programmes operating exclusively for women's welfare in the sampled villages, which were examined for the present study.

Mahila Mandals and Decision-Making

The Mahila Mandals were conceived as an instrument for bringing new ideas and skills to village women in a participative manner. The objectives of these Mandals are to equip women for better home-making techniques; craft work, sewing, knitting, kitchen gardening, basket making, nonformal education and entertainment, thereby enhancing women's decision-making status in the family. These objectives are generally achieved through demonstrations and lectures by Gram Sevika and Mukhiya Sevika. Membership of the Mandal is voluntary without any fee. Table 13.1 details relationship between participation in Mahila Mandals and decision-making status of the respondents within the family.

Table 13.1 *Participation in Mahila Mandals and Extent of Decision-Making*

Nature of Decisions/Beneficiaries	*Level of Participation in Decision*			
	Low	*Medium*	*High*	*Total*
Money centred	**X2 = 132.25* C = 0.498**			
Nonbeneficiaries	256 (85)	045 (15)	—	301(75) (100)
Beneficiaries	023 (23)	071 (72)	005 (05)	099 (25) (100)
	279(70)	116(29)	005(1)	400(100)
Child centred	**X2 = 100.77* C = 0.418**			
Nonbeneficiaries	204 (68)	87 (29)	10 (03)	301 (75) (100)
Beneficiaries	13 (13)	63 (64)	23 (23)	99 (25) (100)
	217 (54)	150 (38)	33 (8)	400 (100)
Farm centred	**X2 = 4.36* C = 0.152**			
Nonbeneficiaries	96 (93)	07 (07)	—	103 (56) (100)
Beneficiaries	65 (81)	15 (19)	—	80 (44) (100)
	161 (88)	22 (12)		183 (100)
Recreational centred	**X2 = 139.47* C = 0.508**			
Nonbeneficiaries	154 (51)	131 (43)	16 (06)	301 (75) (100)
Beneficiaries	09 (09)	35 (35)	55 (56)	99 (25) (100)
	163(41)	166 (42)	71(17)	400 (100)
Miscellaneous	**X2 = 237.85* C = 0.610**			
Nonbeneficiaries	160 (53)	131 (44)	10 (03)	301 (75) (100)
Beneficiaries	05 (05)	19 (19)	75 (76)	99 (25) (100)
	165 (41)	150 (38)	85 (21)	400 (100)

Note: Figures in parentheses denote percentages.

*Significant at 0.05 per cent level of significance.

An appraisal of Table 13.1 reveals that out of total respondents 75 per cent did not join Mahila Mandals while only 25 per cent participated indicating lack of interest among substantial number of rural women in this women welfare activity.

Similarly, 70 per cent rural women had low level of participation in decisions relating to money matters while only 29 per cent had medium level of participation and only 1 per cent respondents participated highly in such decisions. Among child-centred decisions, 54, 38, and 8 per cent respondents had low, medium and high level of participation respectively. Furthermore, 88 and 12 per cent respondents had low and medium level of participation in farm-centred decisions. It may be concluded that women's participation in money matters, children activities and farm-centred decision was at the lowest level. Devi (1982) also noted that role of women in money-centred decisions had been affected greatly by their educational and employment status. On the other hand, respondent's level of participation in recreational and miscellaneous decisions was considerably high. In order to understand the association between level of participation in decision-making and beneficiaries of Mahila Mandals, chi-square as well as coefficient of contingency was calculated. These values were found significant at 5 per cent level of significance in descending order for decisions relating to farm, money matters, children, miscellaneous and recreational. It may be summarised that the level of participation in decision-making was significantly associated with participation in Mahila Mandals. Hira Nand (1979), Spencer (1981) and Achanta (1982) reported that women as wives and mothers have a considerable part in decision-making in the farm and at home.

Craft Centres and Decision-Making

Integrated Rural Development Programme (IRDP) launched in 1978–1979 is basically an instrument to attack rural poverty in its entirety. It is the beneficiary specific major employment-cum-income generation programme. IRDP is a synthesis of the various developmental strategies tested and experience gained through implementing rural development programmes at village level. Sewing, knitting and other functional activities such as basket making and caning of chairs were identified as the potential programmes through which the women could get additional income. So, craft centres have been established in villages where training is provided to farm women. The financial assistance in the form of a stipend of ₹ 50 and one-third subsidy on sewing machines is also given. Minimum duration of training is six months and after the successful completion of training, they get the sewing machine as incentive.

Here, an attempt has been made to know difference between beneficiaries and nonbeneficiaries in the decision-making power. By joining craft centre, women may attain a sense of economic independence; therefore, it is assumed that there is some impact of these programmes on the status of women over the years. Table 13.2

pertains to association between participation in craft centres and decision-making status of the respondents within the family.

Table 13.2 *Participation in Craft Centres and Extent of Decision-Making*

Nature of decisions/ Beneficiaries	*Level of Participation in Decisions*			
	Low	*Medium*	*High*	*Total*
Money centred	X2 = 64.78* C = 0.373			
Nonbeneficiaries	241 (81)	56 (19)	—	297 (74) (100)
Beneficiaries	38 (37)	60 (58)	05 (05)	103 (26) (100)
	279 (70)	116 (29)	05 (1)	400 (100)
Child centred	X2 = 93.67* C = 0.435			
Non-beneficiaries	199 (67)	90 (30)	08 (03)	297 (74) (100)
Beneficiaries	18 (17)	60 (58)	25 (28)	103 (26) (100)
	217(64)	150(38)	33(8)	400(100)
Farm centred	X2 = 32.48* C = 0.388			
Nonbeneficiaries	115 (98)	02 (02)	—	117 (64) (100)
Beneficiaries	46 (70)	20 (30)	—	66 (36) (100)
	161 (88)	22 (12)		(183) 100
Recreational centred	X2 = 146.33* C = 0.517			
Nonbeneficiaries	154 (52)	129 (43)	14 (05)	297 (74) (100)
Beneficiaries	09 (09)	37 (36)	57 (56)	103 (26) (100)
	163 (41)	166 (42)	71 (17)	400 (100)
Miscellaneous	X2 = 127.54* C = 0.491			
Nonbeneficiaries	157 (53)	115 (39)	25 (08)	297 (74) (100)
Beneficiaries	08 (08)	35 (34)	60 (58)	103 (26) (100)
	165 (41)	150 (37)	85 (22)	400 (100)

Note: Figures in parentheses denote percentages.

*Significant at 0.05 per cent level of significance.

A perusal of Table 13.2 indicates that of the total respondents, 74 per cent did not join craft centres while only 26 per cent participated, indicating lack of popularity of this programme among a sizeable number of respondents. Similarly, 70 per cent rural women had low level of participation in decisions relating to money matters, while 29 per cent had medium level of participation and only 1 per cent respondent women had participated to the greatest extent in decision-making. Among child-centred decisions 54, 38 and 8 per cent respondents had low, medium and high level of participation respectively. Furthermore, 88 per cent and 12 per cent respondents had low and medium level of participation in farm-related decisions. It is evident from above that women participation in money-centred, child-centred and farm-centred decisions was confined mainly among educated and employed respondents. Devi (1982) also reported the favourable impact of education and employment on decision-making status. On the other hand, respondents' participation in recreational and miscellaneous decisions was quite high. Chi-square as well as coefficient of contingency was calculated in order to know the extent of association between participation in decision-making and beneficiaries of craft centres. The significant values of aforesaid statistical tests proved significant association between decision-making involvement in respect of recreational, miscellaneous, children, farming and money-related aspects with participation in craft centres at 5 per cent level of significance. It may, therefore, be concluded that the decision-making participation is conditioned by participation in craft centres that means the respondents who had participated in craft centres had a higher decision-making status in almost all aspects of family life. Dixit (1985) and Verma (1986) also reported a notable change among women before and after taking up the IRDP activities. Decision-making power was also shifted from husband and parents to respondent herself. Singh (1988), however, noted that benefits of any rural development programmes are reaped by rural rich at the cost of rural poor.

Adult Education Programme and Decision-Making

The significance of literacy, particularly among the women as an instrument of galvanising and mobilising the people, arousing the community consciousness and community participation for bringing about social change, is universally acknowledged. Women constitute a most important section but are deprived and neglected in the Indian society, especially in the field of education. With a view, to bring the widening gap in male and female literacy, the Directorate of Adult Education and the Department of Social and Women's welfare has implemented a number of effective schemes to improve the literacy status of women. The major objective is to strengthen the component of family life education in general and mother and child care in particular. So, enrolment of women in adult education has steadily increased from 38.58 per cent to 52.24 per cent over the Sixth Five Year Plan period (1980–1985). Here, an attempt has been made to know the participation of respondents in adult education centres, of the selected villages and its correlation with decision-making status of the respondents. Table 13.3 details such information about respondents.

Analysis of Table 13.3 depicts that out of total respondents 87 per cent did not join adult education programme while 13 per cent participated in it, thereby proving decreased popularity of, this programme, among the respondents in spite of the fact that half of them were illiterate. Furthermore, 70 per cent rural women had low level of participation in decisions relating to money matters while 29 per cent had medium level of participation and only 1 per cent of them had participated extensively in decision-making. Among child-centred decisions 54, 38, and 8 per cent respondents had low, medium and high level of participation respectively. Similarly, 88 and 12 per cent respondents had low and medium level of participation in farm-related decisions. It may be deduced from above data that the educated and employed women had participated to a great extent in money-centred, child-centred and farm-centred decisions. Devi (1982) also observed that education and employment had encouraged women to take active part in decision-making within the family. On the other hand, respondents' participation in recreational and miscellaneous decisions was considerably high. The significant values of chi-square and coefficient of contingency in respect of farm, miscellaneous recreational, child and money-centred decisions indicate significant association between adult education programme and extent of participation in decision-making at 5 per cent level of significance.

It may, therefore, be concluded that decision-making participation is also conditioned by participation in adult education programme, which means respondents who participated in adult education programme had a better decision-making status. Dixit (1985) observed that women welfare programme have only benefited a small segment of rural women. While Joshi (1985) concluded that nonformal education for women is expected to help women to raise their status, become economically independent and politically aware. The findings of the present study are in line with most of the earlier studies on the topic.

Table 13.3 *Participation in Adult Education Programme and Extent of Decision-Making*

Nature of decision/ Beneficiary	*Level of Participation in Decision*			
	Low	*Medium*	*High*	*Total*
Money centred	X2 = 9.31* C = 0.150			
Nonbeneficiaries	252 (72)	91 (26)	05 (02)	348 (87) (100)
Beneficiaries	27 (52)	25 (48)	—	52 (13) (100)
	279 (70)	116 (29)	5 (1)	400 (100)
Child centred	X2 = 19.48* C = 0.215			
Nonbeneficiaries	198 (57)	129 (37)	21 (6)	348 (87) (100)
Beneficiaries	19 (32)	21 (40)	12 (23)	52 (13) (100)
	217 (54)	150 (38)	33 (6)	400 (100)
Farm centred	X2 = 59.113* C = 0.617			
Nonbeneficiaries	136 (95)	07 05	—	143 (78) (100)
Beneficiaries	25 (63)	15 (37)	—	40 (22) (100)
	161(88)	22(12)	—	183 (100)
Recreational centred	X2 = 66.91* C = 0.378			
Nonbeneficiaries	156 (45)	157 (43)	41 (12)	348 (87) (100)
Beneficiaries	67 (13)	15 (29)	30 (58)	52 (13) (100)
	163 (41)	166 (42)	71 (17)	400 (100)
Miscellaneous	X2 = 110.87* C = 0.405			
Nonbeneficiaries	160 (46)	143 (41)	45 (13)	348 (87) (100)
Beneficiaries	05 (10)	07 (13)	40 (77)	52 (13) (100)
	165 (41)	150 (38)	85 (21)	400 (100)

Note: Figures in parenthesis denote percentages.

*Significant at 0.05 per cent level of significance.

Women Welfare Programmes and Deviance

Traditionally ascribed behaviour pattern is expressive of the subordination of women in the family. The respondents observing traditional practices such as the female members eating after male members, preference of boys over girls and purdah system were considered to have lower status in the family. Deviation from these customs leads to the enhancement in their status. The last five decades have seen ceaseless efforts among the planners and the programme executives to bring about a change in the Indian countryside through various programmes of rural development. Here, an attempt has been made to find out the differences in the status of beneficiaries and nonbeneficiaries of woman welfare programmes functioning in the selected villages. Change in the social status would be assumed, if by joining these programmes, there is a change in their traditional behaviour pattern. Deviation from the observance of traditional behaviour pattern was noticed on the basis of three-point scale and their level of deviance was associated with the participation and nonparticipation in the development programmes. Table 13.4 elaborates information in this respect.

Table 13.4 *Association between Deviance from Traditional Customs and Beneficiaries of Women Programmes*

Welfare Programmes/ Beneficiaries	*Level of Deviance*			
	Low	*Medium*	*High*	*Total*
Mahila Mandals	X2 = 191.78* C = 0.569			
Nonbeneficiaries	169 (56)	122 (41)	10 (3)	301 (75) (100)
Beneficiaries	14 (14)	20 (20)	65 (66)	99 (25) (100)
	183 (46)	142 (35)	75 (19)	400 (100)
Craft Centres	X2 = 156.86* C = 0.530			
Nonbeneficiaries	170 (57)	112 (38)	15 (5)	297 (74) (100)
Beneficiaries	13 (12)	30 (29)	60 (59)	103 (26) (100)
	183 (46)	142 (35)	75 (19)	400 (100)
Adult education Centre	X2 = 1.02 C = 0.02			
Non-beneficiaries	160 (46)	124 (36)	64 (18)	348 (87) (100)
Beneficiaries	23 (44)	18 (35)	11 (21)	52 (13) (100)
	183 (46)	142 (35)	75 (19)	400 (100)

Note: Figures in parentheses denote percentages.

*Significance at 5 per cent level of significance.

As appraisal of Table 13.4 reveals that 46 per cent respondents had low while 35 per cent had medium and 19 per cent had high level of deviance from traditional customs. The significant values of the chi-square tests in respect of participation in Mahila Mandals and crafts centres in relation with level of deviance from traditional customs indicate that participation in Mahila Mandals and craft centres were directly associated with the level of deviances. It means respondents who participated in Mahila Mandals and craft centres had deviated greatly from the observance of traditional customs, hence, enhanced their status and vice versa within the family. However, participation in adult education programme did not associate significantly with the observance of deviance of traditional customs as was the case in Mahila Mandals and craft centres. But, a peep into the data established some sort of relationship between these variables indicating marginal impact of adult education programme in raising the status of rural women. Meher (1971) also reported that status of women is enhancing due to women's employment and breaking down of traditional barriers. Lata (1990) observed that beneficiaries of TRYSEM programme were rarely following the rigid customs and practices of the traditional family system. Therefore, it may be inferred that participation in women welfare programmes had a favourable impact on deviance from traditional customs by the respondents.

It may be concluded from above interpretations that the respondents' participation in Mahila Mandals, craft centres and adult education programme was far from expectations. It may be attributed to a number of factors such as half of the respondents were employed, so they could not afford to participate in these programmes; second, these programmes may not be attractive, so, respondents were not interested to participate and third, lack of spare time may have forced many respondents not to join these welfare programme. The findings further reveal that the beneficiaries of aforesaid welfare programmes had participated extensively in decision-making process within the family and deviated from the observance of traditional customs, thereby indicating favourable impact of these programmes in improving the status of rural women in the countryside. Dixit (1985), Verma (1986), Singh (1988) and Vermani (1989) also reported similarly while studying the impact of women welfare programmes in enhancing the status of rural women.

References

Achanta, L.D. 1982. 'Role of Rural Women in Agricultural Development'. *Kurukshetra*, XXXI(2): 16–17.

Baig, T.A. 1976. *India's Women Power*. New Delhi: S. Chand & Co. Pvt. Limited.

Bansal, P.K. and Chamola, S.D. 1986. 'The Impact of Rural Development on Women: A Study of Hisar District'. Paper Read in a Seminar on Role of Development Programmes on Socio-Economic Status of Women, held at HAU, Hisar, March 21–22.

Bhat, A. 1989. *Development and Social Justice: Micro-action by Weaker Sections*. Delhi: Sage.

Chamola, S.D. et al. 1986. 'Impact of TRYSEM Programme on Income and Employment of Women in District Hisar'. Paper Presented in the Seminar on Role of Development Programmes on Socio-economic Status of Women, held at HAU, Hisar, March 21–22.

Devi, L.U. 1982. *Status and Employment of Women in India*. Delhi: B.R. Publishing Corporation.

Dixit, A. 1985. 'Experimental Project on Non-formal Education of Rural Women of Rajasthan'. *Prasar*, 12(1/4).

Joshi, V. 1985. 'Research Priorities in Non-formal Education for Women'. *Prasar*, 12(1/4): 38.

Kripalani, S. 1975. 'An Unfinished Autobiography'. *The Illustrated Weekly of India*, 7–8(96): 29.

Lata, Vidya. 1990. *Developing Rural Women: A Case Study of Trysem*. New Delhi: Discovery Publishing House.

Leibenstein, H. 1957. *Economic Backwardness and Economic Growth*. New York: John Wiley and Sons.

Meher, M.H. 1971. 'Problems of Women's Employment'. *Indian Journal of Social Work*, 32(2).

Nand, Hira. 1979. *Techno-cultural Profile of a Dry Land Village and Dry Farming Technology: An Interactional Study*. Ph.D. Thesis (unpublished), HAU, Hisar.

Singh, M. 1988. *Rural Development Administration and Anti-Poverty Programmes*. New Delhi: Deep and Deep Publications.

Spencer, D.S.C. 1981. 'Women in a Developing Economy: A West African Case Study'. *A.I.D. Research and Development Abstracts*, 9(i): 31.

Verma, G.L. 1986. 'Women Beneficiaries and IRDP'. *Journal of Research Rural Development*, 5(1/6): 19–21.

Vermani, S. 1989. 'Programme of Training of Rural Youth for Self-employment'. Paper Presented in XIX All India Sociological Conference, held at HAU, Hisar, March 3–5.

14

Role of Nonformal Educational Schemes in the Education and Empowerment of Women

Raj Mohini Sethi

In the structuring of the National Policy on Education (1986) due emphasis has been given to adult education as a means for the promotion of women's equality. In addition to that it has also been stressed that adult education under the new policy should not be treated as merely a mass literacy campaign but also emphasise the acquisition of functional knowledge and skills by the learners. The idea is to create awareness among the recipients about the existing socio-economic realities. These broad objectives of adult education outlined above clearly indicate the tilt in the New Education Policy from mass literacy to nonformal education. Thus, the recognition and inclusion of nonformal educational schemes under the National Policy on Education (1986) can be a real leap in the attainment of women's equality, if it is implemented in its true spirit.

Nonformal education is a flexible approach to education and recognises the utility of 'need-based vocational programmes' in educating women and youth. For the developing societies, especially it is supposed to have an immediate and practical utility. Nonformal education is generally imparted outside the school and the performance of the learners provides a proof of the knowledge rather than certification. Generally it involves a voluntary participation on behalf of the learners and is a part-time activity (Kleis et al., 1974: 6).

Objectives

The present study was undertaken with a view to find out how far the tilt towards functional education and nonformal education under the Adult Education Schemes will benefit the women in the rural areas. It also aims at finding out how far functional education accompanied by need-based vocational programmes helps in the education and empowerment of women. To achieve these aims, the author has made an in-depth analysis of the Adult Education Centres, Mahila Mandals and other vocational programmes conducted for the education of women in the Dharampur block of district Solan in Himachal Pradesh and has tried to show the relative importance of each in urging the women on to the path of achieving equality and in making them responsible citizens.

Adult Education

In 1971 only 20.23 per cent of the women in Himachal Pradesh were literate and in district Solan the proportion of literate women was only 17.38 per cent. By 1981 their proportion increased to 31.39 and 28.88 per cent respectively, but these figures were still far from the national objective of universal literacy, although they were above the national average of 24.9 per cent (Table 14.1). In view of the fact that very large proportion of men and women were still illiterate after more than three decades of independent India, it was felt that an all out emphasis on adult education would be a viable solution in the attainment of universal literacy. Adult education schemes were therefore renewed and new centres for adult education were started in different parts of the country. Various governmental and nongovernmental organisations were given the necessary inputs to run adult education centres in their regions. One such centre chosen for the purpose was at Jagjit Nagar, in district Solan of Himachal Pradesh.

A Social Work Research Centre was established at Jagjit Nagar in 1977 for bringing about an integrated rural development of the area by providing various types of socio-economic services and training facilities to the people, especially the youth.

Table 14.1 *Percentage of Literates to Total Population*

State	*1971*			*1981*		
	Persons	*Males*	*Female*	*Persons*	*Males*	*Females*
India	29.46	47.69	19.36	36.20	46.7	24.9
Himachal Pradesh	31.96	43.19	20.23	41.94	52.36	31.39
Solan	29.31	40.31	17.38	40.90	52.09	28.88

Source: 1. Statistical Abstract of Himachal Pradesh, 1981.
2. Provisional Population Totals, Census of India, 1981 and 1971.

Table 14.2 *Distribution of Learners by Sex and Caste*

Sex	*Caste*		*Total*
	Non-scheduled Castes	*Scheduled Castes*	
Female	328 (29.02)	291 (25.75)	619 (54.78)
Male	309 (27.34)	202 (17.88)	511 (45.22)
Total	637 (56.37)	493 (43.63)	1,130 (100.00)

Source: SUTRA, 1979, Annual Report, SWRC, Himachal Pradesh.

In 1978, the centre was made the focal point for the Adult Education Programme of the government in the region with the establishment of 33 adult education centres. In 1979, the number of centres increased to 60. In all, 1,130 persons were enrolled in these centres. Out of these, 511 were men and 609 women (See Table 14.2). Around 55 per cent of them were from the scheduled castes. However, it was difficult to sustain the interest of the learners over the year in spite of the impressive initial enrolments. Thus, the dropout rate was quite large and only 54.87 per cent attended the course in the last month of the year. On the other hand, about 55 per cent of the learners were quite regular in attendance, in the sense that they attended the 10 month course for more than 20 days in a month. Those who dropped out of the course did so because of the vagaries of the weather, or because of the preoccupation with agricultural and other household or social activities. The dropout rate was more among women learners as compared to men learners. Hence, new strategies had to be chalked out for involving women in the developmental process.

Mahila Mandals

In 1979, SUTRA took upon itself the responsibility of organising training camps for rural women along with the adult education centres. The main aim in organising these camps was to educate women about the usefulness of different community services provided by various voluntary and nonvoluntary organisations. In other words, they tried to inculcate an awareness of the existing socio-economic realities and made the women realise the need for cooperative action in the implementation of these programmes. Thereafter, in 1983, these training programmes culminated into new groups called Mahila Mandals under the new policy of the Government of India for rural development. Thus, around 40 women's groups called Mahila Mandals with an enrolment of 1,000 women were established in Dharampur block of district Solan alone. The Mahila Mandals hold their meetings in almost every village. Literacy and some type of vocational and recreational classes are held in these women's groups. Once again the primary objective in the formation of these groups was to educate women of the utility of the different developmental programmes organised especially for women and children, so that they are willing to undertake cooperative action. This venture was quite successful in the sense that one of the major contributions of these Mahila Mandals was that they provided the village women with an alternative framework, where they could meet one another and discuss their common problems in spite of their geographical isolation. Coming together and showing common problems in exclusive women's groups helped them to shed off their difference and break out of the bonds of tradition, uncertainty and insecurity. They inculcated in women a desire to change their social set-up by making them aware of the existing inequalities and also of various social problems that had a bearing on their lives. A demonstration to this effect has been amply provided by the women of the region in spearheading a strong movement for prohibition. In fact, it is the first all women movement that aims at achieving prohibition by making a demand for holding a referendum before the licensing of liquor vends by the government at the level of Gram Panchayats (Sethi, 1986). The fact that 500 rural women marched from Dharampur to Solan in March 1986, and thereafter to Shimla in October of the same year, braving all odds of five days speaks volumes for the self-confidence gained by these women.

Thus, it can be said that there occurred a major shift in SUTRA activities in the 1980s. From a mere service input centre, it progressed on to an awareness raising programme and helped women to organise themselves for various activities.

Smokeless Chulha Scheme

Along with the establishment of Mahila Mandals, another experimental programme that was introduced in the region was the smokeless chulha scheme to provide employment opportunities and technical know-how to women. This scheme was introduced in 1982–1983 in seven different states. Through experiments in other states it was found that in order to popularise the demand for smokeless chulhas local women have to be trained for the purpose. The necessity of training local women was also felt because in each region the chulha has to be modified in design to suit the local environmental conditions and also the availability of material. The local *chulha mistrees* were also supposed to provide follow-up action if there arose any problems in the working or repair of chulhas and also they were supposed to act as change agents for other developmental programmes by maintaining a regular contact with the village women (Sarin, 1986).

Under this scheme, 20 village women were trained as *chulha mistrees* and they were able to construct around 2,000 smokeless chulhas by 1987.

This scheme has benefited women in several ways. First, it has improved the working conditions for an average housewife by making the kitchens smokeless and consuming less fuel. The *chulha mistress* has gained a lot of confidence and independence because of their new knowledge and acquisition of skills along with an opportunity of being employed and having their own income. They are often considered as role models by the women in the village and are, therefore, important change agents in the developmental process.

At present, the demand for the construction of new chulhas is almost nonexistent and the services of *chulha mistrees* are only required for skilled repairs or for providing advice or follow-up action. Therefore, for all practical purposes, the *chulha mistrees* has joined the ranks of unemployed persons. To obviate frustration and find an alternative employment avenue for these women, a new programme has been launched which is known as the *Dungar Dai* programme, which is aimed at training women as veterinary *dais* (midwives) or as paraveterinary personnel.

Dungar Dai Programme

When women became conscious of the social realities around them, they discovered that the division of labour in their society was such that the work-load related to cattle care was almost exclusively borne by the women in the household. For instance, all the major tasks related to cattle care such as cutting, fetching and making provision for fodder and water, cleaning and bathing of animals, removal and utilisation of cow dung, cleaning of the cattle shed, and also the milking of the animals are all done exclusively by women in the household. Most of these activities are not only arduous but also time consuming. Transport and provision of fodder and water is taxing because of the hilly terrain and many a times, to avoid this animals are taken to the *ghasnis* (grass lands) and streams or *bowlis* (ponds) for grazing and bathing.

The women also discovered that the milk yield of their cows was very low and the bullocks used for draft power are also of poor quality. The disease and mortality rates of their cattle are quite high and the provision of veterinary services is very poor and, at times, inaccessible. Combined with these is the fact that although women take care of the cattle and do most of the agriculture-related work, it is the men in the household who are actually listed as beneficiaries under the different IRDP schemes, which provide credit to the villagers. Such a situation arises because women do not have coparcenary rights in land and, therefore, are not in a position to mortgage the land for getting the loans sanctioned. The women, therefore, felt that they were being systematically kept out of the power nexus by keeping them away from the decision-making process in the care of their cattle or in making improvements in agriculture. The women then decided to make a beginning in this direction. They evolved the idea that a few women should first be trained as veterinary *dais* or pharmacists who would cater to the immediate health care needs of the cattle and help in the prevention and management of illness because of the impending need of a veterinary pharmacist in every village. Hence, the concept of *Dungar Dai* was evolved and it was decided that SUTRA would take upon itself the responsibility of training *Dungar Dais.*

In the initial stage, it was decided to train 20 *Dungar Dais*. Financial help for the training of *Dungar Dais* was provided by OXFAM (America) and the training facilities by the Himachal government. The project was put into action in June 1987. It aimed at inculcating among women the importance of cleanliness and balanced diet in the health care of the cattle and also a realisation of the importance of immunisation and artificial insemination for the care of the cattle and the improvement of its breed. This programme not only envisages training women as *Dungar Dais* but is also to be used as a module for generating among women an awareness of their powerlessness in their community, thereby encouraging them to formulate alternate support structures through which they could lessen this powerlessness and be effective decision-makers in the family and community. Thus, the *Dungar Dais* are also supposed to act as catalysts of change.

The scheme not only proposes to provide employment opportunities to women but also envisages making them efficient managers of their own affairs by empowering them to act as independent, worthwhile citizens. However, the success of this scheme has still to be watched and nurtured as it is still in its formative stage.

Conclusions

On the basis of the above analysis, a few conclusions may be drawn:

1. The attainment of mass literacy (universal literacy) through adult education programmes is a long drawn out scheme that fails to achieve its objectives in a specified period of time.
2. Making women just literate is not a sufficient condition for making them responsible and aware citizens; therefore, more

emphasis has to be laid on functional education under the New Education Policy (NEP).

3. Functional education through nonformal educational schemes such as Mahila Mandals and other employment generating schemes is more useful in the empowerment of women and in urging them on to achievement of women's equality.
4. The Mahila Mandals and other nonformal educational schemes not only provide the women alternative support structures but also instil in them a self-confidence and independence through sustained interaction and exposure. The leadership that evolves through these organisations also provides the village women with alternative role models.

In the end, it may be said that a proper development of the educational methodology of functional education may ultimately pave the way for an alternative strategy for the empowerment of women at the grassroots level. This method of teaching illiterates in the Third World as advocated by Paulo Freire (1972) and others of his ilk helps the subjects to participate in the transformation of their society by becoming agents of change rather than being passive recipients of it.

References

Freire, Paulo. 1972. *Pedagogy of the Oppressed*. New York: Penguin Books.

Kleis, R.J. et al. 1974. 'Towards a Contextual Definition of Non-formal Education'. Program of Studies in Non-formal Education Discussion, Paper No. 2, East Lansing: Michigan State University.

National Policy on Education. 1986. New Delhi: Ministry of Human Resource Development, Government of India.

Sarin, Madhu. 1986. 'Sukhomajri: A Development Experience'. *Manushi* (37/38).

Sethi, R.M. 1986. 'Rural Development, State Policy and Emerging Tensions: A Case Study of a Woman's Movement in Himachal Pradesh'. Paper Presented at a Regional Seminar, Punjabi University, Patiala.

SUTRA. 1979. Annual Report. Social Work Research Centre, Jagjit Nagar, Himachal Pradesh.

15

Impact of Government Schemes on the Status of Women in Punjab

Bindu Duggal

The endeavour and sustained efforts of the central and state governments and the society at large are now enabling the women to attain the ability to alleviate her to the stature of a man. In any case, the clutches of social impediments have all along been preventing her upward social mobility with regard to receiving education, and economic independence. Over five decades of independence have generated a great deal of awareness among women about their rights, yet it is observed that only urban literate women in general have been largely coming at least out of the shackles of social inhibitions. The rural women, particularly those who are poor and belonging to disadvantaged communities, have yet to get free from both social and economic strangleholds. Even with substantial governmental efforts for uplifting her socially as well as economically, these women have yet to make a desired level of progress.

This chapter is based on a study conducted by the Centre for Research in Rural and Industrial Development sponsored by Department of Women and Child Development, Government of India. The aim of the study is to assess the benefits to women under various governmental schemes during the Eighth Five Year Plan and how these government benefits have made dent in the social, political and economic upliftment of women. Table 15.1 gives the details of the schemes surveyed and the number of beneficiaries covered under each scheme.

Table 15.1 *List of schemes Surveyed, Number and Percentage of Beneficiaries Covered*

Name of Schemes	*No. of Women Beneficiaries*
*TRYSEM	64
**DWCRA	62
Attendance Scholarship to S.C. girls	239
Old-age Pension	151
Financial Assistance to Old and Destitute Women	140
***IRDP	123
Mahila Samridhi Yojna	73
National Maternity Benefit Scheme	28
Supplementary Nutrition Programme	34
National Family Benefit Scheme	4
ICDS	9
Indira Awas Yojna	8
Total	935

Source: Field Survey (2000).

*Training to Rural youth for Self-Employment.
**Development of Women and Children in Rural Areas.
***Integrated Rural Development Programme.

Literacy and Education

It is said that if you educate the mother, you educate the entire family. At present, all movements for welfare of women have emphasised the importance of women being given an access to education.

Although the literacy rate figures of total population of Punjab is above the national average (52.51% in 1991 and 69.95% in 2001). But it is still low as compared to other states and UTs such as Kerala, Lakshadweep, Delhi, Pondicherry, Andaman and Nicobar Islands, Daman and Diu, Uttranchal, Mizoram, Goa, Maharashtra, Himachal Pradesh, Tamil Nadu, Nagaland, Gujarat, Tripura and Manipur.

The female literacy rate was only 50.41 per cent in 1991 and 63.55 per cent in 2001 in Punjab, which shows that in spite of enumerable education and literacy missions for women, still 36 per cent of the women in Punjab are illiterate. In fact the female literacy is unevenly spread. The literacy rate ranges between 60 and 70 per cent in the districts of Patiala, Amritsar, Kapurthala, Fatehgarh Sahib, Gurdaspur and Nawanshehr. The literacy rate is less than 60 per cent in the districts of Moga, Faridkot, Batinda, Ferozepur, Sangrur, Muktsar and is least (45%) in Mansa. In fact in Ferozepur, the total literacy rate of women was 38 per cent in 1991 and is still only 52.33 per cent in 2001.

Therefore, the state has to make special efforts for accelerating the existing pace of the female literacy rate in this pocket. If we look at the literacy rate of district of Patiala, which also forms the basis of our study, it is observed that literacy rate of Patiala is comparatively better, that is, 58 per cent in 1991 and 70 per cent in 2001 as compared to Firozepur (48% in 1991 and 61% in 2001). Although the total female literacy rate was 50% in 1991 and 63 per cent in 2001 in Patiala but the female literacy rate of Scheduled Caste (SC) women is very low, that is, 27 per cent in 1991. Thus, special attention needs to be given to SC women so as to improve their literacy rate.

Literacy and Education in the Selected Blocks of Firozepur and Patiala Districts

The situation of total literacy and especially female literacy in the selected blocks in Patiala and Ferozepur is indicated in Table 15.2.

Table 15.2 *Literacy Rate in the Blocks of Patiala and Firozepur*

Blocks	*Total*	*Male*	*Female*
Dera Bassi	60.13	69.69	49.12
Samana	37.30	45.68	27.78
Abohar	38.24	49.99	24.91
Ghall Khurd	47.06	54.81	38.19

Source: District Census Handbook of Patiala and Firozepur.

Table 15.2 shows that although Patiala forms a part of the central Punjab but the block of Samana is quite near to the Southern Punjab and hence there has been less impact of schemes. In fact, Samana block in Patiala district has the lowest literacy rate (37.3%) and is at the bottom in comparison with the other blocks in Patiala.

Ghall Khurd block in Firozepur district is on Ludhiana-Firozepur National Highway and Dera Bassi block in Patiala district, situated on Delhi-Chandigarh National Highway, is closer to the state headquarters. It is highly industrialised and so the impact of the scheme has been more and hence these blocks show better literacy rate.

Abohar is situated far away from the state headquarters and hence has low literacy rate, that is, 38.2 per cent and the lowest female literacy rate, that is, 25 per cent, which shows that women in the richest pocket of the richest state are very poor so far as the literacy is concerned. It has the second lowest total literacy rate and lowest female literacy rate in the entire Firozepur district. Patiala district is more developed than Firozepur district and Dera Bassi is the most developed block as compared to the other selected blocks.

Although the female literacy rate in all the four blocks is low but the women belonging to the SC category have the lowest literacy rate. The literacy rate of the SC women in the Abohar block is as low as 7 per cent followed by Samana where the literacy rate is 10 per cent. It is really surprising that in spite of government's claim of implementing literacy and education schemes especially for SC girls at block level still 93 per cent of the women in Abohar, 85 per cent of the women in Ghall Khurd and 90 per cent in Samana, 65 per cent in Dera Bassi are illiterate. This calls for an urgent need in policy improvement for SC women.

For improving the literacy rate of women in various age groups, the schemes on education and literacy need to be redesigned so that the girls/women in the various age groups who are still illiterate are motivated to enrol themselves in the literacy centres/schools. The Deputy Commissioner, State Level Functionaries and other Panchayati Raj Institutions (PRIs) should be actively involved in enrolment of girls/women for attending the classes as the empirical study revealed that people in none of the villages selected for survey purposes were aware of any literacy mission.

An effort to improve women's status and to achieve the goal of women empowerment should start right at the tender age of the girl child. Punjab Government started the scheme of giving scholarships to the SC girls at the primary and secondary level. The state government provides scholarships of ₹ 30 per month to the girl students of *Vimukat Jatis* at primary levels and also at the secondary level in order to check the dropout rate among the students of the weaker sections of the society. The government claims that the dropout rate has declined ever since.

The survey has indicated that out of 935 households, there were 699 SC households out of which 239 households, that is, 34.19 per cent had taken benefit of this scheme (Table 15.1). The empirical study reveals that 67 per cent of the children receiving benefits of the scholarship scheme are also getting the other educational benefits such as free books. A total of 66 per cent of the non-SC households have not been able to draw benefits of this scheme despite the fact that these households are below the poverty line because the scheme is limited to only the SC households. However, if the objective of empowering women is to be achieved and if education is to be ensured to all girls, the reach of scheme should be broadened to cover all girls below poverty line without any distinction on the basis of caste or creed.

Further an attempt was made to study the percentage of SC population to the total population block-wise as the scholarships were only restricted to them. In fact, Attendance Scholarship to the SC girls was the only one scheme, which was operating in Patiala and Firozepur districts in the area of education. Adult Literacy Programme was not operating after 1992 and the Total Literacy Campaign started only in 1997 in Patiala and Ferozepur districts. The DPEP (District Primary Education Programme) has also not reached the schools of Patiala and Firozepur districts.

More than one-fourth of the population in selected blocks belonged to the SCs. However, the scheme for SC girls being implemented in Punjab does not cover the entire proportion of deserving children. This is obvious from the survey conducted, which reveals that only 34.19 per cent of the SC children from the total SC families in the selected sample were drawing benefits from the scheme on attendance scholarship for the SC girls. However, in order to ensure the scheme is reached to all girl children in the age group of 6–14 years and to wean away those engaged in labour activities, there is need for additional fund allocation for augmenting the resources being provided under this scheme. For ensuring 100 per cent coverage of scheme, effective monitoring by involvement of PRIs and NGOs along with the state functionaries needs to be worked out. In order to motivate the parents of the children presently engaged in labour activities, the scheme may also provide self-employment for parents specially mothers for making up for the loss of income resulting from sending such girls to schools.

Although majority of the women felt that the scheme helped in supplementing the income of household and the scholarships helped in educating their girl children as well, however, the impact of the educational schemes has not been tremendous in either of the district as a whole. Only a very small percentage of SCs have gained from the attendance scholarships so the scheme needs to be broadened to include all the girls below poverty line. Scholarships without any distinction on the basis of caste or creed should also be given to children belonging to poor families. The economic factor instead of the caste criteria should be adopted in selecting the beneficiaries. NGOs and PRIs along with the government functionaries should be encouraged to promote literacy programmes for women and children in the villages.

Health and Nutrition

Various schemes relating to health, birth control, nutrition and sanitation especially for women have been in operation in the state during the Eighth Five Year Plan. The data captured from the beneficiary households relate to the following schemes (a) ante-natal case of expectant mothers, postnatal case of nursing mothers and care of new born babies as also care of the children under six years of age is taken by providing iron and folic acid tablets during home visits. (b) National Family Benefit Scheme (NFBS) under this scheme, central assistance of ₹ 5,000 is provided in the case of death of the primary bread winner due to natural causes and ₹ 10,000 in the case of death due to accident causes is given to bereaved family below the poverty line. The survey could net four beneficiary women. (c) National Maternity Benefit Scheme (NMBS) is exclusively aimed at assisting pregnant women financially by providing them ₹ 300 cash for the first two live births. The surveys could net 28 beneficiaries.

There are other health-related schemes, which are operated under the programme of Integrated Child Development Services Scheme (ICDS). The main objectives of these schemes are related to improvement of nutritional and health status of children in the age group of 0–6 years. The scheme is also designed to reduce the incidence of mortality, morbidity and malnutrition of children. It also envisages enhancing the capability of the mother to look after the health and nutritional needs of the child. The delivery of various ICDS services is indicated below:

1. *Immunisation Programmes*: Immunisation of all children less than six years of age against diphtheria, tetanus, whooping cough, polio, typhoid, tuberculosis and measles is done by the health functionaries in coordination with the *Anganwadi* workers as also tetanus is administered to all pregnant women.
2. *Supplementary Nutrition Programme*: Under this scheme, supplementary nutrition is given to children below six years of age and to pregnant mothers belonging to low-income families. Pregnant women and nursing mothers belonging to the families of landless agricultural labourers, marginal farmers, SCs, Scheduled Tribes and other poor sections of the community are provided relief under this scheme. Children are given the nutrition amounting to ₹ 0.90 and women for ₹ 1.10. Of the total women beneficiaries selected in the sample study, 34 women had availed the benefit under their programme.
3. *Health Check-up*: The health check-ups are conducted particularly in case of antenatal care of pregnant mothers, postnatal care of nursing mothers as also newborn babies and all children under six years of age. Iron and folic acid tablets are being distributed to them and the usefulness of breast feeding to children is also promoted.
4. *Referral Services*: Serious cases of malnutrition and illness are referred to hospitals, PHCs/Community Health Centres or district hospitals.

The data also reveal that a doctor attended to only 38.29 per cent cases, whereas 60.81 per cent reported that ANM and trained *dais* made visits to village. Households (47.75%) have responded that trained *dais* have been attending to them at the time of pregnancies and they have come to depend on their advice as the visits of doctors are few and far between as also the high fee charged by them also inhibit them to seek their consultation and care.

Further, the extent of medical assistance made available to the pregnant women is, by and large, rather dismal. Only 34.76 per cent pregnant women have reported that they had been provided folic acid tablets/iron tablets/vitamin A as also vaccination was provided to 41.53 per cent women. Overall, there has been no assistance/aid coming from PHC/HC or by the doctors, ANMs or health guides. Even financial aid seems to have been made available to 7.14 per cent women.

Regarding availability and access to the various immunisation programmes, the empirical data collected from the sample households indicate that except for Samana block, BCG and DPT and polio programmes had reached majority of the households. However, hardly any prevention of diphtheria and typhoid is undertaken. Similarly, the supply of folic acid and iron tablets to the pregnant mothers is very scarce.

The data on the frequencies of visits of government health functionaries have been scarce. Only 25.93 per cent women reported that government health functionaries did visit them during normal times and while during pregnancies, 27.51 per cent functionaries had treatment from the government health functionaries in the sample village.

The nonattendance of government health functionaries and their apathy in not attending to the health needs of rural women, especially at the time of prenatal and postnatal periods, are having a telling effect on the health of rural women, which also supports the view that the government health care system has very rarely reached to the women in rural areas especially when there is an emergent need for rendering health care at the door step of the needy mother during and after the pregnancies.

The data indicate that dispensaries and private clinics are more accessible to households in the village, whereas PHCs, sub-health centres and community health centres are situated far away from their villages and thus private practitioners have become more accessible to the village folks. Eventually, they have become more and more dependent on them being easily approachable in normal times as well in case of other emergencies. The study has revealed that only 9.63 per cent beneficiaries have availed medical facilities from PHCs, community health centres or hospitals.

The empirical evidence suggests that the inhibiting factors largely relate to women not being able to go on their own for seeking medical consultation from a specialist in the PHC, which is also attributed to lack of transportation facilities in the village. Thus, many complicated reproductive health problems of women remain ignored, thus giving rise to maternal mortality, births of under weight babies and infant deaths.

It is not the economic progress alone which could bring about significant changes in the social and demographic structures of the women but efforts have to be translated into action for universalising education among girl children and women. Health facilities also have to be brought very near to the rural folks to enable them to gain, apart from the awareness of the programmes relating to reproductive child health. Access of medical facilities at the time of pre- and postpregnancy periods is also to be delivered to the women and child. These could be the main issues to be dealt with at the highest level in the government by way of restructuring, strengthening, capacity building, advocacy and upgrading the skill of the functionaries including involving of PRI as also voluntary organisations and NGOs at the village level/block level.

Income Generation

Development of Women and Children in Rural Areas (DWCRA)

The main objective of DWCRA is to improve the quality of life of women living in rural areas below poverty line and for creating more awareness of avenues of income for them. The operation and modus operandi of the scheme envisages formation of a group of 10–15 women. A total of ₹ 25,000 is provided as one time grant equally shared by the central and state governments.

As per the data collected, ₹ 448.13 lakhs was released by both the central and state governments for promotion of DWCRA scheme, which could benefit women only for generation of income. However, ₹ 453.85 lakhs, that is, 101.28 per cent, was incurred for achieving target of giving training to 25.61 groups of women. Only 2,490 groups were formed, which had a membership of 32,347 rural women below poverty line. The share of SC women out of the total membership was to the extent of 49.47 per cent, while the women belonging to other communities had a share of 50 per cent. Of the total groups targeted, 72.82 per cent women groups targeted started generating income.

Training to Rural Youth for Self Employment (TRYSEM)

The objective of TRYSEM is to provide entrepreneurial skills to the rural girls and boys belonging to the families living below poverty line to enable them to take up self-employment in the broad fields of agriculture and allied activities, industries, services and business activities. The schemes also provide for payment of stipend to trainees and honorarium to trainers and training institutions and free tool kits to the trainees and raw material for trainees in the training institutions.

During the Eighth Five Year Plan (1992–1997), a total amount of ₹ 239.66 lakhs was allocated for TRYSEM to enable both rural boys and girls receive training skills to enable their wage employment in various ventures. A total of 15,925 youths were brought under the ambit of this scheme. A total of 10,657 women in rural areas received necessary benefits under this scheme during the Eighth Five Year Plan.

Women's share in self-employment generation was to the extent of 58.38 per cent of the targeted beneficiaries under TRYSEM programme during 1992–1997, whereas 38.6 per cent of SC youths have also benefited. A total of 64 women beneficiaries were trained under this scheme in the sample collected for the present study.

Indira Awas Yojna

The main objective of the scheme relates to generation of additional gainful employment for the unemployed and under employed persons of both sexes in the rural areas. Eight beneficiaries were netted in the sample.

Integrated Rural Development Programme (IRDP)

IRDP is a major poverty alleviation programme. The objective of this scheme is to provide self-employment opportunities without any distinction to the rural poor living below poverty line through instruments of government subsidy and bank credit with a view to bringing them above the poverty line.

The expenditure has been proportionately higher than the allocation made under this scheme, which is of the order of 104 per cent. On the achievement side, there has also been 153 per cent against the targeted side in respect of advances made as subsidy to the needy. In case of target advances fixed on account of loan, the targets have been exceeded by 157 per cent. The reach of SC beneficiaries has been only 48 per cent.

Other Welfare Financial Assistance Schemes for Women

Besides the aforesaid income generation schemes, other welfare schemes, which benefit women under special circumstances being implemented in the state are as follows:

Mahila Samridhi Yojna

The schemes relates to empowering women, especially through their confidence building and economic independence. It is available to women above the age of 18 years belonging to rural areas. Under its purview, women are encouraged to open their own accounts in the local post offices, and incentives are offered for more deposits and lesser withdrawals. The schemes benefited 7.24 per cent of the total beneficiaries selected in the sample. The data indicate that in district Ferozepur, 55.313 beneficiaries have received monitory help during this year, whereas ₹ 0.77 lakhs has been expended in the district as a whole.

Financial Assistance to Older and Destitute Women

Under this, women *below* the age of 60 years who have no economic means and have been deprived of the husband's support due to death, physical and mental disability or prolonged absence from home are sanctioned financial assistance at the rate of ₹ 200 per month. The amount is granted to those whose monthly income from all sources is less than ₹ 1,000 per month. The schemes benefited 140 women in the selected sample.

National Old Age Pension Scheme

Under this scheme, women as well as men can take the benefit of old age pension, if they are 65 years or above and little or no regular means of assistance is available to them from their own resources of income or through financial support from family members or other sources. In this regard, central assistance is ₹ 75 per month. A total of 14.98 per cent beneficiaries have been netted in the sample survey.

For launching the schemes relating to Financial Assistance to Older and Destitute Women and National Old Age Pension, the state government expended about ₹ 120 crores during Eighth Five Year Plan period. Whereas Patiala and Firozepur districts had allocation to the extent of ₹ 4.03 crores and ₹ 6.23 crores respectively during this period, together these two districts have expended 8.55 per cent of the total financial achievements under the schemes.

Training for Skill Formation and Upgradation

The data collected through the study indicate that only 10.42 per cent beneficiaries have availed training for formation of skill or upgradation of the skills already possessed by them.

With regard to establishment of ventures by the beneficiaries, 1.59 beneficiaries have reported establishment of an enterprise. In fact, 7.34 per cent beneficiaries in the sample have indicated that by obtaining training skills they have not only been able to modernise their enterprise but also helped them in augmenting their family income.

It is only 2.18 per cent beneficiaries who responded that they had received some kind of tools/kits for improving the agriculture/allied activities. A total of 40.91 per cent respondents claimed that the tools/kits provided by the government agencies helped them in making value additions to agriculture and allied activities, while 18.18 per cent reported that this equipment enthused and motivated them at least to enable initiating the establishment of their own ventures.

Table 15.3 indicates the financial benefits received by the beneficiaries.

Table 15.3 *Financial Benefits Received by Beneficiaries*

Financial Assistance	*Percentage of Beneficiaries*
Less than ₹ 1,000	53.27
1,001–3,000	10.42
3,001–5,000	8.43
5,001–8,000	8.83
8,001–10,000	2.68
10,000 above	2.38
No response	13.99

Source: Field Survey (2000).

Majority of the women respondents (53.27%) indicated that less than ₹ 1,000 as financial assistance was provided to them under a scheme. However, 18.85 per cent had availed the benefits to the extent of ₹ 1,001–5,000, while 11.51 per cent beneficiaries reported that they availed between ₹ 5,001 and 10,000 as financial benefits. There are 2.38 per cent beneficiaries who received financial benefit as high as ₹ 10,000 and above.

Thus, the government has invested a lot of money to uplift the status of women through various schemes. Through the direct benefits under one or the other scheme or indirectly through the training taken under some schemes, the women have been able to generate some income of their own. A detailed classification of women beneficiary households in each block by different income groups is given in Table 15.4.

Table 15.4 *Percentage of Beneficiary Women by different Income Groups*

Name of Block	*Less than ₹ 200 (Monthly)*	*₹ 200–400 (Monthly)*	*₹ 400–600 (Monthly)*	*₹ 600 & above (Monthly)*
Dera Bassi	55.41	29.73	12.16	2.11
Samana	82.11	11.58	5.26	1.05
Abohar	67.20	30.40	0.80	1.60
Ghall Khurd	53.84	20.51	16.67	8.97
Total	65.86	23.39	7.53	3.23

Source: Field Survey (2000).

The data in Table 15.4 indicate that majority of the selected beneficiary women (65.86%) generates less than ₹ 200 per month from the schemes availed, while 23.39 per cent beneficiaries have been able to earn ₹ 200–400 per month. A total of 10.76 per cent beneficiaries in the sample have been earning income of ₹ 400 and above.

Since most of the women were contributing to the family income in one form or the other, an attempt has been made to study the impact of schemes aimed to ameliorate the socio-economic and political status of women.

Transformation in the Status of Women

- Transformation in social status
- Transformation in political status
- Transformation in economic status

Transformation in Social Status

Domestic Work

It was found that the household drudgery for most of the women has not lessened. In majority of the households, it was still the women's duty to look after the household chores. As has been indicated by the survey, the women member of the household spend lot of time for cooking, cleaning, washing, looking after children, cattle rearing, collecting fuel, fodder, water and also other domestic chores and has very little time for her own self.

Mobility and Social Transformation

Mobility is one of the significant parameters for assessing how far the women in a particular area/community have been empowered. Historically, Indian woman suffered from such social taboos, which restricted her movement out of her home. Restricted mobility inhibits interaction with other women and thereby blocks her access to information, which relate to her empowerment. Therefore, for impact measurement of the various programmes, it is essential that we should know whether the women have now been empowered to move about freely or not. As all the respondents were taking benefits under one or the other schemes, hence it was thought important to study the impact of these schemes on their status.

The empirical data collected revealed that 89 per cent of the women had freedom to move around unescorted within the village and 62 per cent could even go outside the village alone. A total of 29 per cent of the women reported that they were allowed to move around freely only during day time. However all the women restricted their visits to close relatives and mainly went only in case of some emergency such as birth, marriage or death of a relative.

The primary data collected also revealed that none of the respondents in the village participated in any group activity for recreation purposes. Thus, there is a clear indication that although women felt free to move around as they liked, their visits were just restricted to compulsory obligations and not for recreation purposes.

Decision-Making

It is a general belief that economic independence of the women would free them from the male dominance within the family. An assessment of women's locus of power can also be made by analysing the patterns of her involvement in the decision-making process of the family.

The empirical data collected in the survey revealed that although the respondents were consulted in the household decisions, the males in the households took the final say. The details as to who takes the final decision are given in Table 15.5.

Table 15.5 *Important Decision-Maker in the Household*

Decision-Maker	*No. of Respondents*
Respondent/Daughter/Mother/Mother-in-law	184 (19.68)
Father/Father-in-law/Husband/Son	751 (80.32)
Total	935 (100)

Source: Field Survey (2000).

Table 15.5 reveals that in 80 per cent of the cases, the decisions in the family are taken by the male members, that is, the father/father-in-law, husband or the son. Only 20 per cent of the decisions are taken by either the mother/mother-in-law/respondent or her daughter. Thus, even though the women may be financially contributing to the household, but still in majority of the household decisions and the final say lie with the male members of the households.

Further, the empirical data also show that although majority of the women (62.96%) do have awareness about family planning methods, the rural married women have to take consent of their husband in adopting family planning methods. Except for Abohar block, where most of the married beneficiary women do take decisions themselves, in all other blocks of Patiala district, that is, Dera Bassi and Samana and Ghall Khurd in Ferozepur district, majority of the decisions rest with the husbands.

In brief, although there has been some dent in improving the social status of women, however, by and large, their status in the family remains the same.

Transformation in Political Status

Political status can be defined as the degree of equality and freedom enjoyed by women in the sharing of power.

Right to Exercise Vote

One of the important indicators of the political status of women is their participation in the political process as voters and candidates in election. Indian women were fortunate right from independence in having a right to vote in the formation of the government. According to the study, 70 per cent of the respondents had exercised their right to vote in the last elections in our sample (Table 15.6).

Table 15.6 *Number of Respondents Who Exercised Their Right to Vote*

Response	*No. of Respondents*
Voted	658 (70.37)
Not voted	197 (21.07)
No response	80 (8.56)
Total	935 (100.0)

Source: Field Survey (2000).

Amazingly, though 70 per cent of the respondent had voted, the empirical data revealed that 52 per cent of the respondents were influenced by someone or the other in taking the decision as to whom to vote for. Table 15.7 gives the details.

Table 15.7 *Distribution of Respondents According to the Influence by Others While Casting Their Vote*

Response	*Percentage*	
Influenced	340	(51.67)
Not Influenced	318	(48.33)
Total	658	(100.0)

Source: Field Survey (2000).

With the female literacy rate of 49 per cent in Dera Bassi, 27 per cent in Samana, 24 per cent in Abohar and 38 per cent in Ghall Khurd, it is not surprising that 52 per cent of the women, who voted, did not exercise their right to vote according to their free will. A large majority of them were influenced by the male members of their households, that is father/husband/son. Community organisers, female peer groups or the in-laws of the respondents influenced the remaining. Only 48 per cent of the respondents took their independent decisions while voting.

Right to Contest Elections

Not only it is important that a woman should exercise her right to vote but it is equally important that she exercises her right to contest the elections.

Rajiv Gandhi realised that despite provisions in the constitution/law, women representatives in various political forums were far from satisfactory and hence he proceeded to provide 33 per cent representation in PRIs. He thought of giving reservation to women so far as their representation in various levels of grassroots democracy was concerned. So it was thought relevant to find out women's representation in various forms so as to know how far they have been empowered to take decisions on their own.

The secondary data revealed that in Patiala district, there were 1,063 seats of sarpanches out of which 357, that is, 33.58 per cent were women sarpanches. The total number of panches was 6,264 out of which 2,258, that is, 36 per cent were women panches. In Ferozepur district also, nearly 33 per cent were women sarpanches. Although women were occupying the positions of panches/sarpanches, when contacted it was perceived that the husbands were main decision-makers and thereby usurping powers of their sarpanch/panch wives. However, it is being felt that it is a step in the right direction because in the course of time, these women will become confident/competent enough to take their own decisions. The empirical data also revealed that 50 per cent of the respondents felt that the reservation of seats for women in PRIs had benefited them in one way or the other. They felt that women should be encouraged to become elected members as it enhances not only the status of the women in power but also increases confidence level of the women folk. They somewhere feel more comfortable and secure in approaching the elected women representative rather than men. They felt that their accessibility to women representatives had increased and hence had benefited them in one way or the other.

The political status of women does not seem to have undergone a major change. Although the women are fortunate to have their political right to vote, all the women do not exercise this right and the male members of the household mostly influence those who exercise it. Further only one-third of the women exercise their right to hold positions and that too since the government has reserved a quota of 33 per cent for them. Although women have become sarpanches and panches but it has again been observed that they are mere rubber stamps and their husbands take the main decisions.

Transformation in Economic Status

A very important aspect for evaluating the status of these women is whether the women possess any immovable property/land/plot or a house in their names. However, the empirical data revealed that 95 per cent of them did not own any property in their names. Most of the women who had some property in their names inherited it only after the death of their husbands.

Thus, although all the women under this study were receiving the financial benefits under one scheme or the other, their economic status was very low.

Conclusion

The Government of India has been floating schemes after schemes for uplifting the status of women. The resources utilised so far in the launch of various welfare schemes have been colossal indeed and have benefited the women in substantiating their household income and improving their social status to some extent, however the change has not been that noticeable to bring about any change in the attitude of their family members towards them. There is no reallocation of household work, and traditional roles remain unchanged with men as the main decision-maker.

16

Impact of 73rd Amendment Act on Women Empowerment

A Study of Punjab and Haryana

Swinder Singh and Sumita Bakshi

In the early stages of evolution of mankind when civilisations were emerging, societies were evolving and unique cultures were developing specific value systems, men and women shared equal credits. Their natural abilities complimented each other, their individual roles were well-defined and their distinct skills together helped mankind evolve well. But as the process of socialisation gained strength, the power drifted to the relatively more powerful section of society – men. Natural justice lost its hold and the power of strapping destinies slowly slipped in the powerful grip of men. Natural endowments of masculine powers became a weapon of usurping more power, and the feminine virtues of compassion and benevolence became signs of servitude. And soon sexual distinctions became gender inequalities, male protection became male chauvinism and majority of gender neutral societies turned patriarchal societies. In those societies where women had attained the status of goddess, the female community suffered a huge set back. Women eventually became the most vulnerable, marginalised subgroup of society – disregarded by customs, derided by religion and even discriminated by the law of the land. Such gender differences, based on indiscriminate social constructions, became what social scientists would like to call, 'the fault lines' of society. With age, these fault lines grew bigger and deeper.

The situation has not changed much till today. Jakarta Declaration on Advancement of Women in Asia Pacific (1994) sums up the plight of women of today: 'Women represent fifty per cent of population, make up thirty per cent of the official labour force, perform sixty per cent of all working hours, receive the ten per cent of the world income and own even less than one per cent of the world property'.

Defining Empowerment

Empowerment is a term that defies easy translation from English to any other language. Power is a threatening word. Every human relation has dimensions of power and much of our behaviour is governed by the desire to use power, to enhance one's power and to alter the relations of power. Here the word 'power' is used in benign sense, not as the power to 'oppress others' or inflict pain, but in the sense of 'capacity', as in the ability to read and write, which is empowering (Friedman, 1996).

The word 'empowerment' is a consideration of two words 'power' and its prefix 'em'. Empower is to make or cause power. It means to give power, to give authority and to give ability. It can be defined as a process in which power is gained, developed, seized, facilitated or given to a relatively powerless person who elevates him or her from a relatively powerless state to a state of more power through some definite strategies. Empowerment is generally used as a synonym for participation, for speaking out or for meeting some basic needs. It is a process of gaining understanding of and control over the social, economic and political forces around one as a means of improving one's standing in society. In this sense, empowerment also implies questioning the 'monopoly of the dominant paradigm' or to keep alive the populations' resentment against the most visible aspects of political and social discrimination (Rehnema, 1997). Empowerment of women means that the women to whom so far equitable social status and resources such as land, property and investments were not accessible would have a better access to these resources and inputs. The UNDP with a trace of instrumentalism sees the value in investing in women's capacities and empowering them to make their own choices and stresses that their empowerment is crucial to the goal of sustainable development. Women empowerment can thus be taken up as a process geared to raising women's individual and collective awareness about the ways in which power relations affect their lives while enabling them to gain self-confidence and nurturing their strength to challenge gender inequalities (Oxaal, 1997).

The Draft Declaration by the Heads of the States and Governments (1995) asserts in point 23:

> Recognize that empowering people particularly women, to strengthen their capacities is a main objective of development and its principal resource. Empowerment requires full participation of people in the formulation, implementation and evaluation of decisions and determines the functioning and well being of our societies.

Drawing on this women's empowerment is a process of developing negotiating skills from the bottom-up (at family and collective level) with a view to ultimately bring about a fairer distribution of power. This is more than just a call for equitable gender relations in society, for it hinges on the following question. By changing society, can women's empowerment – an attempt to redress unequal power relations and produce new development paradigm – end both general and gender related inequality?

Women's empowerment may have numerous dimensions, which may be categorised as: (1) sense of security and vision of a future; (2) ability to earn a living; (3) ability to act effectively in the public sphere; (4) increased decision-making power in the household; (5) participation in nonfamily solidarity groups and (6) mobility and visibility in the community.

Women's empowerment viewed from any angle is a slow, long run and complex process. It requires conscientiousness and calls for multipronged action by various agencies. People's empowerment, particularly women's empowerment being very significant in any society and crucial for a democratic set-up and also being arduous in nature and process, requires to be taken up strategically.

The concept of women empowerment though came very late in India continued to gain more thrust, allocation and patronage. Women's cause attracted some attention of the government right from the very First Five Year Plan. The same has been treated as a subject of 'welfare' and clubbed together with the welfare of the disadvantaged groups such as destitute, disabled and aged. The shift in the approach from 'welfare' to 'development' of women took place in the Sixth Plan. Accordingly the Sixth Plan adopted a multidisciplinary approach with a special thrust on the three core sections of health, education and employment for women. In the Seventh Plan, the developmental programmes continued with the major objective of raising their economic and social status and bringing them into the mainstream of national development. The Ninth Plan (1997–2002) made two significant changes in the conceptual strategy of planning for women. First, 'Empowerment of Women' became one of the nine primary objectives of the Ninth Plan. To this effect, the approach of the plan was to create an enabling environment where women could freely exercise their rights both within and outside home, as equal partners along with men. Second, the plan directed both centre and the states to adopt a special strategy of 'women's component plan' (WCP) through which not less than 30 per cent of funds/benefits flow from all the general development sectors.

One of the well accepted measure/strategy towards women's empowerment is through their increased participation. Traditionally, the local self-government institutions are known to have constituted the most well-known devices to widen and deepen popular participation in the process of democratic governance. The central question raised was that if only the decision-making power was transferred to subnational constituencies and new levels of governance created, will it be possible for the masses at large to achieve a voice in determining policies that affect their lives. In rural India, the three tiers Panchayati Raj set-up assumed responsibility of local development and empowerment through people's participation after the recommendation of Balwant Rai Mehta Committee since 1959. The Panchayati Raj (henceforth, PR) Institutions in India are the prime instruments of decentralisation at the grassroots level. They assume importance due to the need to contain the relentless demographic pressures and optimum use of scarce resources for development. More importantly, they act as vehicle in carrying back to the people the power that really belongs to them (Singh and Singh, 2000)

The PR Institutions have been in operation in almost all the states of India for nearly five decades, but with a number of variants and a number of problems. They failed to attract people's real involvement due to a number of reasons such as political apathy, bureaucratic hurdles and paucity of resources. In order to strengthen these grassroots institutions, government enacted the 73rd and 74th Constitutional Amendment Acts with a view to devolve powers for economic development and social justice. Among the prominent provisions of the 73rd Amendment are the revitalisation of the institutions of Gram Sabha (in which all the voters of the village are the members) and second, one-third reservation for women (including women belonging to SC/ST). Consequently, the issue of empowerment of women in rural India assumed considerable significance because of these constitutional amendments and the subsequent legislations by the state governments. Besides the reservation of one-third seats, the amendment also requires reservation of posts of chairpersons for women in all grassroots democratic institutions. This was a historical step of far-reaching implications and significant repercussions on the political processes in rural India (Singh and Singh, 2000).

It was also expected that with the women becoming panches and sarpanches, members/chairpersons of Panchayat Samities and Zila Parishads, the whole complexion of these institutions and rural scene was bound to change, the awareness level among the women would shoot up substantially, women would play effective role in decision-making and which in turn would transform the rural society as a whole. With this achievement, the leadership pattern and the power structure was also expected to restructure substantially in favour of the oppressed and disadvantaged groups including women.

The present study was conducted to look into the functioning of the system of PR over a decade after the reforms and to assess their impact on the rural society particularly on the depressed groups and women. In this chapter, the impact of new PR system on the women has been examined particularly in terms of awareness level among women, their participation and their leadership initiatives. The survey was conducted in the year 2006.

The Sample

For the purpose of the current study, four blocks were selected, two each from Ropar district of Punjab and Karnal district of Haryana. The blocks are Anandpur Sahib (Pb), Chamkaur Sahib (Pb), Nilokheri (Hry.) and Gharaunda (Hry). Blocks were selected on the basis of their proximity and distance from the district headquarters. Villages/Gram Panchayats were randomly selected and visited to administer the specifically prepared interview schedule. A total of 156 out of randomly selected eight villages respondents were interviewed comprising 98 (56 in Ropar and 42 in Karnal) women panches and sarpanches; 42 male panches/sarpanches and 16 officials. Out of the total women members, 13 were sarpanches while the rest were panches.

Socio-economic Profile

An analysis of the socio-economic profile of respondents would help us to have a better understanding of the behavioural changes among the women panches and sarpanches. Nearly one-third (31) of the total 98 women belonged to reserved categories. As indicated in Table 16.1, a large majority of respondents fall in the age groups ranging from 30 to 60 years. More than one-third of the respondents were totally illiterate, while less than one-tenth had formal education equal to and above matriculation level (Table 16.2). However, nearly one third women belonged to the families possessing substantial agricultural land, while 27.5 per cent belonged to landless/poor category (Table 16.3).

Table 16.1 *Age (years)*

	Below 30 Years	*30 to 50 Years*	*50 to 60 Years*	*Above 60 Years*	*Total*
Punjab	8	22	19	7	56
Haryana	4	13	10	15	42
Total	12	35	29	22	98

Table 16.2 *Education*

	Illiterate	Below Matric	Matric & Above	Graduate & Above	Total
Punjab	20	30	4	2	56
Haryana	18	21	2	1	42
Total	38	51	6	3	98

Table 16.3 *Economic Status*

	Substantial Land	Small Land Holding	Other Professional	Land less/Poor	Total
Punjab	21	13	6	16	56
Haryana	13	13	5	11	42
Total	34	26	11	27	98

Political Linkages

Having direct family links or association with one or the other political party may ensure better awareness level or leadership pattern among individuals. As Table 16.4 indicates, direct family links have been indicated more in case of Haryana blocks (8) as compared to those of Punjab (4). However, direct association with one or other political party has been found more in case of Punjab (16) as compared to that in Haryana (5). Nearly two-third (62) women were found to be the first timers in Panchayats (Table 16.5).

Table 16.4 *Political Linkage*

	Direct Family Link with some Known leader	Link with Political Party	No Link	Total
Punjab	4	16	36	56
Haryana	8	5	29	42
Total	12	21	65	98

Table 16.5 *Experience in Panchayati Raj*

	Past Experience as Panch/Sarpanch	No Past Experience	Total
Punjab	23	33	56
Haryana	13	29	42
Total	36	62	98

Awareness Level

The initial condition towards any empowerment move or participation by the individuals is their awareness about the structure and function of grassroots bodies, the levels of government, system of governance and so on. Another disappointing observation made was the poor awareness level of the women panches/sarpanches. The overall awareness among the respondents was very poor in regard to Panchayati Raj set-up and miserably poor in regard to other levels of government. Most of them failed to explain the function or role of an MLA or MP. It was surprising to find their poor awareness in regard to the constitutional grassroots body Gram Sabha. Even in regard to the Gram Panchayat of which they are the members, their knowledge was either partial or very little. Most of the respondents (81) could point out only one or two civic functions being looked after by the Panchayats, and nothing more.

Other than the PR bodies, the awareness level among the women respondents about the municipal bodies, rural development programmes, other governmental functionaries and organs was not contrary to expectations. Most of them were literally uninformed in this regard and very few had some faint idea about the ongoing rural development programmes, nature of urban local bodies or the broader set-up officials at village, block or higher levels. Less than 5 per cent respondents, who had received some formal education, were able to mention some details in this regard. Only two of these respondents were having some idea about the Constitution of India and the government set-up at union and state level.

Participation: Nature and Extent

The bottom-up style of grassroots bodies is rooted in their commitment to the active participation of local communities and other beneficiary groups in their activities. However, low level of participation particularly by the weaker sections and women has always been a matter of serious concern for the policy makers. Before moving further, it would not be out of place to examine briefly the concept of participation. Some use this term to mean active participation in political decision-making. For certain activist groups, participation have no meaning unless the people involved have significant control over the decisions concerning the organisation to which they belong (Samuel, 1989). Viewing from any angle, participation may be taken as an activity by which individual beneficiaries or groups influence the decision-making process or their execution. An attempt has been made to assess the intensity of participation by women panches/sarpanches in the PR bodies as Table 16.6 indicates, the level in participation by women is not at all encouraging. The starting point, their attendance of Panchayat meetings, has been found to be quite unsatisfactory and so is their knowledge of Panchayat resolutions and activities. The scene in regard to their participation is really pathetic. The data indicate that nearly three-fourth of the women panches and sarpanches have been merely the passive members. Most of those who have indicated some kind of activity had some political background, past experience as members of PR bodies or had acquired some formal education.

Table 16.6 *Intensity of Participation*

Activities	*Regular*	*Occasional*	*Rarely*	*Never*	*Total*
Attending the meetings	24	31	26	17	98
Seeking information	7	9	7	75	98
Participation in Decision-making	5	10	8	75	98
Interaction with other member	11	10	18	59	98
Knowledge of resolutions/activities	12	16	25	45	98
Interaction with officials	7	5	8	78	98
Discussion of village issues with villagers	13	16	20	49	98

Leadership Pattern

One of the expected impacts of the 73rd Constitutional Amendment Act was to be on the pattern of rural leadership. With the inclusion of one-third women panches and sarpanches, a new stream of leadership, breaking the gender barriers, was expected to emerge in the due course of time. Information collected for the purpose of the study was on the lines of leadership initiatives by raising certain common issues during Panchayat meetings, role in decision-making, initiation of certain community schemes, motivating co-members towards taking up of such schemes/tasks, and community sensitisation and mobilisation.

Table 16.7 *Leadership Initiatives*

	Frequently	*Occasionally*	*Rarely*	*Never*	*Total*
Raising of issues	4	4	6	84	98
Role in decision-making	5	4	8	81	98
Initiating schemes/works	3	2	3	90	98
Motivating co-members	4	5	5	84	98
Community mobilising	4	2	5	87	98

On the leadership front, the overall picture is once again quite dismal. The new breed of rural leadership, whether women or the so-called lower castes, seems bold on papers yet the truth is that it is far away from reality.

As Table 16.7 indicates, except in the few cases, leadership initiatives by the women panches and sarpanches is as forlorn as ever.

The male attitude towards women empowerment has never been inspiring. The male chauvinism has always been deep rooted in our society. The constitutional and statutory provisions relating to women reservation in PR bodies have not been delightfully accepted by the menfolks. All the male respondents (42) had the knowledge of the provisions for women and SC reservations in the PR bodies and as chairpersons. However, nearly one-third (13) were not clear about the purpose of reservation. Again, two-third of the male respondents were not hopeful of any gain for rural society out of reservation system. With regard to the faith in women leadership in rural areas, nearly three-fourth (30) respondents viewed it a futile exercise only.

The officials' attitude towards the above issues was found much better as compared to those of male respondents. Nearly two-third of the total officials (16) interacted with were hopeful of transformation in the leadership pattern. However, they viewed it to be a long process and stressed on big efforts by governments, NGOs and women themselves.

Major Findings

Major findings of the study are summarised here:

- The overall picture of empowerment of rural women is dull and dismal.
- The awareness level among women about PR bodies and their functions is very poor.
- There is ineffective participation of women in Panchayat functioning.
- The attendance of women members in Panchayat meetings is not regular and their knowledge of Panchayat resolutions/activities is very poor.
- Women in general are playing no significant role in decision-making process in Panchayat meetings and are not instrumental in initiating new schemes/measures.
- In general there is no significant change in the leadership pattern since the implementation of 73rd Constitutional Amendment Act.
- The Constitutional body, Gram Sabha is virtually nonexistent in most cases, thus defeating the basic purpose of bringing out direct democracy for ruralites especially women.
- Women have shown some interest in orientation cum training programmes introduced by the government with the help of certain NGOs. However, these programmes are too short, deficient, scarce and unprofessionally managed.
- Although pushed into PR bodies by the men, women in certain cases have shown a definite spark, interest in Panchayat and village affairs and are willing to accept the challenges and in some exceptional cases challenge the male dominance.

The overall analysis indicates clearly that there is no substantial impact of 73rd Amendment on women empowerment. Except the regular elections, reservation of seats for women and SC/ST, enhanced power and resources, these grassroots bodies are yet to make a mark on the rural scene. As per the statutory requirements, now at least one-third of total panches and sarpanches are women but this is merely on papers and not in reality. Stories of women acting as dummy members to satisfy the constitutional provisions seem to hold true in most cases. The traditional inhibition of women against the male dominance is still a prominent feature of rural society. In a large number of cases the de facto panches/sarpanches against the women seats are the household menfolk.

Suggestions

In the light of the present and previous surveys made by the authors, it would be appropriate here to put forward a few suggestions for the top leaders and administrators and those who are concerned about women empowerment particularly in rural India. These are as follows:

- Orientation cum training programmes for Panchayat members should be an integral part of the PR system. These programmes should be frequent and should be of sufficient duration as against the current one-day programme.
- These programmes need better planning and organisation.
- Such programmes must be conducted at places, either nearer to their villages or at the most at the block headquarters. These programmes should be open for all women voters of the village and members belonging to other disadvantageous sections – SC/ST and economically poor.
- Special arrangements should be made to regularly inform the women in villages regarding the ongoing and forthcoming programmes relating to rural development, women-related programmes, employment generating programmes, family welfare and child welfare programmes.
- Proper publicity/information in regard to the proposed meetings of Gram Sabha/Gram Panchayat must be provided to the villagers particularly to the women. Also the decisions/resolutions of previous meetings, action taken and other related information must be available or announced at designated places and time.
- Gram Sabha/Gram Panchayat meetings should be supervised by the BDO or some other official authorised by him.
- Attendance of rural girls in the schools needs to be monitored regularly so as to ensure their literacy as a long-term measure towards women empowerment.

Conclusion

Mere passing of PR Legislations cannot serve as a panacea to mend the orthodox rural society or to uplift the real status of women. The women will get empowered only when their awareness level is improved, they develop some interest in a village and community affairs, participate in PR bodies and they are able to demand their rights and exercise power. Educational policies for girls, proper implementation of women welfare schemes and rural development programmes are bound to play a definite role in women empowerment but in the long run only. There is a need to mobilise the women folk to come out of the traditional web, to get organised and raise their voice effectively. Above all, the policy makers, and the bureaucracy, need to play a positive role towards empowering the women.

References

Draft Declaration by the Heads of the States and Governments. 1995. Third Preparatory Committee, New York, United Nations.

Friedman, John. 1996. 'Rethinking Poverty, Empowerment and Citizen Rights'. *International Social Science Journal*, 48(148): 161–172.

Jakarta Declaration on Advancement of Women in Asia Pacific. 1994. New York, United Nations.

Oxaal, Zoe. 1997. *Gender and Empowerment: Definitions, Approaches and Implications for Policy*. London: Routledge.

Rehnema, Majid. 1997. 'Participation', in Wolgang Sachs (ed.), *The Development Dictionary*. New Delhi: Orient Longman.

Samuel, Paul. 1989. 'Poverty Alleviation and Participation'. *Economic and Political Weekly*, January 14.

Singh, Sahib and Singh, Swinder. 2000. *Local Government in India*. Jalandhar: New Academic.

17

Empowering Women

A Sociological Perspective

S. Gohilavani

Women empowerment is perhaps a vital component for reaching gender equality, hence refers to equitable access to resources, power and decision-making. Aspects such as women's development, performance, skill acquisition and participation in policy decisions all make women empowerment a positive concept. Feminists refer it to women's capacity for self-action, power to change their course of life and also to adapt to the challenges in time. It is viewed as a process that requires a realignment of power in decision-making at all levels vis-à-vis household, personal, institutional and social levels.

Women empowerment is a multidimensional process, aiming at establishing an equitable partnership between men and women that can be built on the strengths of shared living: in terms of knowledge, energy, creativity and skill. Equitable partnership – a state of empowerment – becomes vital as it is perceived to bring positive benefits to the society and solutions to global problems that are pressing the world's economy, environment and social living. Women empowerment as such is viewed to facilitate a joint venture of men and women in combating the global problems.

International Scenario on Women Empowerment

There had been women's conferences held at the international level: one in Mexico in 1975, one in Copenhagen in 1980, another in Nairobi in 1985 and the last one was in Beijing in September 1995 that includes an NGO Forum in Huairou. Discussions during such conferences revealed the potentials of women's movements at the international level in maximising advocacy efforts towards empowering women worldwide, which are as follows:

- in creating constituencies free from male-dominated governments
- in establishing a new government, sought to be influenced by women. Subsequent conferences of the United Nations held in Rio de Janeiro, Vienna, Cairo, Small Islands, Copenhagen, and Habitat II paved way for multiplying international contact and networking among women.

In all these conferences, the key issues affecting women worldwide were identified as follows:

> Women's economic survival, global economy, empowerment of women, poverty, affordable health care, human rights, workplace rights, educational equity, reproductive and sexual rights, struggles against violence, protection of healthy environment and end to wars and militarism. (Anand and Salvi, 1998)

Beijing Declaration on Women Empowerment

The largest United Nation's conference the world is said to have seen was the United Nation's Fourth World Conference of Women held in Beijing. It was reported as a consensus of official representatives from 189 countries and 30,000 NGO representatives consisting of 20,000 women and the rest being men, which manifested the power of women as a force for global change towards developing countries and benefiting the human kind. The desired goal of the conference was gender equality, which could be achieved by mainstreaming perspective in development process.

Feminists acknowledged that Beijing Conference spoke of many things, but emphasised categorically on paradigm shifts, women empowerment and the male–female relationship. The need for considering these things was stressed not as somebody's business but as everybody's business. The success of the conference was in its contribution towards a change of mindset in people all over the world.

Of course the seed for women empowerment was sown even earlier at the International Conference on Population and Development held in Cairo, in 1994. Women representatives from all the countries of the world confronted over the population policies that remain still abusive to women and declared recognising the centrality of women empowerment both in the population policy and in development policy. Thus, women empowerment received the first attention in the priority list along with gender equality, women's ability to control their own fertility and elimination of violence against women. Such a view was also endorsed in Beijing Declaration, that states

> We, the governments' participating in the Fourth World Conference on Women, dedicate ourselves unreservedly to addressing the constraints and obstacles and thus enhancing further the

advancement and empowerment of women all over the world and agree that this requires urgent action in the spirit of determination, hope, cooperation and solidarity now and to carry us forward into the next century. (Anand and Salvi, 1998: 17)

The agenda for women empowerment named as the Platform for Action prepared unanimously at the Beijing Conference seeks to promote and protect the full enjoyment of all human rights and the fundamental freedom of all women throughout their life. This agenda called for establishing the principle of shared power and responsibility between women and men at home, at workplace and at the level of wider national and international communities. Thus, women empowerment is conceived to be the whole bundle of women's rights vis-à-vis to freedom of thought, conscience, religion and belief, intending to contribute to the moral, ethical, spiritual and intellectual needs of women and men at the personal or communal spheres.

Women's Concerns in the Context of Empowerment

The critical areas of women's concern have been identified at the Fifth Regional Conference on Women held in Africa (c.f. Anand and Salvi, 1998: 35-83). They are women's:

- poverty,
- insufficient food security and lack of economic opportunities, inadequate access to education, training, science and technology, vital role in culture, family and socialisation,
- improvement of health in general and reproductive health in particular,
- relationship and linkages to environment and natural resources, management,
- involvement in peace process,
- political participation,
- legal and human rights, and
- mainstreaming gender, desegregated data as well as
- the status of girl child.

Women empowerment is closely tied with health and education guaranteeing them the possibility of realising their full in society, and shaping their lives concomitant to their aspirations. It is thus a fundamental factor for achieving equality, development and peace in the country, ultimately leading to full participation of women in all spheres, that is, decision-making process and access to power.

Empowerment Framework

Empowerment need to be treated both as a process and as a goal, indicating the fact that it is an end, by itself and a means as well, to reach this ultimate. Similar to socialisation, empowerment takes women to the extent that they think and act self-decisively; it becomes a stage of self-thinking, self-acting, self-made and self-decisive in all walks of life with a positive role performance and role fulfilment. At this stage, the roles and statuses of women and men become common, equal and jointly ventured aspirations and ambitions. There will not be stereotyped, sex-based division of labour, rather merit-based, skill-based allocation of tasks. Rewards and punishments are geared towards the skilful performance of the individuals rather than on the sex of the individuals. Societies particularly the governance aims at reaching that state of affairs through women empowerment. When empowerment is treated as a goal, then there are steps to reach the goal, which is explained as empowerment framework (Sahay, 1998). Empowerment framework is found inclusive of five major stages or levels of equality, such as welfare, access, conscientisation, participation and control. Each stage advances further into the next, one finally resulting at empowered stage.

Welfare

Welfare is the first and foremost stage, in which the governance addresses to the basic needs of women, such as economic, health, nutrition, legal, psychological and social. Obviously the role of state is greatly required to formulate welfare policies and plan for welfare programmes to be implemented. The privileges, provisions, concessions, assistance and other services of the state are being utilised by women. Women at this stage remain as passive recipients and beneficiaries of the target groups. As a consequence, the governance attempts to identify the problems of women such as poverty, literacy, poor health and malnutrition and backwardness presented in terms of statistical, demographic, health and other data documents. Targeted women categories become beneficiaries of these programmes without addressing to the cause and consequence of their problems and the redressals respectively. However, welfare measures do form an important component of empowerment framework. Perhaps it is the stepping stone for women to be empowered.

Access

Access is following welfare because all the welfare services made available to them must be practically accessible to women for use. It is the effort of governance to make the resources accessible to women especially in the field of education, health, media, employment, land credit, marketing, administration, training and other opportunities. For example, every village is supplied with a television, kept in the community hall, with lock and key and under the custody of somebody such as the village president. Women are not allowed to view television as and when they like to use it.

Similarly, agricultural trainings are given to women on the application of fertilisers or pesticides on the paddy/cultivable land, which does not belong to them as the land is in possession of some male member in the family. These are typical contexts of availability of resources but not being accessible to women. Thus, women should become accessible to resources, in this second stage, where women and resources are to be brought closer to each other.

Conscientisation

Conscientisation is a crucial stage in that women are exposed not only to realise their problems, interests and needs requirements but also to recognise the causes, consequences and remedial measures to end those problems. Especially the structural and institutional arrangements of the society to have caused their problems are made known to women. For example, women might come to know that the traditional roles of the society have not only domesticated them but also restricted women's growth and progress outside home. Hence in this stage, all women are involved in the process of consciousness raising, by which they develop feminist consciousness, and throwing away the female and feminine consciousness from themselves. Awareness camps tend to awaken women by arousing their 'We-feeling' and mobilise them towards achieving their cause.

Participation

A woman, raised with consciousness about her role and status, comes to realise her contribution and importance in the society, that motivate her to participate in all spheres. In this stage, women not only think and decide by themselves but also initiate performance and fulfil their aspirations with respect to literacy, employment and public life, thereby they begin to mobilise themselves and carry out activities in an organised way, thus work collectively for the cause of women. Formation of women collectives, women organisations and emerging women leadership in public life is nothing but participatory stage of women empowerment.

Control

Control is the ultimate stage of equality otherwise to be viewed as empowered stage. The end product of all the three stages of this process can be realised in the form of goal setting, formulation of policies pertaining to women's issues, framing women development programmes, devising strategies for implementation and preparing a plan of action for their own benefits, so as to fulfil their interest in every walk of life at the social level. As a consequence, at the individual level, women begin to take decisions over their own lives, children, environment and living atmosphere. Women gain control over all matters pertaining to them, which develops a balance between men and women as equals. Neither of the gender dominates the other and women's contributions will be duly recognised, valued and be rewarded wherever in the society.

Implications of Women Empowerment

Women empowerment implies a lot of sociocultural, economic and psychological changes in women both as individuals and as collectives. It signifies fundamentally a change process in women perhaps begins from letting female consciousness out to that of acquiring feminist consciousness. Female consciousness, according to Keohane et al. (1982) is the deep-rooted age-old experiences of women in giving and preserving life, nurturing and sustaining, considering women as close to nature, that is, self-image of women as life givers and sustainers. Whereas feminist consciousness is developed and defined as women reflecting on women's experiences, envisaging an alternative way of living without restraints imposed by rigid and impersonal sex roles. In this process, women undergo a lot of change in their psyche, personality and in role performance. Women empowerment, hence, signifies a lot of changes on the following lines according to Kamla Bhasin (National Policy for the Empowerment of Women, 2001: 10).

1. Women are being helped to fight their own fears, feelings of inadequacy and inferiority.
2. They are enabled to enhance their self-respect and self-dignity also to control their own bodies.
3. They are prepared to be economically independent and self-reliant.
4. They are made accessible to land, property and other resources.
5. Women's burden of work in domestic chores is considered.
6. Women's contributions and knowledge are being recognised.
7. Women groups and organisations are created and strengthened.
8. Qualities of new outlook and approach are promoted in women.

Thus, empowering women starts with individuals and ends with women collectives, resulting in an ultimate stage of gender equality in the society. Social institutions free from sexist approaches get converted into non-sexist structures, placing men and women on parallel points in the social continuum. As a multidimensional process, empowerment of women includes personal, social and political power, referring to women's capacity for self-action and the power to change the course of their life. Women are helped to build a positive self-image especially to develop basic respect and dignity as capable individuals in their work at the personal level. At the societal level, attitudinal changes take place in women for which consciousness raising campaigns/camps are organised and public opinion are generated in view of eliminating social ostracism of women belonging to weaker and deprived sections. Social empowerment of women is also made by organising remarriage of young widows, separated, divorcees and destitute, which are dowry free, nonluxurious marriages. In addition, supportive services to employed women and alternative vocational skill trainings to girls who are school dropouts and women who had discontinued education, health education to poor and prostitutes, extended with rehabilitative measures are to be provided.

Empowerment of women at the economic sphere includes employment opportunities to women in organised and unorganised sectors. Women's involvement in trade union activities, formation of thrift societies through self-help group activities, extending credit and marketing facilities, making available land, water, and other productive resources to be accessible to women, all empowers women economically. Political empowerment of women is possible only through equitable women representatives in parliament, assemblies and also in local self-governance. Women become legally empowered through legal literacy camps, awareness camps on women legal rights, family and legal counsellings.

Structural and Institutional Rearrangements towards Women Empowerment

Scenario of women empowerment has undergone a lot of changes, ranging from the most oppressing to the just liberating stage in India. There are historical evidences to show that the medieval ages right from eighth to eighteenth century AD had witnessed a most obscure and hazy picture of women. Pandey (2002) narrates it by saying that 'it is perhaps the darkest period of Indian womanhood where she was subjected to all sorts of tyranny, oppression, atrocity, exploitation, and the customs like sati, thuggi, devadasi, dowry, child marriage, hypergamous marriage, polygyny and restrictions to widow remarriage, ousted and uprooted the dignity and decency of Indian womanhood'. The sociocultural renaissance and subsequent movements such as the Arya Samaj, Brahmo Samaj and Theosophical Society attempted to annihilate those social atrocities on women during nineteenth century. But today perhaps the age-old problems of women are removed socially and legally, yet another dimension of atrocities continue to exist. Incidences of rape, wife battering, dowry harassment/death/murder, female infanticide, abduction and inducement to prostitution are high and are enhancing so fast indicating the perpetuation of gender inequality and injustice and the persisting problems of women. Changing such a scenario is the crucial and critical task of today's society in India.

Women's education, employment and independent economic status are of course the influential factors for women empowerment. Agarwal (2002: 9) opines that

> a positive attitude of family members and women's own positive attitude towards themselves is more important for changing women's status towards empowerment. Unfortunately it is lacking, yet it can best be developed by following human and spiritual values in life by all which will help in developing congenial social climate for empowering women.

However, women's position has undergone a significant change especially in post-independent India. Most importantly, the theory according to Maharajan (2002: 17) is that

> women's capacity and physical strength limiting women's range of occupations were discredited after the two World Wars. Thousands of woman voluntarily entered industry, agriculture, substituting men, handling machines and taking part in many new tasks in heavy industries including metal, engineering trades and transportation.

Despite women's entry into various sectors of development, their problems are perpetuated, of course, in a different dimension. Today women in India are the victims of rape, dowry, female infanticide and wife battering, revolving around one social institution, that is, family. How are women going to encounter such a situation? Women are ambivalent about the direction of change and strategies for the rural empowerment.

Women empowerment is thus closely associated with effective changes in all social institutions vis-à-vis family, marriage, religion, economy, education and polity. Syed (2000) presents strategies for bringing out social change in view of achieving protection and empowerment of women in general and Muslim women in particular. They consist of 'changes in legislation and awareness'. Hence, the role of all social institutions such as the family, marriage, polity and economy has to be identified in bringing out an empowered stage of women's life. Generally it is felt by feminists such as Nath (1997) that the paternalistic family and male-dominated political structures do not provide space for women in participating in decision-making bodies and processes. There is always a wide gap between women's de jure and de facto positions in spite of various legislations implemented to repeal discriminatory laws against women.

Similarly changes tuned to effect women's economic empowerment are also tried but are found in vein in the last few decades. According to Jakarta Declaration,

> empowerment of women is not only an equity consideration, but was also a necessary precondition for sustainable economic and social development. It expands the views by stating that women's involvement in the political arena and in decision-making roles is an important tool for empowerment as well as monitoring standards of political performance. (Nath, 1997: 13)

The feasibility of achieving women empowerment can be picturised in the figure below. Categorically E (Empowerment) = three E's (Education, Economy and Employment)

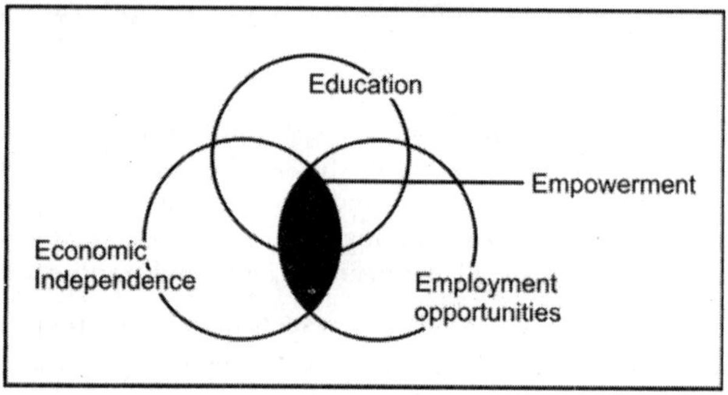

Hence 3E's = E* (E* empowerment)

Empowerment of women is thus a net result of changes in all the institutions concomitantly and not merely due to changes in any one or two of social institutions. As a continuous process, empowerment needs an art to form a group of women, whose efforts have to be mobilised so as to overcome a lot of obstacles that they face in their day to day life'. Pandi (2000) views that women can face the challenge of life with the principles and ideology of self-help formation only by means of empowerment. The following topology would facilitate the direction with which all strategies would achieve women empowerment in the long run:

Women empowerment is a continuous and simultaneous process that initiates awareness of the situation and of their problems, a change in their mindset and attitudes of both men and women. Every social institution should initiate a change by providing space for

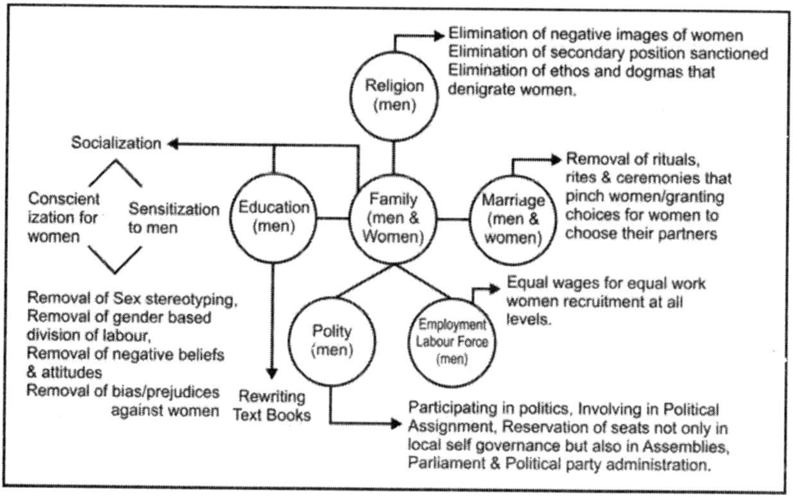

women to voice their interests. Women's questions must be accommodated in all spheres of developmental discussions and debates. It is in this situation of empowerment process, a woman becomes aware of where she is, understands why she is in that situation, then gets motivated to change it with her own efforts, seizes the opportunities, decides what she wants and chooses her own future ... says Mayoux (1988). Thus, an overall change in the social institutions facilitates change in the attitudes of men in general and women in particular. An empowered woman would strive to break sex-based stereotypes, questions male domination and superiority, becomes knowledged, skilled, capable and be informative in all aspects of life as equal 'partners'. Ultimately, it is the rights of women that enables them to act, followed after thinking, deciding, choosing and consenting in such a way as to attain equality and fulfil their ambitions and aspirations.

This view has been endorsed by Nath (1997: 11) who perceives the issue of women empowerment as central to the achievement of goals: equality, development and peace, that is, the Beijing Declaration. It is essential that women occupy in decision-making positions, as it will ensure the restructuring of institutions that are responsible for women's health, sexual harassment and other issues as top priority. Women empowerment is an end by itself and it is also a means to achieve gender equality. Hence, necessary structural institutional arrangements must be made for initiating women empowerment, which in turn paves way for a new structure and institution built on gender equality. At present women's entry to all fields has broken the masculinity of occupations and also the monopoly of men in such occupations and economy. Women in these areas of employment and economy may be less in number and be disproportionate to the total women population, yet they become, 'role models' to a vast majority of women, through their achievements. The real empowerment of women is possible definitely in near future if there are:

- intensive awareness camps on legal rights conducted among women;
- skill training and vocational trainings provided to dropouts and adult women,
- legislative amendments guaranteeing women to think and act independently especially on social causes, social evils and social problems affecting them so long;
- women collectives are formed and mobilised;
- mass women's movements demanding the state to provide reservation in all spheres such as education, employment and in politics; and
- the counterparts perceive correctly women's interests and women's questions.

All these are possible only if childhood socialisation becomes effective in imparting a new culture that preaches and practices gender equality, gender justice and gender development. Family is thus the crux of socialisation as well as empowerment processes. Noeleen Heyzer, Director of the UNICEM, has brought out four important, components of women's empowerment. They are as follows:

1. A woman's sense of worth;
2. Woman's right to determine her own choices;
3. Power to control their own lives within and outside home; and
4. Her ability to influence the direction of social change and to create a just social and economic order nationally and internationally.

A woman is said to be empowered only when she exercises her own rights and powers without the intrusion of any other members of the family/occupation particularly of the opposite sex namely the man. The moment she acquires all abilities in such a way that have enabled her to exercise these rights and powers, she is empowered. Thus, the above are not only components but also the indicators of empowerment in women. Necessary skills, such as psychological approaches, motivation, exposure, training, awareness and awakening, leadership traits and so on, have to be given to women with the ultimate aim of empowering them to be self-reliant, self-dependent, self-sufficient, self-contented, self-achieved and self-satisfied.

References

Agarwal, Kuntal. 2002. 'Empowerment of Women', in Seminar Abstracts, *Environment and Empowerment of Women*, Bharathidasan University, Tiruchirappalli, March 28–29, p. 9.

Anand, Anita and Salvi, Gouri. 1998. Beijing: The United Nations Fourth World Conference on Women. WFS, New Delhi.

Keohane, N.O., Rosoldo, M.Z. and Gelpi, B.C. 1982. *Feminist Theory: A Critique of Ideology*. Brighton: Harvester Press Ltd.

Maharajan, K. 2002. 'Working Women and Empowerment', in Seminar Abstracts, *Environment and Empowerment of Women*, Bharathidasan University, Tiruchirappalli, March 28–29, p. 17.

Mayoux, Linda. 1998. 'Women Empowerment and Micro-finance Programmes: Strategies for Increasing Impact'. *Development in Practice*, 8(2).

Nath, Kamala. 1997. 'Political Empowerment of Women', in Susheela Kaushik (ed.), *Knocking at the Male Bastion-Women in Politics* (11). New Delhi: NCW.

National Policy for the Empowerment of Women. 2001. Department of Women and Child Development, Ministry of HRD, New Delhi, pp. 1–19.

Pandey, P.N. 2002. 'Women in Rural India: Some Concerns about Social, Economic Awareness and Employment', in Seminar Abstracts, *Environment and Empowerment of Women*, Bharathidasan University, Tiruchirappalli, March 28–29, p. 20.

Pandi, S. 2000. 'Self-help Group and Women's Empowerment', in Seminar Abstracts, *Environment and Empowerment of Women*, Bharathidasan University, Tiruchirappalli, March 28–29, p. 13.

Sahay, Sushma. 1998. *Women and Empowerment: Approach and Strategies*. New Delhi: Discovery Publishing House, p. 9.

Syed, Sadiq A.J. 2000. *Status and Rights of Muslim Women in India: A Report*. Proceeding of a Symposium, New Delhi.

Index